A PEOPLE
SET APART

A PEOPLE

SET APART

Chimezie Anosike

ARPress
ILLUMINATING IDEAS
EMPOWERING VOICES

ARPress
45 Dan Road Suite 15
Canton MA 02021
  Hotline: 1(888) 821-0229
  Fax: 1(508) 545-7580

Ordering Information:
Quantity sales. Special discounts are available on quantity purchases by corporations, associations, and others. For details, contact the publisher at the address above.

Printed in the United States of America.

  ISBN-13:   Softcover   979-8-89676-107-5
                eBook   979-8-89676-108-2

Library of Congress Control Number: 2024927096

This work was first published in 2020 and lovingly republished in 2025 to share its message with new readers and generations.

A People Set Apart

By: Chimezie Anosike

Book Review by Mari Carlson

"Biafra is that jigsaw puzzle of Africa's woes, that loose nut when found all our mechanics are aligned."

In this fictional epic set around the war for Biafran independence from 1967 to 1970, also called the Nigerian Civil War, young Chance, sent to America for safety, returns home to create a Biafran town with his American friend, Turnkey. This is the story of Turnkey and Chance becoming friends despite their initial doubts and the origin story of the prejudices behind those doubts. It is also a story of nefarious networks left over from war. Bucknor, a young Biafran like Chance, uses these channels to realize his dream to live abroad. He, too, returns to mete out justice and reparations.

Sweeping and thorough, the novel digs deep into its main characters' projects through the histories of a wide-ranging supporting cast. Its language is saga-like and dramatic, evocative of the oral tradition, painting pictures with metaphors and idioms. Characters give long speeches and hold in-depth conversations with developed and distinct voices. Its pace, like its characters' ambition, is driving toward a vision. The men struggle to balance romance with their vocational aspirations, which the book mirrors in some domestic spats between lovers. The result is a convincing extended fable, portraying Biafran values of dignity, integrity, and self-supporting freedom, and the challenges these values face.

Focused on building suspense as storylines weave together, the book also expresses the spirit of the age in historic figures and events. The villain characters are not short-changed. Their stories show, in greedy deals, the systemic corruption the heroes are up against. The vehicle for change is an exchange of ideas. In the end, the place Chance, Turnkey, and Bucknor design (sometimes together, mostly separately) is not unlike the novel itself—a physical manifestation of ideals wrought by a combination of happenstance and hard work.

This work is dedicated to the millions of Biafran children, men, and women, who were fried with starvation to a slow death in a genocidal war where starvation was used as a weapon of war—a most unnecessary war levied in order to confiscate their God-given wealth.

It is also dedicated to the souls of all Biafran soldiers who died and those who survived the genocide, among them boy soldier, Theophilus, my brother, who was martyred for the cause of wanting to be free, and my other brother, Christian, who walked away from the trenches of war.

And lastly, it is dedicated to my children: Chidiomimi, Esimnachi, Ebubechukwu, and Amajuoyi, who are looking forward to the Biafra that is here.

CHAPTER 1

The weather was wet, and the atmosphere murky with an intemperate wind. There had been steady drizzles these past few days. In a parched land in front of the house lay a heap of gravel and sand mixed with cement. There were several shovels, head pans, three wheelbarrows. Standing over and about that heap were three young men in their late twenties and five others, not so young, in their midforties. They were just starting their work, intermittently interrupted by interchange of drizzles and noisy downpour that lasted but a few minutes. The downpour was ominous in its short span intensity. The rains were sudden pit-a-pat that relented, and then came a bit of sunshine, and then some drizzles, and then briefly the tempestuous downpour. The atmosphere gave no room for cheers for the men whose next meals depended on their accomplishing the day's assignment. The men had nowhere to turn, no time to waste, no chance of rest. At any chance, they worked feverishly to salvage their material and work, or else all their effort would be in vain. They just had to save the work they had started or watch the mixed gravel, sand, and cement wash down the drainage down the dilapidated gutters.

All of a sudden, the rains stopped and serious sunshine blossomed the earth. In the distance, there filtered a dim of noises, moving and cacophonic. It was as if the noises were bringing with them the sunshine. It had driven the rains away, far away than they had imagined. They were beginning to accept that it was going to rain all day that day. Finally, it was an opportunity for the men to resume their labor in earnest. They never trusted the weather. So harry they must. However, the cacophony became more cacophonous. The nearer it drew toward the men, the less it became a dim and an understandable song of solidarity. Nearer and nearer the men could decipher it. Nearer and nearer it was not just a song of solidarity. Nearer and nearer, it was also a traditional war song, a battle cry.

It was a most hallowed song in the whole of Biafra. It was beautiful in its rendition. It made the lily-livered want to lay down his life. It made the infant want to grab a cudgel. It manned a woman. It awakened a man in deep slumber. It was a rallying call. No one wanted to be left behind in its wake.

The song filled the air and filtered its way down the road. In the horizon, far off where the clouds touched the trees, the sun shone in adorable splendor. The earth beckoned it, but it was the journeymen that needed its rays most. As the song continued to waltz through in the distance came the sight of throng of people like a horde of locusts. Jogging and marching, chest-thumping in mob bravado and complemented by the willing-to-die solidarity, this throng of young men and women, boys and girls were headed in the direction of the journeymen who had just resumed their works.

"Nzogbu, nzogbu," chorused a section of the crowd.

"Enyi mba, enyi," refrained the other section.

"Nzogbu nwoke," chorused the other section.

"Enyi mba, enyi," refrained another.

"Nzogbu nwanyi" chorused the other.

"Enyi mba, enyi," chimed in another section of the crowd in roaring accord, as they stumped their legs to convey their sure-footedness and now living without fear.

No one in that area of the town knew what was going on. The journeymen laid their tools down and glared in the direction of the marchers as their song became music but eerie in its rendition. It was no longer cacophonous. It was harmonious, soothing, and delirious. However, everyone understood its ominous awakening. A chant for anarchy and total lawlessness.

The crowd was sizable, too numerous to be counted off like that. As they marched across streets, recognizable and nondescript, they grew in number, adult males and females, teenage boys and a few teenage girls. The purpose of the march was hidden in the will of the elders, incommunicated to the majority of the marchers, among them some displaced individuals, troublemakers, jobless folks, rabble-rousers, freewheelers, and majority of them apprentice boys, let loose by their masters. There was no leadership among them, but their purpose was straightforward. They had been infiltrated by some dyed-in-the-wool scoundrels, irredeemable anarchists, and some other bad boys who had little or no stake in the undertaking. As long as they did not obstruct the original purpose of the enterprise, they could partake in this free will show of understanding for their collective abject experiences. The battle cry went on, and in a twinkle, they had turned into a mob, and in a dash, they had reached their first port of call.

The journeymen understood what was heading their way and laid down their tools and disappeared. While the battle cry raged on unrelenting, a section of the crowd raised the ante in a call for action.

"O she bay," roared a section of the crowd.

"Yeahhhh," answered another segment.

"Boys, o yeh," demanded another segment of the crowd.

"O yeh," answered another.

"O she bay," the crowd ranted.

"Yeahhhh," another section rented the air.

Block against block, brick against block, brick by brick, hammer against block, hammer against wood, the crowd roared and sang and proceeded to tear down the house. Before the bat of an eye the one-story building went from carcass down to its foundations, stripped and reduced to rubbles by the indignation of the people of Eureka. Some with bare hands. Some with improvised cudgel. Some irons. Some sticks. Some nothing! Just rabble-rousers! At this point, nothing mattered. There was strength in numbers. A finger pointed was as mighty as the sword. Mayhem was let loose on the land. That was the beginning of the rampage, and the targets were clear and unmistakable.

The crowd was still spoiling for a fight when suddenly a gunshot rented the air from the direction of the house just across the street. For all intents and purposes, it was a warning shot, to scare the crowd away and perhaps to let everyone involved know who the boss was. But in actual sense the fate of the uncompleted building was the precursor to the whole exercise in that area of Eureka. The shot just highlighted the next port of call. And with one voice the crowd, with nothing to lose except their checkered lives, shifted their angst toward the building.

Then another shot. And another shot. And more shots came flying in the direction of the crowds now driving into a frenzy. Besides De Tom, young Chinweogo lay writhing in pain and anguish. The owner of the house was a well-known bandit of the first order. Famed for his fearlessness and devilish brigandage. But today those shots echoed one underlying instinct of his wretched humanity. How admitting fear could overpower the bravest of men and lead them to do more foolish things instead of choosing options that would ameliorate their state.

A group gathered to attend to young Chinweogo. Others docked. Others scampered for inner safety. The battle cry became frenzy as others braced themselves for action. Momentarily there was despair among the crowd. However, the battle cry frenzy energized them more than allowed despair to conquer their will.

"Boys, o yeh," echoed again and again.

"O yeh," chorused the crowd

Bazooka was a young man, a very young man. He was handsome, a very handsome man. He was always in his own company, a very lonely man. Those who had dealt with him said that soft was his speech. Almost taciturn to a fault. Bazooka was all these and more. He had a heart of steel. Careful in his dealings, unperturbed by any challenge in his path. But careless in managing his accomplishments. He was never afraid to walk the streets of Eureka brandishing his arsenal of trade. He was a rogue before he became a petty thief. He was a thief before he became an armed robber. He was a highway robber before he became a murderer. He never moved an inch of his house without being prepared for what the locals called any eventuality. It was never unusual to see the butt of his revolver sticking out of the top of his hips. He was a reserved man, minding his business. No one had seen him in any operation, but he had a famed history. He was never seen in the company of any of his neighbors. Behind the steel mien of all men there was still that pedigree of fear, difficult to admit but always present, and pinching the tentacle of all their existence. Bazooka's shots were admittance of that consuming fear, and the mob inadvertently understood that and turned their gaze at the house while young Chinweogo lay down dying.

It had been nine years since Biafra fought her way to independence. But not once had such a thing happened: one of their own sons shot in the street of Eureka by their own, with their own weapon. The mob understood the invitation and descended on the house across the street. Three more shots and there was utter silence.

With the battle cry, songs, choruses, and refrains the mob set the house ablaze just like that. In the midst of that pandemonium came two young damsels in their thirties, scantily dressed. They were in grip of fear for their lives as they walked out of the smoldering house barely cladded with nothing but themselves. But the prized jewel was nowhere to be seen.

The mob descended on the women and stripped them naked and were about to be set ablaze with discarded tires when some cooler heads among them prevailed and the women were dragged away in handcuffs. Jubilant as the mob were rampant they waited for Bazooka to appear to no avail as the blaze raged and the house became a carcass of its old self.

The one-story house was small, but the compound it was situated in was massive covering about three plots of land. Bazooka, though young, was famed also for his wizardry. It was said that he could disappear into thin air. He could also turn into an old woman, or feigned a disable man, or a goat, or a sheep, or a cow, or anything besides being himself. As the house smoldered, elderly neighbors gathered and stared, the crowd reveled, and the euphoria was loud and clear.

Fear was banished from the mob, and in upsurge of vigor and trepidation they braced themselves to invade the compound looking for Bazooka, dead or alive. Inside the garage was a brand-new Mercedes Benz that was still smoldering in the fire. Inside the compound were another Mercedes Benz and a Peugeot engulfed in the blaze that brought down the house. But Bazooka was nowhere in sight.

The truth of the matter was that when it became obvious to the bandit that the end was in sight and that the mob was prepared for the worst he lowered himself from the top story with a huge rope that was in some ways part of the accoutrement of the house and made his way across the lawn to the back of the house. He could not jump his own fence because he did not want to risk being captured.

Wily as a cat Bazooka had other plans. He had constructed for himself a small bunker in the middle of his backyard equipped with enough ventilation and a few supplies. It was in that bunker that he found a safe haven to the consternation of those who were desperate to find him. The top of the bunker was level with the ground and grassed over it. It was obvious to the searchers that he was nowhere to be found. Other groups were sent right round the house to inquire from neighbors if anyone saw a glimpse of the famed armed robber. To the consternation of the mob no one had any information of his whereabouts in just a short span of time. Some were mortally afraid to proffer any information even if they knew anything about his whereabouts. In his young age his sphere of influence loomed far and wide and foreboding. Some other times for the mere fact that he had found an abode in the neighborhood was an assurance of security against any intrusion of other bands of thieves who had made thievery and intimidation an art of the era.

The siege was on, and the waiting game just begun. The atmosphere in and around the compound was frenzy and frantic. The battle cry raged on. It was believed that the ladies who made their way out of the burning house would provide a clue as to the whereabouts of the bandit, but that was not forthcoming.

Bazooka was master in his own art, wickedness and survival instinct. He could sacrifice anything or anyone to make it to the next level. When it finally dawned on him that the mob was after him and all that he stood for it did not take him a fleeting second to understand what he had to do to buy himself more chances of survival and escape. The last shot that rang out of his house was fired into Binka.

Binka was a lady of immense beauty, and she knew it without having to flaunt it. She had known Bazooka for as long as people could tell. And of all the people in his world she was the one that seemed to have known him inside out. When he coughed she knew that it was time to hide. When he buckled and tripped she understood that it was time to flee. Whenever he wore a wry smile she understood that it was time to get out of his way. Such were their lives. But she also understood one thing: he did not trust her to say the least. He made it clear for her to understand that he did not trust her. She had been around him all this while because her beauty compensated for everything else she did not have. She had been with him all these years because he was a bulwark. For her he was the king of the jungle. Nothing could happen to her from without. What she feared was the enemy within. Within him and within reach. But she was unfazed.

Even though he did not trust her, she trusted him so much so even with her life. And the bandit knew that. That settled she got everything she wanted now and longed for. With that, one would think she would be close to his heart. She was kept at arm's length in his heart. She made no effort to change all that because she understood her man. What she did not understand was that in the calculation of crude and wicked men survival was measured in both solid leap and bounds, not the flimsy and ephemeral. When the mob was making circles around his house, it was not clear to him that the end was nigh. One thing was uppermost in his mind. He did not want to leave much of a trace. Of all the ladies he had kept company, Binka was the most loved but the least trusted. Of the three ladies in his company that eventful morning Binka was the most likely to betray him. She was the only one that knew him much, much more than anybody could tell. As he lowered himself with a rope through the back window of the top floor he pulled his .38-millimeter-caliber revolver and fired one shot to her chest. She sprawled and slumped, dying. That was the last shot. And then silence.

The crowd splintered and moved to other targets. Others lingered for the emergence of Bazooka. The two ladies were giving a beating of their lives, short of being set on fire. They were stomp and trampled. They were kicked and thrashed. Yet they held on to their secret of their boss's whereabouts. They were dragged to a secret location to spare them of further torture and perhaps see if they would change their minds. But to no avail.

As the day wore on, sunshine encapsulated the earth. And then. And then, words filtered in that Bazooka was holed up somewhere in his compound. Where? Where in his compound could he be hiding, for heaven's sakes!

The thing was in other areas of the town where similar rages and anger of the people were ongoing, another bandit of the first order was glimpsed trying to make an escape into his hole. He was unlucky, very, very unlucky. The mob grabbed him and summarily made a bonfire of him right in front of his house. The chips that were long down had succeeded in claiming one of its sought-after targets.

Tondo was a criminal's criminal. He was born a criminal. As long as he was not caught in the act, he was a will-o'-the-wisp. Growing up, if he was caught on top of a woman, he had to be tied in the act to be proven that he was doing anything. Or else he would pull his pants up and challenge the so-called witness to prove that he was doing what the witness had thought him to be doing. Such was he going up. He would beat up his mates and challenge them to go and fetch the mothers. Such was him growing up that he was avoided as a bag of uncanny things to be avoided. He was street savvy. If he had applied his wit and brawn to noble challenges of life he would have turned out great. But he expended his acumen being a great thief.

When the mob came for him that morning he did not have time to react and fathom what was brewing in his neighborhood. He heard the uproar right and about but did not know what was heading toward his safe haven. Life lived with impunity was effervescent in their alternate world, so nothing ever untoward was imagined. After all, they were law unto themselves. Before he could do anything to salvage the situation the mob had surrounded all approaches to his area. He was a man of immense connections. He tried to make a few calls to begin to understand what was going on right and about him, but the phones rang off the hook. One of the few he tried to reach was a police chief in one of the neighboring towns. On this day of the people's rage the police were, taken by surprise at the turn of events. It was a mass movement. At one section of town the police could do nothing to contain the angsts of the people, so they deserted their posts and fled beyond the grasp of the raging mob. In one instance a police post was burnt and razed to the ground.

The time he took to make his futile contacts brought the cruel fate of justice toward him faster than he could have imagined. All of a sudden, his house was being attacked and stripped. All of a sudden there was bonfire in front to his house. All of a sudden life without the trapping of confiscated power delivered an ugly blow to his rumbling entrails. This brigand who had led armed bandits and stripped men and women of the hard-earned money with a gun butt to the groin and a nozzle to the head saw himself incapacitated in a moment of collective bravado. All of a sudden power became a will-o'-the-wisp. He had no other better choices. He gathered his self-deprecating self and made a dash to his hideout. Because it was known that all days for the thief but one day for the owner of the house. He was about to lower himself into his hole when he was spotted by some vigilante-eyed boys who never thought that this day would come to this bravest of thieves, wiliest of animals, but cruelest and most cowardice of men. Justice, mob justice, had come to town!

Tondo was seized by a group of young boys who stared right in his face and punched his nose. They delivered blows to his face and saw his jaw sag. He wanted to plead his case, but they gave him no opportunity to open his mouth. He was pulled toward the front of his house. Included in the instruments of the mob were used tires. One was placed around his neck. He was doused with petrol and set on fire. He fought and writhed till he died. The crowd jumped and hollered. How the mighty had fallen!

The end of Tondo and the manner his life was extinguished moved through the streets and localities like a wildfire. Before the dissipating mob in front of Bazooka's house there were others who held their ground. As the news of what had happened to Tondo filtered to them there was a certain kind of uproar of exhilaration, a renewed sense of eureka in Eureka. It was a pandemonium. There was a certain kind of rush into the compound. Grassland covered with foliage of fallen leaves and tiny deadwoods littered the whole area. Some were standing on top of the lid to inside the bunker without knowing where they were. As they began to litter the ground with petrol Bazooka felt a sense of urgent foreboding. His choices were fewer, and his chances were minimal and diminished. He would rather die fighting than to be caught up in this hole without a chance. If he had to die, he would rather engage his assailants than to perish without a whimper. As he pushed up the lid to the entrance of his hole, a boy in his early teens staggered and scampered away.

"Wait a minute!" he echoed away.

Immediately bodies of much older boys and young men rushed toward him.

"There he is!" snapped another.

"Boys, O yeh," ranted the crowd in mob revelry.

Gradually, a nozzle of a gun began to jut out of the hole, and shots rang out. Gradually, the cover of the hole was flung open, and more gunshots rang out. It was the sound of a Kalashnikov, a.k.a., AK-47. The weaker and younger boys scampered away, but the bravest hung on, lying belly down. The men among them knew what was coming on. They knew that for this marauder to have a fighting chance he had to crawl out of his hiding place. He who wanted to stealthily steal a look across the other side of the wall must expose his temple first! He or his gun had to come out first. But whichever one there were no good choices. As he continued to shoot into the air as he continued to make his ascent out of the dungeon, one of the men threw a liquid into his face. It was kerosene and it smelled kerosene. And that told him that something more ominous was afoot. It threw him off guard. One of the men lay down and grabbed the barrel of his gun, and a struggle ensued with other men joining forces to wrestle the weapon from this most violent of robbers.

Bazooka held the trigger, and the men who wanted him at all costs held the barrel. His shots were directed to nowhere but the heavens. It was a futile effort. The mob subdued him and dragged him out. They gave him no chance that he sought. They still thought him to be wily. They still thought him to be capable of magic and wizardry. All of a sudden, his chicanery was not as mind-boggling as he was held. He was now just a small boy they went to school with. He was one of them. He was just savvy. Street savvy. He was just smart. Smarter than smart. He was beaten more than a tinker would beat a pan. He knew that he was a dead man walking. They already had kerosene poured over him.

He was dragged to the front of his house, and like Tondo a bonfire was made of his cruel self.

He went down fighting. For the umpteenth time he pushed the tire away from himself, and for as many times the crowd jeered and with sticks they lifted it back on him. The smell of his charred and burning body and tire and petrol and kerosene rented the air. As the crowd began to move on one by one and the fire began to douse, a woman walked leisurely close to the burning heap and spat in the fire. Before the glare of still a few onlookers the woman pulled up her wrapper to the edges of her buttocks and urinated on the embers. That was Bazooka's graveyard. The message was loud and clear, and everyone understood what that was for. The stench was awful and choking, but this woman did not care a hoot. As she was walking away another woman from nowhere came by and threw what looked like a gallon of fuel in the smoldering fire. It ballooned the fire into the high heavens.

She still held Bazooka responsible for the death of her promising child.

Chikwerem was a promise from God by every definition. He was everything a mother would ask of God in a child. As a child he minded his own business. He looked for no one's trouble and offered restitution if any adjudged him offending them. Because of that even when he erred he had defenses. No one queried his character or motive. They were always tailored toward good. He could do no wrong.

His mother did not have much to spare. His father cared less about his children. He was father by name only. If you snatch those kids from him he would not care more. For him, life was what it was: a flowing stream. Keep moving. With it. If it augured well it was what it was. If it augured badly it was not meant to be good. The man had five issues, and Chikwerem was his second child. The first child named Chimamkpam was a chip off the old block. But, Chikwerem, his second, was off a different hew.

As he was growing up he understood his father well enough. Because he understood who his father was early on he inadvertently aligned himself with his mother. It was a choice that served him well. And his mother intuitively saw something in him that was unspeakable.

Such was their understanding that when she could not fend for his academic pursuit beyond elementary levels, she approached one of her distant cousins to have him, Chikwerem, take apprenticeship under his business tutelage.

Under this man's roof, Chikwerem shone like a star. He was different. When his fellow travelers in apprenticeship enterprise grumbled about the cold, Chikwerem clasped his arms across his chest and trudged on because he knew that sooner than later the sun will bend its rays toward the west. Because of his mien and approach toward issues and people his boss placed a huge amount of trust in him and some pieces of authority to boot, sometimes to the chagrin of the other boys.

After four and a half years of apprenticeship and stewardship his boss set him up to be his own boss, his own man. His boss blessed him as a man would bless his own child. He was set off on a good footing, and he started out good. He made an instant progress, and in a space of two years the signs were there that the stars were his limits.

Then on one of those trips to purchase items to replenish his stock of goods, danger struck! They were waylaid by a band of bandits. They were stripped of their cash, and after the robbery, as they are wont to, to scare off further those who had been striped to their underwear, the thieves began to shoot mindlessly, and one of the bullets struck Chikwerem in the cages of his lungs. Before medical help could arrive in the early morning hours seven people lay dead. Among them was Chikwerem!

The news of the attack was one too many and devastated the town of Umudom once again. Nmanma, the mother of Chikwerem, was distraught beyond consolations. As she mourned, the whole town mourned with her. She was not the only one touched by the event. Two other families lost their beloved sons in the attack, but hers was the most high-profile. Chikwerem suddenly was growing in stature. Even one of the women, a few miles away who lost her child, also came around to console her over the death of Chikwerem because every member of the community understood what a promise Chikwerem was.

Everyone seemed to have a tale to tell. In the attack that took the life of Chikwerem, rumors had it that the attack was carried out by Bazooka and his gang. That was erroneous.

It was true that Bazooka was a thief and had proven to be a terrible bandit at that, but no one had seen him in any operation. He never operated close to home. He had chosen his locations far away from home so that he would not have the unsavory encounter of meeting someone he knew, someone who would stare at him and force him to take action against his own person, his own kinsman, his own blood.

Even those who constructed his hideout he stole from far-off places. They were hijacked, blindfolded, and brought to build his bunker. After their work was done he blindfolded them and drove them to where they were plucked up in the first place. As Bazooka was cruel in thievery he was generous to his laborers. He paid them handsomely for the number of days it took them to finish their jobs. They had so much wage than they had ever had in their lives. It was worth the while being declared wanted by their community. They had a tale to tell but had nowhere to point out where their tale took them for nineteen days. It could have lasted longer but they worked feverishly night and day for those nineteen days fearfully having in the back of their minds that Bazooka had no business with a hanky-panky attitude.

Bazooka made his name owing to the kind of weapon of operation that he held close to his heart: bazooka. Bazooka was a most cherished weapon of rampage. It may not be the most lethal weapon out there, but surely it was as good as the best. Even before he became a thief and even before he knew that bazooka was a gun he had aliased himself Bazooka because the first time he heard the name he heard the sound of a gun and he liked it. Growing up it stuck with him. When he eventually discovered that it was a gun, it did not faze him. Actually, he liked the fact that he had chosen the name of a feared weapon to be his alias. He had started carrying himself with some authority and order. He had started seeing himself as dangerous. Growing up he had started pulling imaginary trigger in the direction of his adversaries. And a lot of adversaries he had. And eventually when he turned out that he was of no good, altogether bad, a careerist criminal, it was natural that he

13

chose bazooka as a beloved weapon of violence and intimidation and cruelty and murder.

But the truth of the matter was that Bazooka was also running guns. Bazooka was like a banker's bank. As a state has a banker's bank, Bazooka was such in the banditry world. When fellow bandits ran short of arms, it was Bazooka that provided a lending hand. When it became emergent he was there to close the gap for his comrade in arms. The trouble with Bazooka was that one never approached him with an empty hand or refuse to meet one's end of the bargain. He was as ruthless in his dealing as he was good as a go-to guy. No one wanted to mess with Bazooka. His colleagues understood that if there was anyone that would bail them out in their hours of need, he was him.

On this day of the people when he was pulled out and away from his hole, the supposed leader of the mob world jumped into his abode and found what every gun-trotting, gun-loving bandit would call collector's items. What Bazooka had in his armory could raise a small militia of men to defend a section of the community of Eureka. Among weapons stashed in his bunker included over a dozen of bazooka, eight Kalashnikov rifles, nine .38-millimeter revolvers, nine .36-millimeter revolvers, and a bunch of other guns the young men that invaded his hideout had not seen before and did not even know how they function. There was also an uncountable number of bullets, cache of bullets. They were so afraid with what they had found, and not knowing what to do with them, that they threw them back inside the bunker and fled. Their work was done. It was time to move on.

What happened in Umudom and its environs was not an isolated event contrived by a group of miscreants or gang of troublemakers. No. It was a well-organized traders' uprising, a pseudo civil coup d'état against men of the underworld. In the west end of Eureka, the traders vented their bottled-up anger, and just like in Umudom three well-known robbers were brought to the public square and set ablaze for all to see. In the south section of Eureka, a great many of the mob stormed the house of a well-known bandit, and to their chagrin he was nowhere to be found. He was away the day before and did not make it back into town. In the central section of the town six wellknown robbers were not that lucky. They were nabbed by the angry mob and were not given the chance for any fairy tale. However, the seventh bandit on target list made a miraculous escape. How he succeeded to slip out of their grasp was everyone's guess.

Again and again, they had fallen victim to these too often attacks. Each time these had happened the attackers seemingly had disappeared into thin air. The towns and communities had nowhere to turn. It had become routine that these incidents had become a way of life for the people and their government. When it became obvious that the people of Eureka had a massive uprising without any boundaries, schools were closed and also shops. Market women scurried home. It was for the common good. Men and women and children on their way to the farm or to their other businesses laid down their tools. It was understandable. They could take it no more.

Because armed bandits had grown so powerful, the police became powerless and incapacitated. Because the police were no match to the firepower of the marauders they began to operate with impunity. All they had not done was to form an army and march the streets of Eureka waving their flag of conquest. In one or two known instances, they had the police in their pocketbooks. Some of the guns found inside Bazooka's bunker were police's. On that day of fury of the people the police understood what was going on. They feigned ignorance and were incapable of stopping the rampaging mob. At some posts in and around the city instead of confronting the mob they locked up their armory and deserted their posts. Some shed their uniform and joined the angry mob in a show of solidarity. The people had taken the law into their own hands. They were doing what the police could not do or were ill-equipped to do. It was that pathetic. In that uncertain time people cared less of the repercussion of what may be in stock for them. Life had come to that, and because desperate time required desperate measures the people seemed to have had their own field day with some abandon.

It was toward sunset, and the mob had started to dissipate and disperse when out of nowhere the police began to show up in the streets. They had lain low for some understandable reasons. They did not want to confront the demonstrators who had genuine reasons to be taking the law into their own hands. The vision of the people was intertwined with their own vision. But for years they had seen their work hampered by neglect by the authorities, almost abandoned to themselves. The call to duty had become a very dangerous enterprise. On occasions when they had answered the call to duty they had found themselves outgunned and deflated. Morale had been low within the rank and file of the force. The police never showed up when their need was most utmost. As it were today, it was a culture for them to show up after the fact. Situations like that had made the police to be held much more in disdain. As morale sagged, men of character had avoided the force completely, and in some cases, some of the men who joined had done so for some ulterior motives. Just to have a job at the end of the day. It did not bode well for the force. It opened the gate of recruitment for folks of questionable character to pass through the sifting process to be given the hallowed badge of police honor. The police, as had been known through the ages, had been regarded as friends of the people, but in Eureka, just as in many parts and towns and communities in the fledgling Biafra nation, they had been seen as enemies. They lacked the respect of the people and were despised for all their efforts. It was understandable for the people to feel the way they did. The relationship between the community and the police was poisoned by people's distrust of the police and the force's lack of honor. The grudge was that the police rank and file were perceived to be colluding with thieves to decimate the communities. They looked the other way while bandits ran rampage on the communities. It had to stop, and these traders had no further choice than to take the initiative to save themselves. Even when some people felt that the police were hampered in their work they also believed that the police were their own worst enemies. Neglected and without enough fighting power the police sometimes were just invisible bystanders to the people they were paid to protect and serve and the bandits who had a field day hitherto.

As they drove through the streets they began to round up some layabouts here and there. Of course, they had to have evidence that they did something to curtail the mob while the demonstration raged. How else could it be explained that such carnage and wanton destruction could occur and no one was held accountable, no one was held in custody? Among those caught in the show of force was Chukwubuikem who spent the night in police custody.

Slowly but assuredly dust came real quietly. There seemed to be peace in the land. Over the night there was sporadic gunfire possibly by the police to show their essence and probably by some low-level inconsequential miscreants who wanted to send some signal that the ilk of Bazooka, Tondo, Mascara, Tomfull were not completely gone in their midst. What they did not know was that the traders of Eureka were not done yet with their exercise to get rid of all thieves small and big, at least in the meantime. And morning came really fast. Events of yesterday seemed a few hours ago. Every known bandit in the whole of Eureka who happened to be in the confines of Eureka and within grip of the demonstrators was killed. If one was lucky to be away, then his house was burnt to the ground. The fury was complete and knew no bounds. When an idol became too stubborn, too heady, recalcitrant, acting like a pack of wolves, too great a trouble for the community, its owners, the people, would tell it the stick it was crafted from, hoist it up on a pole, and make a bonfire of its nonsense. That was what the people of Eureka just did.

As the sun began to rise the demonstrators were out and about, sniffing for any action that they had left undone. The police were also out and about with their megaphones warning the people to vacate the streets. It was a call heard with one ear and zapped through the other ear. These people were determined to drive home their grievances, and today they were not in the mood to pick a fight with anybody, let alone the police. However, they did not want to be stopped. They wanted to make their case louder and clearer. They wanted to be free to carry out their businesses without having to keep watching over their shoulders, without being accosted and ripped off their hard-earned money at gunpoint and at cost of their lives, especially while the police seemed to be a disinterested bystander. Action, they said, spoke louder than words, and the authorities got it.

Turmoil was still simmering. The peace was delicate. It was an uneasy calm. The demonstrators were headed toward the main police post where it was reported that a group of young men and boys were being detained for questioning. The police were trying to figure out how to proceed. Lives had been lost, and they did not want to be seen as not wanting to make some arrests. They knew who the leaders of the traders' union were. But to bring them in for questioning had to be done with the utmost delicateness. So, rounding the small fries may perhaps ensnare their masters to come to their rescue. They were the baits and cannon folders. However, that was not going to happen. Rather, these young men and boys who did not want to go through what their masters were going through in the hands of highway robbers wanted to flex their muscles a little bit. They were out and about to confront the police to have the police release any of their colleagues picked up by the police in their lily-livered operation in the aftermath of the demonstration yesterday. The police were not going to have it either. They were determined to assert their authority at least for now. They used tear gas to disperse the crowd. As the demonstrators fled momentarily they regrouped and surged forward again. Again, and again they were pegged back, and again and again they surged forward. What the demonstrators wanted to be accomplished was not written for anyone to understand. Events of yesterday were statements made in bold letters for all to see. Today's event was like putting a cymbal on top of a gong. Skirmishes with the police were normal. Handling it in a way to nip it before it could become a conflagration was the art that was tutored in every academy, yet it was also normal for it to get of out hand and became a vortex. But the police were not going to have it, especially at their doorsteps. Even though the action of the people yesterday to take the law into their own hands had an unspoken, unwritten tacit approval of the rank and file, but that was yesterday. Today they wanted to be seen to be in control of the proceeding. In conference, they had a list of people to be issued some warrants of arrest. If not for anything, at least, to assure some folks who had objection to how the masses carried out the operation the day before that the event was isolated. That effort to send out the warrant had been delayed by the renewed demonstration right in front of their vicinity that morning. As they pushed back and forth with the demonstrators it was becoming obvious to the police that the mob was not in a hurry to disperse. Rather, their number seemed to be swelling. Yesterday was a victory against thieves, big and small. Today was a test to see how far they could go to show the police how not they could do their job.

For the umpteenth time the mob had retreated and gradually the crowd had grown in size, but the difference this time around was that ahead of the pack and marching majestically was Mr. Guzo. Mr. Guzo was a prominent lawyer in town who had had a running battle with the police over the years. His prominence on account of his luminary victories were even reckoned nationwide. The police never liked dealing with him. But today he was a welcome arbiter. At this time, his valuableness could not be quantified. As he marched ahead of the implacable mob the police began to reckon that their problems were half solved. Mr. Guzo had been representing the traders' union organization for years. The leaders of the union had contacted him to pay a visit to the police post to help douse the angst of the irate mob. At this juncture, only Mr. Guzo had the caliber and mental resources to quieten the people. At this time, the leaders of the traders' union knew that something needed to be done or else the police may be heavy-handed or the mob would become more riotous and given the slightest of chances may torch the police post. So, Mr. Guzo's appearance from nowhere was a big relief for the police, and his intervention was most highly appreciated without verbiages.

Mr. Guzo was a man of average height. However, his influence was towering and overbearing of man of his stature. Sometimes his voice had the menace of a gong. He laid emphasis on every word that he uttered that they ring a bell in hearers' ears long after he was gone from their presence. Such was his endowment that it was believed that he could talk to a marauder to lay down his arms. He was such a man! And such a man was who that was needed to quell the fire that if it were not handled with utmost care could well get out of hand.

"I understand your long-suffering anguish," he began gingerly.

"Enyi mba, enyi," the crowd roared in salute.

"Lend me your ears," he started to speak again. "I do not need to ask you what to seek for? Every Mbonu, Iheonukara, and Onunaka knows what your grievances are. I identify with your anguish. I see your pain. I feel it as well. The scars of your physical wounds are there for all

19

to see. Anyone who says he or she does not see what you go through day in day out belongs to the other side of your battle and should be seen as an enemy of the people."

There was utter silence in his immediate vicinity. However, far at the back among the crowd that had now become mammoth a pocket of young boys had started their war song again, rendered in a passionate, victorious cadence.

"Onye akpala nwa agụ aka n'ọdụ ma ọ dị ndụ ma ọnwụrụ anwụ oo; Onye akpala nwa agụ aka n'ọdụ ma ọ dị ndụ ma ọnwụrụ anwụ oo."

They were making a revelry of the situation, a victory lap. Do not touch the tail of lion cub whether dead or alive. And repeatedly, they rented the air.

"You, the people," he began again, "had spoken, and your speech is reverberating and echoing in all directions. Action speaks louder than words, my people. If you were going home and haven't reached your house you keep on going. But, when you reached home you stop and relax. You've reached home. You need to relax. You've made your point loud and clear. But, when you are running and gotten to the wall then there is nowhere else to turn to. You have got that inalienable right to fight back or perish. That's what you just did! That is the first law of nature. The right of self-preservation. That is the right every man and woman has got to stand up and defend. I'm not here to remind you who you are. You are Biafrans, and when Biafrans cannot take any more anguish they let the world know it and proceed to do something about it."

At this time, the crowd roared in acquiesce, and some whispered as basic truth to their neighbor an agreement with what the barrister reiterated.

"But you must understand when enough is enough. You must abide by the law. I do not ask you to leave in hurry. But I do ask you to do no further damage or be a threat to life or property. I know that you have some of your colleagues or neighbors in police custody. I know that you want them released. You will get them released, but I want you to understand that these things take a process. That process is afoot as I am speaking with you. Leaders of the traders' union are in consultation as I am talking to you. They are not leaving you to your own devices. Once again, I do not ask you to disperse. I ask you to remain calm and do no further harm."

There were hisses of murmur among the crowd. However, they were going to trust him to take charge of the situation in the meantime.

"I have an appointment with the police chief. I want to hear him out, and I believe he wants to get this restive town under control."

As the diminutive legal luminary entered the precincts of the police post there was an uneasy calm in and around the walls of the building.

"Mr. Guzo," the police chief started, "you've gotten what you wanted."

"What you wanted!" the barrister charged back, staring him in the face. He's been in the business of dealing with the police for so long a time. He understood that one of their many repertoire of antics was to put you on the defensive at the earliest of an encounter.

"Yes, I mean what I'm saying," the police chief posited again. "You have sent your wards out and about to kill and cause all kinds of mayhem in the restful city. And I and the rank and file of this force are not going to allow it to happen," he continued.

"If their intention were to burn down the whole city, we are determined to stop them in their tracks. The city has taken it in the chin. The police have taken it in the chin. Your wards can declare victory and go home. The police have taken a beating in this saga. I've restrained my men because we wanted to deescalate the situation. We are a professional force, and we want to be seen as such," the police chief went on.

"Mr. Sansom," Mr. Guzo started to interrupt the police chief.

"No, no, no, I don't want to hear from you," the police chief charged back.

"You don't even know why I'm here, and neither have you offered me a seat," said the lawyer.

"I do not want to know why, and I do not have a seat for you, but you can have a seat if you so wished. Your people have destroyed

21

the neighborhoods, taken the law into their own hands, killed innocent people wantonly, and still spoiling for a fight with the police. What else do they want, Mr. Guzo? I'm not asking you a question," Mr. Sansom continued to badger the lawyer

"Take them away from the streets. They should go to their businesses and let law-abiding citizens go about minding their own businesses."

"They will leave quietly if you will permit them," the lawyer began again.

"So, why are they still milling around the streets and most absurdly in the vicinity of the police post?"

"Well, that is why I am here."

"That is not why you're here, my friend," retorted the police chief. "You're not here to take them away or make them leave the streets in peace."

"Then, why am I here?" queried the lawyer.

"I don't know why, but my hunch tells me that you've come to prize away these hardened criminals we have in custody."

"Gradually, we're coming close to the truth," the lawyer began again. "But most importantly, I am here for peace. I am here to help your force. I am here to lend a helping hand. I am not going to tell you how to do your job, but we have to recognize the anguish of the people of this land in the hand of some marauders who had ruled the land hitherto. The marauders are your hardened criminals and they are in flight. And I tell you something in case you don't want to see the handwriting on the wall," he continued. "Let me tell you something, mister man, these angry people are not going anywhere until you do the right thing for them without having to flex your small muscles."

"I do not understand what you mean, Mr. Guzo," the police chief feigned.

"Get it right, Mr. Sansom," said Mr. Guzo.

"What do you mean by 'get it right'?" the police chief said, his voice slightly elevated once again.

"Mr. Sansom, as if you don't know," the lawyer put it to him. "This restless crowd you see outside are not going anywhere until you do something."

"Do what!" the police chief charged back again.

"You must use your power to free their men."

"Free what? That's not going to happen like that," Mr. Sansom snapped. "You want me to set open the door of these detention centers to your miscreants and some other never-do-wells. What am I going to tell the community we serve? If you were in my shoes, are you telling me that that's the way you are going to handle the actions of these people? Misinformed people who had taken the law into their own hands."

For a while Mr. Guzo brooded seriously. He knew the task was daunting for himself and the police chief. For a while he said nothing. He did not understand how he would leave the presence of the police chief with nothing to show for his efforts and assurance his personality had conveyed. He could not leave empty-handed. His journey would be ending in futility. He was about to belittle himself in the eyes of those who had held him in heavenly awe. The crowd would have nothing else to hang on to. Restless already, they might go violent. He thought hard and long and began slowly.

"You know, Mr. Sansom, the events of the past two days are acts rooted in frustrations and discontentment. I tell you most solemnly, the people of this community you claim to serve are staunchly in support of the mob actions you saw yesterday. They had wanted it. They longed for it. I understand where you're coming from, but at this juncture you've given yourselves no good choices." The lawyer paused. "The chickens have come home to roost," he continued. "Over the years, some few bad eggs in your force have infused your rank and file and infected it, aiding and abetting criminal elements in the society, and you, the police chief, seemed to have turned a blind eye or incapacitated by your own indifference, ineptitude, acquiesce, or even connivance, to say the least. You just refused to lay a glove on these people who had made our lives pitiful."

This was like a dagger jarred in the rib. It was incredulous for the chief to hear this from this rugged of all lawyers. He was stunned beyond belief. In a few languorous years of dealing with this lawyer, he had come to know him as one who did not bite his words or mince them either. But in this he had touched the lion's tail and for that matter a live lion. The police chief was livid. He stood on tiptoes.

"How dare you say that," he roared. And his voice was heard reverberating in adjacent rooms. One of his commandants came to his door to eavesdrop in the wake of the rising tension in his boss's office. These police functionaries were aware that whenever this dueling lawyer of a man visited the precinct it was always a tough passage of time. They had always tried to avoid coming in collision course with him. It was, as always, a bruising affair. He lived his life arguing. That was his trade. He may be bruised if that opponent was that good. But at the end of the day that person would be sprawling like a rolling stone without a moss.

"You're head over heels in your thoughts, Mr. Guzo. You can't come here and open your mouth thoughtlessly and say things like a man who never suckled his mother's breast. I tell you, Mr. Guzo, men and women of this force cannot be held in your ignorant view and be allowed to stand. You must make your points, but you must not make insinuations that have no foundation in logic or facts or even in your gymnastic judicial antics."

"Wait a minute, my friend," interjected the lawyer, "I'm making no insinuations. I'm making statements, I mean, factual statements."

Like a frightened porcupine facing an existential threat the police chief's spines were raised ready to be ejected. It was obvious that Mr. Sansom was rattled to hear that from the legal luminary even though it was not something he would want to admit to himself, let alone admit it openly to his face.

"Statement! Factual! Factual statements! Where do you get your statements of facts from? You better be clear with your statement, or I will get my men to throw you into the dungeon."

"That is not why I am here. If you were looking for those facts to be presented then you have to come to my turf. And if you were contemplating that throwing me into the dungeon will solve the problem, then you are making light of the situation and fueling the embers of fire. How much of this town do you want to burn down?

And be it known to you that these people milling out there make no differentiation at this point in time. Before the city goes up in flames, this post will go down first, with you first and I second, counted among its ashes. Do you understand that, Mr. Sansom? And lest you forgot," continued the lawyer, "how many people are your men ready to kill?"

"I do not know how many of your people out there are ready to die!" countered the police chief.

"So, you are ready to dispatch as many as anybody who presented himself in opposition or open confrontation with your men…"

"It is not my job to count those who want to die or willing not to live," said the police chief offhandedly. "I'm trained to maintain order and make sure that peace is not ruffled. That peace must be maintained at all cost. When you gave yourself thought to brood over collateral damage en route to keeping the peace, you dissipate your effort. You run the risk of allowing disorder to slip through your fingers. I do not understand your rambling." The police chief paused, subdued, flippantly sounding ominous. "It is your stock in trade to fish in troubled waters. To say things that you know would not stand the taste of serious scrutiny just to add to your popularity. You seem to have forgotten," continued the chief. "You must know as indeed you are acting as if you don't know. There are people among your mob friends out there whose life ambition has always been to be killed by others or be counted among those missing in action. Yes," opined further the chief, "psychologists are yet to tell us why their lives are bent toward that inexplicable horizon." He finally paused for a longer period of time.

"It is you who seemed to be rambling, Mr. Sansom, I'm not in a popularity contest here. My own record speaks for itself. I'm not going to belabor those points any further than you have made them stand out. But I put it to you, and I want you to know that some of the artillery recovered by these brave souls outside your vicinity have police marking on them…"

"You need to stop, my friend," said the police chief, more subdued. "Lawyers like to start an argument so that they can demonstrate and burnish their judicial acrobatics…"

"Yes, always lawyers," said the lawyer.

"Yes, always the lawyers…," mimicked the chief.

"Not without a reason," Mr. Guzo interrupted him. "I would rather tell you stuff like these than to have you in my court and spilling the bean for all to see. You have bad elements and continue to nurture more in your rank and file. Their continuous employment by you, Mr. Sansom, is the reason why you have these guys out in the streets. Do not give me the opportunity to demonstrate my judicial gymnastics or acrobatics as you put it before my learned friends. The youths you see in your vicinity are here on invitations by your actions or omissions. You cannot inadvertently commission them and suddenly throw your hands up in the skies, that you do not know what is going on. Your actions or lack of it"—the police chief wanted to jump in, but the lawyer would not yield to him that chance and raised his pitch as to the next torque— "have necessitated what is going on today and will continue if you do not change course right now. You cannot eat your cake and still have it. I tell you," said the lawyer with all certainty, "in no uncertain terms, I want you to understand that the crowd have borne the brunt of the rotten eggs in the midst of your men. They are not going away on your assurances. They will go away on your actions, not gestures, and the actions must be manifest."

Mr. Sansom was a veteran of the police force for solid twenty-nine years. He had risen through the ranks by dint of his shenanigans, sheer grit, and ability to convince his superiors that he got the job done beyond the satisfaction of his superiors. In every post and assignment, he had excelled with distinction. That had presented him with more challenges and every challenge, more laurel, and every laurel a higher challenge. When the chips were down he never delegated the toughest assignment to his subordinates. He liked to handle those tough issues himself. As he was wont to say, he liked to nip thorny issues in the bud. He had absolute assurance in his own personality. Believing that the sheer force of his personality would blunt the cutting edge of any army arrayed against him. That was the way he had won his battles. That was the way he had succeeded so far, in a force that was entrenched in guile and streetwise rather than anything that was in the book of survival by instinct. He was not among the crops of officers that loved to beckon on danger for a wrestling match to prove their ability to get the job done. He had succeeded in his assignments by seeing every situation as innocuous first but wrapped up danger that had the potential to snowball and subsequent potential of becoming a hydra with its Frankenstein concave head.

He had been also lucky. But, he had not ridden on his luck. In nine years, he had moved to three different posts, sometimes in the hinterland, sometime in the coastland. It was the difference he made in those areas and the sure-footed he left those command posts that had compelled his superiors to send him forth to other places, each time more troubling than the last one. He had been in Eureka three years already, longer than his last posts in Ngele and Nkanu.

When he came to Eureka, it was not quite clear to him the enormity of the task before him, but he was not indifferent to what it presented to him either. Eureka was a sprawling city, growing at faster pace than any other city after the war. The criminal elements' activities were also famed. So, he had a clear view of what the present assignment had in stock for him. He had convinced himself that he would apply the same paradigm he had used at other places he had been to before Eureka. While every situation may be different, there was no need whatsoever to change a winning formula. That paradigm had won him success. It had won him friends and accolades and, of course, few enemies. He was sure that it may not give him the same result. However, he had something to start with, to use as a starting block moving forward!

Six months into his calling at Eureka, he had made no appreciable impact on the crime level in the town. Sansom was a man who liked to corral a rampaging fire toward the riverbank rather than trying to dissipate its power by striking a hole in its heart in an effort to weaken its flaming force. A hole in the heart of the fire will dissipate its force into impotent powers not enough to galvanize themselves into a raging force and with time withered without angler link for further convergence. That, too, was good! But, Sansom was a Fabian! He loved the Fabian tactic of war, victory by wears and tears, conquest by piecemeal.

When he got to Eureka, he got a dossier of every man and woman in the force to try to have a grip on the men and women under his command. What he was presented with troubled him. To succeed in the way he saw success in the force he loved he would be left with no man or woman in the rank and file. He began the whittling process. In twelve months after his coming to Eureka, he was left with less than half of the men and women he inherited on his arrival. That was brave in implementation. But, that created a new brigade of malcontents. Some of the men that were thrown out joined the band of crooks, brigade of behind-the-scene troublemakers, miscreants, petty criminals, common thieves, full-fledged bandits, and armed robbers. He felt that his efforts were undone, rather. Yet, he felt undaunted even though his spirit sagged. But he had never given up on any assignment he was presented with. He never failed. He had never contemplated failure. His worldview had been honed on positive paradigm.

He looked up to see the reaction of the police chief, but it was expressionless. His mind was buried in august thought. He thought that he was grabbing his attention and would not let the opportunity to press home his point slip away.

"I tell you something, Mr. Sansom, and that is, the people of this town have done what would take men and women in your force donkey years to do, accomplished in a jiffy. In the life of a nation, one day of riot and mayhem is a jiffy, if you do not know."

"But, there must be order," Sansom ventured to say.

"Yes, you are honed from the bricks of order. I am fashioned in the tenets of the law. But, these people out there want a harmonious convergence of law and order for their daily lives to be somewhat meaningful. Devoid of it all our trade, I mean, our occupation, I mean, you and I, are nothing to them. You have a job to do, but I am going to remind you that these people have a life to live. And without them you have no job! You must be bold in action and thought. And it has to be swift and decisive. Not swift and decisive to burnish your ego or flex your authority. But, swift and decisive in such a way that this crowd would go home not feeling vanquished."

"And the police not defeated either," charged the police chief.

"It's a balancing act, my man. We're not unaware of the work you have done in this community since your arrival over thirty months ago. Yet we're aware of the daunting task you have not done since your coming. We're not unaware that some of your efforts have created new problems. Yet, we're aware that when you're pressed against the wall, the only reaction is bouncing off the wall, ricochet toward the only direction. When you're traveling toward a certain horizon, as long as it was not a mirage, you keep going until you get to your destination." He paused for effect as it was obvious that he had gotten the police chief's ears. "Again, I'm here to make a difference. I'm here to quell the fire. I'm here just to help you get the monkey off your back…" He was in the middle of a sentence when the police chief's office phone rang.

It was the commissioner of police himself calling. The police chief asked the lawyer to kindly move to the adjacent room where two of his lieutenants were copiously busying themselves taking some notes.

The police commissioner and the police chief had known each other for some many years. It dated back since their primary school days. From primary school, they attended the same secondary school. They found divergent ways after their secondary school years. While the commissioner went up north for his studies in social science engineering in one of the best universities in the country, the police chief veered westward to the oldest university famed for the number of technocrats it had churned over the years. However, that separation did not put a wedge in their relationship over those years. Both had worked hard not to slip up. Both had shared their experiences. Both had shared their aspirations with each other. There was nothing to hide. The commissioner's earlier plan was to take a path to the air force for a career as a flight pilot. The police chief was intent from day one for an aspiration to the police academy as a careerist police force general. He never had a second-guessing about where he was going and what he wanted to be in life. So also the commissioner though somehow truncated. The scripts were going as planned without any hitch as it were for the police chief. However, it was difficult getting into the flight academy school, yet as fate would have it the commissioner had a thorough breakthrough. He passed every test placed before him. Until it came to aptitude test. He gave less than satisfactory answers to a lot of the questions. These were nonnegotiable. He was a risky option for the school. The examiners, based on his performance in the aptitude tests, had adjudged him to be a risk in charge of any flying object in the sky. They had found him as one of those that were wont to engage their tongues before the brain was geared. It was like having a tendency of putting the cart before the horse. The air force would not countenance it no matter who was pushing the paper or the candidate. His ox was gored. He was crestfallen. But, he was brave enough to dust himself up.

His parents did have their connections to men of immense caliber. But, in the air force there was no compromise, as the top guy in the academy admission brooded no nonsense. He was always ready to walk away from the job than to allow political expediency and pressure to bring calamity to the force, either in the short run or in the long term. But, Obikolo himself had his own fledgling connection. He sought his friends in the police academy, and to his surprise chances abound for fresh recruits. The point was that he got admitted to the academy on his own merit. He needed no one to soften the landing for him. And the other point was that at that time the police force was advertising for position in the force for some sort of holders of some sort of university degrees. For that class rotation, there was still time to squeeze a few more people into the program. Among them was Obikolo.

Obikolo would not be classified as a short man. Neither would he be classified as tall. He did not have what anyone would classify as a big-body-framed man. Neither would it be said that he was lean. His physique was none of these. However, it was looking obvious that when age began to set in he would appear diminutive rather than lanky. But, he did have enough of what it took to be given a chance to have a career in the police force. His eyes seemed to have been screwed inside their sockets. Sometimes they appeared as if they were dented. But they were not. It was just the way he was. Sometimes they appeared as if they were contorted. But they were not. It was just the way he was sculpted by his maker. Those features gave him a stern-looking visage, a visage that left him with the impression of a man with a hollow heart. All these were accentuated by the fact that this guy's smile appeared wry on few occasions he ventured to wear one. Actually, he never wanted to be caught wearing one because that would convey a false impression of his personality. It had served his world well. Hard to say what was what, between his smile and a grimace.

"Hey, San," came the voice of the caller.

"Hello, boss," echoed Sansom, with a tinge of the voice of someone who had his boss's assured support.

"I got all your reports and briefing and feedback on events happening in your community." He paused for some effects as the police commissioner's words filtered through the handset as the police chief nodded in agreement. "We're not unaware of the goings-on in that area of the province. And you should not be unaware of the occurrence of these kinds of events and angst of the people. You've been in the force even longer than I've been."

"I do understand," said the chief.

"But I say to you…," filtered in the words of the commissioner. "The whole world is watching you…," continued the voice of the commissioner. "In the work we do, we're not evaluated by how much peace and order we have in our communities, we are judged by how many riots we put down…We are not evaluated by how many riots we prevented, we're condemned by them…We are not honored by how many lives we saved, we are condemned by how many that were lost sometimes through no fault of ours." The police chief nodded bitterly.

"I tell you, my friend of old," continued the commissioner, "there is more honor among the miscreants…the hoi polloi of the community you serve…" As he continued to listen, the word of the lawyer began to thaw on him like pieces of ice cubes under the gaze of a severest summer day. "Remember…," came back the words of his friend, now colleague and boss. "Remember…," he echoed again, "our first call to duty is to maintain order and peace…We are not given to maintaining the law or enforcing the law without a writ…and that writ must be presented in the torchlight of judicial sophistry…polemics and…acrobatics…," said the commissioner matter-of-factly.

"I don't envy your position as things were in your community," continued the commissioner as his friend continued to absorb the hammers of the word of the lawyer as they landed on his head as a hammer continues to flatten the iron on top of the anvil. "If you must succeed…as we were all thought in the academy…prevent an agitated people from forming groups of twos…threes…tens…That would be tantamount to beckoning at trouble. There's strength in numbers, even when not armed…"

"Yes, sir," for a long time the chief managed to mutter.

"Don't let the opportunity to make peace slip through your fingers…Reach out to the leaders of the community…"

"But, Obai," said the chief informally, interrupting his friend and boss for the very first time with a fond name reserved for old time sake's camaraderie. "Our major problem here is the so-called elders of the community. They are the fuel behind the fire…"

"Then your problem is half-solved…," jumped in the commissioner. "It's they who would drag back their wards off your streets…I know that you're saying that they are encamped before the approaches to the station…Do the smartest thing I've come to know you for… Send an emissary out through over the wall of your camp and have… to those whom you said started the fire…meet their demand halfway or even fully and surreptitiously corral them to your pen…as fire is corralled to the riverbanks…," said the commissioner as his conversation with his colleague continued to filter in.

"And I'm going to say…something to you off the record… These people have done your force a favor…You're beleaguered… overwhelmed…perhaps outnumbered your…men and outgunned you…They did what you will never…the manpower and resource… You can chide them all you want…You can corral them all you want to let the world…that you still have charge of order…They did you a huge favor…for a long, long time to come…You will have peace in your land…I wish you the best of luck," echoed the commissioner as he offered his friend his last piece of advice a colleague can give to another, not just because he was his friend but because they had remained good friends.

"Do have a nice day, boss," said Mr. Sansom.

Obikolo may be headed toward diminutiveness. He may have three times flunked his attitude test to join the air force. His vision in life was clear-cut and focused. He had what was required to succeed in any chosen career. He was well connected both to high and low places. Shake him off one stair in the ladder of influence and trapping of success, which was not too bad either. Deprive him of a chance at laying claim to a fixed goal, he had the trappings to make something good out of the other. He had the knack to hold an opportunity with ironclad resolve and maximize it to the fullest there was of it. Throw him out of the lowest rung of the ladder and he saw it as an opportunity to move to the next level. He came from a family of movers and shakers of the soil and had entrenched himself in those connections and even better. In actual fact, he had made the best use of them. His attitude had always been to ruffle the feathers and chide the wind, to win the game first and then talk about how ugly it was afterward. In the years to come all that would be of matter would be the victory and not how ugly it was achieved which would be a mere footnote if it would ever matter.

If a relationship was not going to benefit him, he would let it be known and forge ahead toward a different horizon. If across the bridge was the final destination, he would gallop across when the sinew was bursting at the seams and then wait for whoever that was that wanted to make it a slouch toward Gomorrah. Having achieved that he could slouch for all he cared. There was no time to waste; get it done and get it done fast.

To whom much was given not little was expected. To whom little was given not much may be expected. He was the quintessential hallowed disciple. He loved to live in both worlds. When one of his uncles was mocked because people were quick to remind him that the foundation of his stupendous riches was laid by his great-grandfather, Obikolo was quick to badge in into that pedestrian thought process. Reminding his uncle's detractors that the guy who made hay with such a largesse should be commended because not everyone entrusted with such windfall made it better. Not many would account for theirs let alone making it something to be handed down to the next generation. Kudos should be given to he who had improved on his own inheritance. He himself had built on the connection of people before him and had made them even better. His rise to the commissioner was meteoric. It gladdened him a lot. Not because he had been helped by people who knew his father. But also, because his course to the post had been made easy by friends he himself had cultivated. He had established himself. He now had his own circle of movers and shakers of events. And more so he was now adept in cultivating those friendships that mattered most. He would not obstruct anyone crossing the bridge. However, he would want to get to the other side of the bridge first before anyone else. He would allow anyone to cross the same bridge. However if another person crossing that bridge posed for him some known problems, he will sever the bridge when that person was at the point of no return. All the person's efforts will be laid to waste, most of the time, at the point of losing all that one had worked for, and perhaps losing one's life. Obikolo was that ruthless.

Failing the aptitude tests was some kind favor to him. Sometimes, he felt that he could have made more strides if he were to have been in the air force. Sometimes, he assured himself that he had not lost anything. Sometimes. But one thing was certain: he knew and he knew very well that when he found himself in a good position, he made it better, and a better position was made best. And then best was left in the dust moving forward. He knew that he was not going to fall out of the sky, just like that, had he joined the air force. He loved life. He loved to live. He was not given to taking unnecessary risks. Success for him was alluring, a sure banker. He held it true, and he held it dearly true. Rather than diminish his purpose and pursuits in an effort to improve he would hold the ground on which he was standing. A bird in hand was worth twenty in the bush. Rather than losing a bit of what he had in an effort to improve it he would hold tight to that which was his. Risks must be measured. When he lost his ground a little he doubled his efforts to regain the measure lost. Was Obikolo averse in taking chances? No! He loved chancing for an opportune and stopping anybody else in the track because his middle name should have been chance.

When Sansom hung up the phone, he was humbled rather than subdued by his exchange with his friend he now called boss. He took a deep breath. While the scars remained, time was the healer of all wounds. The intervening period to talk to his boss had given him a fresh start. Frayed nerves became relaxed. The atmosphere was calmed. He did not need to be reminded or schooled on how to handle the situation, he thought to himself. They were textbook axioms and commonsense, streetwise truths. It was just that he had to hold out for some measure of integrity for the men and women under his control.

He gathered himself and urged his assistant to usher in the combative lawyer.

"Mr. Guzo, where did we stop?" he resumed with a gambit that was neither here nor there.

"It doesn't matter where we stopped. But, of importance to you and to me and this community is to make this restive town quiet, and the restless crowd go away. We stand nothing to gain in a state of constant turmoil," cautioned the lawyer.

The police chief did not specifically want to offer anything without being asked. He wanted the lawyer to throw the gambit.

"I'm going to help you although I know that you're playing on our ignoramuses," fired the lawyer. "Get this town under your control. Get the demonstrators off the streets."

"Who do you want? How many do you want?" offered the police chief.

"All of them, as much as there is to make the crowd go away, for now," he was quick to add.

"You might as well ask me to clear the cells of their holdings," said the chief.

"Well, if that is what it takes to make peace with the land."

"Peace! Peace at all cost," refrained the chief.

"Well. Yes. Peace!"

"Mr. Guzo," began the chief, "you're going to get your wish today. But that is not the end of the matter! Since you've put yourself up to be the facilitator in this matter. I want to see the organizers of this upheaval."

Mr. Guzo understood what "to see" means in police parlance.

"What you had was a demonstration. But, I can tell you without mincing words that the organizers of this demonstration are your men in uniform and their collaborators, I mean the bandits and marauders they had rented to harass and decimate the people of this town."

The police chief did not want a rehearsal of old squabbles with this man that knew the act of going for the jugular when he got his opponent with nowhere else to go. He was no longer incredulous. He just had to listen.

"Prepare your writ," continued the lawyer. "Get me your warrant of arrest. Serve them your warrant," advised the lawyer.

"I'm inviting them to the station tomorrow. This is not a jungle." snapped the chief.

Once again, the lawyer understood what "inviting" was meant to be.

"Put it in writing," he counseled. "Serve them to my office, and I will make sure that they appear in court, and not to your dungeon. You made here a jungle and you get some jungle justice. As a lawyer, I say it with the utmost sense of responsibility for the people of this land have suffered grievously in the hand of your men. You want to prosecute those that have done you a great favor, did the job you and your men are afraid to do. Unbelievable," he drawled as his tone petered out.

When Mr. Guzo walked out of the police station later that hour he had in his company more than three dozen men. First there was an uproar of hooray and the gonging went up into a crescendo. What he got from the police was sizable, notable folks and enough to assuage the crowd, and gradually they began to disperse.

CHAPTER 2

The plane had just landed. Everyone on board bated their breaths. It was a huge relief for Chance, Jason, Candie, Jewel, Dusty, and Turnkey. It was about ten o'clock in the morning. The air was fresh. The sun was sighted in the east. The rain earlier on was heavy. Heavy indeed that one would not be faulted to wonder what about the birds. There was no hiding place for any. Now, it was a drizzle. Perhaps, lighter than a drizzle. Not anything to worry about for anyone who wanted to venture about their businesses. Then. Then, suddenly the voice of the captain of the flight came on through the plane's public address system. He informed everyone on board that there was some situation that would warrant a delay in disembarking from the plane. He urged for patience from the passengers. Having enjoined them to hold tight he proceeded to find out what more was the matter.

Mr. Footwright was the captain of the flight from London to Eureka. He was a frail, gaunt man. Gaunt in his gait and somehow gaunt in his speech. He had thirty-six memorable years under his belt. He had flown to all imaginable and unimaginable places on the face of the earth. He had seen many turbulent flights before, but they never bothered him. He had seen a lot that they had become part of his person, part of his life's mission. He had been to Biafra so many times and for so many years, even when it was part of defunct Nigeria. And he had been to Eureka for a number of times. He loved her people, and the people of this land loved him. He felt free among them in close quarters even though he was convinced he would never bring himself to live among them.

When he came back to the address system again after about ten minutes' interval, he informed his expectant audience that they would disembark. However, he made mention of some kind of demonstrations in the streets.

"Was it a riot?" a voice at the center of the belly of the aircraft, quaking with uncertainty, volunteered to ask. It was Jewel, the nineteen-year-old damsel from south Bronx.

"Or is it a coup d'état?" queried a middle-aged woman from south Wales, sitting next to Jewel.

"No, not at all. And to the best of my knowledge, to my understanding, I was made to understand that it was a peaceful demonstration. I was also made to understand that the police have control of the situation. More so, you're protected within the confines of the airport. The air inside the plane is creeping hot. We've got to move before it gets hotter. We're going to stay in the lounge, and from there you all will proceed to your different destinations," he said in rapid succession, to allay their fears and not wanting to entertain further questions on the issue.

"Now, have you been here before?" he asked, poking his neck in the direction of Jewel, now inadvertently opening up a chapter on issues he dearly wanted to avoid: asking questions.

"No," chorused a collection of four or five voices from the place where she was.

"Well, it's well. It shall be well with you," said the pilot, trying to assuage their fears. "When you come to these lands, they always leave you with some memory, memories that you have to remember for the rest of your lives. Chief among the things you've got to understand is that when you come to this kind of lands it leaves you some jagged memories. There's always a tale to tell, but it's not always pleasant memories. Without sounding like a broken record, when you come to these lands, you've to be prepared for a world of experiences, a world of experience," said the English man, fumbling with his own imperial language, as the passengers filed past him near the door to the entrance of his cockpit.

The captain had visited Biafra for so many times that he had started speaking smattering local language namely Igbo, the language of the major ethnic group in Biafra land. In fact, his constant coming and going into Biafra and his conviviality with the locals had made him immerse himself into the idiosyncrasies of the people to the extent that their language had begun to influence and color his English accent, diction, and lexicons. He could speak passable pidgin English without any qualms. And that had made his own native English language proficiency poorer.

It turned out that what was going on in the streets of Eureka was not a small kettle of fish. It was a mass call to arm. For a firsttime visitor, it was not understandable to say the least. It had been five years since Chance left for the United States in pursuit of greener pastures. Not much had changed in his eyes, but actually a lot had changed in Eureka and indeed the whole of the fledgling Biafra nation. It was almost within the time he left that rogues and armed bandits began to express themselves more brazenly and openly with such impunity that did not just raise eyebrows, it made heads to turn. It was not as if they never existed. They did but not with such "you can't do me anything" attitude that defied imagination. It was so bad that people lived their lives in anticipation of the visit by one group of marauders or the other. In such anticipatory situation households prepared themselves by keeping aside a portion of their lives' savings to the benevolent visitor. As soon as a knock was heard on the door and perhaps a kick inflicted on the door, every man and every woman knew that the imaginable had come. The expected spoil was visible on the table. It was there for their taking. The most benevolent of robbers would just take their loot and vanish into thin air while the bloodthirsty would ask for some more with a barrel of gun to demonstrate their hunger for more, in cash or in blood. Life was that brutal and mercy was that merciless. In the life of a nation, the war had just ended and everyone was thirsting for a want, some with gallant enterprise, and some with effrontery and cruel bravado.

The eastern ends of Eureka were well-known as the hideouts of the nouveau riche in the new nation of Biafra. Old men and women who survived the war with nothing left came here to start a living. They were joined by enterprising young men who were working their heels off to make a living. Hidden in their midst were a few new breed of bandits who made their living like pirates, pirates not at sea. Their sphere of influence was on land. They waylaid business travelers and traders and stripped them off their life's savings, most often, painfully, in broad daylight. Their identities were known. They never made efforts to hide their faces. It was their own trade. When mama and papa, brothers and sisters went out to their places of work, these bandits also prided themselves as also going to work. They had become very brazen, and people of Eureka and surrounding communities had accepted them as part of burden of life, living and dying. But all that was about to change. Young men and women of Eureka had decided that they had a right to decide their own destiny. If the fledgling government would not help them then they would help themselves. Such was the mind-set of these people that they had decided to take the law into their own hands.

"What was going on here?" Jewel began, after about an hour of indifferent silence laced with intermittent dozing off.

"I have no clue," enjoined Candie, another beautiful girl as part of a summer adventure into the heart of Africa, as Biafrans are wont to claim. "This is bull," she managed to conclude.

"It's not bull, it's fucking bullshit going on here," chipped in Turnkey, seemingly rather sarcastically and out of fashion.

Jason had nothing to say because as far as he was concerned it was morning. He lived for the moment, one day at a time. But he did not want his hitch to the sub-Saharan Africa be messed up because time was short. He came from the southern Mississippi town of Troublestone that had seen its fair share of demonstrations, riots, and mayhem. He had seen a lot of upheaval in his young life to the extent that he seemed to have been deadened by events around him that they never mattered one bit of a lot. He had learned to take things in strides.

These boys and girls had come to Biafra on the invitation of Chance. Chance had made a good provision for all kinds of accommodation for his friends, none who had stepped out a foot outside the confines of the United States of America. Chance had arranged with one of his nephews to come to the airport to pick him and his traveling band of adventurers. But events of that morning had made it impossible for any game to come as was planned. There was mass of people out in the streets in the whole of Eureka and up to leading to the approaches to Biafra International Airport. There were bonfires everywhere, and the police had condoned off the approaches in and around the airport. The demonstrators had taken up the streets, and no one was allowed to go to the airport, and for safety purposes the police had decided that there would be no entrants into the city until the situation had quietened down.

The airport was under no threat whatsoever. Owned largely due to the fact that though the angst of the people was broad-based, it was also limited. There was no information that any thief big or small had sought refuge in the confines of the airport. If there were, no barrier stood between the demonstrators and laying their hands on that person who had made their lives so miserable hitherto. However, the last flight that left the airport that morning had, in its belly, one notorious criminal, Otokom. He was headed to Gabon. He was darn lucky. It was just a coincidence. He was billed to journey away for another operation on the outskirts of Gaborone. One lucky thief.

Biafra was a nascent nation. Like a newly born child its steps were uncertain, especially pried out of the mouth of wolfish Nigeria. Infrastructures were condensed. There was telephone, but it was sparsely located. In and around the airport they were spotted. However, not everyone in and around the country can boast of owning one, the sort of thing taken for granted in the remotest part of the New World. But Chance and his family were not so encumbered. Services were disrupted but not disconnected, in actual sense. Just movement was at a standstill. In the new country Chance and his family could be counted as people with some sort of influence and some sort of wealth. Chance had called his nephew that they had finally made it from the airport public phone, and understandably his nephew could not come to pick him up. His nephew he had not seen in five years had informed him that there was a huge uprising throughout Eureka. That the traders had organized a mass uprising against local bandits, known and unknown. That there was mayhem throughout the land. That even the police had scurried away, practically gotten out of the way of the demonstrators. And that there was not a hiding place for any thieves, big or small. There were no good options. And in actual sense the only best option and the safest place for any visitor that had not ventured into the city was the airport. The police chief did ask for some kind of reinforcement, and the force headquarters obliged the request. It was in everybody's best interest to stay away from hotels and motels. Motels and hotels were major targets of the demonstrators. Majority of the bandits had no fixed addresses. Motels and hotels were their natural habitats. They had become their bases and launchpads. Chance had organized a two-day stay for his friends in one of the biggest hotels in the city, but as events began to unfold it was natural that those plans were turning into balderdash, completely untenable.

Before their eyes morning turned into afternoon. As Jewel peeped through shutters of the window of the airport lounge she could see the sun bid farewell to the east as it easily journeyed to the other side of the world. The west was beckoning. The airport was agog, not for fear of anything, but because people were milling around. People who got tired sitting down began to move about. Since Chance and his friends arrived and were sheltered in the airport four more flights had come in. This airport received seven international flights on a daily basis. Two other scheduled flights could not come in because the airliners had sent words across Europe. First it was reported that the new civilian government in Biafra had fallen to the ravages of a coup d'état, one of the twin ills that had befallen nascent governments in sub-Saharan Africa. Such was the state of affairs and the situation she was in as dusk began to envelop the environment. She gobbled additional snacks she had loaded that was estimated to last her a week and counting. The airport authority had organized blankets and bedspreads. Everywhere one could find a space to stretch became a bed. Chance and his friend chatted almost all night, and as nature would have it, one by one they fell asleep. All but Jewel.

Jewel was a vivacious nineteen-year-old. Tall and elegant, beauty's beauty. It would not be an overstatement to say that never was a more beautiful sissy borne of a woman. She belonged to such a dying species of women that could be said that they were not born, they were thrown up, regurgitated out of her mother's mouth. As a nineteen-year-old, she was audacious, sometimes brash. She was calculative, sometimes thoughtless. She was focused, sometimes headlong. She was determined to a fault. When she broached the idea of going to an adventure with her friends to a place barely known to her mother's imagination she was rattled. She pressed her to divulge the place, but Jewel had held her grounds insisting that as a nineteenyear-old girl she was overdue to cut her own path. It was her right to choose moving forward. She was an only child and that "onlyness" had perturbed her mother. However, Jewel had no inhibition. She never understood. That really bothered her mother. And as with every mother she was not ready to give up on her only child. She pressed her daughter to let her know where on earth the hell she was planning to visit. It was like a corked gin. Intuitively she was well aware that her mother did not want to lose sight of her for a fleeting moment. Actually, she never allowed her to move or wander away from their little locale in south Bronx, until college. That was their bond. That was their relationship, tethered by not just mother-daughter affinity, but by inherent fears. Nevertheless, tugged in the other direction by her daughter's divergent intransigence. As a mother that wanted the best for her only child, she never gave up. She had always wanted her to be either within sight or sound. Given a chance she would prefer to have her within sight rather than sound. She pressed and cajoled her to no end. But, at long last, Jewel caved in.

She was going to Biafra, she tacitly ventured to say. Biafra? The mere mention of that name conjured up images of ills unknown to mankind in modern history since after the Second World War. The Second World War cessation declaration made it clear that mankind would never allow such to happen again. However, the ink with which those words were etched had hardly dried up when newer man's inhumanity to man resurfaced its ugly head again and the world turned away. It was not that the world turned away that came to her mind. Rather, it was the images etched on the tribunal conscience of the world, the pogrom, the barbarism, the strife, the struggle, the starvation, and then kwashiorkor, of children condemned to die a slow and painful death in the face of plenty, children starved to death, and the image of the countrywide-proclaimed people's general that was denigrated and vilified as power hungry by the west and misunderstood by the east. Even though the war had ended for over ten years now, she still saw an image of an unending strife. She could be right.

She tried to dissuade her to no avail. She was going to strip her of funds. She waved that aside. That had been taken care of. She was going to take away her tuition financial support. That made no impression.

She had told her mother unabashedly that after all she was past eighteen, the Rubicon of all ages. And now she was nineteen. She could take care of stuff. Her mother did not want to lose her completely. She was allowed to go anywhere in the world as long as she had the decency to call home every two hours. If that was the first gambit in the tussle to take control of the chessboard, it failed woefully. Jewel would have none of any encumbrance. Two hours would amount to nothing if push came to shove in the event of trying to save her life from any imminent danger. Yet. She offered her daughter a six-hour interval to call home. But that was not good enough. And it would not even be worth the neck in which the head was screwed to administer a nod. She knew her daughter like her palm. Her character was screwed on a parallel line to hers, running in the same direction and never meant to converge. She was such a rolling stone that at every inch the torques increased in geometric proportion. There was a futility in about having her to change her mind. It would be on Jewel's term, especially since in all calculus she was over eighteen, and there was little her mother or anyone else for that matter could do to stop her. Jewel had told her mother that she was just going away for a short time and that within the interval the pillars that held the heavens and earth would not crumble but if it did so be it. It was hard to swallow. But she still gave her blessing. Jewel was all she got but all she got to lose as well.

While others dozed off, Jewel found herself being chastised by the altercation she had had with her mother. For one moment, she began to doubt herself. Armed with some bight of Biafra coin, the currency of the new nation, she had exchanged earlier the morning of their arrival, she placed a call to her mother, Ms. Counterfeit. Ms. Counterfeit was relieved to hear from her daughter after more than twenty-four hours. Immediately, she knew that things had not worked out well for Jewel in Biafra. If things had been Jewel had no intention or desire to place a call to her mother. And her mother could feel it in her tone. It was flat without trepidation. Without mincing words, Jewel had told her mother that they were all right in the midst of chaos and upheaval. She was looking for a way to get out, but being in the middle of nowhere, her options were limited, she told her mother. She said everything she knew of to assuage her mother's fears. As soon as she finished her conversation with her mother she fell asleep. It was three o'clock in the morning, Biafran time.

No one had a sound sleep or snored. They were all up at the first sign of the sun thrashing through the pane of the lounge's window. Soon afterward, Chance nephew, Chukwubundu, was on hand to drive them home. The streets were clear of pedestrians, and fewer vehicles were on the ply. The police were more in full force to stamp their authority over the town especially this side of the city. It was complete wreckage. Dotted along the way were charred buildings thought to be the hideout of the thieves. Most affected were the hotels especially those of inconsequential status. The police were on hand to shield the big hotels while allowing free rein to the mob to go after the thieves wherever else they could be spotted. Good enough none of the big hotels played a hideout for the thieves. There were so much devastation in the land that it could easily pass for a war zone. Bonfire littered the neighborhoods. Lying at some point were carcasses of some charred bodies, burnt beyond recognition. While the police had played hands-off approach to the uprising they had done much to douse the bonfires and made sure they did not spread beyond the point they were made. It was not nice to behold, and it concerned Turnkey and his co-travelers. What they saw along the way was an eye-opener. It did leave a sour taste in the mouth. The inhabitants of this land could be akin to the Spartans.

The riots and holdup in the airport completely embarrassed Chance out of his wit's end. Nevertheless, he had mustered every ounce in his young, flamboyant personality to reassure each and every one of them that nothing was amiss as far as taking care of them was concerned. As they rode home, he tried to change the discussion to drive away their sensibilities from the matter at hand.

Finally, they had made it to a home. The family house of Chance in the city of Eureka was relatively massive. It had all the comfort of a modern setup. There were showers and running water. It had all the trappings of wealth and good taste. Chance had told his friends to make themselves comfortable after the raw deal of an experience since they made it to Biafra. He planned to take them around to different places and exhibitions, and then to his hometown in the next few days. But, due to the events of the past two days, those plans were shelved. His friends were terrified. There was a popular discotheque just about a few miles from their family home, frequented by foreigners of every nationality. It was the era of soul train, and all the vibes that were the talk of every town and village had a convergence in that particular discotheque. But, this was an uncertain time and in everybody's best interest to pipe down. They had difficulty being persuaded to venture out during the day let alone at night. However, Chance had assured his friends that this was an isolated event. That the long-suffering people of Eureka and the larger Biafran society were like the biblical gentleman that would offer the other cheek to illustrate a point of peace at all cost. However, there was a limit to all endurance. It had come to that point. Chance had told his friend that it was a clash of strengths. A pushback by some good men against some bad unmitigated, irredeemable idiots and bastards who had lived an immense, unchallenged notoriety. The good guys wanted to make a statement and to dismantle all that notoriety and in so doing certainly make themselves out as the people who put an end to their plight and suffering by seizing the moment and countering mayhem with more mayhem. That was a point well taken, but it did nothing to allay their fears.

It took extra persuasion for Jewel to be convinced that the worst was behind her. The arrangement was planned such that Jason, Dusty, Candie, and Jewel would be staying for about ten days before the chaos and telltale upheaval seemed to have gotten everybody's tail up. And Chance and Turnkey would have to stay a few more days. That initial plan was under serious threat. However, Turnkey did not want it truncated. He used the strength of his conviction and personality to convince Jewel to tarry on. So four days after their arrival at Eureka they booked a flight to the southern city of Umudede. It was a journey of about three hundred miles out.

CHAPTER 3

The six men had just arrived at the police unit and took their place on the bench just opposite the police counter. They were the leaders of Ureka Market Amalgamated Traders Union, the umbrella organization that catered for the well-being of the all traders in Eureka. They had been called to the police station to provide statements on the role of the traders' union in the imbroglio of the previous five days. These were law-abiding citizens but united in their opposition to the police and the hoodlums that run the city and its environs. Among them were Kanka, Chiebuka, Chukwudi, and three others.

Kanka, the bulky, swagger-walking individual that was purported to fear no one. He was a believer in the inevitable. If something was surely going to happen tomorrow it might as well come down quickly today and be done with it. He knew that death was a certainty. He never went about seeking its handshake, but if death was meant for him tomorrow it might as well come down quickly today and be done with it. He did not abhor trouble because if trouble must come to one it must come no matter how fast or far one tried to outpace it. He was the leader of the group and well-known in police circles. The police loathed to deal with him because he was a handful. If they could they would like to avoid him at all cost. But in this case, he was at the center of it all or as the police would want everyone to believe someone had to be held responsible for any event big or small. That scapegoat. And in matters of this magnitude someone had got some explanation to render.

"You boys are at it again," began Mr. Ekarika, the police sergeant on duty that morning. "You'd your failed insurrection that did not work, and now you wanted to start another revolution," continued the police sergeant, sensing that the men just wanted to ignore him.

"Now, you all are sitting quietly as if you never knew a thing," Mr. Ekarika went on. He was an Ibibio man and equally of Efik extraction, his mother having hailed from Efik and his father from Ibibio.

"Officer, you are the one who invited us to come to your office. If you had nothing to say to us then we can go home or back to our businesses. We have got no time to waste here with you," said Kanka.

"I need your statements on the uprising you engineered five days ago of which smoldering flames are not yet doused," said the police officer tossing a notepad on the laps of Kanka, and then turned around and grabbed clipboards and pens and gave to the other men.

"I do not know what you are talking about, Officer," said Kanka, staring the officer in the face.

"Now, you don't know what you did. You think that a denial will convince me," said Ekarika.

"If you want me to tell you what every person in Eureka knew about the riot of the past few days I will let you know," said Kanka, fishing out a written paper from his trouser back pocket.

"You just said that you didn't know anything about the riots, but you have a written statement made already. Keep your written statement to yourself. We don't want to hear about your manifesto. You just lost out in your bare-hand insurrection, and now you want to start your own one-arm revolution. Put your statement down on the pad, or I will tear your manifesto up into shreds before your own very eyes. Make your statements and get behind the bars," said the police officer sternly.

That was usual of men of the police force to make derision of the Biafran war. They liked to refer the effort as bare-hand insurrection or one-arm revolution or insurrection. It was said that either of the phrases were made popular by no other than the police commissioner Barnes Obikolo and his gang of saboteurs. Such belittling of that anguish struggle of the Biafran people had riled every Biafran of age. None of the young traders gathered at the police station that morning saw action in the war but were old enough to see the suffering that went with it. The consequence of the war was the limited opportunity that was the lot of the Biafran people. There were paucity of jobs and scarcity of money. Men scraped through to fend for their families. Young boys toiled to contribute to the upkeep of a whole lot of families. A whole lot more abandoned high school for a life of trading as a way to contribute to keep their families afloat. It was an easier route to pinch in a little to the family finance and upkeep. Those who made it to the university came to discover that their earnings were not enough to match those who opted for a life as traders. It was a stark reality of the time. The men gathered at the police station were a testament of the challenges the Biafran people faced. So when people made fun of the struggle they had to go through or the chain of events that got them here hitherto, it was not like adding salt to injury, it was really adding salt to injury. Such thoughtless jeers riled Chukwubundu and he did not speak tongue in cheek.

"Officer, you know that sometimes you do not fight that big guy because you were sure-footed that you would be victorious," began Chukwubundu, "you fight him for one reason: to be left alone. Win, lose, or a stalemate. He most likely would bother you less. At least, you have shown him that you have got some mettle."

"You might as well get a noose than to test your mettle in that brawl in which losing would make your later state worse than the former," said the police officer.

"Have you heard that statement that goes like, 'give me freedom or give me death'?" asked Chukwubundu.

"A wise man chooses his fight diligently. Your people," continued the police officer, referring to the Igbos, "have no place for burial for those who kill themselves. When your people adjudged you to have defiled the land they laid you to rest in the sacrilegious bush. They do not bury you, you know that, they just throw you inside the bush to be feast for the beasts and elements. Make your statements and get behind the counter," he reminded the traders.

"The day will come when people like you will know what it is to be free," offered Chukwudi.

"Wait for that day! But for now, you're the usual suspects, always protesting and causing mayhem. Make your statements and get behind the counter," repeated the officer.

Getting behind the counter was an unsavory experience. It was a euphemism. But, there were two different kinds of counters at the police stations. There was the inner one and there was the outer one. When the police wanted to be benevolent to their victims they placed them in the outer counter where one would be safe from molestations. When they wanted to teach one a lesson they would shove the victim inside the inner counter. Over inside this counter, they would watch the victim from a pouch in their office as miscreants lashed and exerted their authority over the intruder, because those who were there first had lordship over the new entrants. One had to be steel to withstand the mayhem they would inflict on the newest entrant. Kanka had been inside the inner counter before and had learned his lesson. He was so manhandled that he had to fight back to spare himself of further beating. When they discovered that he was ready to defend himself against their battery he was let go. He was not ready to go in there, but if that was what the police had planned he knew that he had to defend himself. But one thing the police were certain about was that they risk putting these men's lives in danger if they were thrown inside the inner counter because the uprising they were purported to have led was against petty and hardened criminals. And most of the inmates inside the inner cellblocks were criminals of all hues.

In their written statements, the men had denied their involvement in the upheaval of the past few days. They had stated that they had planned a peaceful march, but due to police incompetence the police allowed it to be hijacked by some rabble-rousers, miscreants, layabouts, small thieves, some never-do-wells, and malcontents looking for an opportunity to let the world know that they were not going anywhere yet. They had railed against the police, accusing the police of collaborating with thieves in laying ambush and attacks against the traders in their daily pursuit of purpose. They had bemoaned the travails they faced and being left at the mercy of armless and armed robbers and hoodlums. The police they stated had been the ears and eyes of these societal evil men. They had provided arms to the thieves and had been retained by the thieves. They could not sit idly by and watch their toil and sweat go to waste. They reiterated that they were opposed to taking the law into their own hands, but empathized with the demonstrators and had wished it had happened earlier. The traders and other innocent citizens could not continue to live in fear while those who should be living in fear run amok in broad daylight with impunity. The citizens decided to do what the police had deliberately ignored to do even when it was exactly what they were paid to do. They accused the police of dereliction of duty. Exercising their minimal English pedantry, the traders told the police that revolution or insurrection was usually caused by discontentment and dissatisfaction.

These were traders who peruse the British *Guardian* and the *New York Times* every morning as a way to kick-start their day before it became busy. They were aware of the goings-on in their world sans in-depth analytic conclusions of the whole lot of information that came across their purview. Their analytic grasp may be lacking in finesse, but their knowledge of events around them and the world at large was commonsensical and top-notch. They could regurgitate that one liner by famous world leaders past and present to the affirmative holler and hooray of their neighbors and other onlookers.

In their statement, they had reminded the police that stupid obstinacy to peaceful change like the negotiation before the genocidal Biafran war made that war essentially inevitable. They had told the police that peace must be inherently submissive to justice. Destruction was the unintended consequence of any peaceful demonstration when justice is trampled upon. They had opined in their statement that if peace was submissive to justice, devoid of violence must be submissive to peace, and violence must be submissive to subjugation. In other words the traders told the police that subjugation of their free weal to trade without molestation led to demonstration and violence, and that justice led to peace and not peace to justice, and where there was peaceful existence it would be devoid of injustice and violence. Finally, they told the police that they wanted to have their day in court.

There was not much difference in the statement they had come in with that was rejected by the police sergeant even when it was completely ultra vires for the police officer to intimidate and con them not to submit what they had crafted with the help and counsel of their attorney. The police had thought that compelling the men to write their statement at the station would throw them off their guards. That game plan failed woefully. The main difference was some spelling errors. But the major points the men wanted to put across to the police were embedded in the final statements. In the end, it was not much of a statement. It was like a grievance report because what transpired and what the men really knew about the events were not centerpiece of the statements. Kanka, who had more mastery of the issues, had a more voluminous piece and reflected more the opinion of those stood accused.

As soon as they turned in the statements the men were bundled over the outer counter where they awaited the arrival of their lawyer, Mr. Guzo. It was not long when Mr. Guzo arrived, and to his chagrin what he saw was against the verbal agreement he reached with the police chief, Mr. Sansom, that the men would not be placed over the counter. He was further incensed that the statements the men provided to the police were rejected and that they were coerced to make new statements. When the lawyer confronted the police sergeant on the rejection of the original statements provided by his men, Mr. Ekarika had told the lawyer that the men were coached in the statement and had no factual truth, which was what the police were looking for. Mr. Guzo had reminded the police sergeant that his clients had lawyer-client privilege which could not be taken away by an ill-informed and incompetent police force. The determination to accept or not accept those statements in evidence was not the police call to make. The lawyer told the police sergeant that what he did was a violation of the right of his clients, that his action was ultra vires and had no basis in law. He was going to lodge a complaint with the police chief, and he was going to take it up with the judge and demand an apology.

Nevertheless, he was able to post bail for the union leaders and asked the police to send him information on the date of their arraignment before the judge.

From the police station, the men went back to their businesses. They were triumphant and were given some heroes' welcome as soon as they were sighted in the vicinity of the stalls.

It was Monday morning. The businesses were in full swing. Banks were operational again. For five days the whole businesses were at a standstill. Buyers who came to Eureka from far and wide were stranded, to say the least. Now there was peace in the land, and everywhere people were coming out of their crevices. Once, again, the town was teeming with people. There was a sense of relief. It felt like the people can once again have the pockets bulge with wads of money without fear of being mugged. It felt so good again.

Earlier that morning Kanka's wards had gone and opened his stalls. While the town smoldered a very good and faithful customer was trapped in the fracas. Mallam Abokina. He normally traveled from a very far place, about 430 miles away. Each time he came down to buy his goods, Kanka's days were made. Because whatever article he did not have in stock, this customer trusted that Kanka would get it from one of his neighbors at a fairly reasonable price also. He never stepped foot inside anyone else's stall unless he had to. And he rarely did. His intuition had assured him that he was better off dealing with Kanka and Kanka dealing with everyone else on his behalf. That intuition was never misguided. It was spot on the money. The trouble was his language barrier and the interpreter he had employed to help him navigate the language terrain around him; he could not communicate in English language, and he had a pettifogger as an interpreter. That was his undoing.

Mallam Abokina was a very dedicated customer and trusted every word and prices Kanka offered to him. And he usually bought fairly large quantities of materials. One could tell in his body language that he was weary of Mallam Sabo. Plainly speaking, he distrusted Mallam Sabo. In his infantile naivete he had trusted his hunch that if either of the two men would want to cheat him the other would tell. The trader did not want to lose him. All Mallam Sabo needed was a fleeting sign of infidelity on the part of Kanka, and his prized jewel would be gone. And there were other interested men perambulating about for any sign of saber rattling between Kanka and Sabo. In the end, Abokina was in a limbo, caught in the middle of nowhere, between the devil and the deep blue sea.

"You Igbo people, you are always agitating, fighting, and causing mayhem," began Mallam Sabo, in his Indian accent, that morning as he greeted Kanka.

Kanka loathed him inwardly and always tried to ignore him. He never wanted to offend him because he did not want to lose his customer.

"Welcome, Mallam," he said, referring to Mallam Abokina. Mallam Abokina affirmed with a nod of the head.

"You people cannot stop fighting and destroying your own property," said Sabo.

"You can say that because you do not understand," said Kanka. "We are just trying to make it easier for you to come down here without having to lose all that you had worked for."

"It is always one thing or the other. First, you wanted to burn down the whole country and you got what you were looking for and you wanted to burn down your own country. Are you never tired?" asked Mallam Sabo.

"We cannot stand oppression for too long, my friend. You people can but we cannot. If your state in life was unacceptable to you, make an effort to correct it. Every man must work hard, I mean work hard, to rid himself of captivity. You do not sit down on your hind and expect it to go away. That was what the people of this community did," Kanka told him.

Mallam Sabo, the interpreter, was a very shrewd man, who found himself owning the same kind of business as Kanka and Mallam Abokina. He had no training in the business but felt he could make it in that business world by some kind of effort. By inflating the prices that was offered his friend he was able to save a lot of money from his dealings. Then he thought he could use the money he fraudulently made off his friend to trade on his own. And he made a lot of money on each trip. By his antics and threats and guile he was able to set Kanka up against Abokina. He would bargain with Kanka down to his limits, chopped into his margin of profit, and then added his premium to whatever that was the finally agreed price for the goods. At the end of the day, Mallam Abokina would end up paying for the items very expensively which invariably would lead him selling his goods at very high price with minimal profit.

"You know that you are a born thief," Kanka cajoled the interpreter in his native language.

"You are the known thief," Mallam Sabo shot back in Kanka's vernacular.

In between giving him the price of an item, Kanka would interject a curse and the trickster would respond in kind sometimes with a barrage of curse words.

"Amadioha would break your head," jabbed Kanka, in between giving him a price of an item and as the bargain went on.

"It was you that Amadioha would destroy first," hit back Mallam Sabo.

That was his stock in trade. He was not all that fluent in English language, but he had enough mastery of figures to get him by. It was hard to mislead him when it came to figures. He did not know much about the Igbo language, but he knew a lot of curse words and when they were used and directed toward him. Mallam Sabo was not a language fiend, but he had a fairly good knowledge to keep abreast of events around him.

When the day's job was done interpreting he would help his friend and make sure that all he paid for were loaded. The following day he would come back, first he would walk down the stalls and cross-check that he was given a fairly good price on the items if not the cheapest prices. With paper and pen he would come down to Kanka and table his case. The money his friend overpaid he would convert much of it to goods and the rest as change, to boot. He had two other folks he swindled time and again, but those he took to other traders in the areas. Because he had no training he never mastered the intricacies of owning that kind of business. It was a game where somehow everyone lost. His business never grew, but he still had steady supply of goods after every visit and interpretation work was done. He dwelt on it and fed on it. He was craftier than the serpent. Kanka never asked him to send these other businessmen to him because the man's wiliness bothered him a lot.

Truly, time flies. Three weeks later Kanka and the leaders of the Ureka Market Amalgamated Traders Union appeared in court. They pleaded not guilty. It was a formality. The police had no evidence against them. The judge understood the issues involved and the genesis of the whole saga. She did not want to put the police on trial. The evidence was stacked against the police. They had aided and abated criminal activities of every kind. It was intolerable even in the eyes of those who were not physically impacted. In fact, the judge acted with due diligence. She berated the force, calling them names and asking the leadership to come up with a plan to address the endemic rot prevalent in the whole rank and file. She gave the force a ninety-day ultimatum to proffer a blueprint for the plan of action. Inside her court was a small crowd of people. They, too, had gathered for a show of force in support of the men whose plea was not guilty. When the judge lifted her gavel and hammered it on her desk there was a huge uproar, then quickly subdued, in her courtroom. Kanka and his colleagues walked out of the court in Bolshevik salute, clenched fists, the origin and significance they knew naught a thing about. And right there outside the court was a throng of masses of the people, traders and artisans, teachers and pupils. They had gathered for a show of force in support of the men being arraigned. They were witnessing peace in the land. That was an undeniable fact. Problem solved.

But it was an officer standing outside the court building who had something to say.

"These men are surely communists." He, too, did not know what he was talking about.

CHAPTER 4

Umudede was a bustling city. And the air was welcoming. There was no foreboding. It looked every inch relaxing. It was calming to some frayed nerves. And Jewel could feel it. While Eureka was a city full of hustlers, and petty traders and big-time businessmen and women, with great hustle and bustle as a way of life, Umudede was quieter, serene, a little less in population than Eureka. It was in this city that Chance hailed from. It was in this city that Ogidigi pitched his tent, following the footsteps of his great-great-grandfather.

Ogidigi knew that his son was coming home from the United States. He had also been intimated that he was coming with a bunch of friends. It was a rare thing to do especially since after the brutal war that really decimated millions of people of Biafra. He was curious. But he was prepared. He was a man of considerable means. He was in need of nothing except being a continuous check on himself. It had been five years since Chance left the Biafran shores.

It was early evening when Chance and his friends arrived. Ogidigi had dispatched one of his workers to go to the airport to bring them home. Chance and his friends had no need for hotel. His father's house had extra rooms and tastefully furnished. It may not be a hotel, but why need a hotel when every trapping one sought for in a hotel was available at home?

He was happy that his son, now his first child, had come home. However, he did not like the picture of his son. But he said nothing to that effect. Ogidigi was such a man that would never wear the content of his heart and mind on his face, no matter the level of teasing. So, Chance and his friends were warmly welcomed. He asked his son to make himself and his friends comfortable. There were rooms on the upper floor, he told him.

It was painful for Ogidigi to see his son in such a state of attire. Was he going mad? he queried himself again and again. He could hardly sleep, and the night just slouched on. Some would fall asleep and stayed asleep toward dawn but not Ogidigi. He stayed awake all night.

He did not talk to his son upon their arrival about his concern, and overnight since he never slept Ogidigi had time to think about his son. His son bothered him in no small measure.

While everyone else slept that early Saturday morning Ogidigi woke up his son, Osai. His son's company was still asleep. They had gone out last night to free themselves for a moment from the drudgery that had become their travel to Biafra. Umudede was a sprawling city with a nightlife of her own. Chance and his friends had gone out to one of the best discotheques in the whole of Biafra. And the music was good.

As he urged his son to go in and sit on the front passenger's seat of the metallic Range Rover he did not plan to hide his thought as he tried to suppress his emotion. It was like commandeering and Chance understood it. The tone was unmistakable and nearly betrayed him. He was not a man that was given to outward emotion although he was most emotional privately. All he was trying not to do was to convey or give any room for question as to where they were going that early morning from his son. Osai had not caught that much of sleep that morning as it was not long since they came back from their rendezvous.

Osai did not know where they were headed to. It was about three miles' stretch of road. After about the first two miles the atmosphere began to become familiar to him. He began to recollect where that road led to. It was the notorious Atamiri River. Not soon after they got to the outskirts of the river. However, one had to walk about one quarter of a mile to get to the riverbanks. Everyone just had to park their vehicle and walk the rest of the distance to get to the waterfront. Ogidigi, in spite of himself, was no exception. In this side of Umudede everyone knew him. Everyone respected him not so much because he was a well-to-do man but because of who he was. He had hoped that no one would see his son and the way he was attired that morning and in his company. No one could have recognized Osai if it was not for the presence of his father. He looked different. They had not walked long when a young man was coming from the opposite direction. As the young man passed by, he offered his greetings to Ogidigi. Ogidigi acknowledged and continued at his usual pace while Osai followed gallantly. However, the young man, as soon as Osai walked past him, decided that he must look back to make sure that the tall elegant man following Ogidigi was Osai, who left the shore of Umudede about five years ago for the United States of America. The young man was not too sure since the fella in the company of Ogidigi had his hair braided. That was what Ogidigi had dreaded, the chance of any member of their community to see him in the company of his rascal of a son.

"Hey, Dad." began Osai. "This pathway has not changed."

Ogidigi pretended to not hear his son.

"I mean to say that it is what it is," continued Osai.

"No, it's changing," intoned his father.

"I mean to say, it looks like I can still find my footprint of six years ago when I trod this path with my friends," said Osai.

"Well, I mean to say," mimicked his father. "Look at that tree over there. Six years ago, it was like a shrub." He set his gaze in the direction of a mango tree whose branches were being swayed by the early morning breeze.

"Now, kids can climb on it and feel free staying on top of it. Some things do not change. They are fixed by nature," he told his son.

"That is an absolute truth," he concurred with his father.

Not long afterward they made it to the edges of the river. That part of the river was the creek section of the river. Its water moved but not a lot. It seemed constantly a still water. At one corner of the river was a running water that gushed from a pipeline-like hole on the side of the bank or the river wall. The water was clean and immaculate, and people did drink it without having to worry about its purity and safety. Those who had no access to anything better cherished the water from that source and strove to keep it clean at all times. Everyone respected that source and like an unwritten writ kept it sacred. The only connection this source had with the river was just that it gushed out of the wall of the river. It was natural and beautiful, cool to drink at any time of the day.

On the other side was the seemingly stagnant section of the river down the bottom of the river infested with leeches and swam of tiny, little fishes in their hundreds.

"Oh, look at those leeches," said Osai, pointing to a colony of brownish leeches that were sometimes difficult to see in underwater current.

"I thought that by now they would be no more," he continued.

"Well, some were no more. But new issues populate the water. They're ever present in this water," said Ogidigi, tacitly reminding his son the naturalness in that water. "And they're still brownish and bloodsucking vampires of the near waters," he was quick to add.

Osai did not need to be reminded. On several occasions in the past especially when he was little, they had latched on to his ankle and calf each time he stepped his feet inside the water. The memory was evergreen. He hated them so much so because it took a great deal of effort to get them to release that clipper-like jaw on their victims.

It was not that they were in the water of Atamiri for any special purpose that early morning. However, it was kind of a mission accomplished. Like someone who was looking for something and suddenly decided that that very stuff was of no matter and decided to call off the search. Without any known reason, he asked his son that it was about time that they went back home.

"But, Dad, why are we here this morning?" Osai ventured to ask his father.

"You don't want to know," he told his son calmly and quietly as he began walking back to the area where the vehicle was parked.

Ogidigi owed no one any explanation, let alone his son that he still fended for. Even if he was not fending for him, he still did not owe him an explanation. And Osai knew that well enough. However, what he did not comprehend was the import of their trip to the river that morning. Perhaps, time spent abroad had dulled his understanding of his father. He was livid, nevertheless, he understood that it was in his own best interest to keep his ire, especially toward his father to himself.

The short drive home was smooth, quiet, and eerily calm. No one said anything to each other. Chance's friends were still asleep when they made it home. It was not that much far for anyone to take note. Moreover, it was not that much long since they came back from their night outing.

"Now, sit down over there," commanded Ogidigi, as he pointed to the couch in the near corner of his spatial living room. "Now, tell me what you think you're doing!" he demanded of his son.

Osai was somehow confused, not exactly knowing what his father was driving at. He stared his father directly in the eyes and said nothing.

"Don't look into my eyes like that, or I'll pluck them out of their sockets. Where did you learn that from?" he roared at his son.

Osai threw away his gaze momentarily.

"Dad, but what are you talking…," he ventured to say.

"You mean that you don't know what I'm talking about. You mean to say that I sent you to America to lose your head."

Osai was jolted to reality as soon as his father made mention of head. He ran his right hand through his braids, and for the first time he felt a disdain for braiding it. He said nothing.

"Whose son are you?" queried his father, not wanting to elicit any reply but trying to drive the point home. "Look at what you've done to yourself," he continued. "I did not send you to America to effeminate yourself. How dare you dress yourself thus? How dare you pierce your nose and wear a stud on your ears?"

"But, Dad, it is a fad…"

"Be quiet," roared his father. "It is not a fad to unman yourself. It is not fad to unscrew your head from your neck. It is not a fad to give a false impression of yourself. It is not a fad to make caricature of yourself and your kindred people. It is not a fad to be plain stupid." Ogidigi went about listing a litany of fads unexpected of his son. And as soon as he mentioned kindred people, Osai knew that his father was referring to himself. He was a man who in a lot of cases cared a lot about what others may think of him.

Osai had his eyes fixated on his father like a contest of who would bat an eyelid first. It was one of those idiosyncrasies one usually picked up staying in America. His father could not believe that his son could have the effrontery to stare directly deep into his eyes without blinking for so long.

"You must be out of your mind. How dare you look at me like that?" asked Ogidigi.

"But, Dad…," began Osai.

"But me no but! What is that you have in the demarcation of your nostrils?"

"It is nothing," said Osai as he detached the ring he had pinned in between his nostrils.

"If they are nothing, then throw them away. Do not create a foolery where there is none. And the rings in your ears, do away with them before I throw a glance at your direction again," he said.

Osai had no illusion where his father was headed to: his hair. His father had no stomach for trivial. He was closed to being plain as the nose is closed to the mouth.

"Dad, you've not changed," said Osai as he began to remove the stud on his ears.

"But, I'm changing. And I don't want to hear that from you anymore. One thing that is certain is change. But you grow older being wiser. That is change. You change for good. You do not grow older foolish. That is a path to perdition. You did not go to America to forget who you are, where you came from, whose son you are. Anyone who does not care about what the next person is thinking about him hasn't quite grown. Hardly will anyone tell you what they think about you if they seriously think that it will depreciate your regard for yourself especially if they want you to perish in hell," he schooled his child.

"And I tell you," continued Ogidigi, "before you step out of this compound again and before anyone else becomes aware that you are in town and before sunset, I want anything you have on your hair that is not yours to be removed."

"But, Dad…"

"No, we cannot have an argument about this." Incomprehensibly and quite bemused, Osai tried to continue to press his point.

"Dad, I've come of age. I can do whatever I want with my life," he told his bemused father.

"Come of age? Whose name are you bearing? Is that what they told you in America? Perhaps, you don't want to go back to America. Perhaps, it's time for you to come home for good. Can you fend for yourself? And I tell you, son, even when you think that you've grown and can fend for yourself, a man does not outrun his buttocks. I want you to understand that," Ogidigi told him.

Incredulously Osai stared at his father.

"And I tell you, son," he continued, "some things are just too constant they cannot change. You see the pillars that hold the heavens and earth are fixed and cannot change. Whenever they are shaken the foundations of the world will crumble in its ruins and the firmament will smite the earth to mere rubbles." He paused.

"Osai," he intoned, "I tell you most solemnly. Whomever the gods will destroy they first made him mad. The world is going mad does not mean that you will lose your head.

"Osai," said Ogidigi, in a voice mellowed quite unlike him, "you remember that river creek we just visited. We didn't visit there this morning for nothing. I couldn't have deprived myself some sleep this morning only for sightseeing of somewhere I could go to with my eyes closed in the dark," he told him.

"Listen! If you don't want to listen to me. We are going back there, and I am going to feed you to the leeches. I'm going to sit down quietly and watch them suck your blood until their entrails swell to bursting point with your blood. And you know what, son? Your mother will not save you," he warned him as he tried to leave his palatial living room.

"But, Dad, what would I tell my friends?"

"You can tell them that a butterfly buried itself inside your head. But to be truthful, tell them that you are so stupid that you've not behave like your father's son."

"But, Father, these things complement my look."

"What happened to your looks, to start with?" he said, gyrating his eyeballs at his child.

"Nothing," answered Osai.

"Then you're a fool to distort yourself. You do not need them," he told him. "They mock you. You denigrate yourself. You made yourself a laughing stock. The throng of people may not tell you. But you have to tell yourself," he told him as he walked away from his son, before he lost himself.

However, as a parting shot to underline the severity of his mental agitation and diatribe, he added, "You want to look the baddest, but if you kept fooling around like this, then you're on that freedom flight to be among the earth's worsts," said Ogidigi sternly. "If you're still thinking that you're beyond reproach, I'll tell you that it doesn't take the whole world to raise a child because too many hands spoiled the broth. It takes but a village. If you were thinking that I can't subdue and submerge you inside that water alone, think again. I would go and gather chaps younger than yourself across this community to shell you back into shape and tighten your loose nuts. I'm not going to let you be an agent provocateur that would be the harbinger that drives our small world into decadence. You're *the how* it starts. You want to be another progenitor of the ills that have challenged our norms and mores. You're it! I'll nip you in the bud. Nonsense! We don't need you here, and I can't stomach it while I still have that one puff of air within me. Lest you forgot, the okra fruit, no matter how tall its stalk grows, in real sense is never taller than its planter. All it takes is to bend it to level heights. Get it into your big skull and get it straight, or else this community will hear *the you and I* story, and you won't be alive to recollect it. You've a right to deceive yourself or live your life, but not a right to mislead the vulnerable. A butterfly that is burning somehow prides itself as emitting some oil. Straighten yourself and fool around here no more, or else your mother would never know what has become of your bones."

He looked on as his father made it to the adjacent room and to the next room and up the stairs. As he sauntered across the room to the other side of the house where his friends were, he thought deeply about himself and about his father, the man he had known and come to admire, the man he had believed in and come to respect, the man he had seen walked and copied his gait, the man who spoke softly or harshly depending on the issues, the man he knew that wasted no time threatening, but the man whose every threat must be carried out to the letter. He knew that his father was a difficult man but not a difficult man to understand. He liked riddles but had no time for priggishness. He had abundant love for his family, yet anyone who made himself a goat, not a scapegoat, would be sacrificed on the altar of discipline, like that bonehead he-goat that had the idiocy and effrontery to be sniffing and climbing his mother's privacy.

Osai had no illusion what his father was capable of doing. He may be pompously all things to his peers and acquaintances, but he had been chopped down to his own level before his father. He remembered vividly seven years ago. It was his younger brother, Chikwem. Chikwem was a hothead. He was twelve years old. He believed in nothing and conformed to none. In that youthful age, so to speak, he was law unto himself. One early evening hour he had made their father mad, very, very mad. Ogidigi had him in his grip. However, Chikwem had slipped out of his grip and ran toward one of the approaches to the compound. His father had made a dash to grab him, but Chikwem was as slippery as a salmon in water and ran away. Ogidigi bit his fingers in frustrations and walked away. Instinctively, as he turned back to check what Chikwem was doing next, lo and behold, he had a bunch of pebbles in his hands. He was standing in the middle of the road that ran in front of that approach to the compound. He had hauled the first shot at his father and missed. He was about hauling the second shot as his father was turning. He knew that he was beyond reach. But what he was doing was absolute madness. It was stupid of any child to exhibit that kind of behavior. That was worse than a child using his left hand to point at his father's house. Only a bastard could do such. Chikwem was not a bastard. He was rightfully the son of Ogidigi. And that made his father's anger to boil over. He was livid with rage, but made a determined effort to walk back inside the house. Seething with fury at Chikwem, he brought his meat cleaver and sat down.

Never was it heard that a child would have his back to the road and haul a stone into his father's compound, let alone at his father. Chikwem had crossed the Rubicon of decorum. His days were numbered. And his father waited. Then suddenly, there was a knock on the door and it was his father-in-law.

Nwaturuchi had driven a long way. He had come for no particular reason. That was fate in action. The way he was ushered in by Ogidigi conveyed the untold message that something was amiss. When he saw the meat cleaver lying on the table in front of his sonin-law he knew that it was the gods intervening and directing his course to come.

After exchange of pleasantries, presentation of kola nut and all that niceties he was given the full gist why the meat cleaver was out. He knew his son-in-law well enough. He did not like to cross anyone's path, and no one crossed his path and got away with it. Nwaturuchi told his daughter to prepare some extra clothes for lodging for Chikwem. He left that night with him. Thus, Chikwem escaped death by a sharp cut to the jugular. Osai remembered all this, and goose bumps came all over him. He did not allow himself a fleeting moment to think about the repercussion of noncompliance. He just had to do it. The problem was just how to do it in the presence of his friends who had seen him flaunt his new hairdo.

Osai was not the first son of Onuma Ogidigi. But was honed in the image of his father like he was the first son, though it was not necessary that the first child had to be exactly a chip off the old block. He had the lanky gait of his grandfather. At six feet, four inches, he was a tall chap. He was his father in many ways than one. But he was not his father in so many ways. He lived a little bit on grandiosity, measured in speech but verbose in delivery. Osai was wont to say ornithological specimen of identical plumage invariably conglomerates to the nearest proximity.

"What's that?" queried his friend.

"I'm saying that birds of the same feather flock together," he tried to explain.

"You should have said that in plain language," his friend told him.

"That is the way I want it. That is my style."

"You're full of pomposities," said his friend.

"Not without reasons."

"Your reasons are immaterial."

"No, they are in that self-assuredness."

"Life doesn't have to be that much complicated," his friend Nwachi reminded him.

He had always wanted to be different. He had never elected to do anything because it was easy. Actually, he loved to tread along unchartered territory even if it portended to be tasking as long as there was some dividend at the end of the venture. He was discreet and deliberative as if he was in counsel with himself. He was as strong as he was determined. He wholeheartedly believed that intimidation was subtler than harassment. That was his dicta. That was his mantra. A few weeks before he left Biafra for the United States, he had traveled with one of the buses on one of those going and coming from the embassy in that unending scrutiny by the consulate to make sure that one was what one claimed that one was and that one would not be a public charge while in the United States. He was on his way back, and they had just made it to the bus park. The whole place was rowdy. It was hustle and bustle in galore. There was no order. Touts were howling for passengers. Bus conductors were clearing ways for their drivers to move their buses to take vantage positions. It was utter lawlessness. No one was in control of the park. It was a free fall at the park, as always. Mildly put, it was survival of the fittest. To compound matters, there was a light drizzle earlier. The whole place was wet and muddy.

As he alighted from the bus he saw one woman fearfully and tearfully clinging to the hem of the shirt of one of the conductors. The conductor was making way for his driver to take position, and in the fog of the moment one of the bus's tires trundled the woman's bag of rice and broke it. It spilled and then the rains. The woman was clinging to the conductor for some compensation. She was a petty trader. It could have been her last cash invested and now on the verge of being lost.

"But you left your bag of rice on the way," the conductor charged at the woman. The woman sniveled.

"So because of that you have to trample on her good," interjected Osai who was standing a meter away and watching the proceeding.

"What was your own in this matter?" charged the conductor at Osai as he made to leave, his eyes bloodshot.

"My own is that you can't destroy this woman's article of trade and just walk away," said Osai while blocking the conductor path moving forward.

"You need to get out of my way," demanded the conductor shoving Osai away, as he staggered backward to maintain his balance.

"Do not touch me again, or I'm going to hew you here for all to see," warned Osai. "Compensate this woman!" he told the conductor.

"Get out of my way," said the conductor, pushing him away.

Osai rushed forward and grabbed the conductor, who was about his age, on his collar. The boy extended his hands and also grabbed Osai by his collar. But, all of a sudden, in a jiffy, and like a flash, Osai lifted the boy and slammed him against the hood of the bus, denting it. A fisticuffs ensued. The small, sizable crowd whooped and hollered. It was then that the driver noticed what was going on and came to the rescue of his ward.

In this business, as in every business, time was of the essence. Time was money. The bus driver compensated the woman. He also understood that Osai was not going to let them go like that, as his shirt was dirtied and also lost a button. He made a scene to fight both the driver and his conductor and disrupt their business. He was restrained again and again. As more onlookers gathered he tempered his agitation. But not for nothing. He also got enough for his troubles, enough to replace his shirt. As he walked away, he pulled his rumpled shirt straight up, composed himself together, and held his head high.

That was Osai. The son of Onuma Ogidigi. If Osai was deliberative, Ogidigi was contemplative. At six feet, six inches, he was a mountain man of a sort. Coupled with his huge weight it gave him the image of a tough cop, which he never was, and did not want to be. Because of his huge frame it would not be unfair to have one of his hands tied behind in a duel and still come out not vanquished. All he needed was to keep his balance and land a good blow on his opponent. One good blow to the jugular was all he needed to end any duel against any opponent.

He had a tougher upbringing. His father was a petty criminal. It was a life he was bent on getting away from. However, the urge of not working hard to make a living tugged at him strongly, pulling and almost tearing him apart. He never wanted to follow in the footsteps of his father. He wanted to carve a niche for himself. After high school education, he worked in the local abattoir. The family had some herds of different animal breeding. He was in charge of taking care of the goats, sheep, cows, and horses, and turkeys, and even geese and gander. The farm also held a herd of swine that year in, year out had a collection of pregnant sows. He was like the swain, and he dirtied himself and was always there when the sows readied themselves ahead of farrowing. He never cared about dirt, and in acquainting himself with those duties they gave him easy access to the abattoir. And he was able to sell to petty meat sellers from their family herds at the same time was able to make some stipend working there. Then life became monotonous. He got bored.

Over the years his grandfather, unbeknownst to him, had acquired massive pieces of land, either by hook or crook. Some were acquired by concession after some legal tussle in the local council. Some were yielded to him because very few wanted to mess with him or cross his path. So Ogidigi had a lot to inherit. There were so much at his disposal in terms of land that they did not have need for that much. So year after year the family would lease portions of the land to people who had none and wanted a place to do their farming. After about two years of managing his family holdings, he was fed up. One morning, he went to his father and told him that he wanted to join the army. Joining the army in those days without a high school education was hard work made harder by an ignorant choice. His father and grandfather and those before them had tilled the ground for him. All he needed was to water and nurture it and watch it grow and bear fruits. His father objected and ordered him out of his sight. It was about two weeks later that he returned to his father and asked for his blessing. He completely understood his father. He understood the futility of arguing with a man who had already made up his mind. As he lay prostrate before his father on the third asking, his father kicked him in the rib cage. He rolled over his back, got up, and without saying bye to his mother he walked out and disappeared.

When he walked into the recruitment center the next morning at the army post, the guy behind the counter looked at him straight in the eyes and nodded and shook his head at the same time. What was this tall elegant chap doing at his center? he asked himself. He must have missed his way and needed some direction. He looked puzzled when the young man asked about what it would take to fill out the form and get enlisted in the army corps.

"What do you need?" queried the army cadet.

"I want to fill out the form to join the army," said Ogidigi, throwing his glance this way and that way.

"Join the army?" retorted the cadet.

"Yes, sir," said Ogidigi as he looked at the cadet at the recruitment post straight in the eyes for the first time, of his own.

"Are you sure you want to join the army?" said the recruiter.

Ogidigi did not understand why it was a hassle to fill out this military form. But the cadet understood. Military life was hard work in itself. But his concern against Ogidigi was different. He was that handsome. Though handsomeness never disqualified one from joining the force. One had to be rugged mentally. He was not sure Ogidigi outwardly had what it would take to make it through the ranks. He could have put his physique to better use. Were he born in better lands he could have been a star sport fellow. He was very tall, a little taller than what was ideal for the force in those days. His height was just too high, giving him not much room to bend or crouch to take a shot. He was bound to stand out in a military phalange because he would be shoulder over taller than his colleagues. Such was the thinking of the recruiter that he was inquisitive in offering the form to Ogidigi in the first instance. However, it was not his place to make that determination. If he was not going to be good in the front line he could be put to other useful purposes for the force. And that would be the determination of his bosses.

Two weeks later, he had a letter in the mail that he should report to camp. In those days, defunct Nigeria was in dire need of men for her armed forces. The colonial masters were leaving, and Nigerian leaders wanted to indigenize all the branches of the armed forces. So entrance examination was not prerequisite for admission to the force. Actually a high school diploma could get one enlisted into the armed forces. Ogidigi had it.

For six months Ogidigi and his fellow new recruits had their training at the military academy. His height actually posed a minor problem. And for that reason, he was drafted into the intelligence unit of the force. For another eighteen months, all he did was to have the early morning drills, attend classes, polish his weapons, keep himself fit, and do nothing more.

Without wars military life was challenging, drab, and boring to say the least. But he was not prepared to walk away from it. He displayed strong leadership qualities with no penchant for frivolities. Based on attitude to work and excellent work ethics he was chosen to attend the prestigious military school at Sandhurst in Berkshire, south of England. Among his peers he was one of the luckier ones chosen. It was tougher than he had imagined. But he was determined and he hung on to it. He believed that if it were to be easy then the benefits would be not that great. Success surely required steady perseverance. Easy channels were for the lily-livered. Shortcuts belittled the soul of the brave. It was a deviation from his own father, Amakiri.

Whatever begotten of snake must have a long tail. Amakiri was an almost carbon copy of his father, Emeremnini. He tried artfully to perfect what was started by his father and to an extent did not fall far away from the tree. He did things his own way, anyway. He also excelled. He began as a land-grabber. A noisy claimant. He labored in the shadow of darkness, not as armed robber but as a feller of timber of different categories. He was a well-known dealer in timber and woods but cultivated no trees. His day began in the thick of the night, especially during full moon. He and two of his protégés would invade the forest and chop down trees of their chosen. Of course, they had to do a reconnoitering of the environment they wanted to invade, mark the trees they wanted to fell. With their torchlight they can proceed to see the night as day without any inhibition. He owned a two-wheeled truck. For miles, they pushed, and before the earliest of dawn they were done and dusted. When other traders buy stuff to replenish their stock, his own stock got replenished without a bargain.

The good thing about Amakiri was that he never operated at home. He traveled beyond boundaries to the neighboring towns to hew the woods. But at home he was a terror of another sort. He was wont to claim people's land portion with a straight face. He had such magical powers that people did everything to avoid a tug-of-war with him over any pieces of land. Better be late than late over a piece of land. Out of intimidation and actual devilry he was able to accumulate lands of different and sizable portions, far more than anyone of his generation. And owing lands was tantamount to being wealthy. It was such wealth that Ogidigi inherited and the whole family profited and prospered from them.

Emeremnini was adept in his own trade. But he was a benevolent thief, a pirate, things unheard of before the advent of the Europeans on these shores. He was a swimmer of great prowess. He could swim faster than a man could oar his canoe. He owned his own canoe. Nevertheless, he was good swimming. What he did for a living was banditry at high sea, so to speak. His banditry was limited to the sea, closer to the shores, or river as the case might be. He and his group of marauders would waylay boatmen and fishermen and half the toils of the night and disappear in the horizon of the river. They were that considerate in purpose and action still to the chagrin of their victims. He combined his banditry with hunting for games. He was so good with his guns that he could afford to use two Dane guns in both hands at the same time with utmost precision. In fact, most people of Umudede knew him as a hunter of prey. Because he made a show of his prey and made money off the animals he killed.

This was the lineage from which Osai hailed. Emeremnini begot Amakiri, Amakiri begot Ogidigi, and Ogidigi begot Osai. Osai was looking forward to the next generation. It was that generation that he was trying to carve a niche for himself. His father had begun to deviate from the checkered history of his father and grandfather. Buried in that checkered history were all the ill-gotten wealth that would never be returned to their rightful owners. It was wealth that had been transferred or inherited, unbeknownst to Osai, and not clearly understood by his own father either.

"Hey, what's been going on?" said Osai to his friends, with a little bit of disguised brashness in his tone. His friends were seated at the table for breakfast of bread and butter, cheese and custard, coffee and tea, milk, eggs, and honey. Though it was nascent Biafra, the Ogidigi family have the trappings of everything western.

"Who's this?" queried Jewel, curious at the intruder in their midst, interrupting their breakfast and quiet revelry.

"I'm Osai," said Chance.

"Where's Chance?" asked Turnkey, staring into the face of the tall guy standing right in front of him.

"I'm Chance," said Chance, to the bewilderment of his friends.

"You must be kidding me," returned Turnkey, as they all fixed their gazes at him with great astonishment.

Chance had had a great makeover in a twinkle of an eye. He had dismantled his braids. Removed his studs. Combed out his afro hair in such a fashion that it gave him an astonishingly handsomer visage.

"What a fuck were you doing in those braids?" queried Jason.

Candie puckered her lips. Her breasts heaved a little, and there was a rush of blood down her legs as she held herself together, realizing for the first time how handsome this dude had been. His handsomeness had been hidden in the camouflage that was his braids.

"Hey, guy, what happened with your braids?" asked Turnkey.

"And your ear studs," interjected Jewel.

"And your nose ring," chipped in Dusty.

They all came in quick succession that Chance did not have the chance to address them one at a time. And he did not have any plausible excuse for removing his regalia. He told his friends how he accompanied his father to the river and to their landholding that morning. It had been a long time, and his father wanted to familiarize him with the landholdings. While in the bush, all of a sudden a bee burrowed itself inside his strands. He labored to snuff the life out of the bee before it got to his skull. He had had no alternative than to remove the braids.

"After that, I decided that the studs and rings had to go as well," said Chance as he made himself comfortable in a chair around the breakfast table between Candie and Dusty.

"We thought that you've abandoned us and moved back to the States," said Turnkey.

"Hell no, not at all," replied Chance.

"You look a heck lot handsomer in your natural hair," said Dusty.

"Those braids made you really, really ugly," said Candie, looking him straight in the eyes, and then squinting her left eye.

"You should have told me that all along," demanded Chance, throwing a glance in her direction.

"You would not have listened to me, not in your linear worldview," chipped in Candie.

"Me, single-minded thought process? Hell! No, not at all, Candie," said Chance.

"Hey, Osai," came the voice of his father as he came through the breakfast area to the adjoining room leading to the other side of the annex.

"Good morning," said Ogidigi, as he threw a tonal salute to his guests. "How're you doing this morning, ladies and gentlemen?" asked Ogidigi, in his deep-throated British accent, barely understandable to his American guests. He introduced himself to the young folks, and they exchanged pleasantries before he bent his frame under the door.

"See me before dusk," he told his son, satisfied with his new looks.

"Hey, son, what's that your father called you now?" demanded Dusty.

"That's my name," said Chance.

"Is that your middle name?" asked Jewel.

"Yes, that's my middle name."

"And Chance, your first name?" queried Dusty again.

"No, my first name is Hercules."

"Hercules! I never knew that, you motherfucker," said Turnkey jokingly.

"You never asked. Moreover, Chance has taken over my name that it never bothered me. But my official document has 'Osai' as my middle name."

"I didn't know that," said Turnkey.

"I know," chirped in Candie

"Yes, she does know. As you have your blue passport, I have my land of the rising sun passport. Everything official about me is right there," explained Hercules.

"Well, henceforth, we will call you Hercules or Heck, how about that?" said Jason.

"It doesn't bother me," said Chance.

Growing up Chance never liked his first name for no known reason. Maybe for the sound of it and or perhaps for the mythical implication of it which he never knew about. Time and again he had blushed and fought because his peers had mentioned or referred to him by his first name. He completely rejected it. However, over time he had gotten accustomed to it, and with age he had come to accept it as fait accompli. Yet, wherever and whenever he could avoid it, he had evaded it like an artful dodger. As he grew up and became aware and knowledgeable he began to understand that the mythical impetus was not that so bad. He accepted it. However, by then, his nickname had burrowed into his existence and taken over his recognition as his persona.

These guys bantered for much of the morning as they shifted from one issue to another topic to an endless array of issues and jokes to yap and bandy about. Some were just too hilarious. Jason was boisterous in his laughter. Sometimes they sounded like quacking. Even when it was not that funny, he would deliberately quack in such a way to elicit some real laughter from others. Dusty and Jewel were in between chuckle and laughter. They were noisy but not as Jason, who was thoroughly enjoying himself. Chance had tears come to his eyes. Turnkey and Candie, who hardly show their emotion, did partake in the amusement of the day. Candie could be loud, louder with her laughter than her words. But, this day, she was enjoyably calmer. As the group shifted from one topic to another they also moved to the other section of the living room where they played some games ranging from dominos to bingo to Scrabble and to Monopoly. And the day wore on.

CHAPTER 5

"A fruit does not fall too far away from the tree that begot it," began Ogidigi to his son, who sat about two meters away from his father on the other side of the living room.

"When I sent you to the New World I didn't send you out to lose your head," he continued. "Now, you look like my son. I was embarrassed beyond belief when I saw you don yourself in that outlandish fashion you came in yesterday with. A thief is never ashamed of his trade, but his kin and kindred people cover themselves in obloquy. Take a look at the mirror and tell me what you see now and what you were in the morning. It is always good to take a look at yourself in the mirror before you venture out because not all the time people doffed off their hats that they acquiesced with your behavior or conduct. You just have to use your tongue to count your teeth. You must be able to define yourself. And you must define yourself in good light. You must define yourself to fit who you are and where you come from." He paused as Osai listened.

"I got all that," Chance chirped.

"No, you do not understand. How many of your friends came in with you? And how many of them made a caricature of themselves?"

"It is a trend, Dad…"

"What kind of trend is that? Let me remind you that all trends are not worth trending. A trend that you would make a caricature of yourself is not worth it. And why is it trending with you only?"

"They would soon join the bandwagon. Their minds are not yet sophisticated to understand the in thing of the day."

"Now, tell me about that, Osai!" roared Ogidigi. "Tell me about sophistication. You may be in charge of your faculties and still have your

77

head screwed to your neck because you are strong-minded, however not so with every other person out there. You have weakminded chaps that would copy these your fads and trends and begin to lose their heads and sometimes their minds. You should own it to yourself that never through you shall they come to be led astray!"

"It's he who wants to be led astray," said Chance.

"You should not say that, Osai. Some chaps are impressionistic and are wont to copy things that made neither head nor tail, and it behooves on you to portray those things that would edify their lives. You, yourself, do not even understand the head or tail of what you are doing because you do not even know if it edified you or not. But whether it edified you or not it does not even fit on the tree that begot you."

"Dad, whether it fits the tree that begot me or not, I have not fallen far away from that tree."

"What are you talking about, Osai?" asked his father incredulously. "You do not mean what you are saying."

"I mean to say, Dad. You told me that my grandfather was a mugger and a tramp and a petty criminal and that you have decided to move away from all that and that my great-grandfather was even worse, a man that enveloped his conscience in a cocoon. But you are neither of these and that you had decided to carve a niche of your own."

"Yes, I told you all that, and they are true. But I have decided to move away from that."

"Then you're the fruit that have fallen far away from the tree that begot it," said Osai.

"No, not at all. I have extracted their better angels. I have taken what is good of my father and my grandfather. And you should do likewise. Did I not tell you that my father was willing to lay down his life for this community? He was a symbol of strength for this town. He was an umbrella for a whole lot of people. They were saved under his shadows. That was who he was. In that regard, I have not fallen far away from him. That is what I mean, my son. And a lot of people knew him for that more than any other thing you could ascribe to him. You can walk the width and breadth of this community, and no one, I mean, no one will accuse my father that he had taken a grain of sand or an acre of land from him. He did bring shame onto himself but not to his community. And bear in mind that not many people could tell what his stock in trade was. He was mindful of his people," said Ogidigi.

"And I profiteered from it," said Osai

"I profited from it," concurred his father a variation.

"And there's no way to make amends."

"Well, there're a few ways to make amends. Be a good citizen of the community. Give to the community when there's a chance to show your worth. By giving you somehow make a restitution and invariably you are making atonement for the sins of your forbearers. You see the point I am making? I think it is high time we moved to a different issue," said his father reservedly.

"I'm just saying…"

"Keep your thoughts to yourself. If you do not stop, I am going to deal with you in such a way that your mother will hardly recognize who you are," cautioned Ogidigi. "I would rather have you dead than to have you fall far away from the family tree. We are not living in yesteryears. I have no wholesome restitution to make. Where do I start and to whom do you make your restitution? It was in the olden days, bygone years issues. I just have to live an exemplary life of my own. So do I expect of you. Do likewise. As a man borne in this age and clime, and borne to Ogidigi, you must have a mantra, call it the twelfth commandment."

"What is that?" asked Osai curiously.

"Every man has got to have it. There has to be a point in a man's life where he has to stand out and stand up for something, has to have principled himself and live and exude that principle, call it, as I said earlier, the twelfth commandment."

"What's that, Dad?"

"Thou shall not give a false impression of yourself," he told him.

"Hmmmmmmm." Osai demurred. "We know about the ten commandments, and now the twelfth, how about the eleventh, Dad?"

"It's anybody's commandment."

"Hmmmmmmm," said Osai again.

"It's that simple. We should have had twelve commandments. You're thought that Jacob has twelve tribes. But quick-tempered Moses broke the tablet, etched with the commandments. Piecing them together he lost two and left us with ten. One was later found where he lost his temper, which was the twelfth. Eleventh is still missing. And it's anybody's guess," Ogidigi schooled his son.

"It does make sense," said bamboozled Osai.

"Just hang on to that twelfth. Remember it also because it'll save you from a whole lot of trouble, swearing, and protestation of your innocence." Ogidigi paused and quickly added, "And to the next point I want to talk to you about. Why did you decide to bring these white Americans to my backyard?"

"They're my friends," said Chance.

"Good, they are your friends. But you have to keep them at bay."

"They're good people."

"Good people they are, but you have to keep them at arm's length," Ogidigi told his son again. "Bringing them here is too close for comfort. He who dines with a stronger adversary has to have a very long spoon, in case he jumps at you, you have a better chance to gallop away."

"They're not what you think they are," said Osai.

"You do not understand. What you, yourself, think here is immaterial. I am just telling you that this is the way of life."

"Anyway, Dad. They're not all white. Two of them are as black as you and I," Osai told his father.

"I have no doubt about that, but the important lesson to note is that they are all Americans, and Americans of all shades are the same. They never betrayed their country. They will give you up in the interest of their country. You cannot bank on them to hold out for you against their country, not the least of them. That's virtue. I don't begrudge them. Every citizenry of every clan must aspire to attain that. That's the basal benchmark for honor and duty. That's the least you can do for your country. That's the way of the world. I just want you to know that," he told his son.

Osai proceeded to explain to his father the makeup of his friends. Dusty was a short, blonde-haired girl of immense beauty. Her eyes were not brown as are wont of black people. She had a shade of blue that made her stunning to behold. Her skin was as white as any white person would be. The only way to tell that she was black was not by conjecture. It could only be by science or parentage. Her grandfather was a member of the buffalo soldiers, a group of black soldiers that distinguished themselves during the World War II. His father was a Marine in the United States Army. Her mother was an elementary schoolteacher. She, too, was light complexioned however, not as light, white as Dusty. She must have inherited her complexion from her mother. Nothing else can explain it better than that.

Jason, on the other hand, was equally of lighter complexion. His hair was black and tousled, but his skin bore a testament to his mixed parentage. He was reserved but loquacious when he was comfortable with his environment. His father was white but his mother was black. One would believe that since his father was white, that he, too, would be white. But not to be. Many a great number of white folks tend to shun the whiteness of their children when their birth came as a result of relationship with black women. That awesome melanin in the black man became anathematized. He had also gone further to explain to him that paternity was not the benchmark of belonging. The acid test must be less than a percentage point unattainable ruse test. Ogidigi was getting a little bit enthralled and was going to ask his son to expatiate himself but momentarily a train of thought drifted him and that chance was ditched, regrettably. However, in Jason father's case, the man may have had a point. Jason's mother was an inconvenience of the first order. Her flirtations had no boundaries. She had six children from five different men. She could not stand the same man for too long. She believed that varieties of men were the spice of her life. Lovemaking was her tranquilizer, administered, all her neurotic synapses were neutered, for good.

Jason was the second of her children. Six months after his birth, she began to terrorize the man. Faced with battering the woman and going to jail he decided to move away. That played into her scheme. As soon as he stepped away, she corralled other men to move into her life.

Turn by turn men trooped in and out of her life. At first, Dave, Jason's father, thought he could salvage his relationship with her over time. For months, he kept away from her. It was like an abandoned building. Rats and rodents built tracks in its ramshackle structures. It was not long thereafter she was pregnant with another son, Semaj. Semaj's pregnancy was the last straw. Dave had to completely move away. But he kept in touch with his son. However, each of those moments was a thorn in her flesh. His presence tormented her. And quite frankly the continuous presence of any man for a long period of time. Yet she loved men of all sorts.

"Yes, Dad, you're right on that. I know that they love their country, but they also love humanity."

"It is their country before humanity."

"There's nothing wrong with that, Dad."

"There is something wrong with that, my son. You know, children limit bathing themselves to the belly portion. You do not understand. These friends of yours will save their country before they save you, son."

"I don't know about that."

"I know that you do not know that. But that is what I am telling you. These friends of yours are the ears and eyes of their homeland. They move across the globe to further their hegemony. Now, you know. And you better understand that!" said the former spymaster of the Biafran republic.

"Dad, I have got the best of friends in these folks. I trust them. No country has done more to better the lives of a lot of people than these people. And no country has given free weal to man to unleash the fabric of his faculty better than their country. It's there for all to see."

"Really! You believed all that! Freedom without emancipation for all you care. You believed all that," repeated Ogidigi. "You are still a child. America you know is the more you see, the less you understand," said Ogidigi.

"It's a great place and awesome people. See how their inventions have alleviated the wretched course of man. Dad, you can't but love these people. Look at all that's good they have brought to the world at large," said Osai.

"Have you thought about the other stuff they bestowed on the world since the world had become pax America? Agree, they have made wonderful strides, but, son, agree that some epochal events the world has had to contend with in the last five hundred years has had their imprimatur on it," posited Ogidigi to his son.

"It's still God's own country. Whatever they may have done pales in…," began Osai.

That last assertion seemed to have ticked Ogidigi off. He would not allow his son the latitude to hold his views because he believed he was being impressionistic, dazzled by the wealth and magnetism that was the New World. This was the former intelligence chief of the old Biafran republic. He knew it and he wanted to be left alone.

Fifteen years ago, Biafra was a stillborn. It nearly made it then. With bare hands, in hand-to-hand combat, they fought their ways into the trenches. Like a joke, like jokes, their indefatigable spirit carried every Biafran a foot further. It was a spirit borne out of nowhere else to go. Hitherto they were bathed in cesspools of their own blood, in every land and every clime of what was defunct Nigeria. No distinction was made. Children and women, old and young faced the same horrendous fate. Before the watching world they were hunted in every nook and cranny of what was defunct Nigeria. Unborn children gorged out of the bellies of their expectant mothers when there was no infant left to dismember. It was gory, but it was not enough fun for the universe. Pogrom it was, but nobody cared a hoot. Genocide it was, pure and simple. It might as well have been mere drops of blood. It might as well have been a blood sport. In that old century, nothing resembled it except Auschwitz. They made Auschwitz in every of their streets, in our own land, in all nooks and crannies where they could find a Biafran soul. And the world watched as spectators, business as usual.

At a point in life with one's back to the brick wall, there was nowhere else to go. Fight, flee, or perish. When there was nowhere to flee to, it necessarily would be fight or perish. Every Biafran pledged to lay down their lives. Every man pledged to fight to the last man, himself. It was the guiding spirit that squeezed the last ounce of strength in every person left for the cause of survival. It worked well for the collective enterprise. Victory was at hand. Survival was imminent. Biafra was about to hoist her flag in celebration of her liberation born at the battlefield. Nigeria that was in flight came back resurgent. The Biafran bubble was burst. Ogidigi was there. He was the chief of intelligence of that Biafra that never was through the force of sheer will of the people. He knew where Nigeria's newfangled strength came from. It was the Americans' "not in our best interest" attitude. It was the Brits. It was all the powers that be. Biafra had themselves to rely on. And then the little Nyerere and then the big Houphouet-Boigny and supposedly other minnows of blessed memories. That reversal of success was devastating, and Ogidigi never forgot. Cheetah, the fastest land animal, stated that he did not care about those who were pursuing to nab him because he trusted his ability to outpace everyone but that those he hated most were those onlookers that had no business in the matter but were hollering and urging other bystanders saying, "do not let him escape, do not let him go." The intervention of the bigger powers was akin to that. And Biafra once again was back in deeper trenches, faint but fighting.

"Have you heard about fallen angels?" He stifled a disdain of lack of knowledge by his son.

"Who are they?"

"That is what I am saying."

"Have you heard about Lucifer?"

"You mean the devil?"

"You got it," acclaimed his father. "Lucifer was one of the fallen angels. And he had descended on defunct Nigeria. That's all you need to know," said his father.

"What that gotta do with America's greatness and being God's own country?" said Osai, staring his father straight in the eyes again.

His father's frustration was obvious at this point. It knew no bounds. First his son was making a bogus claim, and secondly he could poke his eyes in his face like that. He had had enough, and he proceeded to inform him what he did not know.

"The unspoken truth is," began Ogidigi, "that the heaven was breached long time ago, and knowledge had been siphoned without the express will of the most high. So when you are enthralled by things and events around you, remember that anything that is supernatural is not from the most high God. God never intended us to be on the same pedestal with him. All you have to do is to keep an ear to the ground. That little bird dancing in the middle of the road may have some other birds somewhere in the bush beating the orchestra for it."

Ogidigi was almost holding his son spellbound as Osai was submerged in attention and buried in thoughts. His mind ran amok, but he was not meant to give in just like that even when that proposition was coming from his father, the man he revered thoughtlessly.

"That I do not know, Dad. But what I do know is that their greatness stemmed from the fact of their amalgamation of thought and ideas with oneness of purpose that literally borders on metaphysical spiritualism. It is also their ethos developed and held up over eons and held up for all to see," said Osai, trying to shake off the bamboozlement his father almost succeeded in roping him.

This was not a land one had to insist on a viewpoint against one's superior especially against your own father especially if one had no higher incontrovertible fact to buttress up one's position. Ogidigi had the edge on this matter bereft of any other superior argument of either party. If it was folklore Ogidigi had the ultimate edge. He had seen more years. He knew his grandfather who knew his grandfather who knew his grandfather who knew his great grandfather who may have passed invaluable eyewitness account to them down the line. However, Osai was never known to blink an eyelid especially toward his peers. His father very much loved him more so because of that tenacity of character. Nevertheless, it was not lost on him that his father was not one of his peers.

"Father, you are so much inclined to believe that these folks had their turf tilled by some mighty god."

"Son, I am not inclined to believe. It is the fact."

"Where're the facts?" asked Osai.

"The facts are in the wonderful things that they have made possible. The impossibilities that they had made possible. The world that they have conquered and brutalized…"

"And made better," interjected Osai.

"Those who wanted to decimate heaven were thrown out of it," said Ogidigi, ignoring his son. "They are here to teach innocent humans how to decimate the earth and even destroy it. They had seen God, were with him. They knew God, wanted to be God themselves. The almighty broods no opposition. Having lost their places in heaven they are here to recruit those who would want to touch God, even oppose him and worse still fight him, worst still, destroy him. And there are willing recruits," he told his son. "We are so used and enmeshed in the so-called goodies they brought to us that we no longer ask questions. They opened the vistas of our sights to see beyond our wildest imagination. We enjoyed it that we no longer ask questions. We are used to all that we no longer ask how they came to be," said Ogidigi.

Osai knew it was a fool's effort to try to make his father to see things differently if the conclusion was long established. It was almost futile to argue with a man who had made up his mind especially if animosity had a hold in the man's heart. Ogidigi had the belief, misguided or not, that America's interest or lack of it contributed largely in prolonging Biafra's suffering during the genocidal war.

"If that truth must be told," began Osai, doggedly, "why did the fallen angels only find the white's man world? Did they not see my beloved Africa?"

"They were here also."

"Then, where were their footprints?" asked Osai.

Ogidigi once again proceeded to explain to him a folklore wrapped in myth. Myth had it that the fallen angels, when they lost their places in heaven, they had no abode for their footstool, neither in heaven nor its approaches. Having realized that they had all it would take to mesmerize the world beneath: knowledge almost as God. They took their chances down to earth. And their first port of call was Africa. Innocent Africa! And true to herself, she refused to be cajoled to take another bait as was in the beginning. All knowledge revealed incrementally would have been hers. The more the angels tried, the more she bent her gaze toward heaven. Dutiful and faithful to the Chukwu Okike Abiama, the most high God. She would not do anything to offend the most high God's warrior angel sometimes symbolized in Amadioha, the fiery, intolerant god of thunder. Stubbornly she clung onto her god. Not wanting to be confused, not wanting to be convinced of the goodness that would attend welcoming the fallen angels, Africa got irritable. A huge misunderstanding ensued, and at threat to their lives the fallen angels ran. They run swiftly, so swift that their heels could almost hit their spine. Africa did not want to know that which was hidden away from her by the infinite knowledge of the almighty. In annoyance, the fallen angels blighted her horizon as they flee for their lives. But somewhere out there in the world there were some folks who were willing to entertain them and their incredulous journey. They that welcomed them got all the hidden knowledge and the trappings that came with it. A covenant was established. Knowledge would be bestowed and transferred to their generations, from one generation to the next.

As Osai listened he had less reason to believe but much more at unbelief. Yet he was aware that something was not right with his beloved Africa and had huge hope that Biafra could change all that for the better. He had nothing to say. He was torn between two worlds. But he needed to liberate himself from some mental confusion.

"Now, you cannot be too sure of the conclusions others make for you," said Ogidigi. "Now, if I may ask you, which one is more mind-boggling? The invention of the telephone or the drawing of the Sistine chapel ceiling by Michelangelo in the basilica in Rome?"

"What's that?" asked Osai, referring to the Sistine chapel.

"It is the most wonderful human art drawing credited to man in the basilica of Rome."

"I see! I guess the telephone," answered Osai.

"That drawing has the unseen hand of the most high on top of the hand of magical Michelangelo. Credit to Michelangelo but we know whose handiwork made it possible. By your estimation this work aided by the unseen hand of the almighty pales in significance to the telephone then we needed to find out who really was behind its creation, I mean the telephone," said Ogidigi.

"Anyway," continued Ogidigi, "I have digressed a lot. I mean to tell you that you should be mindful of the company you keep. I can only tell you as a father will alert his child. What a father saw sitting may still be hidden from a child standing tall."

Osai wanted to get his father off this topic and any other topic for that matter. He and his friends were billed to stroll out before dusk, and the sun had already disappeared in the horizon as the full moon emblazoned the earth again. It had been two days since they came into town from Eureka. Last night Turnkey had smelled some stuff, and this night he wanted to stroll out into near town to explore where that wind was blowing that stuff from. Turnkey loved marijuana. He could not do without it if it was within reach. However, what he smelled last night was different. The aroma was somehow exhilarating, so when Ogidigi held his son he prolonged their expectation. Osai had figured out long time ago that listening would set him free and without making other contribution or asking questions he gave his father chance to peter out the discussion and enquiry.

"You have gone to America to get the best there is out there. Do not let it get into your head. America is also the more you look, the less you see," he told his son.

Osai was happy it was all over for now. But it was never over. The mini inquisition would continue somehow somewhere later. Since he came back it had been a barrage of uppercut punches landed with cogent of reasons and for his mind-bending facade and company. But now it was dusk, and he needed to stroll out with his friends, just to stroll out. The whole day they had been virtually indoors. There were some places, a.k.a. joints, where things *happen* fast and sometimes furious. It was obtainable in every land and clime across the world. Where young men immerse themselves in the halo of invincibility. Life became adventures in itself, and adventure of the sort young men always wanted to get themselves in went by the nickname: either we are dead or get lost, in the wilderness of excitement.

When guys or people who were indulged in certain lifestyles find themselves in a new territory, they sniff the air so quickly to know by instinct where it is *happening*. Chance left Biafra a teenager a little less an adolescent. He knew nothing about how to get *high*. However, he learned fast. And once in America, alone and without much scrutiny at

Rutgers University he had found himself in some company that always liked to experiment and sometimes improvised. American universities were littered with kids who always wanted more and like to experiment into excessiveness. Element of choice to get high was marijuana. It was a pastime in most of these colleges, and both Chance and Turnkey and their friends were part and parcel of that institution. They had been in Umudede for three days, and some kind of withdrawal was setting in. They needed to sniff around a little bit. In this business Turnkey had the upper hand. Though he was the real foreigner but he was an old hand in mastering where to sniff for content of need. Chance knew more of the topography, but Turnkey had a more far-reaching nose to find where it could be *happening*. It was not long when they strolled their way to a joint.

There were petty miscreants but no thieves milling in and out of the kiosk. Since the event of last week in Eureka it would be utter foolishness for any sane fellow to pretend to be a career criminal. The environment was too hot. As soon as they drew nearer the unmistakable aroma of wee-wee or marijuana permeated the air. That was it. It was delicious and alluring. It smelled a little different, but it was it. Chance also had in their company Osondu, a cousin who assumed to understand these things more than him. He did not know much about marijuana but pretended to know a lot. And since his cousin, Chance, just came back clutching his friends along with him, Osondu had self-ingratiated himself more, ascribing to himself some level of higher importance needlessly. He acted as if he knew a whole lot. But in actual sense, he did not know much. He was just showing off. After all, there had never been a company of so many young white men and women in Umudede. Chance had caused some stir in the land with his homecoming and the company of white folks he brought along as company.

Turnkey had smoked marijuana for a long time now. He had gotten used to it. So it never bothered him to smell or even taste any kind from anywhere. He could be mistaken. This was different. No sooner had they paid for a few wraps than Turnkey set alight one roll of the stuff. Not soon! No sooner! It was just one inhalation, and to everyone's disbelief Turnkey was off and running full throttle. It was unexpected, so no one was prepared for it. The takeoff was swift and the acceleration was instant. As if he was expecting it to happen Osondu gave chase. Darkness had completely enveloped the earth. Umudede was a bustling city, so people were still going about their businesses. And for others, it was the start of their own market, especially roadside mini restaurants for early evening and late night grubbers. So the environment was still bubbling with life, so to speak. As he tried to meander through the throng of people at that full speed he was an accident waiting to happen. The atmosphere had become rowdy. Chance and his other friends followed in the chase. Osondu understood that his cousin's friend stood a chance of getting himself injured badly. Before he could run too far beyond reach, Osondu threw himself at the cousin's friend. With that daring effort, he dragged two other innocent trekkers with Turnkey into the gutters. Turnkey struggled to free himself, but he was subdued with the help of Chance and his other friends. The two gentlemen that were knocked into the gutter got out and wanted to make some fuss. But when they saw a bunch of white girls giggling hilariously, they chilled, dusted themselves up, and moved on after vigorous intervention of Osondu. Turnkey continued to struggle to free himself, but stoutly he was led to Chance's home.

As soon as they got home Osondu soaked a bowl of *garri* and fed Turnkey. He ate ravenously to seriously assuage his appetite and douse the debilitating sapping of the wee-wee. He neither knew where he was, nor did he know what he was fed. Every poison had its own antidote. In a jiffy, Turnkey consumed the *garri* without knowing what was fed to him. He was dazed by just one inhalation of the strongest marijuana on the face of the earth. It really knocked him out. It did squeeze out the last ounce of food in his entrails in an instant. It was another three whole hours later that Turnkey rose from his slumber, the ephemeral influence of the wee-wee having withered, a little bit weak, fully aware of his environment, and with the passing minutes he began to regain his strength. What the drug did was to sap his sinew but did almost simultaneously rejuvenate his abilities.

The kind of wee-wee Turnkey had was what among the locals and in the *street* was called *a ga anwụ anwụ, e fo efo* or "if I do not die, I got missing." Others called it *ọ bụ ọnwụ, ọ bụ ndụ*, meaning, "it's either dead or alive." Whatever name it went by, it was not to be toyed with. It was no good. It was altogether a bad stuff. It was not meant for the naive. It had to be smelled first, savor its alluring aroma, before a slightest run of inhalation would be tried. That night Chance considered himself a very lucky man.

The group chatted all night. Played a handful of games. Turnkey became the butt of his friends' jokes, but he took it in stride. As the night wore down everyone seemed to be at home with the environment presented by Chance and his family. The accommodation was superb. The comfort was surprisingly unexpected. The land mirrored in the west as land of the savages had not turned out anything close after all. As they retired to bed their escapade to the land of the rising sun was turning out to be a memorable one. The annex had four empty rooms. As had been since they arrived in Umudede, Turnkey retired with his girlfriend, Dusty. Jason took his place with his girlfriend, Jewel. Chance took up one of the rooms with Candie.

Chance and Candie had come a long way. They had enjoyed their ups and downs. Their relationship had moved nowhere. As the other couples laughed and chuckled and in their respective abodes, Chance and Candie played Monopoly to no end.

"Get out of jail free."

"You have won an investment property," said Chance.

As midnight turned to the other side of the new day, Chance and his friend's sister could perceive the duels going on in the other rooms adjacent to theirs, sometimes frenzy and loud. It was also a distraction. They could hardly concentrate on their game. On two occasions Candie would knock on the wall of the room linked to Turnkey to quieten the groan and noises emanating from therein. When she could take it no more, she urged Chance that they should retire to bed. It was an idea that Chance had harbored to himself as he had been fighting the demon in his adrenaline. It was torturous for him but more especially for her. They were called to action, but unfortunately, they would not do it. Usually he would want to sleep on the outside of the bed, but on this night, he chose to sleep close to the wall. That did not bring him any comfort or relief as he lay on his stomach trying as hard as he could to suppress the long, vertical, and rebellious tension hardening and rising in between his thighs. He was in locked gears. And Candie did not try to break the jammed locks. She lay on her side facing the other side of the room. She was very much disappointed, but she did not say it. She could not understand why this guy would not make a move, let alone have it rebuffed. None of them said anything to the other. Osai was not prepared to do it. Even if Candie had asked him for sex he was not going to fall for it. Even if she forced her way on him, he would not bring himself to violate her. She knew that that gambit had to come from that guy. Even though she came from a country where asking to go out with anyone can come from either sex, it was commonplace, but she was not prepared to make that move. There was quiet in the room as the noises emanating from the other rooms died down. As she agonized, she could feel some wetness in and around her vulva. Then gradually she began to drift to sleep. Then she tossed around and turned sleepily toward Chance who was fast asleep with his face to the wall, his pajamas wet. Unconsciously she lifted her long, beautiful left leg and placed it over his legs and, too, finally fell asleep.

For both Candie and Chance, the night was brief and unremarkable. Both woke up tired for nothing. Exhausted for imaging what could have been or should have been. At the height of her longing for him to lacerate her privacy and his obstinacy to stand his ground the little respect she had for him flew out of the window. It was like a wet paper pulled into shreds and crumbled to nothing now. How can a man refuse such a chance given on a platter of gold? Who was that man that such a thing had become so distasteful especially at a time of collective orgy right and about? It was a torture of immense proportion. He was hard-hearted. She was not going to forgive him. Never. But that was at the heat of the moment.

Breakfast was already waiting for them. Turnkey and Jason and their companies were still languid in bed. As Chance and Candie sat around the table Candie took a swipe of a riveting stare at him. Her blue sunken eyeballs captivating even its presumptuous wickedness. Chance just ignored her. But she riveted him more.

"I cannot cross that line," Osai managed to say, all the time trying to avoid her quizzical gaze.

"Yes, you can," she put it to him sternly.

"I cannot just damn the consequences, twenty years down the line, I will be hating myself for having crossed the Rubicon," he said defensively.

"Damn you, what consequences are you talking about. Not having helped me when capable guys are in short supply, for forty years down the line, I will still be hating you, you son of…" She paused.

"As long as you did not veer into the wild wilderness of sin I will still find you," said Osai.

"It was at no cost now. Neither to you nor to me," she said with no tinge of malice but feigning some injury. Chance continued to ignore her. "Ever since you set your eyes on me, you have spent your entire life seeing me, wanting me, wooing me. When you had the only chance to stick me some spanking, you turned inertia, you married the wall," said Candie with such rawness and gusto that was an American girl gone wild.

"You just lay down there pretending to have expired. No sparks. Look at you now alive," continued Candie. "Now, you are pretending you do not hear me. I respect you more, but I do not hate you less!" she groused.

"That's okay with me. I am okay with that as long as you accord me some respect. If I had done it, when the scale fell off our eyes I'm gonna hate myself because I betrayed my bosom friend. And of course, you still will hate me more. I mean, you will like me less."

"Like you less," said Turnkey as he badged into their discussion, drolly and weak to the bones.

"This guy, this friend of yours had learned nothing coming to America," said Candie.

"I'm in Biafra," countered Chance jovially.

"I know, your goddamn Biafra," said Candie.

"I hope that you guys had a good night," chipped in Turnkey.

"No, it was a nightmare," said Candie.

"What happened?" queried Turnkey indifferently.

"Your friend was being sanctimonious all night. Before I could say, Jack, he had turned his face to wall, and snored away."

"Hey, Chance, is she saying that you did not spank the crap out of her. That is too bad. That was your chance going, Chance," said Turnkey.

"I like honor more than I like to smooch the moose. Moreover, she is like a blood sister," offered Chance in defense.

"Fuck! To hell with your honor. Blood sister, my ass! Give me a break! I was looking for spontaneity. The best sex is that which is spontaneous," said Candie.

"You got it and you lost the chance, Chance," said Turnkey again.

"Never mind him. Perhaps, he is gonna lead me to his wild to catch a moose for him or he thought me a moose or he prefers a moose over me. I don't know about this your friend, Mr. Honorable. He's not learned anything coming to America", griped Candie vehemently.

"I was bred to be a gentleman and I am," said Chance with a wink and not meaning a thing of what he just said. While Candie gyrated her eyeballs at him.

In an age of extreme debauchery, it was nothing for Turnkey to urge his friend to take a sexual swipe on his sister. Chance, still displaying the nuances and idiosyncrasies of his rural upbringing, demurred.

"I'm not the fall guy you think of me. If I whacked you, girl, you will stay spanked for weeks and the memory of it you will live with ad infinitum. Do not put me to the test, girl," said Chance.

"Be quiet with your grandiosity. Action speaks louder than words," said Candie, exasperated.

Turnkey did not want to partake further in these guys' internecine argument that would eventually end up in nothing. He had quickly slipped to brush his teeth and returned gingerly to the table. The events of last night had their contradictions. The marijuana was like double-edged sword. It had knocked him out but had rejuvenated him. More importantly, it had acted like an aphrodisiac, pumped up his energy. It gave him more staying power which he exerted with great aplomb. He had had marijuana before, rampantly distributed on campus, but nothing came close to be compared to the Biafran wee-wee. Its flavor was relishing. Its power was sapping. The aftermath of it was a sudden boost in energy. Dusty just lived to tell the whole story. It was somehow bruising, evidenced by the love marks toothed on the left side of Turnkey's neck. Love mark, a.k.a. sex bite, was common depravity in America romantic imbroglio. But if there were to be anything taken away from his Biafran escapade, it was not going to be the scar of the robust affair. It would be the potency of the Biafran marijuana which would remain in his memory for a long time to come. He was already thinking about missing this new nation. It did not seem to him as if people were so much bothered about this stuff. If he had to come back for another visit this would be a good invitation to make an encore.

CHAPTER 6

The first full day of Osai's return to Umudede was frantic and sporadic. He was highly being awaited. But nobody knew that he was coming back with a retinue or an entourage of sort. It was consternation galore, and no one minced their surprise at the throng that graced his heels. First was his immediate younger sister, Somtochi. Somtochi was a fiery personality. Unafraid of danger, let alone stirring up controversy. So when controversy seriously presented itself she kicked it along like a whirl and damned the consequence. Picking up a fight was in her nature. And she was never in a hurry to scamper away from one.

Chance had done something no one in his right mind was going to do. He was not the first to have been abroad for greener pastures. But in actual sense he needed no pursuit for greener pasture outside the shores of Umudede. It was just. But he was the first to have brought a party of aliens in such numbers in one fell swoop. Somtochi was one heck of a girl. Even though she was younger she had learned to impose herself on him and crossing his path. Going abroad seemed to have solved the division and saber rattling. But one thing time and space had not taken away was her willingness to say her mind. She still had her caustic tongue, painful and stinging. She was still brash, sarcastic, and bashful. No sooner had he finished loosening his braids than she cajoled him to one of the rooms in the main building. Serenaded, she thought she could make the jugular move. However, she was stopped in her tracks before she could begin her own very aggressive inquest.

"Hey, I know what you are going to say, and I implore you to please do not go there," said Osai, trying to checkmate his sister from running haywire on him.

"Let me say something, Osai. Has America given you the power of clairvoyance or are you now a sorcerer?" said Somtochi. "Methinks you now have a right to bring home anybody mindless of how your father or mother would countenance it. And then I cannot even talk about it," she added.

"I don't know what to tell you, Somtochi," said Osai.

"But you should not have anything to tell me," she retorted.

"Boy!" intoned Chikwem who was reclining in the other corner of the room. Chikwem paid no heed to anybody. He did his thing the way he wanted. He, too, had a mind of his own.

"These, your girls are something else. I mean that they are provocative to say the least. They would surely make heads turn when they venture out there in the market. They are hot!" said Chikwem unassumingly.

"And they would get the treatment they craved," said Somtochi.

"Why?" asked Osai.

"They're provocative," answered both Chikwem and Somtochi in unison.

"But there's nothing in it," said Osai tamely.

"There's something in it," said Somtochi snappily.

"I don't understand what the fuss is all about," said Osai.

"Well, to tell you in plain language, if they dressed up like that mindlessly, then they don't understand just as you don't understand. When they dress cut-my-buttocks like that and show-my-boobs like that, they caress our sensibilities. They can't be skimpily cladded and command the respect they deserve," said his sister.

"That's normal for them," said Osai.

"That's outlandish for us," interjected Chikwem.

"That's what I'm talking about. It's outrageous and perhaps offensive for the eyes to behold," said Somtochi.

"It may not be offensive that much, it's just that they're stoking my manness. They're making me have a crush on all of them, as Americans are wont to say," said Chikwem.

"Be quiet with that and keep your manness inside your pants," commanded Somtochi.

"I'm just saying," replied Chikwem. "When you dressed to make heads turn, you dressed to raise the adrenaline especially if you're already beautiful, you call attention to yourself, you make the pelvic region increase in size and density…," said Chikwem.

"Be quiet," snapped Somtochi again.

"I'm not going to be quiet on this. Women, generally, are created beautifully to enchant. And these are made beautiful. And they dress highlighting all the contours of their shapes and bodies, and you want me to be quiet and notice nothing. People, I'm mentally challenged and sexually harassed," he said.

"See how you're gonna get yourself into some trouble," cautioned Osai.

"Over what?" asked Chikwem.

"For sexual harassment."

"Not in this land," said Chikwem resolutely. "I'm going to get into trouble for being provoked? Rather than the person who initiated the provocation! That's like turning justice upside down! You're leaving alone the buttocks that just farted and be knocking on the head that did nothing," stated the law student.

"You should hold yourself in check. That's western mind-set. Anything short of that is like looking for some trouble," said Osai.

"I'm going to hold myself in check, but I'm going to have an opinion about that," replied Chikwem.

"You gotta be careful. Acknowledging the femininity of a female could land you into trouble. Complimenting the beauty of a female could in the long term land you in jail and mess up the reputation you've built over the years. That's part of western civilization. That could be litigated as sexual harassment," Osai told his brother.

"The way they're dressed up and jagging their boobs in our faces is sexually harassing me," said his brother.

"Look here, man! Women from time immemorial craved for acknowledgment and compliment," he continued. "Men naturally are created sexually depraved. And men must be men. And women are women. They crave for compliment and they got it. If you present yourself as a symbol we will compliment that. They're created beautiful. They don't need to do anything to be wanted, to be held, and be squeezed by men. And men are wired to be attracted by them just as bees are attracted by honey. Anything else they do is a figment of an inherent inferiority complex and self-denigration," said Chikwem who was in his sophomore year as a law student.

"All I can say is deal with it! Tame your depravity even if you were daily provoked and, of course, you will be. But in the meantime, leave my girls alone," said Osai.

"That's what I'm getting at," said Chikwem. "Which of them is yours, man?" he asked.

"Stay away, boy! Don't dart your eyes in their direction and keep your darts in their jars," said Osai.

"But you can't have all of them to yourself, it's one man, one chick. You can't leave me in the cold like that. Share the chicks, bros," counseled Chikwem.

As their discussion shifted to mundane, macho chauvinistic issues they did not pay attention to the time their sister exited the room. Inadvertently it touched on her own self-worth as her brothers began to talk about erotic male fascinations. But she had made her point, plain and simple. Everything was still pending, to be continued. So she could return to the topic later on without having to lose her ground but further her cause.

If it were to be a blow it was well-taken. He knew the inquest was not completed yet. His mother had not excoriated him yet. He was cocksure that she would take her time. She was measured in her own speech. Though she was a year younger than her brother, he feared his sister much more. In fact, he feared their mother less. So when she was gone he took a sigh of relief. The worst was behind him. Then he waited for his mother, and surely he knew that she was going to put him to the sword.

"I don't think I like this, and I don't think it's in your own best interest, Chance," his mother began.

"What's that, Mom?" asked Osai.

"Don't be that daft, son! Don't be the ostrich that buried its head in the sand and pretended nothing is amiss," she continued. "You need to sit down so that we can iron out our differences because they're mounting."

"Mom, we've got no differences. Nothing is dividing us," said Osai.

"Then, you can't do that, Osai. You cannot do that," she repeated. "You don't know how much furor you have caused in and around this house. First, with your scraggy hairdo, then the ornaments all over your face, and then with your retinue of consorts. It's getting on my nerves, Osai. Go into town, in less than twenty-four hours, you're the talk of the town, you're at the center of every of our neighbors' discussions."

"Mom, you know that people will always have opinions. If you did good, they would have a say. If you did bad they will chatter."

"Then be prepared to do good," snapped his mother. "Don't arm your detractors and stop giving a false narrative of who you are. We've to help you discover your own foibles, or you'll stew in your own juice. We've sent you out to a place where people stew in their own juice because neighbors see other's foibles and allow them to wallow in their own ruins."

"I'm not arming anybody, Mom. I just have my life to live."

"You don't have a life to live that much on your own. You've a shared life. You don't live in a vacuum. You're not an island unto yourself. If you thought that you have your life to live, well, your life is bothering them and they can't just disappear because of you. Think about it, you may be the one to give way to their sensibilities. You may be the one to disappear before them." She paused as those words flew out of her mouth.

Dorothy was a woman of an iron will. A lawyer by training and a solicitor and jurist by trade. She had done well to a large extent. She was committed in her undertakings both in intent and purposes. It was her stringent persuasion that finally compelled Ogidigi to ferry Osai to the United States. She was convinced that the Biafran war was going to erupt again, and while she was committed to the cause of the Biafran people's struggle, she was not prepared to offer any other of her children to the cause. At the start of the Biafran war, there was no choice for a whole lot of families. The only choice was support for the survival of the Biafran cause. Stand up and be counted. Even when there was an overwhelming need to stand and be counted, war was never fun. Some mothers had hoped that Biafra would just be without any ox gored. Since war requires men, men go to war. To get those men to present themselves was never easy even when the cause was right. Families tried to shield their little ones from joining the expedition. Some families hid their young men in closets and ledges. Some in the bushes. Some in the basement. But a whole of the younger men, boys, volunteered. Some others prayed that the recruiters never called asking for the release of the young men in their families. All kinds of reasons were advanced to avoid or dodge the war recruitment efforts. But not Ogidigi and not Dorothy. Literally Dorothy offered two of her boys and literally Ogidigi sacrificed them on the altar of the Biafran cause. They were in unison in encouraging their children to volunteer. So it was no problem for them to join the fledgling Biafran war efforts.

But they did not come back home. Ileka and Oleka perished in the war. When other men wept their eyes off, this woman moved on. She believed in the war. She believed in the independence of a Biafran homeland. She supported the whole adventure. She understood the perils of war. She knew about the probability that they were unlikely to come back home. She wore her sackcloth and moved on. But she was not convinced of the peace that was negotiated when defunct Nigeria feared that they would have nothing to fall back on. In the middle of one night she called on her husband. Osai must be ferried to safety. In case.

Ogidigi was not opposed to it. But where would the haven be? To the United States. Dorothy was insistent in convincing her husband. It was a bitter reality. The cheetah could have made it gingerly, but for the rancorous hollers of the onlookers that had no dog in the fight dismayed and offended him a lot. It was not an easy acquiesce. Osai would go for further studies abroad. But there was a caveat. Ogidigi would have to get a second wife! Losing two kids in the war left the family depleted. He needed to repeople his household. He had imagined that after whole ten years without a visit to the maternity ward or conception that perhaps his wife would not want to entertain the idea of pregnancy again. It was laborious. But he was mistaken. This matriarch of the Ogidigi kingdom wielding the norm and mores of her traditional weal, and of her people, honored and handed down the ages, could really step out of her way and go out there and contract another woman for her husband whom she could mentor and culture to be her own protégé, yet her husband's second wife. She had the capacity to do that. It was within her office to do that! It was a time-honored tradition and everyone seemed to be happy. But, no! She was not incline to toe that line. She was a modern woman! The not-so-well understood modernity that had torn their lives apart and bent their compass away from whom they really were. Dorothy would rather return to the maternity ward than to allow a woman of any inclination to get a foothold in her husband's heart. In spite of her training, she was not going to allow a divided kingdom. And then any woman that tried to impose her influence on her husband or lure him to divide his attention was risking an untimely death. It was understood. Dorothy had no time for games. From her office to the community meeting everybody understood that Dorothy took no chances in such matters. Osai would go to the United States for more studies and escape of the unknown and she would return to the maternity ward. She had never demanded her husband's respect, and she had gotten it without asking. And in three years she had had two pregnancies in quick succession. First was a baby girl and followed two years later by a set of twin boys. Perhaps in the birth of Karachi and Chimaobi came back Ileka and Oleka.

"Birds of the same feathers flock together." Dorothy tried to veer the discussion toward another direction. "I want you to be mindful of the company you keep," she continued and Osai having said nothing. Of course, he had heard an earful from his father and sister and brother.

"I'm Mom," he said almost tacitly.

"You're not. If you were you wouldn't have brought these girls, barely cladded, down here."

"They are just my friends," said Osai.

"Your friends? Are you flying a kite? Testing the waters? I hope that they're just your friends."

"Mom, it looks like you have some stuffs up your sleeve, something you want us to talk about. I've heard an earful already from…," teased Osai.

"Yes, something, your stupidity! You hear me? No, nothing, if it were just what you said and what I just told you, birds of the dissimilar feathers do not flock together."

"But there's no difference between us humans, between you and them."

"There's none if they just get it, if they just understood that, son. There's none," she repeated. "It's just that they're created into an alternate universe."

"It's one world, Mom."

"Well, I don't know about that. It may be one world. What's obvious is that it is one creator, but different creations and they see life obviously differently. They don't believe in what we believe. Our belief paradigms are different. Don't be a numskull, son, and do not fly that your kite here anymore. It's in your own best interest that you keep your relationship at a very, very superficial level. Don't be carried away. None of these are going to be your wife in your own best interest," she repeated.

"I was not even thinking about that, Mom."

"Then, don't give a false impression of yourself. I'm just advising you."

"But, Mom, if I decided when I decide, what's wrong with that?" he asked.

"That means you haven't been listening. I'm going to shred that your kite. It looks like I've been talking to myself."

"You've not, Mom, but this seems to be much ado about nothing. You're trying to preempt me."

"I'm not trying to be preemptive, and it's very much ado about something. I want you to get involved with one who loves you for what you are and not what you aren't. Marriage and love in western culture is sex driven and nothing platonic. It's sex for sale and love at heat of the moment. I'm not going to have you set your life on fire just for the moment. I'm not going to have you get entangled with someone whose love for you is sex driven, who'll abandon you for the next man when she had gotten a test of your sweetness and leave you broken wondering if you'd made the right choice from the onset."

"That's total misconception, Mom. It takes two to tangle. No one claps with one hand. That relationship you're talking about involves two individuals. It takes two to agree to disagree. Schism in a relationship comes as a result of misconduct of two individuals…"

"I should not be telling you this." His mother cut him short. "Men are naturally polygamous," she asserted, biting her words. "Though not licensed to misbehave and disrespect the partner, neither a whim to be held up nor a caprice I subscribe to, but life is not tit for tat, or else marriage will never survive for a day longer. Sex-driven relationship is bad, and for a woman to abandon her matrimony on account of that is not something I want you to look forward to."

"Mom, I'm surprised that you say this."

"Yes, I'm surprised that I say it myself, but that's what I'm going to say to Somtochi when the time comes."

"That view belongs to the dustbin of history and should be left in the heaps of yesteryear's culture," said Osai.

"It did hold true yesterday and will hold true tomorrow. It's one of those things that never changed if our society, and any society for that matter, must maintain its sanity. Again, it's in your own best interest that you look at these things and think through what you've to do moving forward." She paused. "I tell you, my child, there's more to it. Those you purport to hallow have bent the world we live in and turned it on its head. Because they are like torchlight to the rest of the world. When they move the rest of the world will follow, sometimes even sheepishly." She paused again.

"You can't bring any of these kinds here for a wife, when you do, you bring along their foibles, dog kissing, naked walking, all the excesses without let, the decadence with abandon, the menace to our culture and basic, traditional human norms that we hold dear. Worse still they don't know when to stop."

"But it's their culture," interjected Osai after the round of earful.

"Stop! You're wrong. They don't have a culture, as you know it. They've myriad of new-fangled cultures. How can dog tongue licking be anybody's culture? How can naked walking be anybody's culture? And you know what?" she asked rhetorically. "And you know what?" she asked again, expecting no answers but her own. "They export these nasties all over the whole world because they've the means and lots of the world peoples are hungry and tired and have propensity to experiment with new ideas, be rebellious to their age-long ways of life, and you know that this rebellious ilk have America to defend them with the gospel of freedom, freedom to self-destruct. Is that what you want to bring to us?" she asked.

"They bring more than all you just said. They bring emancipation of the mind," said Osai.

"Emancipation of the mind? What happened to your mind?" she scoffed. "Whose minds needed emancipation? We need to face our forgotten truths. I can't let you surreptitiously begin a new conquest here. We sent you away to learn honor and not be thrown at us to school me. It's always a gradual process and comes in subset, then festers, then substitutes, then corrupts. What you call emancipation of the mind is merely but a concept of the systems that beguile." She paused a little then burst out again.

"Get them to go tomorrow! You can't bring to this land friends who would look you straight in the eyes and still not tell you the whole truth to mess our system under any guise. That in itself is a path to self-perdition. How can a people so endowed not know the difference between candor and indecency and self-deprecation? How can they emasculate the truth and pretend nothing is amiss? Hold your nose and do the wrong thing. Not in this land!" she rapped.

Chance had had enough with little or nothing to counter his combative mother. As he made to varnish from her presence, he tried to lighten the atmosphere and put these never-ending inquests to an end.

"Mom, you've taken a stand on America, how much do you really know about...?" he lightheartedly asked as he tried to make it out of the room.

It looked like Chance had opened a can of worms for himself or aggravated a sore wound that was festering. She had looked murderers in the face and unassumingly asked the presiding judges to send them to the gallows. She had won numerous battles in and outside the courtroom. She had never shirked her duty especially when she was challenged to lay her case bare for all to see. She had no stomach for ruinous pittance. Her son had thrown a gambit at her. She was not prepared to allow that opportunity to slip through her fingers. She loved to prove a point when she was challenged with higher standard of knowledge and know-how. It was like Chance had underestimated his mother.

"Look at your head," she cajoled him sarcastically. "I know a lot about the people you are talking about more than you do. That you have set foot on their soil does not mean that you know a thing about them. You don't have a clue. You don't have to be in New York City to know that its skylines are littered with skyscrapers. You don't have to be in Warthampton to understand that the so-called one hundred and one Amendment is a reminding pillar of vestiges of America's ugly past relived with pageantry pomp in the present."

"Goat!" she almost bleated as she continued. "You don't have to go to Wonderland to know that life isn't what it should be in our present world, that one could lose one's life and the real culprit standing accused let go scot-free under that trumped-up guise of probable quaff. That's what we may call here judicial sophism. I don't have to be with you there in Turnkeytown to know that your life is in constant danger because one homeless man has a right to bear arms and really own a gun but not a means to rent an abode or pay a tax..."

"But it's constitutional...," began Osai.

"Wait a minute, Sheep. Constitution doesn't make a man. Man makes a constitution. This is one of the horror vestiges of the ancient past and you want to hallow it. You're not emancipated by that. Freedom as you see it is a double-edged sword. It could be a mirage you pursue only to lead you to that unreachable horizon. The freedom you thought is an adulterated nonsense. What you see is that cosmetic hype that gladdens the eyes and destroys the mind. That was not the emancipation we bled for. Freedom has become our yoke.

"You who have been to the New World we have not been. They teach everything you needed to know, did they teach you about the Berlin Conference?"

"What's that?" asked Osai.

"I thought that you've gained knowledge and become civilized, Osai, because you're now a been-to. What makes you civilized if you, Osai, coming of age you cannot stand up and say to your mother's kindred people that they were wrong and that the heinous things my people did in the past weren't a good testament to be touted. Is coconut water inhabiting your big skull? Learn the right stuff, Osai. Your father and I did not send you out to learn foolishness that you never had before you left. You still don't know that the Biafra holocaust was a scramble for Biafra and her resources, a template culled from the scramble for Africa, but a more pernicious scramble. After all, the dishonorable men at the table of Berlin did not fire a single shot. Rather, they gave themselves thumbs up for their crimes against the African people that are not part of humanity. You got that playbook that thou shall not covet other people's property, but they have coveted Africa as a property, even as I speak to you. Does it matter to you, Osai? Does the cost matter? As always, what matters is the end justifying the means," she paused. "Don't you know that all pogroms, all wars, all genocides, all holocausts, are a scramble for something? Are you really what you claim to be? Human! Or human a misnomer, a false ascription? The Armenian genocide was a scramble for something. The Jewish holocaust was a scramble for Jewish industry and wealth. Big-eyed Europeans would rather wash their hands in the blood of a people than take their eyes off something that does not belong to them? You know nothing! The worst of stupidity is to know nothing when you have a chance to know and should know. It is left for you to receive sense, and understand, and work tirelessly to prevent a second death. The Biafra holocaust was the cruelest contrived scheme to demand and snatch from a people that which is dearest to them. That is what the scramble for Biafra represented. Don't come here to teach me new nonsense.

"All of us pay allegiance to something or someone. I pay allegiance to Biafra and to your dad even though I won't let neither Biafra nor your father kill me, neither would I allow him to marry a second wife nor let him cook his own meals. But, if that foolhardiest lion dashed in here to maul us, your dad would be that bulwark that he truly is. He will manfully sever the jaws of the stupid lion with his bare hands and make a mincemeat of it and would rightly be called *Ogbuagu*, the one who hewed the lion with his bare hands, not the irreverent townsfolks who parade themselves as *Ogbuagu* but would dash to the woods and ask the hills to cover them when a cub showed its teeth and yawned at them. You're enjoined to pay allegiance. They school you to pay allegiance. That's alright! But they don't want you to know anything about the conquest of Africa. Instead of starting the First World War on that account, they decided to postpone killing themselves and divided Africa among themselves. Then the wholesome, official rape of the continent began," said his mother.

"Oh, Mom, you meant the scramble for Africa. What has that got to do with America?" asked Osai incredulously.

"They have nothing to do with the partition of Africa, but they were gawking, leering, and salivating from the little corner of the table ceded to them by the hungry Europeans and then they as in a lot of things were one of the chief beneficiaries of the decimation of my beloved continent," said Dorothy.

"Mom, you seem not have anything good to say about these people. If you don't have anything good to say about someone, you don't have to say something ugly either."

"Rubbish, I've lots and lots of respect for the people that made their place your abode. I've a lot of good things to say about your friends and the place whence they come. They're a restless people with incredible spirit. They don't sleep. In fact, they sleep with one of their eyes open. When you slumber, goat, they set their minds ablaze, their spirit agog. I hope you learn something from their sleepless slumber. I hope you learn to sleep with one of your eyes open. Or else one day you are going to wake up and open your eyes only to find out that they have abandoned this ugly, wretched planet and moved on, leaving you in the lurch. If they found another abode in the sky, they would throw their urine and feces and dirt down to earth and in your face and you would do nothing about that. They are the physical horizon you see on top of the hill, a complete mirage. They never set a bar for themselves, so when they scale one bar they quickly raise another for themselves. Life and environment they live in must be conquered and be dominated, perhaps decimated. In doing so they've no respect for danger. They see no danger in their path. But when danger is the next bar, they try to overcome it. If you're that danger they will sacrifice you on the altar of the-end-justifies-themeans. It's always success at all cost. Do you get that, bush animal!

"I've something good to say about your out-of-this world, ill-cladded friends. Without doubt they are also wonderful, in the real sense of wonderful. They're a wonderful people. They gave us the Bell brothers, that invented the wonderful means to chat across the seas, though with the help of some unsung, good-for-nothing folks. They gave us modern nimbler coaches that simplified our movement on a large scale. They gave us the beautiful bogies and the Ram brothers. They gave us a whole panorama of things too numerous to mention. In fact, they simplified our lives and raised it to the highest standards. It can't be denied them. But, goat! My goodness me, you know that they are the only one that had figured out how to harass the hell out of the rest of us with mass fear and mass peace. And more so, they are spurring all of us to more freedoms. Freedom to live, yet not emancipated by it. Damndest freedoms, surreptitiously like a laser, guided at people like you. We've mastered the sophistry of speaking with tongue in cheek? We don't any longer know the difference between good and better? Our world is weighed down by the tyranny of freedom, and emancipation has become subdual, and like a hunted animal, cowered in a corner frightened beyond belief. Good grief!" she said.

"Mom, is that all you gotta tell me?" he asked as he tried to provoke his mother further.

"Don't get yourself bamboozled like your great, grandfather who wholeheartedly believed that *bekee wu agbara*, that the white is a spirit, instead of human. He died a fool, for up till his dying days, before his bottom fell out, he truly prided himself as a philosopher, though erroneous, still believing that white men are spirits. It was that belief that was the foundation of the abyss we are all grappling to crawl out from as I speak to you. Don't be fooled, Osai. Rather, ask question and more questions. Query every doctrine, especially all outlandish belief systems, pushed down your throat or sheepishly accepted and imbibed.

"Always remember, at a point in your genealogy, Osai, or that string that knots our bloodline for eons, an offspring or some offsprings would deviate from the ills which their forbearers held sacred and pure! My question to you, Osai, is when will you abandon that which your forbearers held pure and true? And for clarity, ask your father about your grandfather and great grandfather".

"I know. I don't know," answered Osai offhandedly, and quickly added, "We're all cultural, even in our erroneous beliefs, and we hold them dear. Hate is cultural. Bloodletting is cultural. Subjugation is cultural. But, love is tribal. If you didn't know, you don't know. If you never experienced it, if you never thought about it, you never worry about it. That's the way of the world. These truths take time to come to."

"I hope you learn something from them. And by the way, when are you taking your friends back?" she asked as Osai tried to make it through the door on his way out of the room.

"I'm going to tell as a mother will advise his child. Remember that if someone was good for friendship she should be pleasing for you to marry her. Contract a friendship with a beautiful and good-nurtured person in case of marriage. You don't contract an ugly damsel for frolicking and when there's a mishap you turned around and tell the rest of us how ugly she was. Or how her legs are bent like a blade. If she was good for friendship she must be good for an unplanned marriage. You've reasons to be happy, but you don't have reasons to be evidently stupid," she said after him.

Chance had never thought about having a white girl for a girlfriend, let alone go beyond platonic flirtations. But as his mother harangued him, having a white girl for a friend had given him food for thought. It had inhabited a part of him. He also knew that his mother had said all that to checkmate him before he dabbled into that winding affair. Methinks there were reasons in what his mother enunciated to him. As he left the room, he knew that the end of the tête-à-tête was not as smooth as they had begun. His mother was combative when she had to be. She was also mellow when she had to be. Some cases are won by a wink and a bang, and some are won by wink only. She never believed in banging to emphasize her point but never shied away when it had to be employed to drive home the point.

CHAPTER 7

It was on a Thursday afternoon and five days since Chance and his gang of friends made it to Umudede. By their schedule they had barely two more days to while in the bustling city about thirty miles to the creeks of the Atlantic Ocean. It had been a remarkable excursion. While the visitors seemed to have enjoyed every bit of their adventure, Chance had taken a beating of immense proportion. However, he had borne it with some stoic forbearance which was every bit a plank of his life. Every member of his family completely disagreed with his brazen experiment, and none minced their distaste for such insensitivity. But he had carried on without betraying the torture and tongue-lashing wallop he had endured. Business as usual he had projected to his friends who were mindless of the inquest he had had to go through for treading audaciously where angels feared to tiptoe.

The group had been to various places of interest, from the zoo that could not afford the famed roar of a lion that was told and held to choking fear in the America folklore. They had gone to the wildlife park erroneously taught in schools to experience all the myopic depiction of what was not true of Africa by any stretch of the imagination. They had also visited the clashing stream. The sight was unique in its wonder. Two streams that were seen to spring from the same source but veered toward divergent ways at a point in their flow as they made daily their journey toward the Atlantic Ocean. Any effort made by any doubting Thomas to bring them together would yield a repulsion to each other. They always flow apart and usually made a clapping sound louder than a ripple when someone tried to bring them together. The adventurers had visited that amazing sight fascinated, and thoroughly enjoyed the scene especially as they tried to see the reaction of this sisterly aversion played out before their eyes when they experimented the reaction that was always wont to occur.

It was that much of a festive period whenever the comet appeared. Though it stood no chance around the sun but when it was seen in the horizon then something big had happened. A beggar had not kicked the bucket. The festival of Okonjo had a schedule. But when it made an unusual appearance then something big had happened, perhaps a prominent personality had given up the ghost. At such a time, the hoi polloi would have a field day and the opportunity to dine at the table of the rich. And that festivity was not because Osai and his friends came to town. No! A very rich man had just died and Okonjo had to come to town to pay him respects.

Okonjo was the monster masquerade. It could make one run. It could make one laugh in his flamboyance. It could make one have one's heart fall inside of one's stomach in its monstrous ugliness and scary visage. Okonjo was not only unique in his monstrosity, but also it was unpredictable in show appearance. It could make his spectators wait and wait almost to no end. It was an embodiment of the mythical African time. If it were announced that Okonjo was coming, one might as well go about their businesses because Okonjo never made it out on time. It was always a waiting game. And when Okonjo did appear he did it with such fanfare and no one could ascertain from which approaches he was going to show up. The music to usher him out could go on forever. But the very music that brought out Okonjo had a distinct tone, and the gonging was metallic as it was somber. His guides and town folks and those well initiated in the culture knew it. For them it was unmistakable. As always it was his music. He knew it. When it was esoteric, it was his. When it was like a dirge, it was his. When it was not any of these, it was not his. The initiated knew, and at the height of the gonging they knew it was time to scamper out of the way. It was his beckoning music in its intensity and frenzy. There was always pandemonium with people running helter-skelter with no place to hide. There was always the danger. Okonjo was entertaining, however. Armed with a bloody machete he could scare the gallantry out of the bravest of men and onlookers unless one was initiated. If one was caught in his stampede, he was not going to slaughter the person. However, he could pin the victim down with the edges of his bloodstained machete that one could feel the jag as in a dagger point. Okonjo was more likely to injure his guide or members of his retinue than an innocent bystander or onlooker who had come to watch and be entertained. Okonjo never hurt anybody. One could get hurt by running scared and falling over one another than from anything Okonjo could have done! It was such a show, and a whole lot of people understood that.

The Okonjo show was once-in-a-while occurrence. It was on schedule to be celebrated once every three years. It was not due to make any appearance until the next two years. But this time it had to appear because a prominent member of the society of Umudede had died. The community wanted to pay their last homage, and the Okonjo crew felt really, really obliged to pay him their last respects. And it so happened when Osai and his friends were in town. And they were there to watch and pay their respects as well. As the community hollered in the chaos and pandemonium the Americans hollered, too, but frightfully.

Chance and his friends had seen all these. What they had not seen were those lions and leopards and tigers that were the tale in teaching classes across their land and for which they had been scared to death. They had seen what they were never told: the merrymakers of Okonjo.

But today they were out in search of some souvenir. And to the biggest market in sub-Saharan Africa they were headed for. It was a beehive of people. Kind of impregnable in its mass. There was no space for much movement. It was body against body. Vehicles crawled because there were not much extra inches for pedestrians to tread. It was bumper to bumper, fender to bumper. To make matters worse, it was hot, extremely hot. Nevertheless, it did not deter folks. They were used to it. It was natural for the people of these parts of sub-Saharan Africa. It was in that atmosphere and environment that Jewel found herself that afternoon. It was kind of enjoyable initially. But at a point it was not that much of a fun. Coupled with the fact that she and her friends had to brush through a throng of people to find the path forward. Movement was very, very tight, and she could feel her boobs brush in between people of all walks of life, just to make it to the next point. She was riled. But Dusty and Candie seemed to be enjoying it all. Now she was finding herself in the minority. So she trudged on at war with herself. As if that was not enough, the noise was just seemingly deafening. That atmosphere was like both a bazaar and an auction. She could neither make a head nor tail out of it. And then there were the *gwongworo*, the ten-wheeler vehicles that share the roads with everyone and everything else. It was chaos at its highest stage. The traffic was a crawl in most places and in some places at a standstill. Frustration was the order of the day sometimes accentuated by the blare and honking that accompany such testy atmosphere. Every inch of space gained mattered a lot. But because of the din in the noise it was possible that a lot of people had become deaf to anything, even the beat of their own hearts.

Jewel was trudging behind her friends, almost cavalier like, unmindful of the commotion about her. It was like vying for space with man and machine. She came from a country where it was law for pedestrians to have the right of way. Not so in these lands. Then all of a sudden, she felt a pair of hands on her sides. Before she could turn around to see what was happening she was lifted and swept off her feet and gingerly dropped on her feet a little bit away from the road. She staggered a little to keep her balance and she did.

"Hey, woman, you are on the verge of losing your small last toe," said a young man in his early twenties, who quickly dashed forward and heaved open the front passenger's door of a pickup Ford truck and jumped back in.

The young man had just alighted from the truck as it crawled on its way forward. They had been crawling slower than they were afforded, but having Jewel walk elegantly on the edge of the road like that made their progress even slower. And no one could afford or want to lose a space there to gain because it was hard to come by.

"Hey, hey, hey, take your hand off me," shouted Jewel, petrified as she gathered herself.

"You need to get out of the way," said the young man as he threw an ugly, rebuking look at Jewel with one hand hanging out of the door of the moving vehicle.

"I've the right of way," she said to him, pointing a finger in the man's direction.

"You're lucky, ewu. You stand a chance of losing your legs, and no one will care a hoot here. Be careful," he counseled her as the vehicle moved a little bit with increased speed but a speed that could still be overtaken by someone doing a race-walk in an alleyway.

When that young man lifted Jewel out of the road it attracted a little bit of revelry uproar among some onlookers and passersby. That also attracted the attention of Chance and company who were about five steps in front of her. They did not see what happened to her, but the look on her face was not amusing. She was bemused. The quizzical inquiry on Chance's face did not need to add any other utterance to boot.

"That son of a bitch just lifted me up and hoisted me off the road," Jewel told his surprised friends.

"Who?" asked Chance

"He was gone with the truck right in the distance," she said, pointing in the direction of the Ford truck just about to gather speed.

"What do you mean?" asked Dusty, bewildered and wearing some kind of a mischievous smile.

"I mean what you just heard," said Jewel, a little bit amused, almost smiling.

"You mean, he just carried you off the road like that," quipped Dusty, now smiling.

"I'm telling you and you can't believe it, what a shorty he was. He just grabbed me by the waistline and gingerly dropped me off the road," she told her friends as they now made light of the whole incident and continued their stroll inside the main market.

"Young men and women you need to get out of the way," said an onlooker who was a few yards behind Jewel when the show happened.

"What's your dog in the fight," Jewel fired back sarcastically. "I think I should tell you that I've the right of way." She tried to school the man.

"Dead men have no right of way. They cannot even give an evidence in their own case," said the man who continued to walk forward slowly on his way as the human traffic jam went on unrelenting.

Chance uttered no words. He was torn between the droit du seigneur of Jewel, his guest, and the mishap the story would be if any of them would have a toenail chopped off on account of making a trip into desolate village of torn Biafra.

If the road was compact the approaches to the market were jampacked. At some points, one virtually had to pause in one's track to give way to the person trying to beat the pedestrian traffic logjam in front of one from the opposite direction. And the cacophony of voices was even louder as traders tried to win customers or even lure them to disregard the approach of their competitors and neighbors. Here everything was up for bargain. Every sale tactic was fair. No complaints. No stopping. Keep moving was the mantra unless some stuff or ware caught one's eyes. To say that the marketplace was densely populated was to make light of the phrase. Actually, this was the biggest market in the whole of Africa. The whole place including the market was denser than densest. People brushed one another to afford access. It was not unusual to feel the boobs of one damsel brushing the bicep of an apprentice boy trader who was trying to weave his way past the pedestrian traffic holdup. It just happened to Dusty. It was intentional. It was just a way of life. Startled as she was she chuckled to herself. It would be just a tale to be told. One of those things!

"Child of a white man, I got what you are looking for," said one of the apprentice traders trying to draw the attention of the group as they made their way past the vicinity of the stalls.

"Pfffffffffff," came a whistle from the other side of the pedestrian demarcation between the line of stalls.

"I got it here," beckoned another boy as his boss who sat at the corner of the stall kept fanning himself, trying really hard to cool himself in the suffocating heat.

"Wow," echoed another boy who just became his own boss after being settled to be on his own by his boss after seven years of apprenticeship. "These kids are from a different planet," he quietly added.

"No, they are from the outer space," quipped another. "They are not born of a woman," he concluded.

"What do you mean?" demanded his neighbor.

"That one there," he said looking in the direction of Jewel, "was vomited. The mom did not give birth to her. She is too beautiful to be borne like that. She threw her up." He concluded.

"You are right," agreed his neighbor.

"That one packs some punch," howled another neighbor pointing at Dusty.

"Front and back," concurred his friend, standing about six feet away.

There was not much of a souvenir they could pick on this lane. As Chance urged his friends to move on, another whistle came through the din.

"Man without cojones, you mean to say that we do not have anything that conquers your attention here. Buy me, I am for sale?" said a young man, known for not biting his words or mincing them. He was referring to Candie who led the rear this time around. She was wearing cute short pants that had all the beauties of her physique embossed. Her behind was it. It was the proverbial figure eight, rotund, rounded, portable, cute, noticeable, provocative, but most importantly a beauty to behold, charming like the damsel on whose frame this body part was hung.

In this land for a woman wearing trousers was a rarity. To wear a variant so tight and so close to the edges of the buttocks was an aberration. It was an affront to their sensibilities, and they got it and expressed their aversion to it in the strongest terms. It was the least the girls had expected, but it never bothered them. Actually, somehow the girls seemed to glow in the ululation and brouhaha, attention or admiration they were receiving. They did not understand some of the language, but they did understand that much of comments were directed at them and perhaps unsavory.

It was a short drive home from their picnic of the day. As usual, Chance manned the wheels. Night had descended on the land. The streets were well lit. It was enjoyable. The picnic had not been totally enjoyable. The Okonjo show did not live up to expectation in terms of excitement. On many occasions, the Okonjo made many forays in the direction of Chance and his friends, and on many occasions they were forced to scamper for their dear lives even though Okonjo had never seriously harmed anyone that graced his revelry. And the visit to the zoo did not assuage their disappointment. But anyway, it was night and they were headed home. Jewel was impetuous. When she remembered how she was picked up by that young man and hauled off the road, she tried to suppress a little flicker of chuckle that perched on her lips. The trouble with her was that she was imperial without a crown. She was impervious without a bulwark. In spite of her shortcoming she never failed to assert herself and be heard.

"So you felt good taking us to a zoo without even a cub," began Jewel imperially, addressing Chance. This was important since when she broached the idea to visit Biafra her mother had tried to dissuade her by telling her the usual fallacious elementary tales that were bandied in classroom discussions by those who knew but nothing, that she may be devoured in her sleep without a chance to save herself. She brushed her worries aside. It made the prospect even more exciting. She wanted excitement and she wanted it in galore. So her disappointment had no bounds, and she wanted to poke a jab in the side of Chance for the fun of it. Since he was unable to provide them enough memories to hang on to, he might as well be the boot of his friends in spite of his effort.

Jewel was a character. When she referred to the guy that heaved her out of the road and out of danger as shorty, it was by no means that the young man was that short in stature. No. The man was more than average height. It was just that by any measure Jewel had no appreciation for those she was by an inch taller. The young man was not by any estimation of shortness. It was just that he was by an inch shorter than Jewel and in that estimation, she saw him as a short man and diminished his worth by all measures. She was imbued in some many measures. She was endowed. Nevertheless, she had so much going for her. Anyone else's guffaw could be shadowed by her chuckle. She could elicit a convergence of help for a stumble than anyone else who was felled by a stumbling block. She was such that she could charm a total stranger to buy her tale against the veracity of eyewitnesses or onlookers to an incident. She was such. And she was such that anyone would want to engage her in any polemics because in most cases they ended up exercises in futility. She was difficult to deal with. She could wag her tongue and she could wag her tail. It was such that her friends understood that aspect of her life that they tried all the time to steer away from anything that would bring her to a collision course with any of her friends. Just leave her alone. In spite of her tilted favor they still cherished and loved and longed for her company. And in some ways, she had taken their devotion to her for granted.

"Where're your famed wild gorillas and orangutans? Your hyenas and wild dogs. Where're your lions and tigers famed to live among you? And where are the leopard and these other carnivores?" she asked. "You must be hiding them from us. That was what I wanted to see," she continued.

"You're asking for a myth told in tales," Turnkey told her.

"No, it's not," said Jewel.

"Well, they are in the wild," said Turnkey resignedly.

"It can't be wilder than this," chirped Dusty.

"If you were looking for anything wilder than what you have seen, we can find those in the Appalachian valleys or the Cherokee lowlands," said Chance, trying to refocus their attention.

"If that was all you got we could have gone to the Yellowstone National Park."

"That's all I've got. Anything else is a figment of the imagination of those who never left their homelands but with binocular in their heads see far and wide in ignorant spectacle," said Chance. "They've conned you. If they were paid they had taught what they weren't paid to do. You need a refund."

"Where're the coyotes?"

"It seems that you're not listening, Jewel! I know that you wanna do what you wanna do. But, now, you go and ask your teachers that were teaching you nonsense. I know that my people have a long way to go. But, you've gone a long way off the track. And even then, my people are making efforts to get out of the bush while you're just walking right back into its thickets. Get off it, Jewel. And tell your teachers that I said so."

"You're right," she drawled, "I hear you. And then that spectacle of a show. What do you call it?" continued Jewel.

"It's the Okonjo revelers," answered Chance.

"What's that! Is it part of your heathen tradition?" asked Jewel again.

"What do you mean?" asked Chance, in typical Biafran idiosyncrasy.

"I want to know if it was part of your pagan custom?" she asked.

"I don't get what you're talking about. It's part of the things that make a society what it is."

"You know what? This is one of your heathen celebrations that I think the time has come to be discarded in the dustbin of forgotten anachronism," said Jewel offhandedly.

"Really?" snapped Chance.

"Be a decent guest," Candie counseled.

"Candie, allow her to go on. I see her crying over the refusal of her mom to buy her some Halloween costumes or even take her out for a trick or treat parade," said Chance mockingly. "There's nothing more heathen than Halloween."

"What!" yelled Jason.

"Believe you me. There's nothing more heathen than the day of the ghoul. Children are escorted door to door demanding for candies dedicated to the demons."

"Please, I don't want my name bandied in Halloween discussion. Do not get me involved," Candie cautioned.

"My bad. It was pun unintended," apologized Chance.

"Please, don't say anything ill about Halloween. Growing up it was my most hallowed day," said Jason. "I always look forward to the coming of Halloween. Trick or treat was good. Candies were in abundance. It was holier than Christmas. But that was then," he added.

"I really enjoyed it," chirped Dusty.

"But that was then. It doesn't matter to me now," said Jason.

"It was then for you, Jason, but there are those who still celebrate it more than Christmas or even Fourth of July. And all they do is nothing but pay homage to strange creatures. I mean to say, the ghoul," said Chance.

"I don't care what you think of Halloween. I love it and still do. It's celebration rooted in history," said Jewel.

"So, Jewel, your history of unknown origin dedicated to the demon is worth celebrating, but time-honored revelry of the Biafran people is for a dying heathen culture that scared the hell out of you. Give me a break!" demanded Chance. "It is an agelong misconception," he continued. "You know how if a cockroach is tired of life or hungry-looking, tattered, they would say that it's an African cockroach, but if it's big, obese, and perhaps morbidly obese, it's an American roach, because it's well fed."

"Hey, you guys are bogging me," said Turnkey at last. "Can we just stop for a second at the joint?" he demanded. All along his mind had wandered toward the wee-wee rendezvous. No one was more in dire need of this species of marijuana than he. He loved it. He wanted it. He enjoyed the taste of it and the feeling it left one with. He loved the aura it made him exude. They had another night to say bye to the town of Umudede, and he wanted to take advantage of this penultimate night to saturate himself and his body with what he had come to believe to be finest marijuana on planet earth.

Turnkey also remembered a discussion he had with his mother before he ventured with his friends to Biafra when he intimated her he was going on vacation in far-off land in Africa.

"Say it again, let me hear you clearly," she demanded of her only son.

"You mean to say that you're going to the enclave of the lions and tigers and, worse of all, the land of the monkeys," she had demanded again and again.

"Have you been to Africa? How do you know that, Mom?"

"I see it on television. I read it in the books," she said.

"Who wrote the book you said that you read. And who made the stuff you saw on telly?" asked Turnkey vehemently.

"It's in the books. I saw it on telly," she said again. "People share their balconies with monkeys, and on their front lawns you see them scamper all over the whole place."

"Mom, you must have seen something different or heard somewhere else. Perhaps, you are referring to Gibraltar. And Gibraltar is far away from Africa. And if I were not mistaken, the last time I checked, Gibraltar is somewhere in Europe. And you know, Mom, we may have more lions here in the United States. Check out the plains of Chattanooga or the wood of Kissimmee for more dangerous animal than the things you put in your massive head as distinctive features of African wilds," he said to his mother. "And, Mom, I've heard you say things about the naked people of wild Africa. You've more naked folks in the Amazon basin than anywhere else in Africa, and the last time I checked, the Amazon basin is in the Americas."

"That I don't know. How do you know that, son?"

"I see it on television. I read it in the books," he told his mother. "And worse still, the Amazon basin is closer to you here in the States than it's closer to berated Africa."

"Then they must have come from Africa," said his mother.

"That I don't know. But if they came from Africa, your great-grandfathers and uncles must have brought them here and abandoned them here without clothing, without caring, leaving them to live in the wild like that. And now without knowledge you're having an erroneous opinion because you read or saw on telly concocted stuff by some of your ilk who have the pedigree of your great-grandfathers and uncles," said Turnkey.

"You need to stop, son. I knew it from the outset. When you began your relationship with that wizened African kid, I knew it. I knew that you will never be the same again. How I wished that your uncle was still alive today!"

"You need to stop, Mom. Perhaps when next you hear from me I'd be calling you from deep inside Africa, in Biafra."

"That's if they had a phone to reach me," said Splendor.

"We shall see, Mom."

As Chance held on to the gas and brought the Land Cruiser to a halt, Turnkey was out of the truck before that stop could be ascertained. For a week now the patrons of the wee-wee joint had come to know the little white boy as one of them and a friend to Ogidigi. They had come to accept him and had no fear that he could be a mole for the police. He just wanted a few days' supply for tomorrow and onward journey to Eureka. Tomorrow they had planned to go nowhere but spend the day indoors, relax and prepare for the three hundred miles to Eureka. It took a matter of minutes, and he was back in the belly of the truck and as Chance heaved the truck forward Turnkey was the happiest of the friends. Not far from there Chance made the turn to the annex, and the guards opened the bulwark gate as the truck made its entry.

What happened that night was epic. Jason retired with his friend of two years. Turnkey had some whiff of inhalation and exhalation and felt good with himself before he joined Dusty in bed. Chance chatted with Candie most of the evening playing some Scrabble.

"Play your game and stop throwing that kind of look at me," said Candie.

"I'm minding my business, girl," swooned Chance.

"If you were minding your business then you should not be throwing that furtive, flirtatious look at me," said Candie.

"It doesn't hurt me looking at you straight in the eyes. I've no need to look at you with the tail of my eyes, girl," said Chance.

"Then play this game. I'm not taking you home even if I won. Of course, you'd be of no use to me. Even if I hung you as a trophy you're not worth the space you'll occupy on the wall or in my heart," said Candie.

"You must be kidding me," said Chance.

Ever since their first night at Umudede and subsequently when Chance left her hanging their relationship had stagnated. On many occasions Chance had actually made effort to avoid looking her directly in the eyes. But he never felt that he had done anything wrong. Actually, in the privacy of his being he had thumped his chest for not succumbing to tasting the forbidden fruit, especially from such a close family friend. He had no regrets. On the other hand, Candie had not forgiven him.

However, she had mellowed a lot. Her angry reaction to his failures had regressed a lot. But she had made up her mind that even if he came back to himself and effusively asked her for copulation, probably he would not, but she was certain she would never grant him that request even if he was on his knees doing so. She had moved on. There was a thaw in her initial perception of him, but the opportunity of mating her had gone. Yet, one thing that may have been lost on her was that he had no intention of making any overtures or even asking to have a sexual relationship with her at this point in their relationship. It was not quite long after they also retired to bed. They lay with total understanding of each other's motives. The companionship had become really platonic. It was acceptable to both. She lay innocently with her head right on his broad shoulders, inadvertently or not, no one could tell. He could feel her breath cascade down his face and ruffled the broad spat of hairs on his chest. It was innocent. Her right leg was right on his, but his muscle neither moved nor were his thoughts challenged. Of course, he was deep asleep, but there was this feeling of conquest for him than any act of sexual escapade, consensual or imagined.

CHAPTER 8

"**G**entlemen, good to have you in my presence for a while. Osai told me that you are set to set forth tomorrow for onward journey back to the United States in the next few days," began Ogidigi, as he ushered Jason and Turnkey inside his palatial living room.

"You are?" he asked, looking at Jason even though they had been introduced to him previously.

"I'm Jason. Jason Deville," said Jason.

"And you, young man?" he said, looking in the direction of Turnkey.

"My name's Turnkey Ghoostte," said Turnkey.

"Mr. Ghost and Mr. Devil, make yourselves comfortable," urged Ogidigi with intentional, deliberate malapropism. *What names!* he muttered to himself.

Ogidigi had not changed from whom he had always been. However, he had adapted to doing things a little bit differently. Since after the suspension of hostilities of the Biafran genocide he had withdrawn from public life. He had thriving businesses before the war. Those businesses were decimated by the war just like everybody else's business. It was frustrating to him and a number of his comrades. He did not want to go and challenge for a place in the negotiated government. He did not want anything to do with governance although he dearly wanted it to succeed and flourish. He invested his whole being in the Biafran struggle, but when the ceasefire was agreed he left every instrument of the war on the battleground. He wanted an outright victory. However, he was fine with the war that was waged and the peace that was reached. Being a soldier he would have preferred an outright victory on the battlefield. That outcome was not achieved and that sometimes frustrated him. But he had moved on. He quickly began to rebuild his businesses. He had a large landholding, obtained ancestrally and more recently through land speculation. That had served him well. And he had expanded his influence and his business had also flourished of late. Though it was slow for Biafra picking up the pieces of its remnant, but business seemed to have gathered pace. There was influx of money from the world that watched while men, women, and children were butchered with impunity and now had turned benevolent benefactors, investors in cruel nobody's blood. Businesses had boomed and Ogidigi had benefitted from it all. That had kept him busy. Very, very busy.

As soon as they sat down, Ogidigi requested of his son to get him some kola nut to officially serve them in his own capacity although they had been around for over five days. Kola nut was usually the first gesture of goodwill to welcome a guest to one's home. It was customary in Biafra land. When Turnkey and his friends arrived Osai had offered them some kola nut in his own capacity. It was not appetizing. It was not one of those things consumed with some relish. But surprisingly Turnkey had munched it with no concern. Even if he had some misgiving about its bitter taste he never showed it. If he had consumed vodka then there was no need to complain about the bitter taste of kola nut, a bitterness that was ephemeral. Actually, he had munched it with some surprisingly native relish, to the consternation of Dusty who put it in her mouth and hastily spat it out. Jason did not like it then, but he hung on to it now.

Ogidigi had prayed over it, blessed their coming to Biafra and going back to the States, and asked Osai to split one of them and pass it to his friends. He did something else: he gave one whole kola nut to Turnkey and one whole kola nut to Jason.

"When kola nut gets home it narrates where it was coming from," Ogidigi had told his young guests. "Take it home and it will tell the rest of your journey. It will tell people that you had been to the land of the Igbo, the land of the Biafran people. In some cultures, they may welcome you with water, and some others will offer chewing stick. But here in Biafra it was always going to be kola nut. You may not understand what I am talking about, but kola nut is the foundation of our welcoming and hospitality, gentlemen," said Ogidigi.

"We appreciate," muttered Turnkey and Jason in unintended unison.

"I am glad you guys thoroughly enjoyed your stay here," he said.

"Oh no, we do appreciate your hospitality," said Turnkey.

"And your beautiful home," added Jason.

"Now, if I may ask, you seem to have a good relationship with Osai, how did it start? Of course, if you never had, you would not have accompanied him to this far-flung land of ours," said Ogidigi.

"Yep," began Turnkey. "I've known Jason for upward of six years, and we have been good friends since then. And Chance I've come to know him ever since he came to the States. First, it was frosty and antagonistic, but then it quickly thawed and we've been the best of friends since then. Now, he's not just a friend, he is like a comrade in arms, a brother. He had told me a lot about his people and the struggle of the Biafran people, as well. I do appreciate him so well, and he had shown me esprit de corps in more ways than one," said Turnkey.

As he said these, Ogidigi's eyes lightened up. When he saw a faithful servant, he could tell. In an instance, he saw a good fella in his son's friend. The words he was using gave him up. This chap could have been a Bolshevik but for the fact that he was an American. He saw his child as a comrade, and their relationship tinged with the military parlance of esprit de corps. In the years gone by if he was found to be a liker of such doctrines that would qualify him to be under some form of surveillance. For some reasons, he was almost sounding like a communist. Part of the reasons why the Biafran struggle was not allowed to succeed on the battlefield was the notion that her leaders had communist bend and inclination. It was error number one. It was a pretense, an excuse. And excuses are pretenses, false reasons.

"It wasn't for nothing that we are so close. When I was walking in the wrong direction he was the one that pulled me back. As he explained it to me then. It was he who told me that no matter how far one had gone in the wrong direction that the only option was to stop and make a reverse course since at the end it will only lead to an effort in futility.

He taught me those words of the wise, and I've never regretted it ever since then. I take pride in knowing him, and I'm proud of myself for having the judgment to know that he meant good for me," Turnkey told Ogidigi who was even prouder of his son on hearing such things said of him.

"It was nice to hear such things said of Osai," said Ogidigi.

"So when he offered me an excursion of Africa, I didn't give it a second thought," said Turnkey.

"He's such a nice dude and a good sport," said Jason in collaboration.

"And have you heard from your parents…?" asked Ogidigi striving to move the discussion away from Osai.

"Yes, I spoke to my mother just yesterday," said Turnkey. "Even though I didn't have to," he added.

"Why is that?" asked Ogidigi.

"She didn't know where I am. All she needed knowing is that I'm safe and as long as it wasn't reported that I was in harm's way, she was all right," said Turnkey.

"Why is that?" asked Ogidigi again, with bewilderment written all over his face and his tone tinged with wonderment. "You mean you did not tell her where you are. How about your father?"

"He was always away. But he would not have cared less," said Turnkey.

"You mean that you can wander all over the world without your parents knowing about your whereabouts," said Ogidigi in muffled consternation.

"Yah, I can. I have the freedom to do whatever I want," jumped in Jason.

The mere fact that these kids could boldly tell him these gave him instant goose bumps. If these kids would tell with such audacity he shuddered at what influence it might be having on Osai. Ogidigi was not given to prevarication or fear for nothing. However, he felt that he had a reason to be worried. Now, Ogidigi was not sure how to deal with these kids so that they do not break his child's backbone and lead him to self-destruction. He was sure of his son before he went overseas but not any longer. Osai came back with a bizarre hairdo and piercing of the ears and nose.

"Is that what freedom is all about?" asked Ogidigi, never trying to conceal his consternation.

"Yes, that's it and much more than that," said Turnkey.

Ogidigi was at home with every discussion unmindful of age and status. As long as there was something to be gained, something to be learned in every discussion he would immerse himself in it so it was not out of order for him to engage chaps as young as his son in this new thoroughfare of thought.

"Well, that being the case will never ever happen here," he said.

"That's the difference between America and the rest of the world," said Turnkey.

"When you give unfettered freedom to every child it makes discipline an act of the law of children," said Ogidigi.

"Not necessarily, Dad," chirped in Chance.

"Well, I got to say this though: America's greatness is hinged on the tenets of granting freedom to its people. It unleashes the inner capabilities of man. That's why America has thrived on the global scales far beyond the reaches of her next competitor. When we limit freedom, we shackle the reaches of our capabilities, we stifle the driving force in the self, we kill innovation, we kill enterprise, we limit risks, we limit the lingering thought to touch the horizon. It may be a mirage, nevertheless the urge to touch it makes it possible for us to find new lands and all that is hidden in them. That's why we're never fearful to venture into the world of the unknowns," said Turnkey.

"The chances are in most cases," he said. "In most cases, you chip away the clout of parents to rein in on their wards. And the unintended consequences of that is that it becomes like a Pandora box full of cankerworm. It becomes a cancer. Young men, I know what I am talking about. What you guys did, to leave home without proper agreement with your parents where you are headed for, is enough to get Osai into such a trouble that he may not live to tell the story," said Ogidigi.

"I did tell my mother," said Jason. "But we were not in agreement where I was going," he told him.

"That is what I am saying. You probably may have told her that you were going to Biafra and she would be wondering where in hell is Biafra. Telling her that you were going to Africa would make more sense to her, at least, she erroneously would assume that Biafra is synonymous with Africa and that Africa is one hinterland tucked away somewhere along the equator line," said Ogidigi regrettably.

"No, no," said Jason. "She always refers Africa or Biafra as the motherland." He paused as if he had misspoken.

Ogidigi momentarily paused himself.

"Why would she say that? Is she black?" asked Ogidigi in quick succession.

"I'm of mixed parentage. She's black and my father is white," answered Jason.

"I see," said Ogidigi, a little bit taken aback. It dawned on him that the very handsome chap before him was actually not white yet white enough than black enough. He did not want to betray his ignorance or misconception of Jason, in spite of the fact that Osai had told him earlier that Jason was black by official classification and demographic purposes.

"Anyway, young men," began Ogidigi again. "The point I was trying to make is this, freedom should not be mistaken for a show of the imponderables. I get the *Dukedom Times* every morning and we watch it on television. The world is turned on its head, and you can never make a head or tail of what is going on. We've muddled up some stuff here. Men have lost their fibre and become rudderless. People are frolicking in the streets and in the parks. It is appalling. Our world has gone topsy-turvy…," said Ogidigi.

"Those are trends," said Turnkey. "They ain't gonna last. It will go away as it came," he added.

"Those may be fads. It may be a trend. It is what it is. Freedoms needed to be checked. Frolicking in the streets is an aberrant and a symptom of a decadent world" said Ogidigi.

"It will go away just like all fads before it. When I was growing up, a couple of years ago, my uncles used to wear high-heeled shoes and had the hem of their long pants cover their shoes. Men actually walked like women then," recalled Jason.

"Young man," Ogidigi cut in. "That was a fad. Here in Biafra, I partook in it. But what we are seeing and reading is not like that. It is a symptom of an ailing world, decadent universe, and if you do not know, free weal like that festers like cancer and it has staying power to linger. And you know what is worrisome about the whole show in our world and more importantly the western world, if your country showcases it the rest of the world copies it. If you do not oblige they would shove it down your throat one way or the other in the guise of defense of freedom. Tell me what is laudable in aberrant tendencies, young men?" queried Ogidigi.

"It's unfortunate," quipped Osai.

"In your country," continued Ogidigi, "you are allowed to kill yourself and others even in cold blood. But it behooves on us to make an effort to stop anyone who was found wanting to kill themselves. You have freedom to kill others but not freedom to want to kill yourself. If that freedom, to want to kill oneself, could be abridged why would we hush-hush ourselves into inimically loudest silence?" Ogidigi asked his guests.

Both Turnkey and Jason remained silent for a while as if they were trying to absorb the tenacity of Chance's father's polemics.

"You see," Ogidigi began again. "I do not so much like the government we have in our country. It is a potentate. It is fledgling. It is a by-product of those who installed it. One thing I think that they are right on the mark is on the issue of focusing ahead. I know that right now we're in an aberrant world because of a lot of man's contrived hope, fancies and ideas but, this land had determined to do things differently. I hate fighting a losing battle. And I agree that people can do whatever they like; it's a given. We've no new heaven and new earth, but we, as a people, are weary of new-fangled behaviors, habits, and cultures. I'm saying..." Ogidigi paused.

"But we have had these kinds of freedoms and trends before since time immemorial," said Turnkey.

"Yes," shot back Ogidigi. "Yes," he repeated. "Freedom has existed. But in every society some freedoms are always looked at differently. It is now a whole new ballgame for us to be frolicking in the street with such gusto, in broad daylight. This is a challenge to critical query. It is a mess of thought. This is the height of relapse to ancient topsy-turvy. This is standing logic on its head," said Ogidigi.

"Dad, this is this, this and that, we may disagree with but it has come to stay. If people are not spilling other people's blood, then let sleeping dogs lie. Those who condemned Galileo Galilei to terrible inquisition later discovered that they were all wrong. We've to keep our chins up. It's part of the new world order," said Osai, in surreptitiously stinging rebuke and with a furtive glance of his father with the corner of his eyes. He knew that that was his chance, in the company of his guests, to make one flippant assertion before his father.

Ogidigi cleared his throat. A hush filled the room, and momentarily an uneasy calm, broken by the clear voice of Jason that pierced the silence.

"And the world is changing, Mr. Ogidide," said Jason with his own unintended malapropism.

"Old chap," said Ogidigi, referring to Jason and ignoring his son. "Some things do not change. For instance, the pillars that hold heaven and earth do not change, or if they did, you may wake up one day and discover in your helplessness that the heavens have crumbled and we are all buried in its rubbles. Some stuffs are immutable as Chukwu Okike Abiama is immutable. Nonsense! Stupid ignoramuses!" he said, exasperated with his son more for being easily convinced and joining the bandwagon of new-fangled habit.

The night was well spent. Again and again Turnkey had yawned aloud after he could not muffle them anymore. They needed sleep for the drive tomorrow down to Eureka. Ogidigi was an absorbing man. Every discussion seemed to be his turf, and he held back no punches. He never hit his opponent below the belt, but he would always give you signal of what he intended to do. Perhaps, a little of the local brew helped to weaken Turnkey and sapped his staying power. But Ogidigi made a huge impression on him. The constant idea that people should cocoon in their places gave him food for thought. Freedom, after all, could be subjective. Conscience is subjective. But, real science is not, and nature is not, either. What was a man's meat in one household could be a man's poison in another. That, too, is subjective. Really, some stuff are immutable, and tinkering with them may be affront to what was sacred and true. It may be a slippery slope and would wallop the soul to decadence. But, Ogidigi was beginning to understand. At least, he had come to accept that it was a given that people could do whatever they liked.

"Gentlemen, I know that you are tired and worn out. I'm going to say this: there is the demon in all of us, and no one stands with arms akimbo in the face of an enormous, cascading change. But, if there is nothing you took away from me tonight, I want you to know, my father used to tell me that but for the work of the evil one what would a person be looking for in the secret places of another person," he told his guests. "It is that chimera in all of us. Be wary. If you gave him a finger, he wants a hand. If you gave him a hand, he wants your wrist. If you gave a wrist he wants your elbow. If you gave an elbow he wants your arm, and then an embrace, and then you are finished. But who am I to stand in the way of the world? Nobody can!"

After a short pause, he added.

"I may not have time to see you in the morning before you depart. I am wishing you a safe journey, be good and be of good repose. To yourself be true. I hope you enjoyed yourselves staying here with us these past few days."

"Oh no, we had a blast," chorused Jason and Turnkey together.

Chance walked his friends to the annex and came back to his father. Ogidigi looked at him straight in the eyes and said, "Son, you have got some interesting young men for friends. That mulatto is very interesting, but that gangling chap," he said, referring to Turnkey, "is most engaging. He seems to me to be full of contradictions. He seems to have a grasp of everything and rooted in the American sense of freedom. I am afraid he is bent on reshaping his environment. It looks like he is more dogged than you. You must assure me that you have the grit to have yourself rooted on firmest ground. You must not be distracted. You must to yourself remain true." He informed his son.

"By the way, is he a southern Democrat?" he asked his son.

"No, not all. Actually, he is neither here nor there. The thing is that he has moved from being a Democrat to be a Republican. And today he is unaffiliated. But I think that he still has a soft spot for Republicans. He comes from a family of carpetbaggers. When I ran into him for the first time he was torn between the realities of the time and the lost vision of his great-grandfathers and uncles. He did not know who he was and had believed in the absolutes of the olden days. I think that he was starstruck by my will. And by the way," he said, borrowing a cliché from his father, "no one bends me to his will. You know me, Dad. I am the son of my father. You may be iron. I do not mean you per se, Dad, I mean to say that anybody else. You may be iron. Dad, but I am the ironmonger. The work I have done on that boy has been massive. He would be unrecognizable by his uncle who taught him to hate if he were to be alive today." He paused. "I am a formidable force," he reminded his father.

"You may be. But you came back looking like a scalawag. You are a few steps away from being mad," he told Osai.

"Dad, that was one of those things," said Osai.

As Chance left his father's presence, Ogidigi felt some reassurance that his child had been reset to default setting without having to do anything outlandish. If Chance was carried away by some childish exuberance he had assured himself that he had brought him back to normalcy. Never had a child promised so much and all of a sudden had the wheels come off without a moment notice. Not while he still had one ounce of breath within himself.

Back with his friends at the annex. Quite unexpected Candie came after him gushing.

"Boy, you scared the crap out of us. I thought that you had taken Jason and Turnkey to the slab of your altar to satisfy the demand of your heathen gods."

"What are you talking about?"

"I was thinking it would be turn by turn. That after Jason and Turnkey you would come for us, having taken care of the hardest parts," said Dusty.

"You all are joking. And that is the dumbest thing to ever imagine," said Chance.

"Look, I'm down to my fifth bottle," said Jewel, pointing to the empty bottles of Berghoff before her. "Before you place me on that anvil, I want my whole body to be encased. I want it painless and perhaps quick if they will."

"You are a jerk, Jewel. You will be the least my pagan gods would desire for sacrifice. They don't appreciate a riotous spirit. They don't want someone who would come to their enclave and lead a revolt against the order of the netherworld. When someone of your ilk is brought before the gods, there's always pandemonium. They don't want that. They would not want anything to do with you. You're an unwanted spirit. In fact, you'd be the hardest part for them to deal with," teased Chance.

"That's what I'm saying," said Jewel, as she rose from her chair, cupped her boobs, tugged on her bra, and gyrated her waist in defiant body positivism culture and some kind of dance moves to the delight of her friends.

"But, if I may ask, why were we not invited to this august meeting that was so important to warrant our exclusion?" asked Dusty.

"It was just a gathering of men's thought," volunteered Turnkey.

"What's that?" demanded Dusty.

"There's nothing in it," said Chance. "It's just that my father has a way of doing his own thing."

"What do you mean?" queried Candie, who neither drank nor smoked, but has an unquenchable knack for soft drinks of any sprite and taste. She also had an uncanny nature. She never drank coffee but loved its aroma. She never smoked cigarette but loved the smell of some of its species. She never liked weed but did love the aroma as well. She was choosy with food. But she was ravenous with the much she loved. She was simple but at the same time complex in some ways.

"My father believes in sifting the chaff from the wheat," Chance began awkwardly. "Kind of separating the corn from the weed."

"What does that mean? What's that?" she repeated.

"He likes to keep some company mainly manly. He's nothing against women, after all, he has daughters. He, if a situation doesn't warrant involving women, keeps everybody in their places. It's as simple as that, folks. It's not a big deal. For him the world is divided into two folds: man, woman, and anything else is a miasma of rubbish."

"I do not get it," said Candie. "He must either be a segregationist or chauvinist or even both."

"No, he's neither. He's just a realist, pure and simple. While he's color-blind if I may say, he sees things from the purview of blackand-white. Men parley with men and women, women. He makes no apologies for it."

"I think he needs some schooling," said Jewel.

"Be quiet!" demanded Chance calmly.

"But what did you talk about? Did he pull your ears not to marry any of us?" Candie wanted to know.

"Hey, girls, let's move on. We leave tomorrow morning," said Turnkey, trying to change the subject.

"Oh, he would love you to be his daughter-in-law," said Chance.

"Married to who?" asked Candie.

"That, I don't know," said Chance.

"You still do not know. You all can have Jewel," said Candie.

"Not me," said Jewel. "If I'm not good for their idol goddesses I would not be good for her worshippers. That's a good thing."

"You've not told us what you guys talked about behind our backs," demanded Candie.

"It was men's affair. You are not supposed to be privy to it," said Turnkey.

"It's a man's world here," said Chance.

"Explain yourself," demanded Candie.

"You don't wanna know, girl," said Chance.

"Please, I'm dying to know," urged Jewel.

"I mean to say. If a lion bursts into our midst now, I see you trying to shelter yourself behind Jason, your heart falling inside your belly," said Chance.

"You must be kidding me," snapped Jewel. "Jason will be out of here in a blink of an eye. Jason will be saving himself," she concluded.

"Well, that isn't what men do. I will be here battling the beast. I don't have to do it for honors, I do it as a duty, and I can understand why Jason would dash for the hills and allow you to stew in your own juice," said Chance.

"That's mean," said Dusty.

"Nothing mean about it, girl. When girls claim to be men they are asking to bear their own burden and fight their own fight. Folks, nothing goes for nothing. There's no free lunch as Americans are wont to say. Or when there is, someone somewhere out there picks the tab. You can't eat your cake and at the same time have it again," said Chance.

"That makes sense," said Jason.

"It's just what it is. If you counseled your guy behind closed doors and allowed him to take charge in both private and public he will serve his arm to the lions and wolves to keep you safe. But if you perched on his every word he would go about a sunken man and on the day of reckoning he would feed you to the wolves, get a chair, make himself comfortable, and watch them make a mincemeat of you, lick your blood, smack their tongues, and thoroughly enjoy themselves," explained Chance.

"Methinks a lot of sense in it," said Turnkey. "But we got to go," he concluded.

"That's mean," howled Jewel.

"It makes sense for nothing," said Dusty.

"Candie, you now know how you could be saved from yourself," said Chance.

"You can have this kingdom to yourself," she said.

"Then beware of the day of the lion," he advised them. "In the olden days when men were the hewers of wood and drawers of water, they run the show," he continued. "When the men coughed the womenfolk cowered for cover. In those days squirrels had their abode on the tree branches. Not anymore. Today they want to yank you out of the way. They want you to scurry onto the trees and vacate the landscape for them," stated Chance.

"You know Herk," began Jewel, "if you are nostalgic about the years gone by, about eon, your ilk were the hewers of wood and drawers of water but they never run the show. Actually, they got the slipshod," said Jewel.

"I got what you mean, Jewel. But that was an aberration then and is an aberration now. And if I may say I think that you are digressing away from the point. It's not fair, it's cold," said Chance.

"Whether an aberration then or now, I said what I said, and I'm not ready to lose an inch of what I've wrestled from you guys, and you can have this kingdom to yourself," repeated Candie.

"Then be ready to hew your own wood and draw your own water and beware of the day of the lion," cajoled Chance.

They bantered from the trivial to the mundane to the frivolous on and on, and suddenly Turnkey and Jason slipped to the corner of the annex and lit the weed and took some inhalation. When they reappeared shortly afterward it was time for them to retire for their last night in Umudede.

CHAPTER 9

The journey to Eureka was smooth. Close to the approaches of the city there were debris of destruction emanating from the uprising of the past week. It was like a war zone. Burnt tires and burnt vehicles found their final destination in the beleaguered streets of Eureka. It was not a protest that they were feeding the eyes on. These American kids had never seen anything of this nature in their streets, not even during the Vietnam War protests or civil rights movement. As they fed their eyes and had their senses etched with the relics of what seemed a massive wanton destruction of property they could not stop imaging whether some destruction of this magnitude could ever happen in America. As they reached the interception of Umulihilihi and Emeremnini they found some three houses in the corners of that junction left in ruins. When they reached the junction of Brigandry Avenue and Palace Court they noticed two exotic houses charred with only the skeleton to tell the story of the once beautiful architectural designs. A week ago when they touched down at Eureka they did not have the opportunity to see the wreck that was done to the land. They had to travel by another means to Umudede. But now that they had to drive this side of the town they were able to see more of the mayhem like firsthand. In Umudede they saw the relics of the ravages of the genocide many years ago still assaulting the eyes of every visitor and resident of the city. And now this sight.

"Herk," began Jewel, "it looks like your people are given to civil strife. Did you say that this was a protest? Who gave the permit to cause this level of havoc? It looks like a civil war. This is wanton," she said.

"It was not a war. It was the venting of frustration and anger at the system. And you don't need a permit to protest. The permit is in its spontaneity. It's the people's inalienable right. Moreover, police permit to protest is a facade designed to protect the rich and powerful from the legitimate angst of the downtrodden and oppressed. Imagine asking for police permit before the people can go after the hoodlums and miscreants. It's merely a signal for them to take flight," said Chance as they sped past another junction.

"That's an absolute truth," said Turnkey. "To ask police for a permit before a protest is to limit the people's will to vent their spleen. It's a ploy by the powerful to control the will of the people to register the anger to the fullest of limits. It's our rights, and it should be part of any people's right of self-determination. People's right to protest should not be shackled by police permit. It doesn't make sense! But this looks like wanton."

"Wanton indeed," said Candie.

"That's one of the collateral of protests without a permit," said Jason.

"You said that this was a protest, a demonstration. And I say that it was a riot, an upheaval. Where were the police?" asked Jewel.

"Which police! The police are not for the people. They are here to maintain the system," said Osai.

"Then, take it to the judge," said Jewel.

"Jewel, you don't get it! You forgot that you've to have the police to take it to the judge and don't be reminded that judges are also for system maintenance, and no judge is wiser than the people, girl," Osai tried to school her.

"Take it to the jury…"

"You still don't understand. Some of these things are delay tactic wove in the system. And justice delayed is justice denied, for your information, girl. The will of the people long abridged could be redressed and reclaimed. When the rights of the people are brazenly taken and pinned down the only recourse left for a long-suffering people is what you ignorantly called riots and upheavals."

"Then, this must be a jungle…"

"That's what they told you," said Osai

"Yes, that pilot said it all that when you come to these lands they leave you with some haunting memories," said Jewel.

"He said that you leave with jagged memories and a world of experiences," Candie finally chipped in.

When they were at Umudede, Chance had taken them around the town and shown them buildings that were left carcasses of their old selves. Houses after houses with potholes in them that showed the ravages of the Biafran genocide. None of his friends had heard about the genocidal Biafran war and if they had it had not registered to stick in their memories. Chance himself did not know a whole lot about the war. He was rather told by his father in what he called the Biafran revolution. Chance did not want to refer the Biafran imbroglio as a revolution. The mere mention of revolution to an average American sounds like a reference to the coming of the communists in Russian and an American, young and old, never liked the mention of communism, and worse still a communist. The American kids were accustomed to wars and are at home with it. As Chance tried to explain, it was fleeting and not a deep knowledge of what to say or how to expatiate on the little he knew. Nevertheless, the Biafran trauma was no revolution as in the Bolshevik revolution or the French's. It was a statement of intent to say let my people go, set my people free. The genocidal Biafran war was a clarion call for survival in a concerted effort to decimate a people and those people to stand up and put up a resistance.

The Biafran people were not given to revolution as were the Bolsheviks or the French. They were not even given to a civil strife as were the Mau Mau people of the Kenyatta land that stood up to the British and forced them to come to the table of justice. They were not given to all that. They were a people that sought to dominate their own land. They are Republicans in every sense. However, they are not part of the Grand Old Party. They may have something in common with the GOP: they want to be left alone, they want to emancipate themselves and the people right and about them. They are such a people.

The Biafran people are not given to equivocation. They never cuddled a child whose body is festered with craw-craw just to be nice. They never swallowed the sputum just to evade being shamed if the disgusting sputum was spat in public. They are not given to telling a parent that their baby was such a beauty just to please the parent only to go behind and spit out their disgust, telling themselves in their privacies, what a treasure! A treasure? It would be nice to be buried as such. They did not mince their words just to be seen to be nice for all its worth. When one made oneself irresponsible, when one looks irresponsible they would tell the person that they were such. When one brazenly beckoned on attention of a notorious kind they shower the one such demand in galore. That was why when Chance and his friends donned their worrisome attires provocatively they got the attention they wanted for it. They tried to remove the log in their eyes before haranguing someone else to take out those tiny specks in their eyes. Like the Spartans they endure pain to the extent that their stoic forbearance would sustain. A Biafran man was not given to foolery. When Chance ran into Candie for the very first time in close quarters he had told her with ocular gyration of some sort that he was not going to play the fool for all she cared.

It was the first week of college. Chance had just arrived. A Johnny-just-come of a guy. He did not understand the idiosyncrasies of the people he had come to live among. He had thought that it was going to be life as usual in his rugged Biafran homeland. He had come to a *civilized* people. And Candie was such a damsel that could not be ignored especially if she was approaching from the opposite direction. On their first encounter, she had seen Chance coming from the opposite direction near the science building. She could not make an about-turn and could not evade the piercing glare of Chance as they came across each other. Then her defensive mechanism came into good use in full gear. She was taught to appear nice whenever she came across a black man. It was cultural. It was inherited. It had become intertwined. It had been reinforced in school. It was a survival instinct to appear nice to persons who for all intents and purposes were not out to do you any harm whatsoever. It was a badge of dishonor, and Chance rightly fitted into that mix. So on that fateful day in that first week of college in that science building area for this innocent Biafran boy Chance was one of them. As Candie approached, she did not know whether to continue on her way or walk back her steps or grow wings and fly or disappear into thin air. In an instant, she flashed her clenched dentition toward his direction. Chance did not know what to make out of that. He only gyrated his eyeballs at her in total disgust. He did not know that that was a kind of being nice and courteous. He also did not know that as a black person he stood accused of a propensity to do harm. Then a few days later almost in the same area there came Candie again. From a bit far off, she began earlier to flash her dentition for a smile toward Chance, and this time Chance was not going to play that fool again. As she continued to veer toward the edges of the curb wearing her fake smile Chance continued to walk toward her stepby-step pushing her away from the road and more and more toward the curb and then face-to-face, eyeball-to-eyeball. Scared of life, she was frozen thinking that some harm was coming to her person. That was what Chance was angling for: stop her in her tracks. But more importantly a chance to warn her to be nicer. It would rather be nicer if she should stop deceiving herself and keep her teeth in the closet of her mouth. He was going to take out her dentition if she ever flashed a fake smile at him again, he warned her. He told her that he was not that flesh-eating cannibal her mother had told her about. That she needed not be afraid of him. That he was neither a Nat Turner nor she or her father a Colonel Joshua John Ward or Stephen Duncan. He reminded her: who was to be feared? The one who enslaved or the one that was slaved? The one who still had power to enslave others or the one who could still be enslaved? He told her that she needed to be afraid of herself or her kindred people and not him. He told her that he was not a predator but rather than that he was human as she was. Those who lived by the sword never wanted anyone wielding a machete behind them. Do not be afraid of the sins of your forefathers or the vengeance of your former hillbillies. It was a warning and lesson well delivered, but whether it was well learned was given to debate. But for Chance it was bravado in ignorance. In years gone by, not too long ago, that attitude could have been enough to warrant him a day at the gallows or the noose treatment. In later years when he began to imbibe the culture of the people he came to live among and remembered his foolery and the great escape he had it gave him a feeling of a man that got reprieved from the death row. Chance who gave no chance to fear thought himself a lucky man. He learned his lesson even without a reprimand. Self-teaching was common sense!

"Why are there still some dilapidated building in these parts years after the war?" asked Jewel.

"First, girl, this was not a war. It was genocide. You got that! Mind you, before you guys came here this naked land was littered with the bones of children fried with starvation, ain't that genocide? And crusts of dried up pools of blood. What you see right now in the dilapidated buildings and their potholes are relics that are ephemeral to us and infinitesimal. Those that are permanent are in our hearts, huge, never going away, never to be forgotten. Second, people are yet to recover from that experience. This was the epicenter of the newest effort at extermination of a people. They were decimated, and a whole lot of families lost their livelihood. They were left with nothing. It has been hard for a whole lot of the Biafran people. For a long period of time people could hardly fend for their families. It was food for the stomach first and repair later," said Chance.

"I see. It was just that you guys began an adventure you were not able to bring to fruition on the battlefield," stated Jewel.

"We were nearly there. But for the conspiracy of the biggest powers we would have joined the comity of nations without much blood and tears or even a single bullet fired. Aburi gave us that chance," said Chance.

"That must have taught you a lesson learned the hard way," said Dusty.

"Who is Aburi?" asked Jewel.

"Aburi was the last dice for peace. You know, folks, you can't argue with a man who's made up his mind. It would end up as an exercise in futility. If you were dealing with someone over a serious issue and your opponent is completely absentminded, just know it that it wasn't worth your effort. Everything you're talking about would be a waste of your goddamn time. Defunct Nigeria came to the table absentminded because their plan A was to drag Biafra into a war of extermination… There was no plan B."

"So, who's Aburi?" asked Jewel again.

"Yes, Aburi was a peace conference held in the city of Aburi in Ghana brokered by the then Ghanaian head of state to avert a fullscale war with defunct Nigeria. The conference seemed to have gone well for all sides, but the bunk head, the Nigeria leader went home and began to sing a different song. In fact, he forgot that he attended a peace conference. He thought that he attended a war conference. How could that be?

"So when the Biafran leader came back home and was telling the whole world what was agreed, the nonplussed Nigerian idiot denied that he was at the conference. 'On Aburi, we stand' became a refrain of every Biafran child and peace-loving people all over the world. But it did not matter. But Nigeria forces and their colonial master had their armies marshaled at the gates of Biafra, knocking and leering and sneering. They wanted to make a mincemeat of every Biafran. They were baying for blood of the innocent, and they got it. Let me tell you, there would have been no bullet fired if Aburi had stood. Aburi was a road map for trapped Nigerians in that contraption to say to themselves: to your tents O brain-dead Nigerians" He paused.

"Ileka and Oleka would not have perished if Aburi had stood," said Chance solemnly.

"Who's Ileka and Oleka?" asked Turnkey.

"Ileka and Oleka are my brothers. They fought gallantly. Report that got to my father was that before they died, Ileka drove his dagger to the hilt in the heart of one of his assailants. They were joy to be with, but when Aburi failed it cost us their lives just as so many other families in Biafra land."

"Ouch," cried Candie.

"Didn't they have guns?" asked Jason.

"They had guns. But everything was in short supply. They triumphed more in hand-to-hand combat and wrestling the enemy's guns and turning the guns against the enemies. From seizing one gun they were able to seize an army post and more guns and ambush a tank and then strengthened our defense and attack. Many of our units equipped themselves with weapons they wrestled from the enemy. It was gallantry at its best. We acquitted ourselves. We made our own weapons in the most dire of circumstances. I'm proud of my people…"

"Not enough guns, just gut-wrenching will…," began Turnkey.

"You do not go to war you don't have enough men and materials, and you are not certain to come out triumphant," said Jewel. "America never been to war she was not sure she was going to win," she added.

"You're not listening, girl. The Biafran people did not go to war. War was levied on us by the British because without the British, Nigeria stood no chance. War came to us. We had to face the reality of the time and defend ourselves. It was not a decision we made lightly bearing the consequences in mind. At the point we were, we had no choice but to fight. It was a choice of fight or perish. It was fight because there was no place to run to. And we were not fighting because we were wholly convinced that we were going to win. We engaged in the duel because for us at that point that was the only thing to do. Sometimes, the little guy does not engage the big, fat fool because he was convinced he was going to land the fat, ugly bully a blow that would dent or stagger him but because he knew that he was more likely to be left alone win or lose. But the Biafran scenario was far worse than that. Do nothing was practically a death sentence. Even in the midst of overwhelming odds stacked against the Biafran people the spirit of the Biafran people was very high. Children starved of food and basic social amenities could be pictured dancing in the streets, cheering every Biafran soldier in sight. Those children even understood what triumph would mean. So every inch gained was like a triumph in toto. That explained the tremendous inroad we made toward the enemy's territory, almost taking over their capital, and the enemy in full flight out of their cities and strongholds," said Chance who had his listeners spellbound.

"And you know, folks," he continued. "The truth about it is that your country has been to wars and triumphed. Even the battle of Saigon was a setback. I would say that it was a stalemate because America did not want to reach deep into the capability of her armory to achieve victory at all costs at the expense of the people of Vietnam. Sorry to say that, but, that was the truth. But another truth is that the Biafra genocide was never to be abandoned, it was meant to be won at all costs. Have you heard about Warsaw?" he asked his attentive listeners. And the chorus was a resounding no.

"Warszawa was the capital of the polish people," he proceeded to informed them. "When Warsaw saw war, she shook her head! When her villages, cities, and towns, metropolis, and counties saw war the Warsaw people demurred war and clamored for peace, perhaps at any cost. When war came to Warsaw, the Warsaw landscape was never to be the same again. The potholes you see in Biafra that looked indelible in their permanency are a child's play. Believe you me, my friends, Warsaw had a day of reckoning for us all. This is our own Warsaw. But, ours is worse than Warsaw." He paused.

"Destruction is so good as long as it's not your ox that's gored. It's fun to destroy if it wasn't your neighborhood that's decimated but hard to rebuild. Rebuilding is difficult folks, and it will never be the same again for the Biafran people." He paused again.

"Methinks there is truth in what you are saying, Chance," admitted Turnkey.

Jewel wanted to say something. Rather she lost it and pouted her lips as the group approached the entrance of the supermarket having detoured to a shopping complex to stretch their nerves, and the sliding doors swung open and they walked in.

The party arrived at the property of the Ogidigi in good spirit. It was a long drive. Tired but energetic. However, they decided that they would not be going out that night. Turnkey had spare wee-wee for days, so he was not bothered about going out for the night. They soon retired to bed. Jason, Jewel, Dusty, and Candie had their flight back to the States booked for the day after tomorrow. Chance and Turnkey would follow in a few days later.

CHAPTER 10

As usual the scene at the airport was hustling and bustling. This was the most densely populated parch of earth in the African continent. Passage in the airport building was tight. People were milling about. Travelers were coming and going. Newly arrived were making their way out of the arrival section and then mingled with the rest of the people. About-to-depart passengers also mingled with the people for their chance to be called to line up for crossing over to the side of the boarding process. It was no chaos, but hardly could anyone hear the voice of the person next to him or her. It was maddening. One had to talk at the top of their voices to make out a thing of what was being said in the din. It was cacophony. It was not everybody in the airport lounge that was coming in from overseas or traveling to another country. Among the people at this airport that day were tramps and pimps, rabble-rousers and hustlers, loafers and layabouts, pickpockets and muggers, businessmen and women, politicians and swindlers, pen robbers and miscreants, and a few urchins, visitors like Turnkey and sons of the soil like Osai were also there. As always it was a no-man's-land. It was everybody's turf. And at one end was one tramp named Osisioma. A small distance apart was Bucknor. Both were unknown to each other.

Osisioma was an astute young man, rather a boy. He was neither a boy nor a man by looks. But he could pass for either. However, he was more of a boy than a man. Because of his stature he could be consumed in the midst of people with modest height. But that never bothered him. He liked to be underrated. In his trade, his record was unblemished. He had never ever been held in suspicion or worse nabbed. He had to be caught pants down before he could be pinned with anything unbecoming. He never wore it on his sleeves, but he knew what he was capable of. He was as slippery as a fish in slimy water, hard to catch. He had no allegiance to any master. He was his own boss. One would think that the events in Eureka in the past ten days would deter him. But he figured out that that was the time for people to momentarily lay down their guards. And because of his physique, it was hard to suspect him to be capable of picking people's pockets with that much dexterity. The art of picking pockets was risky to say the least. But Osisioma was a master of the art. He took fewer risks. He usually did his homework very well. He snared and pounced on his targets with a snap. He understood that missing could be catastrophic, especially in those days.

Chance had taken a walk to the restroom. There was a small crowd of people waiting to use the restroom, so it took him a little bit longer to come back. It was in that split moment that catastrophe occurred. It happened in a flash. Turnkey had kept watch over their traveling luggage as Chance went to the restroom. He was not bothered by the noise about him. He knew that in a short time they would be airborne to the States. All of a sudden, he saw a flash of hand across his face. The thing was a slap across his eyes actually. He writhed in pain and bent over as he clutched his eyes. His wallet in his back pocket was gone in a jiffy in that physical and mental confusion. It was almost at the same time that Chance reappeared and found his friend bent over. As he grabbed him, he knew that the worst had happened. In the immediacy, the departure line started to inch forward. Chance struggled to decide what their next move was going to be. But first he had to get his friend to open his eyes. He led him to the restroom to see washing his face would help him see. Rather to his chagrin, he could smell some peppery odor on his face. It was then that he realized that his friend may have been blinded with a slap across the face with a palm laced with pepper. Washing the face with water made it sting more. Turnkey could not try to open his eyes and could not try to look at a shining light or an object straight on as those efforts made his pain more excruciating. And from the din came an announcement over the public address system urging traveling passengers on flight 2852 to come forward, and prominent among them were Turnkey G. Ghoostte and Hercules O. Ogidigi.

Turnkey could talk. He told his friend that they had to go and board the flight. With passage of time, he would be better and if he required medical attention he would get that in the States in the next twenty-four hours. Chance labored with his friend to move to the line. But the stark reality was that when the customs agent at the point of no return demanded to see Turnkey's passport, it was nowhere on him. It was gone with the bandit. Chance gawked at the agent with a sightless sight to no avail. There were no two options. They had to call off the departure. It was botched.

No one around Turnkey took notice of what had just happened to him. The moment he clutched his face his wallet was gone. Osisioma first meandered briskly through the crowd as he shoved his way by. Then he galloped a little bit. Then he darted. Having made himself a few distances away from the scene of his desperate deed, he reverted to his normal gait albeit faster than fast. In a short moment, he was at the staircase exit of the floor. As he hooked his grip on the rail and jumped the whole flight of the staircase, right on his heels was Bucknor. Osisioma was not given to fear, but instantly he recognized that he had no chance against the guy right behind him. He ignored him and made another flight down to the next level below. Again on his heels was Bucknor.

"What do you think you were doing?" queried Bucknor of Osisioma.

"I am minding my own business," said Osisioma.

"What's your business? What have you got there?" asked Bucknor in quick succession.

"What is your own? I am minding my own business," said Osisioma, sensing some danger. By this time Mr. Turnkey's wallet had disappeared inside his winter jacket he wore even when there was no need of it at this time of the year.

"You are making a mistake, you upstart urchin and thief," barked Bucknor. "And do not answer my question with questions. What you got there?" he asked him threateningly.

Sensing the cruelty of danger, sizing the guy's height and weight against his he knew that he needed acting swiftly. He was after hard dollar. Nothing mattered any more than that. He needed cash. He pulled the wallet out from his jacket and dexterously pinched out the dollar bills in Turnkey's wallet in one swoop with the precision of a wild hawk. Bucknor did not need the money. At the instance Osisioma was pulling out the money from the wallet, Bucknor, with eagle eye shot, saw the tip of a blue shining matter in the wallet. It was the American passport. Bucknor was after the passport. If a blind man missed the opportunity to grab the fig fruit he stepped on his chances of eating one would be gone. He knew that fact. He had longed to have one. He had worked to have one American visa, and not even the passport, to no avail. And now the passport. The pursuit of an American visa had always been an exercise in futility. Swifter than Osisioma he grabbed the passport and threw the wallet at him and walked away. The wallet lay on the ground, the better parts of its content gone. Its main spoils shared and the rest of its content laid waste for nothing.

Bucknor was the son of the police boss, Obikolo. He was at the right place at the right time. He was never a thief and had no inclination of being one himself. It was that at the stage where he was in life ultra vires means may present itself as a vehicle to get to the next level in one's pursuit of glory. The end may justly justify the means after all. He was at the airport that afternoon to see off his friends board his flight back to the United States. But what was he going to do with a stolen passport with someone else's name on it?

Being the son of Obikolo he was privileged. There was no doubt about that. He knew it. The name could open doors for him and other members of his family that shared the pedigree of that name in Biafra land and some other places. But one place that name made no difference was the American embassy in Biafra or anywhere else for that matter in the world. The name was a pariah to many western countries led by the United States government. The name has become a burden for Bucknor. It had limited him so much. Being a police boss had various avenues to acquire wealth either by hook or crook in nascent, fledgling Biafra. Not just wealth he was able to amass he had aggregated power and had corrupted himself and the institution of the police force with extrajudicial measures that the American government had noticed and taken a stand. He and members of his family were placed on the list of government officials that would not be allowed to set foot on American soil or any of its principalities or potentate states. On several occasions

Bucknor had gone to the embassy on his own recognition for a visa, but on each occasion his last name had become a major impediment. He was turned out. His connection and the clout of his family name took him to nowhere. He had begun to dislike his family name. Since he had come of age he had hated what his father did for a living. What he had not disavowed was the wealth he had amassed and other trappings that come with the position. His father's wealth was his mother's as well. And his mother's wealth was his, no doubt. And through his mother he had access to as much money as he had wanted on any particular day for any particular issue or any particular endeavor. Having given up on going to the American embassy, the passport he squeezed out of this upstart tramp had given him a new lifeline. He would try it even when he was opposed to acquisition of anything by hook or by crook. He just wanted to carve his own niche detached from the connection to his father.

The following day Chance and Turnkey were at the visa section of the American embassy in Biafra. Access was easy because there was a separate door for American citizens to make it easier for them to gain entrance into the building. As soon as they got into the waiting area, Chance pulled out a ticket from the dispenser and they sat down. Shortly afterward they were called to the window. Behind the counter was a black young man in his thirties. As soon as Chance noticed who was going to attend to them, his countenance changed and became somewhat ashen.

"Yes, how can I help you, gentlemen?" asked Mr. Oguchi, the man behind the counter.

"We would like to talk to your boss," demanded Chance.

"But, how can I help?" asked Mr. Oguchi again.

"We want to talk to your boss," Chance demanded again. He had looked at the visa agent and felt that that black man behind the counter had not got enough powers to make a final determination on any issue. That he would eventually have to report to his boss sitting somewhere in that office. If the visa guy had to run behind to obtain maximum power to solve their problem, then why deal with him in the first place?

And why not talk to that guy hidden somewhere in that office who had absolute powers to ameliorate or mar the situation?

"How can I help you? Talking to my boss is not how I can help you, gentleman," said Mr. Oguchi "Things go through a process here. You have to give me a reason why I should bring my boss right up here. If you told me what you are here for I would determine whether or not it's something that would involve my boss. If it's something I cannot help you with I would have to escalate it to the next level. I can't just bring my boss here because you asked for him without giving me any reason. You need to give me a chance. That's how things work here. Meanwhile, I'm the boss at this window. And by the way, if I may ask, the issue you're here for is it for you or for this other gentleman?" asked Mr. Oguchi in an undisguised American accent, sensing that the guy talking to him may be a freelancing advocate fronting for the little white guy in his company.

"Does it really matter? It's for my friend," said Chance, riled.

"Can he talk? What's his name? Can he write?" asked Mr. Oguchi in quick succession.

"Yes," said Turnkey who yet had not spoken hitherto.

"Guy, what's your name?" he asked.

"My name's Turnkey, Turnkey Ghoostte."

"Mr. Ghoostte, fill out the form for me and bring it to the window as soon as you are done. There is a reason section on it, briefly state why you're here, and that would help us deal with your issue as quickly and expeditiously as possible," said Oguchi.

Turnkey collected the form and the clipboard and sat down. Chance felt sulky. A few minutes later, he was back at the window to turn in the form. Again, he sat down and Chance stood, pacing up and down.

A few minutes later Turnkey was called to the window.

"Hey, young man, you forgot to provide your Social Security number," Mr. Oguchi informed Turnkey.

"You do need that also?" said Turnkey.

"Oh yes, we do need it. You're on US soil, but because you're not in continental USA we surely would need it for some verification. In the States, there are other ways to verify one's information. But outside, Social Security number is imperative," he told him.

Turnkey did not understand what US soil in Biafra means. Nevertheless, he went ahead and gave the man his Social Security number. Then Mr. Oguchi adjudged that the information he was looking for was complete and told Turnkey so.

"Mr. Ghoostte, on issues as yours you have a solid request. We are sorry for what happened to you, it's one of those things. You now have another experience added to your life stories. When you come to these parts of the planet earth there's always some tale to tell," he told Turnkey. Turnkey had heard it before, "Resolving your case doesn't have to go beyond this level of consultation. But usually it takes a few days to check out your information. And due to the nature of your case we are expediting it. It's obvious that you have a legitimate request here. However, I'm not going to urge you to make traveling arrangement until your case is resolved, nevertheless I will urge you to come back in the next two days to check out the outcome of our consultation with the passport section of the State Department in Washington, District of Columbia. I'm positive that your case would be resolved by then, but if it wasn't resolved in two days and you happen to make traveling arrangements, it may warrant you having to change those arrangements again. That involves money and could be darn frustrating to say the least," Oguchi informed him.

"That's why we want to talk to your boss," complained Chance.

"Gentleman," said Oguchi, calmly addressing Chance, "there's not much we can do at the moment. I can assure you that we're going to work diligently to set you guys on your way back to the United States as soon as practicable and as expeditiously as possible."

It was Turnkey who pulled his friend away from the window and urged him that they should go home.

"And if I may ask, gentlemen, have you made a police report?" asked Mr. Oguchi, as Turnkey and his reluctant friend were about to turn and leave.

"No" was the answer that came back from Turnkey.

"I would advise that you go and get a police report and bring it along with you when you come back in two days' time. We've all the information we will need for proof of citizenship. However, the State Department in DC would want that piece of information to be placed on your file and for the records and for statistical purposes. And you know what? You would need it for future reference. You never can tell, my young man," said Mr. Oguchi.

Based on the information Turnkey had provided the verification process was easier. It was a routine business phone call. The information he provided collaborated with the information the immigration services that handled, processed, and issued passport had. When the duo came back two days later, Turnkey's traveling papers were ready and waiting. The police report was not vital to the process, yet Ms. Patricia Cornfield who attended to them on their return visit requested for it and had it tucked inside his file.

"We could have gotten this the last time we were here, instead of going and coming back for nothing," complained Chance

"Well, gentleman, it doesn't work that way, and we needed that police report for reference purposes," she reminded him again.

Again Turnkey pulled his friend out of the window.

"Be safe. Be careful out there. And do have a safe trip back to the States. I hope you do come back and see us albeit for something nice and sweet," offered Ms. Cornfield as they made to leave.

"Thank you, ma'am," said Turnkey.

CHAPTER 11

One day after Chance and Turnkey traveled back to United States, Bucknor made his way to the village, the notorious counterfeit capital of this part of the world. At this village, everything was possible save to clone any legged animal or a homo sapiens. Whatever that could not be rehashed elsewhere would be replicated here. It was famed for its dexterity in honing stuff and even making some duplicates better. It was here that pound sterling could be coupled and the British ambassador to Biafra could not tell the difference between the real sterling and the fabricated one. And as a matter of guesswork he was confused enough to choose the fake pound sterling. The American ambassador knew the notoriety of the village that he would not venture a guess between the real dollar and the fake one. He would rather have the two dollar bills than risk embarrassing himself. Here at the village, they invested a lot of finesse in all their works that the finished product would at all times fool the most knowledgeable in any trade. It was in the hallowed corners of the village that Bucknor walked into that fateful morning, clutching the blue passport, the most sought-after traveling paper in the whole world.

Bucknor was a very, very realistic young man. He was streetwise and had no desire for wishful thinking or pursuit. In his own objective reality, he employed not only critical thinking but reasoning as well. Given an array of options he always went for the one that portended less risk even when the ones that portended more risks have much in them some stupendous prospect in dividends. He would always want to gallop past those minor risks and collate the aggregate. At a point, he had overcome tremendous risks and built a storehouse full of dividends, and then he would want to have a stake in riskier ventures. Understandable!

He was always taking the least common denominator for risks. As he walked inside the village all by himself, he had on him some wads of the Biafran bight, the national currency, and two passport photographs.

"Why do you not want to insert your real name in the passport?" asked the apprentice boy who was going to help him transpose his photograph on Turnkey's.

"I don't want to tinker with a lot of things on the passport," said Bucknor warmly, who did not want to expose his real name to this small boy who was merchant of trade in outlawries. But the apprentice boy was suggesting additional tinkering with the passport since he knew that more work on the passport meant additional charges. Yet charges were of no concern to Bucknor. He just wanted to limit the alteration done on the passport. The more alterations, the more it would give up on its originality.

"How about the birthday? You will be looking ten years younger. We can change that to reflect your real facial appearance," suggested Odinakachi, the apprentice boy.

"No, I'm okay with that," said Bucknor.

"So, all you wanted is to have your passport photograph superimposed on Turnkey Ghost. What a name is that? This name sounds bad. White people and their ugly, meaningless names! This one is bad and ugly and no good," concluded Odinakachi.

"Do what you are told to do and stop making a noise. How does that bother you? If you saw me tomorrow and call me Mr. Ghost, I will beat you so much that your mother will no longer recognize you," Bucknor warned him.

"No vex, Oga. I am sorry, Oga," the boy offered apologetically.

"How much is your work?" asked Bucknor.

"It is one thousand eight hundred and fifty-eight bights."

"Why so? Did you catch a lion for me? Or you want me to give you enough bights to build a house for your father?" asked Bucknor.

"That is the price. You do not know what you have here. When I finish this work, you will understand that what you have is worth more than catching a lion for someone. You are getting it on the cheap.

This is the ultimate. That is why it is so expensive. If you have the British passport I will be happy to beat down the price for you. If it were defunct Nigerian passport, it is nothing, and I will do it for you free of charge," said Odinakachi as he paused to gauge his customer's unspoken reaction.

"Oga, but you can afford it." Bucknor said nothing. "You can afford it," Odinakachi continued. "Look at your skin. You look like someone who is already living abroad," he added.

For a while Bucknor ignored him and then said, "Can I see your boss?"

"No, you cannot see him."

"I bet you, he's hiding in that office behind you," said Bucknor.

"But, you cannot see him."

"Why not?" asked Bucknor.

"He is not in, but I can go in and see if he would approve some discount for you," offered Odinakachi as he made to slip into the back room behind the counter.

"But you said that he's not in," said Bucknor as Odinakachi stopped in his tracks.

"I wanted to make sure," said Odinakachi as he disappeared into the back room.

The thing was that his boss was never available in that office. It was a racketeering business. The truths came in halves. The only truth was that his master would slip in through the back and to check whether there was any job to be done. If there was he would pick it up and take it to the workshop far from the prying eyes and scrutiny of the police. Odinakachi just feigned he was consulting his master when he just walked into the adjacent room and made it back as if he had spoken to anyone higher than himself.

"He would give you a discount of fifty bights," he told Bucknor.

"Go ahead and do it. How long would it take?" asked Bucknor.

"Yours is a simple but complicated one. I would say two to four hours at most."

"Can I get it earlier? You want me to pay for the work and receipt now?" asked Bucknor.

"No, you do not pay for anything upfront here until the job is done. And we do not issue any receipt here. What we do here is strictly on trust, our work is our bond. You can make additional inquiry and come back. We are big on reputation. If you do not believe me, *biko*, you can take your work and go elsewhere."

"You do not give receipts, what do you give?" asked Bucknor.

"Our work is based on trust. Check it out, nobody issues you a receipt on this matter. But I can provide you with a tiny plaque-like ticket which you must return to me when you come back. Of course, if you lost it our relationship would be arduous. Just do not lose it!" said Odinakachi.

Bucknor was rattled. He looked at the boy who had the audacity to push him around and could not believe his eyes or what he was hearing. How can he bring himself to trust fraudsters? Honorable thieves! Was he going to lose this thing he had longed forever to obtain and fought to acquire against his own principles? For a while he thought really hard. Momentarily his mind began to wander to his father's office and the power it could bring to bear as he made an effort to shut up that choice, that was, if things did not go down well with these tinkerers. As Bucknor made to leave with the passport Odinakachi said to him firmly, "But trust me, you are in good hands. If you do not believe me you can sit down at the lounge and I will get it ready in about two to three hours."

Bucknor relinquished the passport with Odinakachi, trusting only his instinct and not what the little urchin had given him as an assurance. He also grabbed the token. He held it in his fist for a while and on second thought put it inside his rugged jean trousers. As soon as he did that, Odinakachi once again slipped through the door into the adjacent room and dropped the passport and back again to the front office. Bucknor went toward the lounge and sat down in one of the empty chairs. It was comfortable indeed. But he was not all that at peace with himself. He felt that he would lose Mr. Ghoostte's passport. He gathered himself. He did not want to dwell on it. One thing was certain:

he had made up his mind that if stories were told of the passport he would finally ask his father to raise a battalion of police officers to come and make a sweep of the village. But when he thought about the many people in the lounge waiting for one thing or the other his fears were allayed. Then he reminded himself that he was in a dangerous terrain. He needed to go away from that vicinity in case the police decided to raid the whole place which they did very often. He did not want to be caught with his pants down. He would rather be seen perambulating or loitering about than to be caught waiting in any of those offices whose stock in trade was known to be shady. He did not want to start swearing his innocence.

He left the comfort of the chair and walked out of the office. He had nowhere in mind in particular. All of a sudden, he realized that he was close to the lagoon and he headed toward it. The ocean breeze constantly made its way to the mainland and with it cascaded the water of the ocean as it landed on the sandy shores. Again and again the waves rose and formed valleys and hills, made their way to the shore, and petered out. Back to the seas the current flew, gathered some momentum, formed some waves, and came back crashing at the seashores. Such was the repetitive rhythm and circle when Bucknor made it to the lagoon. And sat down on one of the benches. Staring down the horizon he could see the cyclic, unending returns of the waves. As he looked farther and farther afar, he could see nothing anymore except the vast waters that appeared to be at level with the heavens where the horizon touched the seas, limitless horizon and in his mind's eyes he could see the American skylines, just beyond that horizon, nigh the skies. Then, he could see no more. At that moment, he was back to earth.

From his shirt, he fished out a pack of cigarettes. If there were one vice he copied from his father it was the culture of smoking. Much as he tried to give it up he had never succeeded. He tried to light one of them, but the breeze would not let him. He tried to cup the light against the weather and only succeeded to light one after numerous efforts. Back-to-back he did not realize that he had downed six sticks in less than two hours. He had never done that with much frequency before, and as soon as he realized what he had just been doing he threw away the one he currently lit and buried it with the ocean sand. The waves ebbed and then gathered strength and buffeted the ocean banks. He sat up and slouched the thirty minutes' walk to the village. As he sauntered in he was greeted by Odinakachi with a smile. That in itself assured him that not only Mr. Ghoostte's passport was safe but also it had his image superimposed over Mr. Ghoostte's. He paid his charge and collected the passport. He opened the picture page, and what he saw pleased him. It was actually his passport photograph. He thought about it. Henceforth he would want to be called Mr. Ghoostte, Turnkey Ghoostte. He pocketed the passport and bounced out of the door, darting his eyes across the faces of those who were still there waiting. Without tarrying he dashed out of the door and disappeared in the village, not quite incognito yet.

CHAPTER 12

Bucknor never quite knew his father. He was married to his job as a police officer. He had no time for his family. He spent much time with the force headquarters trying to make the force better, one would think, both in outlook and productivity. When he was not engaged with myriad of issues at the headquarters, he was on the move. One eye on the force headquarters and the other on the road and no time for the family. Not enough eyes for all his responsibilities. And the family suffered most.

One who sought for justice must come with a clean hand. The force he purported to wanting to make better had its hands mired in avoidable challenges and self-inflicted injuries. He had been in the force for better of thirty-two years. So he would be said to belong to the old guard. He was there in the then colonized Nigeria police force. He was there in the defunct Nigerian police force. He was there in the new Biafran police force when Biafra was at war with Nigeria and had been since the peace that guaranteed the end of the war. So he had seen it all. And he felt that he knew it all. Yet not so much. At a point in his long career, it seemed he had his sight set on self-aggrandizement than truly doing the work of a careerist police officer. He became mired in pursuit of personal gains and interest group protection rather than focusing wholly on the work of a thoroughbred police officer. He became a perfect example of absolute power that corrupts absolutely. He amassed a lot of wealth for himself and family. Landed property here and there. Empty plots of land scattered all over the country. Some given to him in appreciation. Some bequeathed to him to curry favor and have the protection of someone with some might, connection, and clout. It was obvious that he had made himself a very, very rich man.

Obvious also was the fact that his life's earnings would never support such a grandstanding of wealth and opulence for a police officer. The murmuring had grown and became widespread. He had become the epitome of corruption, and the force he led was the quintessential corrupt force.

At twenty-seven and out of the university Bucknor had heard enough and knew enough of the name Obikolo. He had his father's clout to be anywhere he wanted to be. In Biafra. However, he never wanted that route to get out of the starting block. After a degree in economics at the University of Biafra he wanted to leave for overseas for further studies. First to free himself from the appellation of everyday life being linked with his father and secondly, he wanted the next academic feather on his cap to reflect a foreign trained this or that. He would like to one day be addressed as American-trained economist or American-trained accountant. He had chances to go to London, even to the prestigious London School of Economics, and the traveling papers and visa were there for the asking. But he was bent on not taking it for all its worth. The reason why he did not like to be called British-trained economist or British-trained accountant was best known to him. Perhaps, as a young boy he understood the abhorrent intrigue of the British playbook in the Biafran genocide. Then the raison d'être was not far-fetched. Perhaps, he had most of his friends studying in the United States of America. It was unheard of. But that was the degree of his chances. But that was the level of his loathsomeness of his father's influence and the Brit. But that was also the extent of his fixation. That fixation took him to the American embassy in pursuit of some kind of visa to be able to make it onto the American shores. But each time he visited the embassy his last name and pedigree became an impediment. It had become a burden. It used to be that if one could sustain one's stay in the United States one would be guaranteed access to entry, but in his case, the proof that he was not going to be a public nuisance was not the benchmark. It was in his gene, why was he so fathered?

He wanted to detach himself from being so linked. But no matter how much he tried it stuck like a leech. In those days, American universities did place some advertisement for entry position into their college and university programs. It was easy to find schools as long as one could fund one's passage. It was also easy to get admission letters from these schools. Just under three months ago he got an admission letter from Accord University to study banking and finance. It was a good fit for someone with a graduate degree in economics. While one needed that for where one wanted to go and what one wanted to do in America, to obtain a visa one did not have to apply for admission into an American university or college. Rather when one applied for an admission into a university or college and got approved, that admission letter and all other particulars that come with it became part of the supporting documents for visa application. Without that admission letter of where and what one wanted to do in the United States, the request for visa looked purely like a request of a vagabond. The very rubbish America detested most. Now, Bucknor had a Mr. Ghoostte as his de jure name for passage into the United States. And he had admission into Accord University to study banking and finance. His papers were complete. As a guy carrying the blue American passport he needed no bloody American visa to gain entry into God's own country.

Everything seemed to have fallen in place beautifully. Then the what-if questions began to sting his mind and began to tear him asunder. What if the immigration officer wanted to ransack his belongings and discover that he had an admission letter bearing a name different from Mr. Ghoostte? He had an already made answer: he would tell them that he was bringing it to a family friend of so many years. What if they found his Biafran passport? He needed not think about that one. He would leave his Biafran passport behind and have his sister mail it to him when he had situated himself with a temporary or permanent address. All bases seemed to have been covered. Moreover, as an American citizen he felt good that the process may not require that much scrutiny after all.

Bucknor was not the favorite of his father's seven children, but he was the oldest. A father seldom had a child of choice among his children. If a father had to have, surely, Bucknor stood no chance. He knew it. But he respected his father immensely. That respect was unconditional despite their different worldviews. If not for anything he had provided for his family. He had put his family on such solid financial and economy pedestal that if the earth were to open up today and he was no more, they would miss only real, solid sense of his touch after all he was never at home, but not actually his presence because what he had done for them will loom over them for a long time to come. His physical presence would still be felt as in flesh and blood as was the little they had gotten of him. His disagreement with his father was not over who he was but over what he was and the degree he had gone being what he was. He was industrious, but he was rich without an industry. Bucknor loathed his father's means, but he had no compunction dipping his own hands directly or indirectly into its largesse to advance his own cause. He enjoyed what being comfortable with finance brought to the table.

As Bucknor sat before his father and mother that evening, for the first time his father held him in a tremendous awe. He could count the many times Bucknor had made fruitless efforts to secure an American visa to no avail, stopped only by the fact of impetus of his last name. And here he was telling him that he was ready to breach the gates of America. He had not told his father the details of how he secured entry papers to go to America. The details did not matter to Obikolo, and he did not want to know. What mattered was that he succeeded wherever he ended up in America. He assured the young Obikolo that if he needed his attention he had a direct line to him as always.

There was fire in Soweto, South Africa. There were constant protests and demonstrations in the land to put an end to the apartheid regime there. The protests and demonstrations were widespread. Stretching to Cape Town, Johannesburg, and to Pretoria and other cities. There were protests outside South Africa as well, including in Biafra for the freedom of the South African people. In Washington, the government called their relationship with President Nico government as constructive engagement. While in London, it was a kind of deconstructive arrangement. Whatever that meant was a matter of conjecture or diplomatic sophism. Late in 1977, Steve Biko, a prominent enterprising black leader, was murdered and that pricked the withered conscience of the unconscionable world. It helped raised the bar of the levels of the kind of oppression that was going on. That was about one year ago. But today was 1978, and Bucknor was ready to ship out of Biafra. He had money. And lots of it in traveler's checks. He did not want to go straight to the United States. He wanted his passport, bearing Mr. Ghoostte, to reflect a man widely traveled. And he chose to take off to South Africa.

As an American it was easy for him to get in and out. And he chose to visit Soweto.

It was easy for him to get into Soweto. But Soweto was everything but easy or peaceful. It was a risk not worth taking. The city was on fire. There were killings. He planned to stay there for about four days. But the rioting made him change his flight. He shortened it to two days as he hitched his next flight to Buenos Aires, Argentina. Nineteen seventy-eight was soccer World Cup year, and Argentina was hosting the participating nations. Biafra had no stakes in it, but Bucknor was a die-hard soccer lover and he had money to spare. So he flew to Argentina, en route to the United States. That would also reflect on his passport that he was a man widely traveled. He knew nowhere in Argentina or where he was going. But as soon as the flight touched down he grabbed a map and tried to figure out where he might pass the evening that day. That was easy. When he had figured himself out he hailed a taxi and asked the driver to take him to Alvear Art hotel, located on the outskirts of the city.

A dictator held court in Argentina in those days. He ruled with an iron fist. The courts were a rubber stamp of his iron dicta. That man brooded no opposition. So anyone who raised his hand in opposition made themselves marked men. The one would either disappear on their own or would be made to disappear. Opposition to his rule just disappeared. Those who would not go away became faceless. The dictator loved those even more. It became easy for him to state to anyone who cared to listen that he was waging a war against some guerrilla warriors. They are stateless. They had no ground to perturb his country. He had a reason to go after them. Some other world leaders bought into his ruse. Some world leaders countenanced him more when he branded his faceless opposition as communist upstarts, trying to cement a foothold in his hemisphere. That was music to the Americans. As long as you were dedicated to putting a wedge on the cascading influence of communism America would listen to you. Every opposition was tagged a communist and an object to go after to decimate and conquer or be neutralized. If you were fighting the communist then you were with the Americans. Americans would overlook some of your stinking monumental sins. Having mastered the art of ruse he clenched his teeth and his enemies scampered and in hiding. But America did not rest on their oars. They invested in mining for secret information all over south and central America. They fanned men and women all over the hemispheres, making sure communist infiltration of the hemisphere was never going to materialize anymore. Cuban debacle and the Bolsheviks' infiltration were never gonna happen again. America slept on duty. But, no more!

He got himself booked luckily in the only room left in the hotel. As soon as he sat down he turned on the television and there was a match already in progress. Bucknor finished watching the live match between Algeria and Yugoslavia that came down to a paltry one goal defeat for the African desert warriors. As soon as the match was over he stepped out, hailed a taxi, and decided that the driver drop him off at one of the biggest supermarkets in the whole of Argentina right on the outskirts of Buenos Aires. The weather was unusually warm. So both visitors, soccer revelers and townsmen, were out. The air was good. As he alighted from the car he knew that he had plenty of time to while away. So he made his way toward the entrance of the supermarket, and a few meters ahead of him was this black guy of about five feet five.

By Bucknor's estimation he was a short man. And he did seem to have much of flesh on his bones. That made his shortness very, very pronounced. He walked with a certain kind of gait in his short strides and a certain kind of bow. That compounded his whole physique and seemed to have made him even shorter than his five-five height would suggest. He was walking leisurely like someone who never had any need for haste. He had one fisty hand in his right pocket. He seemed to be brooding. He had no pigmentation of white. He was black through and through. In the years past, Argentina was nightmarish for black people. It was an unforgettable history.

"Look at his buttocks. What is this man doing here? He looks like someone who forgot something from wherever he came from," said Bucknor, tacitly in his own mother's tongue but enough for the man to hear.

The man cleared his throat, still walking, neither turning left nor right, and said, "Estas hablando de tu madre. Si yo descendiera sobre ti, tu madre nunca te reconoceria mas," (You are talking about your mother. If I descend on you, your mother would never recognize you anymore) he said in Spanish.

Bucknor got it. He knew that the man was referring to him and probably cursing him out. He hastened to pass the man, and the man added in Bucknor's own mother tongue of Igbo language.

"Ọ ka ụnụ si achọ okwu ebe ọ bụla ụnụ gara," (That is how you people look for trouble everywhere you go) said the man in Bucknor's own native language.

Bucknor was rooted to the spot. His earlobes seemed to have flapped in the wind. His ears were tingled, his hand covering his agape mouth. Wearing a smile and suppressing a chuckle, bemused at the same time, he tipped his frame in salute and restitution of respect.

"Ah, dede," he offered him a title name to show respect, "a maghị m na ọwụ gị. Gbaghara m. A kpaga m onwe mụ ihe ọchị," (I did not know it was you. Forgive me. I was just messing with you amusing myself") he told the man sincerely.

"So you have to make fun of every black man you see in this part of the world," said the man in an English accent neither here nor there, neither British nor American but more of British than American, deep and a little bit throated.

"No, not at all," Bucknor pleaded his innocence, "it's just that when you are bored your mind begins to wander about. You know how they say that an idle mind is the devil's workshop."

"I see. Be careful and watch your steps," said the man with no flippancy.

"Who are you, young man?" asked Jorge as they trudged toward the entrance of the supermarket.

"What do you mean?" came the reply.

"Your reply gave you away, young man. You must be a Biafran or an Igbo man. You just confirmed who you are and where you are coming from. It is only an Igbo man or a Biafran that would answer a question with a question," said the man.

The pair entered the supermarket together. They talked briefly but nothing serious, engaging, or deepening. They were very superficial pleasantries. The only thing remarkable in their brief discussion was that Bucknor told him that he was en route to the United States. He was here for a brief period of time for the tournament and that as soon as practicable he would zap. In his job, he loved to work alone, but the man was happy to stumble into Bucknor, someone who really spoke his language as his mother tongue. Bucknor told the man that his name was Bucknor. And the man told Bucknor that his own was Jorge. Surprisingly, neither asked the other his last name or surname. It was not long after they had separated that Jorge came to the realization that he did not obtain the young chap's surname. In his profession divulging personal information to the barest minimum was the gold standard. It gave one the leverage when less was known about one and one knew more of the people right about one. The good thing was that they were scheduled to meet tomorrow about after the day's soccer matches. That was if.

Bucknor went home overjoyed. Out of the blues, he found someone who spoke his language and who probably was his very kinsman. He could not believe it. Then he remembered what his father once told him: if you traveled to any crannies of the world and you could not see or encounter an Igbo man, hasten your exit from that place. If there were to be an Igbo man there then there is habitable air and relax. If you found no Igbo man then the air the inhabitants of the place breathe in was no good. It was not all that habitable. Meeting Jorge who probably was an Igbo man made true the words of his father. Argentina and her suburbs were truly habitable.

But he could not stop thinking about that man that spoke his language so fluently and could even pinpoint where he hailed from and the idiosyncrasies of his people. He could not understand why he was bearing a name that was not Anglo-Saxon, Jorge. Because if he was Igbo and wanted to bear a foreign name it most probably would be Anglo-Saxon. And it did not appear that he came to grace the world soccer tournament. Why was he in this remote part of the world? That was not too vital to understanding the man. After all, if he was truly Igbo it was not out of place to find him even at the utmost ends of the earth if there were air there. Then another thought overcame him. What if meeting this man tomorrow would expose him to the unknown about himself? He wandered if it was actually right for him to meet this man. He thought to himself that the fish would not have been in trouble if it had kept its mouth shut! If he had not begun to make fun of the man he would have walked and be as incommunicado as he had wanted and had his time and proceeded to the United States unobserved by anyone that could trace him to nowhere. He clenched his teeth and made a fist. He thought about the unfathomable. This guy would surely be asking him about his last name, and he wandered how he was going to skirt around it and still be nice. And since his father was not beloved, if this guy was a Biafran as well, it was probably that he would disavow of his father's deeds and conducts as a public official. That could spell trouble for him. He saw that the possibility of he making it to his final destination may be scuttled. He did not fancy meeting this guy again tomorrow and thought hard if it was truly a wise decision. He dwelt on it and dwelt on it and still thought about the fish and keeping its mouth shut. Finally, he yawned and yawned again and fell asleep.

He had dwelt on these thoughts all evening and now slept on them all night. He still decided that he would meet this guy as was agreed.

He woke up languidly early that morning and decided to get a little more sleep. Rolling over to the other side of his body he fell asleep again and slept all morning. When he finally woke up he felt sounder and he took his shower. After the shower, he felt rejuvenated with new energy and strength. He had already skipped breakfast. In fact, he was not a breakfast-hype type of a guy. After a while, he strolled past the lobby and went out to the nearest store to buy some biscuits. He came back shortly afterward and made a call to his sister in Biafra. He told his sister, Amarachi, that he ran into a man that spoke fluent Igbo but bore a Spanish name and possibly could be a Biafran. Amarachi had less to say about that but still asked his brother to be careful. Evening was approaching. After the call, he began the long walk to their rendezvous.

He got there early. He made himself as comfortable as he could on the bench that was there for people to while away their time. People were jogging, some were walking, and some were strolling, ones and in twos. Then he waited. Minutes turned into an hour. Jorge was not coming. Jorge did not show up after all. Not long after dusk began to gather. Not wanting to be out in the dark he strolled back to his hotel. He was relieved. He was not so much disappointed. He had had a mixed feeling about meeting this man again. He was traveling with a foreign name. He really wanted to get away from his surname, at least, for now. Though while he could not do much to distance himself from his real name he did not want to flash it for all to see as a badge of honor. Because, there was nothing honorable about Obikolo. While he recognized that a man never outpaced his shadows or outrun his buttocks he did not want his buttocks to protrude so much to be a drag on his flight. He went to his hotel room a relieved man!

If he had thought to himself that he was early, Jorge was earlier, but far removed from where Bucknor would see him. He knew the terrains. He just took a spot at a non-descript angle and was all eyes. Meeting this guy was not worth it after all! At least, not now.

Of course, Jorge had had a rethink of his own. He felt it was too soon to bring his countryman that close in this foreign land. And based on the work he did for a living, there were many other pairs of eyes watching and following every of his moves. He did not want to complicate matters or even risk his job. He would be glad to meet his countryman, but he had to tread softly. His job barely allowed him complete liberty to communicate with his relatives. On his current post reviewed after every twelve months he had to tell his employers who those relatives were so everybody else was a friend. Those listed as relatives permanently remained so. Any addition was an invitation for a thorough and new rounds of scrutiny. His job allowed him to contract friends. After all, it was by contracting and keeping friends that hardcore information and intelligence could be garnered. However, one had to keep one's friends at arm's length without letting them know that you distrusted them. For the security of his job Bucknor was one of them.

It was two days later, and Jorge's boss came to town for some briefing. Their briefing usually took place at the same hotel Bucknor was lodging. Jorge, whom he thought he was not going to see before he left, was striding hurriedly, gallantly toward him along the long hallway of the hotel in opposite direction. From afar, Jorge saw him, and from a measurable distance, he began to tell Bucknor in measured tone, not wanting to attract any attention, that he was sorry he could not meet him two days back. Talking and still striding hurriedly he walked past him, imploring him entreatingly that they could still meet tomorrow at the same place and time if he did not mind. He was truly apologetic, and Bucknor understood that this man must have some stuff of utmost urgency he was dealing with. He was suited up. He did not look at him. He was almost rushing by. Their only eye contact was fleeting. Their language was vernacular. It was done in spymaster fashion. The dexterity with which Jorge communicated his message made Bucknor to wander anew. But he also saw something: he was truly sorry and intended to honor the next appointment.

The next evening Jorge showed up earlier than they had agreed. He went and planted himself at a vantage position where he could have a good sight of the approaches to where he was. He wanted to make sure that Bucknor would come to him alone on this day. The hotel Bucknor was lodging was close to where Jorge lived. But he did not want to invite the young man to his abode, nor did he want to discuss anything with someone he just met near the outside lounge or lobby of a hotel. In his profession, the hunter could also be the hunted. Listening devices could be planted everywhere inside or thrown anywhere outside and be remotely disabled after the job was completed and information extracted. It was a risky job, and one had no added impetus adding another layer of risk to it.

It was not long after that Bucknor made his appearance. Like a chess master Jorge held his jack in a bulwark and decided that he had to extract as much information as he could. He was apologetic that he messed up on their previous schedule, but he was not going to dwell on it. After some niceties, he went for the nitty-gritty.

"I forgot to ask your last name the first time we met," began Jorge.

"I also forgot to ask about your surname the last time we spoke," said Bucknor and quickly added tamely, "my surname is Obikolo."

"Obikolo, I see," said Jorge and slowly added, "my last name is Santana, Mr. Obikolo." As soon as he said that, Bucknor knew it was coming and his heart sank. "Are you the son of Barnes Obikolo, the police boss in Biafra?" asked Mr. Santana.

"Obikolo is a popular name in Biafra," began Bucknor, trying to be evasive. "In my own town alone, I could count three families that bear that same name."

"I know! So your father is the police boss!" said Jorge.

"He has been there for a long time. He needs to retire," said Bucknor and then added to change the subject, "You seem to know much about Biafra and speak the language fluently, you must be a Biafran. And if you were, where did you get these strange names? What are you?"

"Young man, what do you want to do with that? What I am!" That confirmed to Bucknor where he was coming from, not minding his names.

"You could not even confirm to me who your father is," said Jorge.

"I thought I did," returned Bucknor.

"No, you did not, old chap," said Jorge. "You don't have to confirm that, but one thing is certain: you do not have to deny your own pedigree."

"Oh no," cut in Bucknor, "the police chief is my father." Bucknor acknowledged.

"You see, I see that you do not agree with your father. I see that you are trying to carve your own niche. Your father shaped himself in his own image. You did not help him do that for himself or to himself. It was his own choice, his own making. You have to shape yourself in your own image. You see, one does not outpace one's own buttocks, but how you made yourself will also determine the shape of your buttocks or how that final silhouette called shadow will appear as you make that life's race. As for me, I'm here for survival. I do everything I can to survive. I'm journeyman. I'm a jobber. I'm a hunter. I'm an artisan. I'm at home with the local people here. I set traps with them. I hunt with them as much as they allow me. I bother no one and no one bothers me. I'm like a typical Biafran, anywhere there's air, I try to make hay out of it, with or without a sheave." He paused. Bucknor did not want to cut in. He wanted him to continue and divert the discussion away from his father.

His father, Barnes Obikolo, was a quintessential traitor for the Biafran cause. He was a saboteur. He did not veil his disposition toward the Biafran cause. He did not make his wealth from outright bribery. How much could he be bribed? He made a ton of money because he played into the hands of the defunct Nigeria. The government of defunct Nigeria continuously over time paid him some huge amounts of money so that he could betray the Biafran cause. So when Biafra failed on the battlefield and succeeded on the peace table he claimed a prime place of pride. But the point was that the peace process did not start or succeeded because of people like him. Peace began and succeeded because Biafra was dogged and fighting to the last man. He actually compounded the will of the people of Biafra again and again and sapped the sustaining sinew. And then, he reaped the supposedly windfall of peace. He was in the enemy's good books. He became a pseudo potentate. He also was the proverbial dog that liked the company of that potbellied man because if he did not vomit he would defecate. Not a lot of people liked him. But he was the police chief, so people spoke tongue in cheek. The people may have spoken tongue in cheek, but their loathsomeness toward him was there for all to see.

His pause gave Bucknor a window to pounce.

"Why here of all places and where did you get all these names?" asked Bucknor.

"I've not told you that I'm not from there. It's just that I've great affinity to the Biafran people. As for my name, what's in a name? You can call me Amadike," said Jorge. That was another jigsaw in the riddle however this hammered the ball to baseplate more than anything else.

"That must be your Igbo-Biafran name," said Bucknor. "And you don't look like all you said you are: a hunter, a trap setter, a craftsman, a journeyman. Those don't square up. Are you a mugger?" That slipped out of his mouth.

"I didn't say that I'm a mugger."

"I'm sorry about that," apologized Bucknor as he gathered himself and quickly continued. "You look like someone who has connections to the corridors of power. You cannot be a dashing dude in that hotel, dressed up like that when you are a journeyman and a trap setter in this foreign land," said Bucknor.

"It doesn't square up, young man," began Jorge, "when you vacillated to state categorically who you are. I believe that you are not a true son of Barnes Obikolo. Because if you were you would not be bound for the United States. Your entry would be denied, and you would be wasting your time and money. Or you must be traveling with a pseudonym," said Jorge.

That was like a stab at the jugular. Bucknor felt like a caged animal with nowhere else to go. He had wished again he had never met this man. This man could be capable of stopping him from moving forward.

"If you were the son of Barnes I do not blame you for wavering to identify yourself," continued Jorge. "If I were you I may. Or I may take a stand. I may still help myself with his largesse, carve a niche for myself out of it, and distance myself, especially if you had come of age as you have. This is not a pig land thing, where you wash a pig, comb a pig, take a pig to Philadelphia, a pig remains a pig. No. It's not," said Jorge.

Bucknor remained speechless. He did not want to say anything else that would exacerbate his situation, open more cans of worms for himself.

"Time is coming," he continued, "when everyone who had come of age had to take a stand. You, I don't mean you per se, had to take a stand. You don't have to deny your father or mother but you must stand up and tell them the truth. It's not going to be the biblical father against son, son against father, or mother against daughter, and daughter against mother. No! But you must stand up and be counted." He paused to make sure he was creating an impression.

"When I look at you, young man, I see that you want to get away from your father. You didn't come here because you have done so well on your own. No. But, you have done well at school. Not every kid made it out of school with a certificate. But you are able to make it here and further because you have dipped into the largesse that is of your father and helped yourself. I don't begrudge you, young man. It's just that going forward you want to make amends at every opportunity. We cannot make the same mistakes of our fathers, and their fathers, and our great-grandfathers," he said.

There was no retribution in the man's words. There were all axioms. They eased his mind for a while and then he ventured.

"You have spoken like you are Biafran. Only a Biafran could have the interest of the Biafran people at heart like that," said Bucknor.

"You said so. But I could have been a mercenary, paid for fighting a cause I believed in somehow," he said and quickly continued, "The Biafran people will one day come to power. And when they do it will reverberate in all corners of the earth."

"What do you mean? The Biafran people are already in power," Bucknor reminded him.

"No, they are not, young man. I've been a mercenary all my life. I know what I'm talking about. But anyway, when they did, you will see the difference, you will see the fire in them. I've fought in many wars, and I can tell you now, I've never encountered a people like these people. Anyway, that bird that flew-jumped from the ground to the shrub is still where it was. It had gained no ground. When the Biafran people come to power, we would seek out the best accountants wherever we can find them, and fewer lawyers. It is always the fault of the lawyers," he interjected. "We will get the best accountants and number crunchers. We will seek out the best economists, at home and abroad. We will dig deep. We will find out how you can be a billionaire without an industry, just because you are industrious by half. We will dig deep," he said again. "We will find out how you the civil servant becomes a multimillionaire by earning a salary for fifty years. We will tabulate your earnings over the years and the interest it may accrue assuming you never spent a farthing out of it and see how far it can go. Oh, you have invested it. We will throw the books at you, with the accountants and number crunchers, and see how much your earning and investment have yielded you over the years. We will follow the money, for sure. And you are a contractor who was awarded a work and connived with those who would supervise its completion to make sure it was not done or meagerly done or done substandard, wishy-washy way, we shall see. Or that government worker that inflated the invoice to get a huge kickback and then sat back in his swivel chair and became a millionaire, we shall see. He stayed there and fattened himself, moonshined the rest of us and asked us with impunity to kiss his fat, ugly, big butt. We shall see! Oh, you won a lotto, we would be glad to see your numbers. Oh, it was bequeathed by your grandfather who committed suicide, well, we will like to see how he made his riches before he decided that he did not like to enjoy the fruit of his labor anymore and you become a benefactor of his kindest heart. We send people to the jailhouse for stealing a pen and allow pen robbery in government raiment walk freely and receiving our homages and obeisance. If you do not know where the rain started thrashing you, you would never know where its hammer would stop hitting you, young man! Biafra must do all within her powers to make right the wrongs of history. All hands must be on deck. Yours should too." Bucknor was absorbed.

"And I tell you, young man, most solemnly, there is nothing a man can do to his own people worse than treachery. It is the worst kind of cowardice. I can understand that not all of us are made of sterner stuff. Not all of us can hear the whistling sound of a musket and still keep our own machine gun on our shoulders. Some would just lay down their arms, shed their garment, and ask the bushes to hide them. I can understand that not all of us would want to hear the cries and moans of our comrade in arms and still be able to help because of the multiplying danger you faced let alone trying to compound that situation. I can understand that not all of us would look at your fellow soldier in his pitiful bloody, teary eyes shot, not all of us would at the moment that tarrying is suicidal to you and remnant of your men, not all of us would have the courage to look at your brother soldier in the eyes writhing in the throes of death with no chance of making it but a chance of being tortured for that remnant of his beleaguered life and still expend that gunshot into him to spare him further agony, risk of being captured by the enemy, and that ultimate risk of being tortured to death. No. Not all of us! I can understand all that. I can even understand a soldier deserting his post at the height of the heat of battle just to spare his own life. But, young man," continued Jorge, looking Bucknor straight in the eyes, "but, young man," he said again, "I can't understand how a man would just find honor in betraying his own people for some pennies and shelling. That I can't understand! If you were very observant, you will notice that there is clumsiness in my gait, a limp. It was as a result of the shrapnel of war. I was lucky to tell the story. Theo, a comrade and a brother, was not that lucky. We fought side by side, and beside me he lay dying, and holding him in between my arm and hand I watched as the last drop of blood in him ran out and dried. You know what? But for saboteurs or traitors among us perhaps I would have come out of the war without a limp and my brother, Theo, would have been alive today. I'm not going to bore you, young man, in spite of the iniquities of people like Barnes Obikolo, who sold out his people," he said sounding to doubt that Obikolo was his father. "You can still have a say in the government that is to come. You are going to study banking and finance, do it right, and believe you me, there is a place for you at the table. Biafra will never visit the iniquities of the fathers on the sons. Not yet! Unless you're holding tenaciously to the wretched caprices of your father. We will never have an emperor Nicholas II moment or a July 1918 event, or even create a Mensheviks, no, it will never happen, in my estimation. But it will happen if the people bayed for it," he quickly added. "Study hard and secure for yourself a place of honor at the table, my young man," he told Bucknor.

It was like a riot act. He nearly swore that he did not want to see the day those prescriptions would come to pass.

"It used to be government officials hijacking ten percent of all invoices as if it were a right. Then they called themselves ten percenters. That was the requiem Britain bequeathed to her beloved Nigeria. Defunct Nigeria carried it as a dirge to her beloved Biafra. Biafra has nowhere to take it to. And Biafra can't be cuddling a dead child. Biafra must bury it, and from its ashes would sprout a new Biafra. A Biafra that has a clear vision of what its purpose in history is all about," he told his dumbfounded countryman.

"Young man, you know that I have seen more days. I can't be repeating myself. But again, that bird that flew-jumped from the ground and perched on the shrub has made no flight. That was what Biafra had done. There's no difference between the defunct Nigeria and what you call your beloved Biafra. They are one and only. In some scales, defunct

Nigeria may be better than Biafra, God forbid," he swore as he spat out some spittle. "You are going to America. A land made good by her people. They say that it is God's own country! Well, they made their land good, and God saw that the labor of their hands was really, really good, in spite of their generation of atrocities, and decided to have a covenant with them. They didn't do anything worse than David, was it not from the land of Judah that the Messiah was made incarnate and man? Name one individual in the Bible who did anything worse than David, unless Lucifer himself! I'm going to stop thus far. But, I'm going to pour out a libation for you as you go forward. I mean well for you, but you must also mean well for people around you and your own Biafran people. You still wonder where I come from?" he asked him.

"No, but…," began Bucknor.

"Hold it and but me no but," cut in Jorge. "Sometimes you don't have to ask too many questions. Sometimes you may have to sleep with one of your eyes open. Sometimes you may wanna take a deep breath and rejuvenate your heart. Do you know why parents deny their kids some freedom and not expose them to some stuff? It's just for their own sake. Knowing too much too soon is surely detrimental to their well-being. Sometimes you need to tarry. But all the times try and keep an ear to the ground or even lend an ear to your surroundings. Then everything else will be added onto you," he counseled him.

"Having said all that," he continued, "I'll take you to my house so that you can visit anytime before the end of the tournament and before you depart for the United States. That's, if you like." He offered Bucknor.

CHAPTER 13

The mystery of this man bewildered Bucknor even more after hearing all that from him. The man minced no words. The stroll to his apartment was wasted on mundane things. The soccer tournament was the talk of the town, and they dwelt on it as they went along the two miles' walk. Nevertheless, his mind kept wandering to unanswered questions. This man must truly be a Biafran and not a mercenary. But then why all these other names. If Amadike was part of his name, that must be his middle name. And if that was his first name, then what was his surname? Again, he had forgotten to straighten that out with him. And now the man had wisely counseled him to stop asking too many questions. Time shall tell! Going back to start querying him all over again would mean that he was not listening. It would also mean that the little thaw in their understanding would stop and the hardening of the ice would start all over again. He would take his counsel and let sleeping dogs lie. Perhaps, time shall tell!

Both his apartment and the environment it was located was truly unremarkable. Inside the living room, there was not much of appurtenance of someone who was well-off in his skin. Only the rug on the floor told a story of someone who may have been to Persia. It was handmade. It was stylistic. It was beautiful. It was also padded. At one corner of the room was a Sony television that must be of the newest kind out in the market. There were no pictures on the wall that could help expatiate on who he was or tell any story about his family, his wife, and children or the lack of the latter thereof. Nothing! None. There was a door that opened to an inner room which supposedly must be a bedroom. There was a three-seater sofa right behind the entrance door. That was the only couch in the living room. There was an ashtray near the couch, but it had no ash in it and looked as if it had not been used in months. It was that clean. There was no turntable in the living room, but music could be heard waffling out from behind the closed door. On the right of the entrance door was the kitchen. The gas cooker was sparkling clean, and the one pot on top of it was a testament that it had not been used for a long time. There was a refrigerator near the cooker. On the deck platform linking the cooker and dishwashing sink was a toaster. The whole place looked like a bachelor's abode. But Bucknor thought to himself that though this man may be a bachelor but he lived an ascetic lifestyle. He may not be a hermit, but it looked like he was styling his dwelling place as someone who wanted to be left alone. Or someone always on the move.

"Please, make yourself comfortable in the couch," he offered Bucknor.

Bucknor muttered some words in appreciation and sat down. Without going to the inner room or bedroom, Jorge went to the refrigerator and fished out some stuff, opened one of the cupboards, and brought out a saucer. The next minute he was presenting his visitor kola nut to his greatest bewilderment. Kola nut in this part of the planet earth?

Kola nut had always been the crème de la crème of Igbo man's welcoming hand and hospitality. It also made clear to Bucknor where the man he visited hailed from. He did not need to ask any further question in that regard.

"If I invited you to my place or house," he began, "I may not have water. I may not have food on the table. But what I do not miss to present to you is kola nut, unless I did not ask you to come. But even if I didn't ask you to come, traditionally I've to show you some hospitality, and as you know kola nut is the flagship of warmest of…"

"Where did you get that from?" asked Bucknor.

"I always have some. When I travel I buy a lot of it. And since I'm always traveling I replenish it a lot. I'm never out of it. My father used to tell me that that is the best present you can give to a stranger to your house at home or abroad. Unless the visitor does not understand he would not say that he was not warmly welcome. That is the greatest welcome for my people. Food and water and other niceties are mere footnotes," said Jorge.

He immediately prayed over the kola nut and made libation out of it and offered one to Bucknor, cajoling him to take it along with himself and tell the story of the nut when he got to his destination. He had assured Bucknor that he was free to come by anytime he was free to do so. It was an offer Bucknor felt good about. After that, the pair went out that evening and ate at one of the closest restaurants nearby before they retired to their places.

CHAPTER 14

It was still a Monday morning, a week and counting before the finale. The soccer tournament was still ongoing. Bucknor was still in Buenos Aires. By his own estimation he still had a few more weeks to burn. After all, the semester he was angling for still had over a month to its commencement. Everything was still in sync. Money was still not a problem. He had still hundreds of dollars to spend. But it would not carry him to those few number of days he still had to waste before he hooked his next flight to the Windy city of Chicago.

He joltingly woke up that morning for no certain reason. He sat on the edges of the bed and could come to nothing that would make him feel that way. He thought about home and instantly remembered his closest sibling, Amarachi. He had hoped nothing was wrong with her. He would go down to the lobby and place a call home to make sure everything was okay. Not only Amarachi but also to make sure that his mom and dad and his other siblings were doing fine. And then he thought that he also needed to present one of his traveler's cashier's checks to the bank to begin the process of turning it into hard currency. He was told that it would take a few days for any bank to verify its authenticity since it was passing through some international barriers and boundaries. He had no problems with that. Then he brought out the book he had been reading during his itinerary, Chukwunonso's *Europeans Left a Baboon Economy for Africa*, and opened it again. He was a few pages into it again when he decided that he needed to take his shower and go to the bank. Then, he stood up. He stood there, lost.

Then he took another look at the book. Something struck him hard about it. The caption sounded good. He thought about it. He queried it. Was it really true that Europeans left an economy for Africa where baboon toiled for monkey? Yeah! It was true then! But was it true now? It might still. He tried to convince himself. Then he shook his head in confused disbelief. Did Europeans set Africa in perpetual self-confusion in that spell-casting delirium? Does Africa not have right to their own destiny? Are we in continuous spin away from reality and that which was good? In a blink of an eye his mind was running amok, haywire. He remembered his father! He loathed his father. His means. But had no qualms helping himself out of his unaccountable largesse! That largesse, how large it was, he did not know, and even his father, the owner, may neither know, nor could he tell. And worse still they were stashed away overseas in raw cash. If he died today the whole wealth stashed abroad died with him. They become someone else's inheritance. And worse still he was not compelled by any foreign power to store away his largesse overseas, that was, if he really owned it! It riveted him a little bit. The path his father had chosen was wrong. If he would veer toward the right way perhaps someone else will follow suit and then another and then another. Europe may have stolen Africa's resources. They might still be stealing her dry unashamedly. They may have bought a whole lot of young men and women in those eon years. They may have kidnapped lots and lots of healthy young men and carted them into slavery eon years without qualms. And had lived thereon without qualms. But we have repopulated the earth, and our natural resources and endowment were inexhaustible. So why were we still bemoaning centuries-old injustices as badges of honor and held them up as to why we have refused to think right and embrace the future? Why are we holding our badge of dishonor as our signpost? We were mired in some endless blame game, he thought to himself. He had come to his wit's end! That was what it was! Instead of wallowing in self-deprecating snivels we can thrash out the remnant of what we have got left and forge ahead with a new purpose and say to ourselves: never again.

As he was lost in thought he did not even know when he sat down in the couch at the center of his hotel room. Then his thoughts were reverted to his father. His own father was famed not for being a first-class police officer but roundly remembered as he whose effort sabotaged the Biafran war effort. He was not forced to take a stand against his own people during the genocidal war. He got remembered in tales as the man who coined the derisive bare-hand revolution that caricatured the struggle of his own people. What if he could account for all he was purported to be worth? Perhaps that which he was looking for in Nkwume was in his own Okwudo, near Umushishi. Perhaps there would not have been any need for him to be seeking a first-class university in another man's country when there was enough to set up one in his own backyard. Those thoughts engulfed him. It was like thinking about how the world came to be and who created God and who created he who created God and so on and so forth. Again, he had come to his wit's end! It was the unfathomable, fathomable unfathomable! How could it be understood? How could it not be understood? How could it be understood for a people so endowed to be scratching their heads and then never saw beyond their noses? He could not remember when or how he slumped into the couch. It was with a great will that he got to his feet and decided to make his next move. The day was just gone like that! He did not make it to the bank.

He just did not want to be the first person at the Barclays International of Buenos Aires. He was glad to see a branch of a British bank in Argentina. That meant a whole lot to him. And hopefully communication would not pose a problem. He had had it galore since he came in and that had limited his movement and interaction a lot. His wonderment was compounded by the fact that black people were hard to come by in Buenos Aires. He was a young man given to wonder. Why are there no black people in this area of the world? He did not dwell on that for a long time. He was a man on a mission. He just had to mind his own narrow business. So he faced his immediate trouble as if he knew it was coming. And now he was among the first few persons to make it to the premises of the bank that morning. He was straddled between the threshold and another step inside the door when all of a sudden, he swirled around, almost knocking down the lady that was right behind him. It had just occurred to him that he was a Mr. Ghoostte. That he had left his land-of-the-rising-sun passport behind in Biafra. Now he had to think really fast. He had to put on his thinking cap. He apologized to the lady and stepped out of the doorway. He had planned that he was going to call Amarachi when he got to America and identify an address for her to mail to him his passport. Now he was running low on cash and needed to cash one of his checks and would need a passport that reflected the name on the checks. He rushed back to the hotel and asked the service desk if he could receive a mail at the hotel. There was no problem, he was informed. The front desk lady furnished him the right address highlighting his room number.

Five days later a letter was delivered to the mail pouch in front of his hotel room door. Amarachi had sent to him a mail using the fastest means there was to deliver a mail. And he wasted no time in delivering it to the bank. It was another Monday, and the bank had told him that they would do the customary due diligence on verifying the check. It would not be ready that day. He had to check back on Wednesday or Thursday. He went home a relieved man.

He had now grown accustomed to Jorge. He had decided that he would take his bag and spend the night at his apartment that Friday night. It was no problem for Jorge. When he reached his apartment, Jorge was on the phone, but he did acknowledge his countryman's presence. As soon as he got off the phone, he asked Bucknor to go to the convenience store both had visited together these past few days to buy a pack of cigarettes. It was about two blocks away. Bucknor had no problem with the errand. Matter-of-factly he smoked occasionally especially when under serious pressure, or when he had to impress his acquaintances and pretended to be a smoker. Smoking was his father's vice which he had indulged himself for aforementioned reasons. As soon as he stepped out of the door, Jorge pounced. He used his master key that can open virtually any traveling box key in a jiffy. He wanted to know whose pseudonym his countryman was traveling to the United States with. Masterfully and luckily, he was able to reach his goal. There in was the blue passport embossed with his passport picture with the name Turnkey Golan Ghoostte.

He now had the information he was looking for and masterfully replaced everything as he had found them. He left no traces of any intrusion. It was not long when Bucknor returned. Jorge, who gave up smoking soon after the war, lit one stick and pretended to be inhaling and exhaling. For Bucknor, it felt like some unfinished business. He really needed to know this presumably countryman better. Some stuff could not wait. He did not want to proceed on his way without making all the effort to know more about this man he wholeheartedly had come to believe was his countryman.

"If I needed to tell my father that I met someone like you, who would I be telling him that you are?" began Bucknor slowly.

"But you do not have to tell him or any other person about me. It's not necessary," said Jorge, "Or you can tell him, if you needed to, that you met a man of an unknown country but who knew a lot about your country. But more importantly, you needed to dwell on that which is very important to you. More so, you have not been forthcoming with the truth about your family or under whose pseudonym you are traveling with. Nevertheless, these are not important to me. All that's important is that you do well in America. You do not have to come back bringing a diploma but come back clutching their work ethic. It is very, very important. Trying to or knowing all these issues about me will never help you move forward. But it might be in your own best interest if I've an idea of your assumed name," said Jorge.

Once again Bucknor found himself in an unchartered territory. Again his inquisitiveness had let him be boxed into a corner. One more issue he did not want to discuss had come back again to haunt him. And this time around he was his own worst enemy. He wished he had kept his mouth shut or at least remain in his hotel room unperturbed, unbothered, or burdened by any of the issues that kept landing him in trouble. He did not want to come further forth about his new name and did not know how to extricate himself from his own quagmire. He would rather let their relationship sour than to divulge his assumed name. He had come thus far to now want to risk the rest of his effort by his own miscalculations and wanton inquiry about nothing. He tried to change the topic, and Jorge flew with him. Since they had all eaten dinner it was not long when Bucknor fell asleep on the couch.

He slept soundly most of the night. However, to his surprise, each time he momentarily turned in his sleep, he would notice that Jorge was awake. Morning did not come that soon for him, but eventually it did. After a light breakfast of fried eggs and bread and tea he was good to return to his hotel room. It was Saturday, and the third-place match of the world soccer tournament would be taking place. He was not attending. He was rather billed to attend the final match of the competition between the Netherlands and the host nation of Argentina. That was the ultimate show case and prize. He had already confirmed his traveling after the tournament. His check, having already cleared he had intended to leave for O'Hare Airport at the sound of the final whistle.

As they were about to part company that Saturday afternoon, Jorge said to his friend, "I can stop you from getting to O'Hare. It's as simple as a stone throw, a mere phone call. But I do not want to. I could have told you one or two things about the name you are traveling with that would have helped you move forward. But since you want to keep it to yourself and all you cared about knowing is where I got Jorge from, I would let you carry on. But as you go forward, I want you to know that neither Mr. Ghoostte nor yourself can help you in America but I can."

Locusts just swirled in Bucknor's head. To say that Bucknor was startled was making light the confusion that was rocking in his head. He looked at Jorge in the face and saw for the first time a very dangerous man, a man capable of helping him further but also capable of derailing his movement. Then he thought to himself that this man could be capable of killing him without a trace as well. It was too late to tell the man everything about himself. He did not know if prostrating and pleading with the man to forgive him would do anything to correct his prevarications and ill judgments. He was rooted to the ground as Jorge turned around and started making his way back to his apartment.

When Bucknor managed to lift one of his legs off where it was rooted to the ground the other followed suit naturally, and he began to walk tiredly back to his hotel room. He became tired more than he had ever been before. Now more questions had arisen in his concave head. Would he ever make it to the United States? Who really was this man? Why was he an agent provocateur for his own undoing? Was it possible for him to hop into an aircraft and disappear in the streets of United States before this man could finish setting up his web to stop him? Then he realized that he could not do that. Flight travel was not like hopping or hiking a motorbike. It was much more than that. This man could be that dangerous and come after him and even kill him, he thought to himself. There was so much at stake. There was no margin for an error any more. Yet, his paths were littered with errors already. First things first. There was no hiding from this man. And he knew the terrains. He was not moving an inch away from his hotel room again. He was going to forfeit watching the final match of the soccer tournament live. The only movement he was prepared to venture out of his room for would be to hail a taxi and be driven to the airport. Anything else mattered not. And so it was!

The departure line at the Ministro Pistarini International Airport was seamless though there was heavy police presence. Mr. Ghoostte had no problem whatsoever passing the line of final inspection. More so, he arrived much more earlier since he forfeited watching the World Cup final. The first point of problem that had worried him had been scaled without an ado. Mr. Santana had pulled no plugs yet. Shortly afterward they were airborne. Then he began to gather his thoughts. One of his friends in New Haven, Connecticut, had schooled him a bit on how to carry himself through lines of inspection at the arrival terminus at the O'Hare Airport: keep to yourself, guard your own luggage, do not open your mouth unless you have to, if you have to talk limit your response, do not proffer more answer to a question than was required, do not be loquacious, nod your head in agreement if acquiescing was what was needed, try making an eye contact when you were addressing a fellow, but do not try to sweep one off their feet with your gaze in the name of eye contact, do not stare in the horizon as if you were lost, do not start a discussion, and wear a serious visage so that people would recognize that you were a serious-minded individual and leave you alone, but do not wear a threatening look to warrant the security personnel to fix their gaze at you, pay you more attention than was necessary; kind of profile you on the spot. Those were some of the thoughts that crept like mice in his head as he sat by the window of the giant plane. Then his mind veered toward Mr. Santana. What if he was at the airport waiting to hand him over to the police? Could he be that ubiquitous? Could he be that mean-spirited to betray his countryman? Then he was jolted! If his father could side with the enemy and betray the Biafran cause and cause this man to lose his friend and more friends and property and more property and more dignity and more dignity and come out barely with his life and a permanent limp in his gait, then this man could put a dagger in his rib cage without caring a hoot and could be justified doing so. In fact, he considered himself lucky to have stayed with this man and come off unscathed. And in fact, Mr. Santana treated him nicely and could truly be a nice man! He did him some good. He could have done him some bad and be justified. He was jolted back to life when the tall, beautiful air hostess approached the row of seats he was squatted and asked what kind of drink he would like to have. He momentarily thought about it and waved her on. He did not have to open his mouth unless he really, really had to.

The flight from Buenos Aires was calm except on few occasions when the hot humid air coming from Africa through the south Atlantic Ocean clashed with the swirling air of the north Atlantic and the hoopla waves of the Pacific and there would appear like the plane hit a bump on the road and over the announcement system the copilot calmed the people to stay without fear because it was mere turbulence as he put it. Mere turbulence! They were used to flying that when the aircraft characteristically quaked a little bit, it was normal and nothing to worry about. For some of these pilots were more troubled with their cars skidding past a pothole than some turbulence in the air. Somehow the fourteen-hour flight from Ezeira Ministro Pistarini International Airport was smooth.

O'Hare Airport was imposing. The crowd of people was like a throng. The whole place was teeming with people. As they were marshaled out of the belly of the aircraft, there was an announcement that American citizens should be in the line on the left and noncitizens should join the line to the right. For Bucknor, he had his eyes fixed on trying to spot Mr. Santana around. He was nowhere around, yet that did not offer him a sigh of relief. He could still pop up somewhere out there and hand him over to the police. But then why worry about Mr. Santana? He could be working for other entities. He never said who he was working for or what he was doing except living among the locals of Argentina. His thoughts were wandering too far away as the line kept moving faster than he had anticipated. Because it was the citizens line it was pretty fast. There was not that much scrutiny. But he was still far off. Though there was not much scrutiny, there still was because flights and passengers from Argentina still had extra checks because of their situation. But that day the crowds of people coming in were massive than usual. The world soccer tournament just ended, and people were getting back after all the fanfare that accompanied the events. That added to the number of people at the arrival terminus that day. And the marching order as usual was to get people off the lines as quickly as possible. Americans should not be detained passing through checks in their own country. That was where Mr. Ghoostte found himself that late morning hours. And from behind a hand was placed on his shoulders. He remained transfixed. For a moment, he just refused to turn his head. His heart sank and convoluted within his entrails. Then the guy moved over right in front of him. It was Chuck. Then relief came. But he needed a split second to get his act together before everything he had worked for went kaput.

"Hey, Bucks!" shouted Chuck. "You made it!" he continued.

"Old boy, yes, I made it," he said to him, with not so happy a grin on his face, as he dragged Chuck away from where he was in the line.

"I need to cross that man," he whispered to his friend from college.

"But, you need to be in this other line," said Chuck a little louder than Bucknor would stomach, pointing to the noncitizens line.

"Take it easy, old boy. It's a long story," he whispered again to his ears, still wearing that muffled, not too incandescent grin on his face truly like a man with a lot to hide.

"Then, I will see you at the other side after the clearance," Chuck said quietly to him and walked back to his line.

For a moment Bucknor forgot that he was a Mr. Ghoostte. And his line had moved a lot faster within the interval. He had two people ahead of him, a lady presumably of Caucasian origin and a thin-looking man, surely an oriental, perhaps Japanese, Korean, Vietnamese, Laotian, or even Chinese. Ahead of this man was that lady and before them was Mr. Cornerstone, a loquacious Vietnamese veteran, who, on top of his uniform as someone who checked in incoming passengers, had all manners of insignia and badges and epaulettes earned for his exploits during the Vietnam War. Truly they were badges of honor, but he wore his with some aplomb for all to see. Even at a time when war was no longer an honorable habit and that war in particular was not the quintessential of American prowess Mr. Cornerstone, a jolly good fellow, wore his insignia of gallantry and service and duty with some pomp and sometimes some kind of pageantry about it.

He was retired from the military after twenty-two years of service, eight of which he spent in the jungles of Vietnam fighting the Vietcong. Military service was a passion for him, and he could spend all days talking about the life of military men and women. When he was let go for minor infraction of rules, after being reprimanded on a number of times, being very cozy with ordinary Vietnamese children, his life went topsy-turvy. He hated the drudgery that was civilian life and initially did not want anything to do with it. Life was almost spiraling out of hand from him. He began to invest his time drinking. In no time, he had added a lot of weight, and gradually obesity set in before he could tell what was wrong with himself. Weight had shortened his height, and the swagger of his stride was all gone. As he sat down there like humpty-dumpty he found his new job very interesting, and he wanted to make the best out of it. He liked talking, and talking he got his mind unburdened. He had started enjoying his job. He liked to interact with almost every fella coming from abroad. His bosses knew the risk he posed with his cavalier attitude and less attention to details, his old vice, that instead of posting him to the noncitizen section where miscreants of every hue could slip through they placed him at the citizens' section of the arrival wing where all he needed doing in most cases was to make sure that all passengers coming through had the blue passport, matching face with picture, place the admittance stamp on the passport, and wave them bye.

That was all he was doing. And then came the man resembling a guy with an oriental origin. For some reasons Mr. Cornerstone became more animated, while from behind the man Mr. Ghoostte watched with rapt attention, his large ears twitching to record everything and his unblinking, big eyeballs watching what this huge security man must not be doing. He had been paying attention to the proceeding all along with some keen interest. He watched the security guy open the man's passport and scan his eyes across the man's face, then flipped through a couple of pages. That was when his eyes struck a most interesting part of the man's blue traveling paper. His eyes were gleaming with nostalgia and that also reflected in his tone.

"You are a well-traveled man, hopping in and out of airports. Been to Saigon and coming in from Buenos Aires, very hot places," he told the man standing before him expressionlessly. "I was in the jungles of Saigon. Today a part of me still feels left behind there, like missing in action. Oh boy, missing in action, not that I want to relive it all over again. No! But because I still feel that I left a part of my good soul and ugly heart over there. Better forgotten than relived. Hanoi, Saigon, oh no!"

"It was bad and still is," chirped in the man.

"Man," Mr. Cornerstone continued, "you are coming from hell! Did you see Pol Pot?"

"No, sir, I was just at the gates," said the man jovially.

"Well, if you had been to Saigon or Hanoi, you had been to hell. Well, you have to get to hell before you can go to heaven for all you think or know," he jokingly added, hammered his entry stamp on one of the pages, and handed the man his passport, rolling the iron grid gate for the man to make his entry.

Mr. Ghoostte, who was watching very attentively, moved forward and gave Mr. Cornerstone his passport, staring him in the eyes. Mr. Cornerstone flipped open the picture page and then next page and the next page and next.

"You, too, are a man well traveled. Apartheid South Africa, gruesome genocidal Biafra, and now Pinochet's Argentina", reeled off the loquacious security guard, now erroneously and inadvertently swapping Chile with Argentina, "all places with some horrid stories to tell. I would have loved to fight in Biafra and slay all those sons of a bitch that were slaughtering innocent men, women, and children. That was the real war instead of the fruitless exercise in the creeks of Ho Chi Minh City." The man paused, as Mr. Ghoostte muttered inaudibly his acquiesce.

"Your name gave you away," continued Mr. Cornerstone, as Bucknor stood there breathless and lacking anything to say or anywhere to dash to if he had to fly. Momentarily, he thought about why Jorge was saying that he knowing his pseudonym might do him some good. Perhaps, he had recognized that his name might pose some problem somewhere out there and was going to prepare him against any eventuality.

"You must have been an adopted child." He paused as Bucknor said nothing.

The man figured out that he was about to cross some line profiling this young man and quickly added, "You know black folks do not bear such names especially if they have origin in white subculture. Anyway, are you from the famous Ghoostte family in Indiana?" he asked.

"No, not at all," said Bucknor firmly as the man lifted his admittance stamp and hammered it on one of the pages. It showed 09:27 GMT and initialed on June 26, 1978. The trouble with this time stamp was that it should have read 10:27 GMT but because Mr. Cornerstone was talking and distracted he forgot to manually swing the time stamp to the next hour. In that dereliction of duty he may have allowed a lot of passengers entry with wrong arrival time on their passports for about an hour.

"I see! You are welcome back to the United States, Mr. Ghoostte," said Mr. Cornerstone reconciliatorily.

As soon as the man rolled the gate for his entry Bucknor could feel the presence of Jorge Santana all about himself. He turned left, and he could see the image of the man move swiftly further left of him. He turned right, and there was the man's silhouette still about him. He steeled himself. After all, he was the one who made things happen when they were in high school and through college! But he did not know where to go, now made less of a burden by the fact that he had met someone who could be of assistance. His initial plan was to hitchhike a cab that would take him to one nondescript hotel where he would gather his thoughts and plan his next move to Accord University. As he moved a little bit further away from the entry point he looked back and could see his friend giving him a thumbs-up. He tarried, and shortly afterward he was joined by Chuck. It was a difficult plan made easier by the hands of the mighty gods and beyond his wildest imagination. He made no arrangements of any kind because he did not want to expose his plan to anyone. You never could tell who would want to scuttle your plan of a lifetime.

Dumbfounded, Bucknor could hardly remember anything his friend of old was saying to him. It was like what he was saying made their entry through one ear and disappeared through the other. Their ride to Chuck's was all high fives, but Bucknor was not really in the discussion. All entreaties for him to divulge how he made it to the line for citizens and green card holders were met with a stone wall. He was adamant that it would be a discussion for another day. Chuck then concluded that being the scion of a powerful and ruthless police boss everything was possible for Bucknor. But he would not let go and Chuck continued to pester him to no avail. To alleviate their friction over the matter, one day later Bucknor moved into a hotel. He had the bucks. Since he had missed much of the semester, he decided to lie low. Three days later, he flew off to Boston and paid homage to one of his maternal uncles there and then hitchhiked a cab for the one-hour ride to Providence, Rhode Island.

CHAPTER 15

Born in Owere, thirty-seven miles off the coast of the Atlantic Ocean in Biafra, Amadike was three months when his parents moved to Marseille, south of France. Awed by the beauty of the city as soon as he could perceive, he grew up liking everything about Marseille and eventually France and her language. And the city was as beautiful as the language. He loved playing in front of the gold statue of the virgin and child right in front of France's perhaps most beautiful basilica and edifices. He loved the story of Charlemagne, the medieval emperor that labored to unite all of Europe through wars and conquests. He cherished playing in the beaches of Vieux Port and climbed the stony landscape of Chateau D'If, the strange fortress of a prison that was the pride of the nation but now a symbol of her cruel and tortured past. He loved the story of Napoleon Bonaparte, the leading warmonger of his time that terrorized much of Europe and Far East and Africa. He loved everything French. When the British were segregating patches of the African landscape, pitching together people who did not belong together, the French had a policy of assimilation, anchored on the phantom, deceitful tripartite mantra of *liberté*, égalité, and *fraternité*. They wanted every other people to be like French, for good or for bad; feigned lip service for they meant none of them. He loved all that for good or for bad for a young chap.

Marseille was it. A mirror of what France really was! Multicultural. A convergence of people and cultures, of languages. Marseille had become the home for people of different nationalities. North Africans to people of eastern and western Europe: Poles, Czechs, Albanians, Germans, English, Russians, Spaniards; Ethiopians, Ghanaians, Ivorians, Togolese, bloody Nigerians, and a host of other nations! The good thing being that people were not bothered speaking what they could best understand. It was in that babel of tongues and voices that Amadike cut his first teeth speaking French. He was able to communicate freely with French as soon as he could yap just like a kid born into that society, that one could not tell otherwise! It was natural to him. While he picked up French growing up he did also pick smattering pieces of other languages.

At high school, he already knew what he wanted to do for a living. His sense for other languages had heightened. When it was time for him to go to the university there was no hesitation on what he wanted to do. He was bent on knowing a lot of languages as much as he could. He chose to study German as major and Russia as minor. That arrangement worked well for him. Twice every year there was this excursion into other countries where these languages were spoken to kind of get a hands-on feeling of the other languages. His trips to Germany and Russia as part of the class curriculum helped him immerse himself in these languages. At the end of the four years of study and interaction in Russia and Germany and with Russians and Germans in the Marseille neighborhood he was growing up, he was already proficient. He could add some panache to them with some proverbs. Then he decided that he was going to go for a master's degree program. This time around he chose Spanish and Portuguese in his undisguised quest to compare and contrast the two languages. They were much easier for him because he had the rudiment. And for two years he threw in everything he had to it. He became so good in Spanish aphorism. He did help himself. He never spoke French or English unless he had to. Anyone not having known him would think he was born in Germany or Russia, or Brazil or even Mexico. He just had a knack for picking up languages. He was a language fiend! Since his neighborhood experiences in Marseille he had this mix of people that he picked up anything that his ears caught. He did not speak Amharic but make no mistake cursing him out in Amharic because there was the possibility that he had a smattering knowledge of what was said about him. He once manhandled, *boy-handled*, a boy of his age who cursed him out in Albanian thinking that he did not understand what was said of him.

After he completed his postgraduate degrees, his parents decided that it was time to move back to Biafra. Amadike stayed back in France and picked up teaching jobs. Of all the languages he studied he seemed to fall in love most with Russian. But he chose to teach Spanish and German. He found joy on his job, and for five years, he stayed buoyed on the beat. Then for some reasons he decided that he had to move to what was called north of Nigeria. He was there for two years and could not find joy on the job and environment. Then he decided to move to Biafra land. He wanted to impact his knowledge to the forgotten children of Biafra, and the land of the Ibibios was where he pitched his tent. Three years later, there was some kind of cataclysmic vortex. The news kept coming that there was a systematic design to exterminate the Igbos. At some points one event led to the other which culminated in the formation of Biafrans' resistance and a declaration of an independent state for the people of Biafra.

Initially, defunct Nigeria elites thought that Biafra would be crushed in a matter of days. But Biafra was not fooled. Biafrans were convinced that they had an uphill battle to fight. The leaders knew that they had to make enough impact to be left alone. First they began information campaign to arouse the people to understand the task and to give their unalloyed support. The gruesome nature of the events that led to the resistance was relentless so every Tom, Dick, and Harry was aware of the situation, including children who girded up their loins for the worst to come. Evidenced in scenes where children made merry out of the situation because they, too, believed in a free Biafran nation where they could call a homeland.

The information campaign paid off. The conscience of many mothers and fathers was touched in more ways than one. Young men were conscripted, and many a time a lot lined up to be recruited. Many parents, especially the well-to-do, tried to shield their wards from joining the Biafran Army let alone be conscripted. Many a parent found it worthy trying to hide their young men from joining the new Biafran fighting force. On the ledges inside and hedges outside were options. Attic was considered. However, that was the initial place to search for those whose parents never wanted to surrender to the resistance effort. Bushes were also optional, but the danger being that those sent out to find those able-bodied young men usually come very early in the morning. And the bush posed additional problems because one could be bitten by some dangerous snakes or some other dangerous creatures out there. So it made no sense. And then how far or how long would one be on the run. Ahulele had discussed all options left for him and Amadike, and he was convinced they had an agreement on everything they had to do to be safe and avoid direct involvement in the war. Including also that possibility of moving back to France.

It was a gentleman's agreement. An unwritten rule. Amadike was supposed to go to the yam barn and stand erect like one of the columns. It was an early morning raid to find him. Ahulele had quietly opened the gate for the searchers and was almost convincing them that Amadike had traveled back to France when, all of a sudden, behind his father was the ghostly figure of Amadike.

"You are Amadike," demanded one of the men, throwing the glare of their torchlight into his face.

"Yes, I'm he!" he said firmly to the consternation of his heartbroken father.

"Good, you're going with us," said the other man. "If you want to pick up a thing or two, you are obliged to, or you can still come and your basics would be provided on as needed basis," he concluded with some honest dispatch.

Ahulele stood there as he watched his son walked toward his room with one of the men who stood by the door as Amadike gathered a few things and threw them into his travelers' box and went out of the gate with the men.

Ahulele knew that it was coming. When the clamor for independence was growing loud he readily knew the inherent danger that would follow suit. Declaration of independence would surely lead to a shooting war. Godforsaken Nigeria was not going to let her prized jewel just go like that. And a shooting war would require men and men in large numbers. Deep down his bowels he supported the declaration and the independence that was attached to it. So in essence one would expect that he would support every effort geared toward its protection and sustainability. Not so quickly. He would support it while other people's kids are in the front line of danger. But he had in Amadike who he knew could be a different kettle of fish to deal with. His son believed that if one had to support the effort to resist or fight the enemy, one must be prepared to chip in something either in blood or in sweat but most especially desirably in both. He did not want to be conscripted. His desire was to fight with his whole heart. For one to yield to being conscripted instead of volunteering may result to being seen as lily-livered and more likely to be distracted and most likely to be consumed in the heat of fire and smoke yielding only but ashes. So he made no hesitation and left everything else and followed the men. Amadike joined the army on his own volition.

There was no time to waste. It was like the enemy was at the gates of Biafra. The leaders had assured the young nation that they had enough material to prosecute the war. But those who ought to know knew. So to mitigate against these ills, the leadership of the fledgling nation did the most commonsense of things to do. They assembled engineering students, their professors, and other intellectuals around the country and tasked them to apply their hidden ingenuity to the fabrication of war materials, and within months they made light of that challenge. When they doled out their multitude killer mobile gun, *ogbunigwe*, the military leader of the young republic nodded his country's readiness to repel the enemy and safeguard the territorial integrity of the new nation. While these intellectuals and their protégés applied their knowledge to practical use the leadership still recognized that manpower and materials were most likely still to be in short supply and more likely to run lower in a few months. As a stop gap, the military trainers who had seen the loopholes had anticipated that if need be, there may be the need for hand-to-hand combat. No stone was left unturned!

Life at the training camp was tough. It was not Sandhurst, the British royal military academy. It was not Forth Brad, the top American military base. This training camp was nascent, and not even a fledgling Biafran army could make it better. So in that nascent Biafran force all survival skills were taught in case. One of those skills on board and display was martial arts. During the first week of training Amadike had squared up with one of the trainers, a big bulky guy that brooded no nonsense. He was out to punish anyone that squared up with him but not enough to hurt. By all measures he was no match for Amadike. The exercise was supposed to be jab for jab, mindful of security and safety of your partner but tough enough to make one realize that in the thick of a live event submission was abhorred. In a flash Amadike let his guard down, and the bulky guy gave a stinging jab to the stomach to floor him. His fellow recruits thought that he was hurt and wanted to pick him up. He quickly got to his feet, waved them away, and began darting and feigning around the dusty enclosure ready for the exercise to continue. It did continue and he got smarter. Not long after that he landed a southpaw hook on the guy who staggered back and tripping forward supported with his two hands clutching some sand and readily composed himself again. Amadike distinguished himself. Nevertheless, he was admonished: don't let your guard down! As a person or as a people!

The idea of the exercise was not to stand toe to toe with your assailant but to aim for an opportunity to take advantage and hurt your enemy enough for the enemy to seek a way out and retreat, that was, if he was not dead. The instruction was to keep your distance and seek where it would hurt your enemy the most. Having achieved that put your opponent at a dagger point. His weapons became your spoil and your ammunition to attack his brother.

Christened John Peter Amadike Ahulele by his parents who later took him to France. Was he born in France perhaps his parents would have named him Jean Pierre if they had thought about it. Actually, in all the years he spent in France he had been referred to as Jean Pierre by friends and peers and neighbors. He got used to it that he did not worry about John Peter. John Peter growing up loved to assume himself some position of some leadership. Liked it or not he would put himself up to be chosen. In doing so sometimes he had appeared a whole lot opinionated and arrogant. He had come across to his elders as a smart boy and to his peers as priggish. Other people's opinion of him never bothered him. He was concentrated on doing good for himself and let the crumbs filter out to other people who did not fight hard enough. Where he was short in height he made up in assertiveness and proving himself. His not too great a height was dwarfed more by his bulging hips by his sides and protruding buttocks. When any other chap was slow in answering he was quick to raise his hand. His pedantry was in no doubt and that he never bragged about. He was a standout chap. However, because he had worn glasses since age three there was a peculiar kind of way he trained his neck to listen that sometimes gave out the air of being offish. But he was not. He was a highly misunderstood boy growing up and remained a very, very misunderstood man. In a sense, he lived according to the pedigree of his father and his kindred people and seen as such.

The war did not last long enough because peace was on the table after all. The two years and a half it lasted was like an eternity and brutish caldron in every of its ramifications. There was no need for the war after all. However, the bruises and scars of the war were hard to overcome. The way the peace was designed did not go down well with some of the combatants and would not augur well for them moving forward. The fear of retribution, of revenge, or vendetta was palpable. There was not enough provision for safety for those who wanted to win it on the battlefield. For those armistice was a mesh of patchwork meant to calm all frayed nerves, and then let the system that subsisted in Nigeria be superimposed on Biafrans. Among those who would not want the status quo that was in defunct Nigeria be transposed to Biafra was Amadike. In the meantime, he wanted to check out for good!

America had a program and created an avenue for some former combatants and soldiers to escape to a quieter life. As Amadike walked into that camp that morning he had thought to himself that he had a chance to make it to the United States. Being who he was, confident of himself, if he had known that he did not have a chance he would not have tried in the first place. After all he could easily have traveled to Paris. True to kind he loved trying new horizons. So it was not unusual for him to want to go to America.

The line was not as lengthy as he had imagined, so things seemed to have moved pretty fast. He had filled out his papers a few days before, so he was waiting for the asylum officer to call him out. Not long after he had arrived was he ushered before the asylum officer, Ms. Topsoil. Bespectacled, Ms. Topsoil's mien was hard to place. It looked cool and collected. No one could tell what she could offer. Her demeanor was composed. She carried herself as someone who wanted to be accorded all the respects she had earned and demanded of her office.

"Mr. Ahulele, Lieutenant Ahulele," began the asylum officer referring to Amadike who in about three years of fighting and bravado and gallantry had risen to earn his rank, "you want to emigrate to the United States. That is what I understand you're asking for, is that right?" asked Ms. Topsoil.

"No, I'm seeking an asylum to move to the United States," said Amadike firmly.

"So why do you want to go to the United States?" asked the asylum officer. "You were fighting for a homeland for the people of Biafra and a homeland was delivered to you, so also peace. I thought that you would stay here and savor the peace and help nourish the land. And from the information I've of you before me, it doesn't show that you were among the top echelon of government officials that were wanted or targeted for retribution. No one should be marked for retributive justice. My government will see to it that nothing like that would ever happen," she quickly added.

"Yes, it always seems so, but at the end it's always the small guy that gets the stick. For me, madame, it's not the fear of the unknown, it's being weary of the unknown. Being cautious isn't being frightful," said Lieutenant Ahulele.

"I see," said Ms. Topsoil, "but I don't see any need for you to want to go the United States. I don't see any evidence that your life is in any physical danger. You're not among those being sought by the new government, and actually my government doesn't know of anyone being sought out for any retribution. And in fact, America is using her might and influence to carve out a safe haven for those people who may be in danger of any high-handedness of the new administration. It was going to be like an American territory, so it was going to be under the might and control of the United States. So you don't have anything to worry about. If you found your way to that small territory you should consider yourself safe," said Ms. Topsoil to Amadike who seemed to have paid no attention to what he considered a cajoling rigmarole by the asylum officer.

"You're saying that I can move to a safe haven in my own country! Be placed in asylum in my own country! Would rather be raped in a foreign country than to be stripped naked in my own country. I would rather be in an asylum in another country than be in an asylum in my own country," said Amadike calmly.

"Well, Lieutenant Ahulele, every enterprise has consequences. Victory has consequences, so also defeat. In your case, it was no defeat. It just turned out not the way you had envisaged it from the outset. You wanted to fight your way to victory. What you have is a negotiated peace rather than a peace won till the last man. That's a pyrrhic victory. It serves no purpose. In my own estimation, pyrrhic victory is a defeat. Pyrrhic defeat! I would urge you to consider what you got a victory. The main outcome you were looking for was what you finally got, forget how you got it." She paused.

"I'm also gonna remind you that in the armistice that guaranteed peace for the Biafran people no one would face retribution, vendetta. It was enshrined in the piece of paper, no victor, no vanquished."

"Madame, you called it a piece of paper. Submerge it in water and see what would happen to it," said Amadike, even calmer.

"Mr. Ahulele, you might wanna go and come back with more reasons why you should have an asylum passage to America. You might as well try the French or German consulates down the road," counseled Ms. Topsoil. She had lifted her denial stamp to hammer it on his application when Amadike muttered some words.

"And what now? What's that you just said? Do you speak Spanish?" she asked.

"No. Yes," said Amadike.

"What did you just say?" asked Ms. Topsoil.

"I was speaking my Portuguese. But I also speak Spanish to a good measure."

"Really," said Ms. Topsoil in muffled consternation.

"I speak more languages than you can imagine. Name it! From German to Russia. In fact, of these languages, English is my least understood. I would say that I have a smattering knowledge of English as compared to French," he told his bewildered interviewer.

He knew that he had gotten her attention. He had to sell himself in one last ditch effort to leave his frustration behind and try finding new horizons to settle his soul. He also knew that he needed to put his mental demons in check. They were his own worst enemy: self-confidence, assertiveness, and that flip side of avarice, the insatiable need to keep conquering. This was a man who understood his own frailties but could not overcome them.

"Ms. Topsoil," he began, "I know that you are looking at me and keep querying what is that national interest in this man for my country. That is the overriding principle of America's willingness to help. Well, that's where you have veered toward the wrong path again and again," he told Ms. Topsoil, who paid less attention to what he was saying but was thinking what to do with this man who could speak a plethoric of languages and tongues and English the least of them.

"I needed this asylum visa to get out of here," he pressed on.

"Lieutenant Ahulele, this has nothing to do with national interest or whatever you are thinking. What we are doing is purely humanitarian, but you have to prove that you are in an imminent danger. Prove it, sir," she said.

"Madame, I don't have to prove everything. It's inherent in the situation," he told her. "And I must quickly add: the situation we are currently in could have been dealt with differently from the onset if America had chosen to act. Because we all know that your country has the capacity and means to bring positive change anywhere it chooses." He paused, as Ms. Topsoil kept looking at him thinking what to do with Lieutenant Ahulele.

"National interest is not everything. Look at Argentina, you took your eyes off the ball and that butcher ran slipshod on his countrymen, chased them away, or made them disappear under America's gaze just because he claimed that he was pursuing the Bolsheviks. There were no communists in that country. He just waged some *dirty wars* against his own people. And your country turned the other way. Or look at Phnom Penh." Ms. Topsoil's eyes involuntarily became wide open.

"Do not tell me that you speak Vietnamese." She wanted to know.

"No, I don't and I'm not a communist either, before you start thinking that I'm one." he quickly added. "The fact was that Pol Pot was not a communist. He never liked the Bolsheviks and was no friend to the Americans. He was never a good man either. But America made an evil out of him. The need to stop the spread of communism in the jungles of Saigon and Phnom Penh and the utmost ends of the earth played into his hands. It brought out the depravity and beast in him. Everyone lost, but America lost woefully."

"Sir," said Ms. Topsoil, "I don't think that you have come here to berate me or chastise my country. I thought that you have come here to seek asylum to the United States."

"Yes," he said, "but one thing leads to the other. It looks to me like you have tied my asylum visa application to your national interest. You were fighting a war you had no need for, and Biafran men, women and children were decimated in their own streets. Something worse had happened here. Where's that freedom you have promised to defend around the world?"

"No, I've not tied your application to any other interest. And America had not negated its responsibility to the world, at large. And you can neither harass nor intimidate me to do your will. And I can't be bullied, you understand that!" retorted Ms. Topsoil, almost exasperated.

She had seen it all. She was once at a post in Lebanon. And on one occasion a young man she denied his application gathered a crump of heavy sputum and spat it right in her face. She was lucky she was wearing her glasses and that rested on one of her spectacles. On another occasion, she had denied an asylum application to a young Lebanese boy in Beirut and the boy had gotten so irritated that he banged his fist on her desk and gave the middle finger salute. He walked out swearing. She got so scared that she thought he was going to gather some pebbles, stones, and boulders, the typical elements of killing anyone with maximum slow punishment. She called for additional security and her surroundings were beefed up. Nothing happened. She had seen it all. The inherent danger in every job.

"What we do here is purely humanitarian," she continued. "If we grant visa to everyone who showed up for asylum, then the streets of

America, not just Washington, would be overflowing with foreigners of every hue including miscreants, muggers, and hustlers. Look, America has enough of those in her hand, and her prisons are brimming with additional intakes. We would be denying protection to those who legitimately and really needed to be protected. Mr. Ahulele," she continued, "you are one muscle away from being denied your request. But I'm gonna escalate your request to the next level. My advice to you is that you must tone it down. The next guy you would meet might be less tolerant of your assertiveness. I'm gonna set you up for further interview in two days."

"That means you don't care about what happens to me before then," said Amadike.

"That's not the case. The safety of every targeted individual for their politics or views is our utmost concern. But in your case, that's not. There is no mass roundup of ex-combatants going on. I don't expect any harm to come to you," she said as she began making her notes on his application.

In her note, she had made reference to Mr. Ahulele's strength of will, the tenacity of his character, his understanding of world events, and above all his language skills. She stated in her note that he was a former combatant and now very combative, almost venting his spleen on America's place in the world. But she also stated that if the lieutenant were to be a stock he would be considered a gilt-edged investment. She stated that though he may be cash-strapped he had extraordinary skill and would not be a public charge in the United States given his abilities. She wanted her superiors to thoroughly examine him and perhaps co-opt him, possibly use his language skills to advance some areas of national interests. The Russians, she noted, would be thrilled to have him on their payroll.

That national interest lieutenant Ahulele spoke about was then the driving raison d'être for her reconsideration to expedite his request for further examination.

As Amadike made to leave her presence, she asked him to tarry a little bit. She wanted to go to the room behind and speak with one of her superiors to check whether they would like to take an immediate look at this ex-soldier. His potentials were massive. Failure to capitalize on it would be tantamount to a dereliction of duty.

When he was ushered in to the presence of Mr. Bourgeoise he knew that he did have to blow his own embers. But in essence his life did not depend on going to America. He could still buy a ticket and board the next flight to Paris and get on with life. But it was in his nature to explore new places and see things for himself. When he was told the name of the official he was to see he thought he was going to meet a man who spoke fluent French. Mr. Bourgeoise spoke no word of French. It was just that he came from one of the parishes of Louisiana, a French protectorate America obtained from France in the famous Louisiana purchase. Mr. Bourgeoise held a bachelor in philosophy and a master's in psychology and had been working for the intelligence services for over twenty-five years, and he was just forty-two. Over those years he had risen through the ranks and was always on the move. He was employed by the justice department but attached to the foreign service liaison assigned to the asylum portion of the department. He drew his pecks from the justice department but spent his time attached to the State Department collecting information for the intelligent services.

When the lieutenant walked into his office he did not have a ready opinion about him except that note Ms. Leighann Topsoil had made of him. Usually he would. But not in this case. He could not build a character profile of Mr. Ahulele except the physical presence, a man in his midthirties, with a slight bend in his gait, perhaps of some kind of deformity from birth or something else. He offered him a chair and they exchanged some pleasantries. He had an open mind toward Mr. Ahulele, but nothing in his persona assured him that that was a man made for information gathering and collating. Since Mr. Bourgeoise spoke no other language except his American English he could not test the man in any of the languages he claimed in his verbal résumé that he was master in. So for good measure it was all about why he wanted to emigrate to the United States and also trying to know where his allegiance lies. The lieutenant told him that he had no allegiance to anybody or interest elsewhere except to the freedom of the Biafran people and to the proletariat anywhere he came across, any. Mr. Bourgeoise was concerned about that and asked him if he were a communist. The lieutenant told him that he was not and had no inclination toward that ideology however while that concept was utopian it was admirable in that conceptualization. Mr. Bourgeoise could not make anything out of Mr. Ahulele and excused himself and walked out of the office further back to the office of one of his colleagues for many years, Mr. Bismarck.

Mr. Bismarck was German born but America bred. He spoke German and Russian languages with English to boot. So he had tremendous advantage. He was loud and never said a thing in whispers. Mr. Bourgeoise explained to him why he was in his presence, and he liked what he was hearing. Instead of asking Mr. Bourgeoise to bring in the lieutenant to his office he decided that he would walk with his colleague to his office and see the man in question. When he got to Mr. Bourgeoise's office he decided to engage the lieutenant in Russian. That threw Mr. Bourgeoise off his balance. But there was nothing new in their little discussion. It was just a confirmation that the man could speak with some fluency those languages he claimed proficiency in. They also veered a little bit into German and talked about places they had been to like the Brandenburg Gates with the looming, gleaning gold-topped victory columns of the Siegessaule and then back to Russia where they remembered together its spectacular electrifying architectural showpieces and then as the cradle of the 1917 revolution that in ten days changed the whole world and made the world to live in suspicion of one another. That was a discussion that placed his stake in his American dream in slight jeopardy, but if one had to evaluate his verbal résumé then the story of Saint Petersburg must be a centerpiece of it all. Knowledge of the communists posed no discernible problem, but coziness with it did. However, some people all the time equated knowledge with being one. That usually sent chills to the uninformed. These two gentlemen understood and understood what their calling called for. They left the lieutenant and walked back to Mr. Bismarck's office.

Without any doubt, someone with knowledge-based language skills was in short supply at the intelligence agency, and these gentlemen understood that. They had a brief tête-à-tête and tried to come to a consensus. The lieutenant was young, bright, and articulate. He had the language skills sought after by intelligence agencies all over the world but not only that he knew the terrains. That was what Ms. Topsoil called gilt-edged in stock parlance. But they also recognized that since he had all these knowledge-based language skills he may be difficult to control. He may be an albatross, a wild card, a gadfly, and with the strength of his will according to Ms. Topsoil's note they may be left scratching their heads in the long run. However, both men came to the same conclusion that Mr. Ahulele should be given a chance. He who pays the piper dictates the tune. America always had an antidote to every rubbish, and the lieutenant would be put in his shoes if he became recalcitrant. The hunter could be hunted. They would start him off as an interpreter, which was a good area that needed coverage, and watch his progress. He could never be let loose unless his allegiance had been proven beyond all doubts, reasonable or not, and that he would be working for the national interest of the United States of America. In the end both men concluded that it would be in the best interest of the United States not just to grant him the visa but also to give him a job. They were convinced that the lieutenant would survive anywhere in the world, but now they not only gave him a job, but also, they gave it to him on a platter of gold. They agreed that he would receive O-1 visa reserved for people with capabilities extraordinaire.

But they had also concluded that they would engage him and pick his brain on knowledge of the world around him and his understanding of the United States, and perhaps know a little bit more of him. By talking more, they would come to master him. Surviving an unnecessary war and speaking a plethora of languages did not tell a whole lot about this ex-combatant. When both men got back to Mr. Bourgeoise's office a few minutes later they found the lieutenant pacing in short strides up and down his office, looking at the postings on the walls of the office and a world map on the wall to the left of the office table. They offered their apologies for keeping him waiting that much long for however long it was.

"Mr. Ahulele," began Mr. Bourgeoise, "we know little or nothing about you, but that can wait. Tell us a little bit how much you know of the world. You are a highly traveled man, but being highly traveled does not translate to knowing much about the world."

"It could have been a better world, a world at peace with itself," said Amadike. "But the world is convoluted, almost always in constant state of peaceful conflagration and occasional imbroglio. Man engineered conflagration. The trade in human trafficking created the most indelible mark in the psyche of the African man. That experience surely changed his deoxyribonucleic acid, you know that molecule that carries genetic information about whom we are as a people. That's a fact. You know history is always written by the victor, and for too long that basic, commonsense fact had been swept under the scientific carpet. My question was who swept the carpet? The victor. Those who arrogate to themselves the epithet of the first world and to others third world. Of course, as you know there's no second world. You know, as I do, that our world is bipolar, suffering from some bipolar disorders. Because you white people see the world and everything in it in polar extremities: good or bad, vanquished or victor, freedom or enslavement, wheat or chaff, cows and horses, geese and gander, defeat or victory, bad guy or good guy, exploit it or save it, there is nothing in between.

"Our contemporary suffering is neocolonialism which had its foundation laid in the scramble for Africa. That's a fact. But as you know the first world is in denial. I've seen much of the world, and my understanding is that the world is designed for the survival of the fittest. The big powers have arrogated to themselves masters of the chessboard, and the rest of us become pawns used to prolong the existence of the king on the board. We're the jokers in the pack, and the expendables. We are the skunk, smelly and offensive, yet you will not leave us alone. We're being tugged at both directions. The west pretends to be fighting for the soul of Africa, and the east, the Russians tended to be saying that we are defending the heart of Africa. The world game is the survival of the wiliest, and Africa is at the center of it all. You invest in both sides of warring factions because you do not want to lose out in the sharing of the spoils of war, the spoil that is Biafra, the spoil that is Africa. Does that tell you anything about my understanding of the world in which we live in, Mr. Bourgeoise?" asked Amadike

"Well, I would say, yes, and, no, at the same time because something was missing," said Mr. Bourgeoise.

"What was missing?" asked Amadike.

"You seem to have a soft spot for the communists," jumped in Mr. Bismarck who had been listening attentively.

"And you seem to be blaming the rest of the world for Africa's woes," came in Mr. Bourgeoise.

"Not necessarily. Neither is true. Africa had gotten herself to blame! But the point was that the west and the east, the Russians are in denial of the wounds they have inflicted on the African people with the collaboration of the stooges and satraps they had helped to install in the corridors of power. You know how elephants are mindful of holes, and unicorns are weary of trees, Africa is dreadful of those who purport to lead her because they allowed themselves to be easily conned. But we know where governing power came from. We know who has de jure power, and we know who has de facto powers," said Amadike. For a while, he allowed his French accent be wrapped around those words that their meanings seemed to have been lost on his interviewers.

"We can lambast the Russians from here till next circle of the full moon, Africa's chiefest problems are the twin danger of the French and the British," he added and then proceeded. "And furthermore, I've not said anything to uphold their concept of their world and governance. But you might be right. I have some attraction to the philosophical purview of the ideals of the Bolsheviks," said Amadike.

"For Africa, it is always somebody else's fault. She has always blamed someone else but herself," said Bismarck.

"But, you are not a communist," said Bourgeoise almost simultaneously.

"No, I'm not," said Amadike emphatically. "I'm actually a bloody capitalist. But what I'm not is a bloodthirsty, cudgel-welding capitalist. In fact, I consider myself an egalitarianist. As for Africa blaming you, don't give her the chance to point her supposedly cursed fingers at your direction, lay your hands off her back. Pay for the value of her natural resources you exploit and don't allow her leaders to stash away funds meant for the impoverished people of Africa in your banks and financial institutions. Do this favor for Africa and see what would become of Africa vilely raped by foreigners and denigrated by her benefactors while her sheepish offsprings are bamboozled since time immemorial," said Amadike.

"That's fantasizing, Mr. Ahulele," said Mr. Bourgeoise vainly, "that ain't gonna happen."

"So you must believe in the bourgeois culture of the Bolsheviks," Bismarck accused him.

"To some extent," said Amadike unapologetically, "and I hope that does not make me a communist. And if you thought that I'm fantasizing, well, it is unfortunate. But know that your good life may have warranted the miserable lives of millions of other people whose resources your governments have snatched from the jaws of some common hungry folks. Folk, my people do say that when you are holding a little chap's toy and raise your hand beyond his reach, he would keep pointing at his stuff until you release it to him. Africa will never stop pointing her fingers at your direction until you take your fingers off her monkey business! And the way I see it, you are not ready to relinquish that which you've held up as yours, which your uninformed country men and women naively thought to be theirs, and which we are all in denial," he added. "Does it look like I know a thing about the world, or you still think that I'm a communist?" he asked.

"That's borderline," said Mr. Bourgeoise wearing a wry smile on his face. Though his name is French he never understood its linkage to the Bolsheviks and its place in Russian dictum.

"Having said that…," began Bourgeoise.

"But, do you consider me a communist?" asked Amadike to no one in particular.

"Well, that's yet to be seen or disproved," responded Bismarck.

"Having said that," began Mr. Bourgeoise again, "you're aspiring to go to America. Tell us what you know about America. If you knew the world that much you must know America even much more."

"I've not stepped my foot on American soil…"

"But here you are sitting in is on American soil," said Bismarck, animated.

"I was going to say continental American soil," he said. "I've not been to America before. All I know about America was everything I had read or seen in movies and television. But my conclusion was that they are exceptional people, either by acquisition or by creation. They are wonderful in every measure known to mankind. Pathways and roads were here before they came. It was not they who started to build a road, but they have made building roads easier and building better roads. Guns were here before you became a nation, but you have made building guns better. Slavery and enslavement was here before you became a people, but you have made enslavement an art. In fact, as soon as America entered the slavery market, means of capture and futility in trying to escape the hell that was slavery was that massively improved. Mr. Nobel was not your uncle, and he did not teach you how to make a dynamite. In fact, at a point he abhorred his own invention. But as soon as you deciphered how to make one, you made better ones, that is, deadlier ones. Surely, there are no better dynamites! War had been with mankind since eon. Every generation past had always had a warmonger. Napoleon Bonaparte was one that terrorized much of the world and set Europe on a tailspin. Julius Caesar was another warmonger before him. They served their time and were forgotten in that dustbin of history. So war has always been with us. But as soon as America entered a fray, it becomes better. Oh, there's no better war! It became fiercer. It became a game. It became a fun thing, at the expense of weak and helpless. It became a spectator sport! Bloody sport, indeed." He paused.

"Is that a compliment?" asked Bismarck.

"I don't know. What do you think?" replied Amadike.

"I think it is compliment in notoriety," said Bismarck.

"No, it's compliment, compliment of American exceptionalism," said Amadike, and there was a brief silence in the room as both Bismarck and Bourgeoisie exchanged glances.

"You sound like a peacenik or pacifist, you must be one," accused Bismarck.

"No, I'm not. After all we just came out of a tango," said Amadike.

"So, you believe in wars?" asked Bismarck.

"That's a difficult one to tell," said Amadike,

"How difficulty is that! Your people just come out of a just war," chirped in Bourgeoise.

"That's the crux of the matter," began Amadike. "I don't believe that there's anything like a just war. It's fallacious. There is nothing like a just war."

"What do you mean?" asked Mr. Bismarck.

"The so-called just war was nothing but an instrument by the rich to advance their cause. I would rather you told me that it's necessary than to say that it's just. You know why I said that?" he asked his interviewers rhetorically. "I say that because all necessary wars are just, but not all just wars are necessary. It must be necessary to become just. And then that it's just does not mean that it's necessary. It's necessary to spank a child that is recalcitrant, but it's not just to do so. Just wars are a figment of the imagination of the powerful. When you levy the so-called just war on a country, you levy it on a people," said Amadike.

"How's that?" asked Mr. Bourgeoise, ignorantly.

"That's easy. A country are people, my friends. Anything you do against a country, you did that against a people!"

"Ummmhhh, this guy knows something we do not know," muttered Bismarck, inaudibly.

"What did you just say?" asked Amadike.

"No, don't worry about that," replied Bismarck.

"I can't tell you enough about yourselves," continued Amadike. "But it was they whom it was said of, challenged them to run, and they would gallop with impossible strides. There's no impossibilities in their worldview. An average American can out-spur his stallion. Their outlook in life is a horizon filled with infinite possibilities. An average American views the world with a limitless compass. He knows within himself that he's built to surmount every obstacle from every or all approaches. He doesn't need the compass to find his way. He needs it to see that he has endless possibilities ahead of him. An average American is a perfect example of what the Igbo people called Dike. America is a land littered with lots and lots of Dikes, if I may say" he told his listeners.

"What's that?" asked Bismarck.

"Dike is a steeled, strong man. And my people say that sudden obstacles humble a steeled, strong man, but a steeled, strong man is known for his ability to surmount any obstacles, sudden or not," he told them.

"America is an enigma," continued Amadike, "and always leaves you with that wonderment. You try to understand it, and it slips away from your finger grips. It's like a gadfly. I can't tell you enough about your country. She waves this gospel of freedom for all to see, and when the battle cry of freedom sounds she picks and chooses which freedom call serves her national interest most. But national interest is a miasma. The challenge is containment. Yes, it is all about containment. Containing the effervescence spread of communism. Freedom is a front. Nobody cares about anybody else's freedom. It is all about personal or national interest. American intelligence community worry about something else, but Washington worry about a different animal altogether. But we, freelancing unattached surveillants, unemployed, self-schooled, roving our eyes around the world, see something different in the horizon."

That raised the knuckles of the gentlemen listening to him.

"What's that?" asked Bismarck.

"What's it that worries Washington?" Bourgeoise followed.

"You know those technocrats in Washington have sleepless nights over Kremlin. Until Russia became a democracy it will always be anybody's game, a suspect never to be trusted. And that has gotten everybody in Washington always worried. Since it was never a democracy it was never to be trusted. On the other hand, the intelligence community has her eyes set on a more amorphous entity, other actors on world stage. Some are stateless and faceless. Others are stateless but not faceless. PLO falls into this group, so also Columbian FARC. They are non-state actors but are not faceless. Their modus operandi are understood. But the trouble is always with those faceless actors that strike from nowhere. Battles with those sort of individuals are zero-sum game and never a winnable affair because they never go away. Crush one unit, and other units will sprout forth from nowhere, but, gentlemen, they make our world go round, and America loves these kinds of state of affairs." He paused. "That's much I know about America," he added.

"You seem to have a fairly good knowledge about who we are not," said Bismarck.

"Lest I forgot, I must add, America is a contradiction. And her greatness is encapsulated in her contradictions. It spares no expense to maintain her greatness. Every article in her path becomes an expendable force. She can talk about her benevolence after the fact. It is like shoot now and ask questions later, about whose ox was gored. A good heart after the end has justified the means," said Amadike.

"What's that supposed to mean?" asked Mr. Bismarck.

"I mean a great people, willing to help at no cost to their national interest," parried away Amadike with some sort of pun, trying to ameliorate the offense he may have caused. "These contradictions are ever present. For those who don't want to understand they will never understand. Freedom is granted, yet freedom has become a tool to destroy the fickle. It has become a bone thrown out there for the dogs but used to snare it for a fight with the spirits. Freedom has become a trap for a whole lot of the people. Show me who had ever fought the spirits and lived to tell the story, and I'll show you those who had been destroyed by these other freedoms…"

"Well, sir," cut in Bismarck, "let me correct one misconception, our efforts around the world have been at a great cost. But they have been geared toward world peace."

"The gospel of peace is akin to the gospel of freedom or the gospel of Christianization of the African people or the gospel of the civilization epitomized in the scramble for Africa," said Amadike. "They are camouflage for the rich to advance and protect their own cause. What has a poor man and downtrodden got to do with peace? One of the contradictions of your people is that it balances her book on the back of the poor the rich always try to denigrate. And to achieve that they use semi poor people like you and me as fronts. It smacks of some diabolic intent, I mean the rich. Tell me how can Americans split the atom, overtake the speed of sound and conquer the outer space yet it cannot figure out how to equitably distribute her resources? Tell me a contradiction greater than that!

"Freedom and peace are the world two greatest deceits. They bolster the vantage positions of the powerful and the rich and the advantaged. In America, you use middle class as a feign, a ruse. That is a coinage invented by the plutocrats to make the semi poor to feel good and contented with their conditions while surreptitiously they milk the system dry to their own capricious end unashamedly." He paused.

"And you know what baffles me is that the semi poor guys are contented being used by the few rich folks in their midst. Having become contented with their little power, they seemed to see themselves as having some work to do. They are not afraid of losing their positions. They are just contented with their low places, as long as they have lesser humans in far more lower places. These semi poor don't care about changing anything because at the end of the day they got food to put on the table and they're schooled to believe that they have freedom," he said, gesticulating with forefingers and middle fingers of both hands, making a sign of the bracket.

This was a man on a mission willing to air his opinion with little or nothing to lose. If the Americans decided not to grant him an asylum, he had some other options. He could try and book a fight to Lomé International Airport en route to Charles de Gaulle Airport in Paris at a moment's notice. So he was not bothered a bit. After all they offered him the latitude to express his opinion about their beloved country, and he was prepared to offer it at no charge.

"And oh, lest I forgot," came in Amadike, trying to veer off, "America's place in the world is assured and that would be for a very, very long time. How long it would last, we don't know. In the olden days, we had Pax Romana, and that seemed to have lasted forever. People then thought that it would last forever. Then we had Pax Britannica, and that lasted for a little over a hundred years, and Britain used it to cement her place in the world, conquering, raping, making destitute of people, pillaging, thieving, and causing strife around the world. We're in an era of Pax Americana. Maybe it will last forever. That we do not know. But what we do know is that nothing lasts forever. We shall see. But as we speak, Pax America is knowingly or inadvertently transferring a huge part of her power to the orient, building up the People's Republic for cheap labor that would come back to haunt her. History will need no augurs to decipher the rhyme or reason behind this abdication. Your country will vitiate her own hegemony by herself and her people would be at worst in time to come. Then we may have Pax Chinese that would be the last major Pax and for the longest time. After that, surviving banana republics would be Pax themselves, having acquired their own MAD, you know what I mean. Those banana republics, having earned their own respects, too, would be flexing their own irritant muscles, and there would be tranquility in the land and peace in the world at war with itself. And that's what I mean when I said that we, freelancing surveillants, see something different and huger in the offing." said Amadike

"We shall see," concurred Bismarck.

"It might last longer than others before it. Complacency will not dent it. Americans sleep with one of their eyes open. What will would be hubris and lack of humility thereof. You know, celebration is part of sportsmanship, but when you mock your vanquished, you take away sportsmanship off victory. Americans don't celebrate their victories. They mock their opponents. If America will learn to shoulder their greatness and victory with humility the vanquished will walk away with their heads held high, even in defeat. Is that food for thought?" he asked the duo who seemed to have been enthralled by his pugnacious audacity.

"We shall see," repeated Bismarck, almost absentmindedly.

Amadike had given a good account of himself via his wealth of knowledge. The men interviewing him were hugely impressed with his understanding of the world in which he lived. They were afraid that this man might be a difficult one to debate about some facts with. But who was this man apart from being an ex-combatant, speaking a myriad of languages.

"Now, we would want to hear a little bit of who you are," said Mr. Bourgeoise.

"I don't know how to describe myself, but one thing I'm certain about myself is that I have no time for prevarication." The men listening to him nodded in agreement.

"Some people see it differently and sometimes tell me to my face that I'm self-conceited. But I know that I'm not. It's just that manchmal bin ich eigensinnig zu einem Fehler. Das fasst zusammen, wer ich bin" (sometimes I'm opinionated to a fault. That sums up who I am), he said in German that threw off Mr. Bourgeoise and got Mr. Bismarch nodding his head.

"Is that all you can tell us about yourself? Tell us more," said Bourgeoise.

"You seem to know a lot more about other people and places," added Bismarck.

"Yes, in telling about others I've told a lot about myself. The onus is upon you to decipher, but I think that I've said a lot about myself already. I'm like an average Biafran man. What I'm not is an Isoma man," he added.

"Okay, you can tell us more about the Biafran people," said Bismarck.

"And what's an Isoma man?" asked Bourgeoise.

"Well, I'm not going to say a lot about the Biafran people. You may have to figure it yourselves. But I think that the Americans already know who we're as a people." The two men sitting before him seemed to have fallen in love with his guts in that American ethos of free will and freedom to express one's opinion without fear of retribution for your contrary viewpoints.

"In your own words, you can tell us more," beseeched Bourgeoise. These undercover spy agents realized that if they kept him talking that he was likely going to spill the beans, so they wanted to indulge more even when the one they were prodding was only acting on the confluence of his gut and self-assuredness.

"All I would say is that a Biafran never allowed an opportunity to go to waste. We thought that we're a people designed to conquer the world until we ran into the Jews and the Americans. And in a way, we're like the Jews and the Americans. In a way we are both, fused into one. We like to move around. There aren't a lot of us in the world comparatively, but, we are everywhere on the whole planet earth. It's said that anywhere you go and do not see a Biafran, especially the Igbos of Biafra, you need not think twice, the place was uninhabitable. You needed to pack your bag and baggage and vamoose. But when there's air in a place then we can pitch our tent and make a living off the land, till it to submission."

The conversation had turned into a discussion, and in his game Amadike was unstoppable.

"Gentlemen," he continued, flashing his small eyeballs at his listeners, "we, Biafrans, work not for a pity or for a pittance, but make do with pittances anyway knowing that it adds up to a mound in the long run. We, as a people, do not mind scavenging in the chaff to find some remnant wheat, and make hay out of it to the envy of the chaff owner who had found nothing in it and discarded it. Now, we have caused him some chagrin! Now, we have taken that which we should not have had. We have invited hate upon ourselves. We are marked. We are like the Americans sans their surreptitious, stealthy hegemonic tendencies. Challenge a Biafran to work and prove himself, and he would make light of a supposedly difficult task. We're like the Jews with their Midas touch sans chicaneries. We're ready to make something out of nothing. That's who we are. That's me! Oh, you wanting me to define myself. In me you've found Biafrans."

"Hmmmmmmmmhh," murmured Bismarck.

"Really," said Bourgeoise.

"I'm the Biafran people!" said Amadike.

"You must be Baby Duck," said Bourgeoise.

"No, far be it from me. He was a whippersnapper, impostor like the rest of them little tyrants," he said.

"What's this about whom you are not, the Isoma?" asked Bourgeoise.

"They're my father's mother's people. My father's mother is from the Isoma extraction, not anything different from the other Biafran people, but different anyway. Left to them we would still be in the bondage of the Nigerian people. They live for today and never cared about the exigencies of tomorrow. They like to live," said Amadike.

"And you love to die," chirped in Bismarck lightheartedly.

"No, we love life and we love to live. It's not as if we love to die. But we don't die a second death. If a man came to my house and cut down my he-goat in the prime of his life I'll teach him a lifelong lesson, but my father's mother's kindred people will do nothing about such desecration."

"Perhaps, the intruder is stronger…," began Bismarck.

"No, you must do something, or else he'll go further and litter your household with stinking poo."

"He may be stronger than you are and still did it and be capable of beating the hell out of you," added Bourgeoise.

"No, you know the terrains of your house. You must do something. Throw a bowl of shit into his face. A war that was scheduled does not cripple the weakling, let alone the strong. Save the hardest feces for any eventuality. Arm yourself to the teeth with it. Forget about its inconveniences, your survival may depend on it. You just must fight him with all you have," insisted Amadike.

"Your father's mom's people have wisdom and you don't understand," said Bismarck.

Amadike wanted to accuse his interviewers that what they are almost advocating was characteristic of the American psyche. It was acceptable if it were they who were lying on top meting the unsavory acts. They advocate Confucius but never believed in the principle he espoused. He held his breath. He muttered something inaudible in Portuguese. For the first time since the interview he checkmated what he wanted to say.

"Is it not said that cowards perish numerous times before they were actually dead?" said Amadike.

"At least, you have a chance to live another day," said Bismarck.

"That's if you had a chance and if it was worth it. He who littered your house with poo have other ulterior intentions of destroying your abode. Why postpone the evil day? What difference does it make? Is it not said that he who killed someone five years before his death eliminated numerous years of fearing to die?" said Amadike.

"It looks like suicide, it sounds suicidal," said Bourgeoise.

"Well, I don't think so. The Biafran people did not defend themselves because they thought that they can match the strength of the invading Nigerian army but because they wanted to be left alone. Every generation, every people have a duty to say no before their eyes, not in our time! That point was well made. The Biafran people and especially the Igbo people of Biafra have an indefatigable spirit. A people who can't query or challenge and work to change their deplorable state are not worthy of good tiding and fortune. The Isoma people are of such people."

"You epitomize the spirit of your people," Bismarck finally told him.

And finally he also told him that his request for a visa had been granted and would be forwarded to the State Department for processing. He told the lieutenant that if he wished he would be quartered in asylum and refugee holding area in transit to the United States until his traveling papers processing was completed. The mere contemplation of being told that he could be quartered in a refugee camp in his own country set off a conundrum of rumbling in his stomach. He was never a wanted man. He just could not stomach the reality of the character of the people who had taken the reins of power in his native Biafra. He wanted a breath of fresher air. Nevertheless, he expressed his appreciation and left the outpost.

CHAPTER 16

He quickly got acquainted with his environment in the United States. His training went well without any hitch. He combined his training with minimal work. He was almost ready for the job since he was supposed to interpret materials both written and spoken and there was shortage of manpower. Materials were pouring in fast and furious. He distinguished himself in both. However, he still had limited access as his complete allegiance was yet to be fully ascertained. But one thing stood out: he never stopped raising his hands, he never stopped asking questions. But he had also decided to do something else: cure one of his own maladies, curb his own propensity to dominate his environment as so it had always seemed.

His superiors liked his work and his work ethic. The amount of information he dissected was enormous, and no one was in any doubt how accurate they were. Little by little he was given some free weal. However, he had no doubt that he was being monitored and scrutinized. He took no chances. He had a lot going for him, so he did not want to mess anything up. He schooled himself to believe that the Americans would always present you with a second chance, but he never wanted to be at the mercy of others or live the life of a cat with some spare lives when he had none save the one inhabiting his whole being. They like to cut one some slacks. It was always one slack, and one slack was usually one too many. So one thing he had come to grasp with was taking responsibility for his action. It was the mind-set of everywhere in the western world, and he had seen a lot of the western world to understand. However, America had taken it to a new level. Every act of omission or commission must be traced to some desk. So the buck stops at somebody's or someone else's desk. Woe betide you if through you the stone was left unturned. It was a precarious situation which he had accepted with some uncommon equanimity. It was that calmness that set him apart and at a point of conflict with those who never understood that he just wanted to be left alone.

He was cordial to all but to no one in particular. Six months into the beat, he was still enjoying himself. He liked what he was doing for a living. It had no analytic hinge. It was basically interpretational information flow from troubled spots to untroubled spots around the globe, requiring his language equipment in his own armory of knowledge. His work was always based on facts in the material he had before him, so it was fact-based narrative. While he always liked to question things, on his post he made no analytic conclusions. It was the fact he provided in his interpretation that formed the basis of underlying fact. After the daily beat, he would retire to his apartment and watched for the daily flow of news, most of the time repetitive to thrusts of not worthy to be news, concentrated very much on the North America hemisphere with total disregard of Africa and her troubles. Africa never existed except as a footnote of world events, and anything news that came from Africa was anchored on its troubles and unending problems. Nothing was ever said about her golden eggs hatched for others to enjoy while her children were mired in unending needs. The Dark Continent. Alas! But, where every world powers, including minnows had seen the light to conquer, exploit, and pillage. The African universe was a game turf where everything everybody else got was by cheating and defrauding, yet nobody owning up to anything amiss but telling her children to wise up. It was a complete assault upon many a sane mind. But, the generality of the people watched, listened and imbibed. It became boring in itself and offensive to what really would constitute newsworthy in a normal world. Then he would help himself with some books, and eventually became an avid reader. He had ample time on his hands and decided that it would do him some good if he would invest the time in further studies. The one major language he did not have in his repertoire was the most populous language in the whole world: Mandarin, spoken in China and parts of Far East.

It was at the University of Washington and there he ran into Evangel. Evangel was a lady of immense beauty, not beautiful in that flimsy way. There was something about her that made whatever she lacked facially inconsequential. So what she lacked facially she made up with some intrinsic qualities by her comportment and grace. Alluring, beckoning, there was not much about her beauty but she had something inexplicable that made men to turn for a second look. The first time he encountered her he was forced to take a third look even though that first glance captured all that was in Evangel. Hardwood, who never took an interest in any lady, paid attention. His interest in any girl was those childhood flirtations growing up in the rugged terrain of Marseille. And those forays he made into maintaining relationships were in his adolescent and his twentysomething years. And then occasional love incursions later on. Now a grown man and unattached, he had no inhibition. And shortly she, too, was quite interested, and they hit the road running. She was white as any white person could be, but actually she was black. That was a fact he never knew until later. But when he discovered, that pleased him a lot. But she was never happy about her complexion. She was never trusted by her black folks who thought her uppish. And to her white acquaintance or neighbors who had attitude about her that she thought she was white. Now she had a complex. Neither here nor there. She was the bat, a flying mammal, but, neither a bird nor a beast. In a lot of ways nudging her on toward inferiority. Because Mr. Hardwood never trusted anyone he was not accustomed to, he held her at arm's length, in spite of the fact that everything about her pleased him. That disposition toward her compounded her understanding of people around her and especially those who should have known better. Mr. Hardwood had nothing to do with her state of affair. He did not even know the battle she was waging silently inside herself, pleading with forces beyond her control to understand and accept who she was, her state none of her own making. Mr. Hardwood not knowing what she was going through stuck to his gun. Distrust had been his guiding principle not because it was Evangel. Perhaps that unwillingness to trust had helped him a lot. She had visited on a couple of occasions, but that night she decided that she was going to pass the night at his place.

That night was an eye-opener for both of them. Because there were a lot of ground to cover they stayed late into the night. The nagging question for Evangel was what drove Mr. Hardwood to so much immerse himself in many languages, and still wanting more. This was a man who liked to volunteer an opinion. However, on this issue he had no cogent opinion. He could have told her that it was circumstantial, but he did not. Eventually it was time to retire, and Evangel was ready for deep sleep before Mr. Hardwood could gulp the dregs of the red California wine they had relaxed with to wind down the hours before going to bed. He did not have any reason to distrust this lady, but by instinct and intuition he was almost wide awake. Each time Evangel would turn in her sleep she would notice that her partner was either awake or half asleep. It was like he was nocturnal. However, he was never found wanting on his job or in his class.

When morning came Mr. Hardwood took his shower earlier. While in the shower he kept the door to his room open and the door to the shower ajar. It was a one-bedroom apartment. The way he set up his abode he could virtually see anything happening inside his bedroom from the shower. While in the showers Evangel thought she had played a fast one on his host and rummaged one of the drawers and removed what appeared to be some money and tucked it inside her purse. It was botched. Hardwood stayed calm. And as soon as she was in the shower and drew the curtain Hardwood did not allow a minute to elapse before he extracted the exact figure she had taken from his locker. He made sure he left enough for her taxi. When she came and dressed to leave she never bothered to check to make sure everything was as she had executed her plan. If she was a setup, Hardwood told himself, the plan failed woefully. He went about his business. If that was a faux pas it never affected their relationship. He knew that he had a testy job. One could be tried in a number of ways. In the intriguing, and unconventional ways of doing business at the agency, a mouse could be set to scamper in one's way to see if one had the natural instinct to jump, scared. Evangel was never a vagrant or anything less than a sterling character. Unbeknownst to him she worked for the agency, but was sent as a stratagem, and as a continuous check on his dedication to duty and attention to details. Sometimes one would be evaluated for such innocuous things that ordinary folks would consider trivial. Attention to details was paramount to the agency. It was like aeronautical setting or physics where a misplacement of a decimal point could spell catastrophe for any operation.

When he joined the agency and after the initial training he was sent to wait for a certain gentleman in a nondescript building. He took his position on the second floor of the building as was the directive. And waited. The instruction was to pay attention and wait for a young man in a business suit. After crossing the entrance door, this young man was to slip and drop some stuff. Hardwood went as was the instruction and waited, eagle-eyed. For a long time, he waited, almost without blinking. For long no one showed up, and he was thinking that perhaps the gentleman would not show up. At last a young man showed up, and passing through the door he slipped and dropped a pen and a notebook. Following him was another young man in business suit as well who slipped and had all the pieces of paper he had in his folder flying everywhere. They both bent down, and the first guy was helping the second because his stuff were strewn all over the place. The way he was flailing he must have stepped onto some liquid. As they labored Hardwood watched from the balcony of the second floor. He could decipher without telling who among these men had pretentious mishap. The gentlemen went different ways but still came to the entrance of the same elevator on the ground floor. When the door of the elevator was yanked open on the second floor the man who had his stuff scattered all over the place paused and turned right and began walking away without hesitation. The other guy with the pen and notebook stepped out and glanced at his right first and left second. He vacillated. He appeared not to know where he was going. Actually, he was not told whom to expect, but right behind him was Hardwood who accosted him.

"You are Gonzalo," Mr. Hardwood put it to the young man. Mouth agape, the man affirmed. Gonzalo was a new recruit to the agency. He had no inkling about the daily surprises and the unsimplified ways that the system worked or that his job entailed.

"You're looking for Mr. Hardwood?" queried Hardwood. The young man still had a surprised look on his face. He knew that he was going to meet some gentleman but not a black man who had his face covered with beard. His tiny eyes were buried in their sockets, and the sockets seemed to have been lost in the temple. His nose was not large as one would expect of black people with their African curves. His mouth was small, perhaps appearing small having been diminished by imposition of his huge beard. Gonzalo could not tell how the man's chin was having been buried under the facial hairs. And from the look of the whole contour of his face he must have some broad cheeks. The hair on his head was full and thick and well manicured. He had no baldness as far as Gonzalo could see looking at him face-to-face. But there was some style his hair was combed that Gonzalo, being much taller, could tell that the man had started to have a chunk of his hair receding at the center of his head toward the back. He was of an average height, and Gonzalo was perhaps a foot taller.

"Yes," said Gonzalo inaudibly, nodding at the same time, still wearing that quizzical look on his face.

"I'm he!" said Hardwood as he began to march away toward a nondescript room where Gonzalo was being expected.

CHAPTER 17

Three years later, Hardwood had begun to master beyond the monotony of interpretation. Before he came on board this agency had existed, so without him it would still be. That was basic Washington paradigm. With trainings, he had felt good that he could do well with information gathering in the field. He had what many of his colleagues did not and would not be able to acquire. He was a good fit for a whole lot of places. When the opportunity came and someone was needed to be in Brazil he was a good fit: he spoke Portuguese. But not only that he spoke the language but also he had earned the trust of his employers. The veil of suspicion or uncertainty over his allegiance had been dispelled. He was now a full-fledged member of the intelligence community. There was not much going on in Brazil. There was not that much need for many ears in the country. It was stable. There was no upheaval or insurgency or rebel group of note. While he was able to mix with the locals, he was not extracting as much of hard, useful information as would justify his placement in the country. So after less than a year in that country he asked his superiors to find him a new territory to occupy. The request to be withdrawn was granted, and he returned to Washington.

That time the FARC rebels were making some progress in the agitation against the government of Colombia in Bogota. They were brutal in their approach and desperate in their menace. Not many operatives would willingly volunteer to go to Columbia let alone near the outskirts of the jungle where the rebels held court. This time also Hardwood was a good fit: he spoke Spanish. His employers knew his worldviews. When not many were eager to go, it was Hardwood who raised his hand and said, "Send me." It was not a decision he made lightly, and his bosses did not view his offer to go lightly. But they had felt good with him to send him to such ground anyway. He was never a communist apologist. He never believed in their ideology. However, he was at home with their sentiment toward the proletariat representations and that ultimate need for a bourgeois society.

"You've volunteered to go to Colombia," reiterated Mr. Bourgeoisie who had summoned Hardwood to his office, and he was one of the two men that interviewed him in Biafra.

"Send me!" repeated Hardwood, emphatically.

"I can send you. Sending you is not a problem here. The snag was that we have an identification problem here. The work we do of which you're conversant is by no means a mean thing. When we send someone out on a mission, the person becomes our daily concern. Colombia is unlike any other place you have ever been. The FARC rebels are very vicious, and the drug warlords are even worse. So we do everything we can to place our agents undercover." He paused. Hardwood was hanging on to every word he was making effort to mutter.

"What I'm trying to say is that if you had to go you have to get rid of your beard. It's a good marker. A huge identifier. We don't want you to stand out in the crowd," said Bourgeoise.

"Is that what you are mincing words to tell me, trying to chop off your tongue?" asked Hardwood without appearing brash. Mr. Hardwood's facial hairs grew so rapidly, if he had to keep a clean shave he must be prepared to shave two times every day. It had slowed him down. He had decided that for him to lead a near normal life he had to keep his beard sometimes bushy.

"I was saying that because everywhere outside the United States is considered an enemy territory. We don't want you to be an easily recognizable target, easily picked out in a crowd. If we ever had an event, say, missing in action, say, kidnapped by the rebels, we don't want to be looking for a guy who looks like a mullah or some sheikh. No, we want to be looking for a clean-shaved man. But you know what, if there were to be a mishap and you were taken, we now know what you would look like if you were not given the opportunity to shave off your beard. Of course, remember you may not get a chance," said Bourgeoise.

"Still send me! Just tell me when to be ready, and I will shave off this goddamn beard," said Hardwood.

"And you can keep it whenever you made it back to the homeland," reminded Bourgeoise.

When he got to Columbia, he was no different from the local folks. He was black, and Colombia had a great many black people in the population. He was one of them. He immersed himself in the culture and their ways of life. He spoke their language so fluently, so he needed to catch up with their idiosyncrasies and mannerisms. He blended so well that they thought he was a native. He spoke no English, nor Portuguese, nor German, nor Russian, nor French, nor his native Igbo language. He was Spanish in manners and language, and with that he was able to obtain information from the local folks that when he relayed them to his bosses in Washington they valued his input so much that he was dubbed the Colombian. It was an appellation that accompanied him everywhere he went in the hemisphere among field officers that even in Argentina he was known by locals as the Colombian who lived among them. As at the time he met Bucknor everyone knew him as such unbeknownst to Bucknor. Hardly did anyone know him as Jorge Santana. All the time he met with Bucknor, he avoided meeting local folks in his company. The last thing he wanted to be known with was an American especially in the terrain he had chosen to be his habitat. And never in anyone's imagination was he linked to be a thoroughbred African man let alone an Igbo man. He was that shrewd and stealthy, a good fit for the job.

CHAPTER 18

The first summer classes were already underway. Bucknor was supposed to have begun his classes in spring. But the impediment that was his last name did not allow him to make it to the United States and enroll in classes on time. So he was expected. However, when he did not show up the authorities did not go out and about looking for him. The school was teeming with students every segment of the school year that the absence of one student was like a drop in the ocean. Bucknor knew that he was running late so he had already shifted his gaze to the next semester. So that morning when he sauntered into the admission office to present himself for enrollment or clarify where things stood for him he knew he still had a place because his friends had told him so. Ms. Shelby, who was supposed to be behind the desk, was inside rummaging through rows and columns of files and folders looking for other names unconnected to a Bucknor Obikolo. Bucknor waited for a while, and sooner Ms. Shelby was back at her desk.

"Yes, sir, how can I help you?" she asked, staring him in the face.

"I'm here to check on my admission," stuttered Bucknor.

"Which admission? And I'm sorry, my name is Ms. Shelby, Mrs. Shelby Chancellor," said the admission officer, and extending her hand of welcome for a handshake.

"I was offered admission to study banking and finance here," said Bucknor.

"And what's your name?" asked Ms. Shelby.

"Oh, my name's Bucknor Obikolo."

"Bucknor Obikolo! That name does not ring a bell, Mr. Obikolo, but if you give me a minute, I'll check for you," offered the admission officer.

She gave Bucknor a clipboard with a piece of paper and pen attached and told him to fill it out. It took Bucknor some time to complete the filling, and in the interval Mrs. Chancellor attended to the next guy. When he came forward with the paper he had filled the admission officer was ready to assist him further. And she went back to the rows and columns of folders and once again rummaged and was able to locate Obikolo's file lost in the echelon of columns and rows.

"Mr. Obikolo," began Mrs. Chancellor, "your admission was slated to have started last spring semester and now we are right into summer classes. I don't know if you wanted to join the summer classes. Since you just arrived from Africa I don't think you're in the frame of mind to jump in now. I'm just saying."

Bucknor did not say anything.

"But I can't just say," she continued, "but whether you would start now or during fall semester is something you've got to decide in collaboration with your course advisor. I'll be sending you over to the building, Colonel J. J. Ward building, third floor, room 355. There they will explain to you what you have to do moving forward."

"Thank you, Mrs. Chancellor," said Bucknor.

"You're welcome to Accord, honey. Welcome to Providence. I hope you'll have a wonderful experience." Bucknor did not hear all she said. Nevertheless, he understood what the instruction was. While he heard the word "honey" he did not understand the import of it. He was happy. All he wanted to know was to get to his destination. Everything else was unimportant including bees and honey.

At room 355 he met one Ms. Brown, one of the course counselors who explained to Bucknor that his admission had been deferred to the fall semester on account that he did not show up in spring. She empathized with Bucknor for his inability to make it earlier and join the spring classes. That being the case it was no problem for him moving forward. He could still join the second summer classes, but in her estimation, it might be too tedious to start life in an American institution on a fast track since summer classes were designed to be quick and intensive. Bucknor acquiesced, yielding to the counselor whatever she felt was good for him, having just arrived America. Having paid for the evaluation of his certificate earlier which was part of the application process he was set to pick his courses. Banking and finance was his stated course of study. The counselor helped him with figuring out those courses he needed taking for a freshman at Accord University. Bucknor had no objection to the advice of the counselor. He was set. Having done that the counselor pointed out to him the direction to where he was supposed to go and make payment to complete the enrollment process.

CHAPTER 19

"Culex," cajoled Atinga.

Turnkey raised his fist in the air to acknowledge the accolade of his teammate as he headed to their opponent's goal inadvertently almost aimlessly, running in a virtual linear line rather clumsily but full of energy and determination.

"Culex," hollered Atinga again, trying to draw his teammate's attention to look up and pass the ball to another of his teammates. It was frustrating.

Turnkey did not understand the concept of soccer. It was a team sport. It had artistry in its genre. It had depth. It involved ducking and feigning, evading and meandering, dodging and mesmerizing, every bit of these and more. One must possess guile and deft. Ultimately it was about making goals. But it was not about making goals only. It was both physical, and at the same time, it involved some mental investment in cunning, stamina, and art. But, above all, judgment, seasonable judgment! Turnkey did not understand all those. What he understood was goals, goals, and goals. He wanted to win. Winning was counted in goals. That was what mattered, and each time he got hold of the ball it was a race to the goal line, leaving opponents and teammates in the dust. Because he was not schooled in what it would take to win, most of the time he got the ball kicked too far ahead of himself that he lost control of it that his opponents would take it away from him, defeating his individual effort to mount a winning onslaught and to the annoyance of his friends. But Turnkey would not stop.

"Culex," drawled Atinga, as he kept running on the opposite side of the small pitch and making a nonsense all effort of his teammate to attract his attention.

Atinga was such just a cute boy, just nine years old. Uncultured and innocent. He came to the United States just before the war and knew no bounds. He was white. Actually, whiter than white. He was Biafran and black. But he was so white he was called the white Biafran boy by his black and white American peers and others in his neighborhood where his parents pitched their tent. He was not mistaken to be called the white Biafran boy. He was recognized white in his homeland in Biafra that he was nicknamed bekee, meaning a white person. When he came to America, no one could tell the difference. And he carried on. And no one could explain how he came out so white. His mother, though light skinned, was black. So also his father, not so light skinned as the wife, but a whole lot lighter than many of his kinsfolk. Perhaps a combination of their complexions yielded such a deviation, it was hard to believe that he was really black. Atinga was a different breed. His eyes were different to the point that his pupils had a tinge of blue about them that it was said that he had cowrie eyes, which translated to mean that he was white right into the eyes. People made fun of his eyes while growing up. He was the butt of his own family as well. The fun made of him by family and peers was not out of jealousy. He was different. No one envied him. But his complexion had served him well in his newfound land. His hairs were thinly curly and kinky but kind of sparsely populated. It was short and seemed not to ever grow beyond a certain level and inches.

Atinga had four brothers and four sisters. Two of his sisters were light skinned like their mother, and the rest were nothing near them in terms of complexion. In fact, one of his brothers was as dark as a kettle, and another was as light as a pot. But he fitted into the American landscape of his neighborhood. He was courted by his peers. One thing stood him in good stead. He was a soccer lord. He was mesmerizing with the ball on his feet. Without the ball, he was a danger to unnerve his opponent because he seemed to have the agility to dispossess his opponent with guile and pace for his age. His mates wanted him to be in their teams. He obliged. He had no preference. He made no fuss. He was just willing to play.

Atinga learned to play with guys twice his age in his homeland. He was always the odd man out. He was just a boy. He usually made up the numbers when young men were fewer. When boys way beyond his age group played and they were short of one player, Atinga had always been used to make up the sides, fill the void, ahead of his peers. Afforded that opportunity again and again he had coped magnificently. He had improved himself. He had translated that to good use when he played with his peers. To a great extent he loved being the one holding on to the ball, finding spaces and distributing passes to his teammates more efficiently, single-handedly always rescuing his sides from defeat, and in some other instances helping to ameliorate the whopping failures or utter walloping. He had distinguished himself. In this newfound land he had been challenged to the detriment of the will to win. Turnkey had usurped that responsibility, single-handedly driving his teams to defeats. It was in that frustration that Atinga called to mind the name his elder brothers used to label one of their teammates back in his homeland: Culex.

The irony of the whole show was, besides their skin and facial differences, they seemed to share a few things in common. Both were gangling lanky little boys. One would think that they would grow up taller than all their kinsfolk. Both were built to look innocent like a lamb, seeming not to know their left from their right unless they were schooled to know. Atinga never understood what Culex meant even as he repeatedly heard his brothers indulged in its usage. He never bothered to know. But he eventually knew.

He had innocently dared. One day he had dared to call this friend of his brothers Culex, and without warning, Lance, the friend of his brothers, had grabbed him by the scruff of the neck, held him under his left armpit, and powerfully squeezed the knuckle of his right middle finger into his forehead. Lance had held on and squeezed harder, and Atinga had writhed in pain and hollered for help. When Lance eventually let go his forehead was dented, and soon afterward it was bulging at the seams. It was an unforgettable lesson.

Turnkey did not care a hoot. He just wanted to play. In those days, initially Lance did not understand what Culex meant as again and again he would raise a fist in the air to acknowledge the appellation until it dawned upon him. Him, Culex genius? The dangerous, sharp, spear-mouthed, bloodthirsty, spear-headed mosquito? It was a rude awakening that he had saluted when he was disparaged. He took offense. But it was too late. The name stuck with him. He tried to fight his way out of it, but it would not go away, even up till today. He took it on the chin.

"What's that that little African boy hollering at you?" asked Cochran of Turnkey.

"Who?" asked Turnkey.

"That weird boy," said Cochran.

"You mean the white Biafran boy," said Turnkey.

"I mean the weird, funny boy."

"You mean the white African boy, Atinga," repeated Turnkey a variation.

"I mean that weird little boy that has a funny-looking skin."

"I don't know. What is it?" Turnkey demanded of his uncle.

"You need to know. You need to listen. I don't think it's of any good," he told Turnkey. "And I don't think that he's white, either."

"He's white," said Turnkey matter-of-factly.

"Well, I don't think he is. You need to know your kind. You need to grow up."

"What do you mean? He's white," said Turnkey again.

"I'm saying that you need to understand. That someone has a complexion like yours doesn't make the person white. Whiteness is in the blood, and you should be able to tell that even from afar." Cochran proceeded to school him. On and on, he harangued him on the need to keep it straight, to be cognizant of who he was and what stock he was crusted from. As they trudged home it was unending, and little Turnkey was lost in that cesspool of wonderment of who he was and who he ought not to think he ought to be.

Cochran was a rabble-rouser, a separatist. Ever since Turnkey's father's long-distance truck driving job Cochran had moved in to fill the void. He had taken it as a challenge to nurture and coach him. At doing good and unbeknownst to him at doing bad. He had taken him to a different thoroughfare, a wayfarer path. Coolly but assuredly he had started to wean him toward his own disjointed weal. He had taken him to the tip of the layabout and the hill of the vagabond. He had given him a bear hug and urged him to aim at his target without blinking and the viewfinder with a squint in one eye and an unmistakable clear vision in the other. He had taken him to the shooting range and shown him all sort of guns. He had shown him how to handle guns. He had taught him to aim intently in the middle of a deep breath and holding that breath to shoot very measuredly. He had urged him to measure with dexterity and with the accuracy to hit the anus of squirrel on the prowl. He had urged him to never put his sword in ordinary plowshares or sheath his dagger. With the world under his feet he could do no wrong! And young Turnkey had taken all to heart. And at his seventh birthday he had presented him with a real gun as a present. Turnkey did not much cherish it. He never understood. However, his uncle had told him that it was his to keep and should master how to use it. He had told him that he may need it. He was just nine when his life began to turn the corners.

Like all kids, life was normal. The presence of Atinga was normal as he was as white as white. He had played with black kids and fellow white kids. Actually, growing up he knew no colors. He was like his father, open-minded without any inhibition. Then his father zapped, working long hours and many days without knowing home. And that door became ajar and then open. And as his uncle worked on him he found a new vista opened up before him.

The next day when they gathered at the playground he had an ear to the ground. His mind was geared toward a war. He spoiled for a fight. His uncle had planted in him the notion that his friend was no longer white, and it ate deep into his subconsciousness. He could not resist it. He could hardly. There was something about him he believed that made him top-notch. He had accepted the white African boy as one of his kind. And now he was not sure what to make out of the world around him. He was torn between what he knew and what he was being schooled to understand.

As the boys gathered that early evening hours for their game Turnkey did not change his approach to team sport. His purpose was clear: get the team some goals and his name on the scoreboard. What

241

he changed was that he paid attention to the hollering directed toward him. And it was not long in coming. No sooner had he headed to the far reaches of the playground than Atinga began his refrain: C-U-L-E-X. Turnkey heard him well enough and ambled his pace surreptitiously toward him. Atinga, sensing he was drawing nigh him, darted away. When it became obvious to him that Turnkey was coming after him, he galloped. As Turnkey increased his efforts to lay his hand on him, he knew that like a machine he needed to put his engine onto the next torque. And he was gone! No one could match his gangling pace. He was like turbo charged, in spite of himself. No one could catch him on his day especially if he was already a foot ahead of his assailant.

Turnkey was the third child of deJohn who was married to Splendor. Before Turnkey, deJohn and Splendor had another child christened Candie, and Candie had a sibling sister christened Mermaid. They were one happy family. But the trouble with deJohn was multifaceted. He was a man of many innocuous vices that later on became debilitating. A chain-smoker of the first degree. In the life of most men who smoke, the other twin ill that was always roaring its ugly head with it was the love of drink. But he seldom did. His other most enduring ill was the hunger for work. He was a work addict. Though he loved his family but he was so immersed in work of every hue that he seemed to have paid little attention to his wife and children. He could go out days on end without wife and children that it ate deep into the fabric of his family. All he earned he brought home. He was frugal to a fault. In spite of that his family never lacked to the best of his knowledge. And of course, his ability was not lacking. He trailed the smell of any kind of job. Since he had very little formal education he was after all kinds of jobs wherever it had tracked. He was an artisan, a bricklayer as much as plumber, a roofer as much as a carpenter, a construction worker as much as a macadam. Any work that required little or no skills he had a knack for it.

deJohn was a very shrewd man. Growing up he understood the vagaries of life. His grandfather was a living wretch. And without much saving for retirement he labored into his eighties still a pauper. deJohn did not want to go through that kind of ending. He lived not wanting history to repeat itself before his very eyes. To guard against that ending, if he had to attain old age as his grandfather he did not want to stretch his saving beyond breaking point. He had devised a means to put away what he considered that portion of his earnings which he considered to be his. Against all odds, against all circumstances, that portion of his earning had become untouchable, almost sacrosanct. If his family needed more he applied himself to more labor. And before Turnkey joined the family he had learned to drive 18-wheelers. One guy he ran into one day had told him that he could make a more decent living driving around the country and even up to Mexico and Canada than dragging his whole body system into overdrive. He had listened and acquired a license. That in itself had become a license that drove him further away from home.

No arguing the obvious, he loved his wife. But Splendor could not bring herself to understand or accept that. How can a man who so loved his wife and child so much as he loved to labor, perhaps more. Not understanding that their love life began to drift. Provisions for one's family was not all that was to life. How about sitting down on a couch and discuss family business and watch the kids add inches and weight to their bodies? How about the touches? How about the caresses? How about the kisses? How about the smell of his breath? How about the real thing? Starved of love one fateful evening she gathered their child and a few belongings and called it a day. When deJohn made it home after a couple of weeks, he found his abode deserted and the air desolate. She had left with all her valuables, chief among them their little girl, Candie. She did not want to deprive him the knowledge of the whereabouts of his child. On one side of the wall of their rented apartment she had left behind an address about ten miles away where she had decided to pitch her tent.

There was something about deJohn that was intriguing to the common eye. No one could tell exactly how he acquired his sense of work that could tear his young family apart. He was fixated on saving for retirement to the detriment of his family. Foolish intelligence, indeed, but he cared less. As much as he was able to provide for his family he cared less about his presence before them or anything else. But on this day, he was desolate. What could he do to bring back his family? There were no good choices. Something had to give in! It was his wife who made the decision to vacate their home. He hated being idle. He hated beggars. He hated loafers. He hated layabouts. He was a man highly conflicted, perhaps suffering from an undiagnosed ailment. If not how could a man love to labor that he seemed to love his family less.

Splendor was never an awful woman. It was just that she could take it no more. She was hardworking in her own right. One job was enough. Supplemented by the income of her husband, it was good enough. Saving for retirement was never in her orbit of thought. She cared less for tomorrow and far more for today. For her, it was one day at a time. It was not as if the signs from her husband were not there from the onset. It was just that she did not see it as something that would snowball one day to hedge her whole self into the corner of the Lilliputian dungeon. Then during their courtship years, she had noticed that her husband was such a restless man, he could hardly sit still. But because he was a jack in bed it covered all her other fears. Having gotten married, she began to discover that things could at all times not be at ease. For deJohn, with the arrival of their child it heaped extra responsibility on him. He did not want to falter taking care of his family, so he applied himself to more work wherever he could find one. And driven by the constant nagging notion that he must save for retirement at all cost he drifted to the periphery of almost neglecting the utmost needs of his wife, Splendor: romance.

Splendor loved to make love. Whenever she came back from work, she was ready. She usually dusted herself and as always, always ready for her man. If lovemaking was food she never had enough. It was the tonic of her life, the tune-up of her whole being. Perhaps, now, her own vice. It seemed to have bordered on some kind of mental disorder of her own. While her husband played the journeyman, she sobered to have him back. Even though the demon in her was always wanting some more, she never sought courtiers outside the four walls of her home. But as soon as she decided to leave home she decided to run haywire and find that missing link, that hole to be plugged, and that void to be filled.

Though he loved his wife, but he was more afraid of losing Candie than he was afraid of losing his wife. He made peace. He began to allot more quality time to his family, which meant less travel and less work, less money and less saving. In those impassioned moments, both to assuage her and make up lost grounds, Turnkey was in the offing. However, an 18-wheeler long-distance driving was a lonely calling, with a wandering yet an idle mind, and an idle mind was the devil's workshop. That job made him truly a free bird. Before the coming of Turnkey began to brew, out there in the sizzling sphere and freewheeling of New York, he had a tango and an issue was germinating in the womb of another woman of loose calling. A testament of his errant escapades was coming.

Vanderhoof begot deJohn who begot Turnkey. Vanderhoof had an ironclad will. He believed in the pedigree of his kindred folks. He was a separatist who saw life and brotherhood and neighborliness running in parallel lines. What he failed to understand was that time was a moving compass. It waited for no one. One had to tag on and cling to it, or one was bound to be left in its dust. In his frame of mind he tried to raise his children to toe the line. But for some reasons all his kids turned out to be the antithesis of everything he held dear. But he was adamant. He was constant. He was hewed from the stock of those who could be said to be capable of leading a one-man riot gang. He did not see it coming. Or he was playing the ostrich that had its head buried in the sand. Things had begun to turn rapidly like a rolling stone that gathered no moss. Trying to stand in the way of an enormous change could leave the obstinate swept in its wake. Vanderhoof seemed very much immutable, unalloyed, and unbending.

Vanderhoof liked to mess with guns. He liked guns. He loved to have his children love guns. All his children had guns presented to them at age seven as souvenir. It was their inalienable right to own it and to learn to use it. He lived by example and had fun using his guns. Since he was a man that did not understand boundaries nor draw his own line of boundary in the sand to help him navigate the labyrinths of life, he went wayward and rascal. Such was his frame of mind and understanding of the changing tides of time that he did not understand well enough. It was in the early 1950s, before the behest of the civil rights marches and agitation for equal rights and justice, in the woods of central Indiana town of Boonville, this man, bent over and crutched and willfully shot and killed a colored young man. There was no repercussion. There was no intention to disguise his motive. It was cold-blooded. Without thought to what he had just done he began to walk away, thinking that not even the bashful eyes of the heaven saw him and his heinous deed. Especially as the area was heavily wooded, covered with trees that very large logs could be made out of. It was an era that left all colored people at perils of some sort. They could disappear without a trace. And some misguided folks killed with impunity, getting away with murders. It was broad daylight. Though he was shielded from the heavens by the thick forest, but he was highly, highly mistaken. Unknown to him, a block away was his elder brother, Vander Sar. At the sound of the gun, Vander Sar had moved away from the sound of the gunshot but still kept an eye to see if he could see who shot the gun and for his own safety to be aware. In the immediacy, his brother just emerged from the place where the gun rang out. He right there knew that his own blood brother had done something heinous because he heard the aching sound of man, then a whimper, and then silence. He himself had seen that colored man on his way into the woods. He did not confront him there and then because he knew that his brother was volatile. But it was obvious that his brother had taken someone else's life in cold blood.

That sole episode struck a dent in his whole being. He labored with the knowledge of what he knew and his inability to tell on his brother. Though it was most likelihood that if the authorities had known he would face no difficult time trying to prove his innocence. But! Was it not the blood a colored person that was gored to rejuvenate the life of a country in perpetual denial and endlessly salivating for more blood? Yet Vander Sar labored to tell and labored to free himself from being complicit in murder. His own brother could be put away for a long time. That was the worst he could face. How he had wished that they would really throw him in gaol and have the keys thrown away. He had to bring himself to bear witness against his own brother. It ate into him, and it haunted him for a very long, long time, and for a very long, long time he was beside himself with rage. It incapacitated him. But in actual sense he incapacitated himself.

Actually, Vanderhoof and Vander Sar never saw eye to eye, and after this incident their loathsomeness for each other reached the high heavens. They shared a few things in common, chief among them, they were gun enthusiasts. They were raised to game. From a very young age their father thought them how to dismantle guns and put them back together. That seemed to be where their commonality petered out. Where Vander Sar was deliberative, Vanderhoof was spontaneous. Where Vander Sar was quiet to a fault, Vanderhoof was loud as a cymbal. Where Vander Sar was cautious, Vanderhoof was brash. Where Vander Sar was audacious, Vanderhoof was daredevil. Where Vander Sar was careful, Vanderhoof was evidently careless. Where Vander Sar was very lucky, Vanderhoof seemed to have an attraction to bad omen. On this day, no one could vividly say he saw him snap at this man, even though he did kill this man in cold blood. It all portended all ills that trailed his life as a young man. Vander Sar knew that for one thing, his brother was a careless man. That summed up the totality of this man's image.

A few years back, Vander Sar had started a business with money he borrowed from the bank. It was a little over ninety thousand dollars. After a few years that money had grown into a multimillion chain. However, Vanderhoof had complained loudly about the extraordinary rapid rise to wealth of his brother. He had complained and bandied about openly and loudly that any system that made a man so stinkingly wealthy within a space of a few years in multimillions, that that system was rigged against the poor. That that system needed to be overhauled. He had stated that such rise to wealth could only come out of corruption or willful exploitation of the masses of the people. Vander Sar had taken such comments and views as a deliberate act to impugn his name and diminish hard work. As his wealth grew his influence grew in bounds. He began to have access to the corridors of power. Making huge and small contribution to party men of both parties. And when he could no longer take the haranguing of his brother, he had threatened him with exposure of his shooting an unarmed colored man in the wood without provocation. When it was obvious that he was about to be given up, one morning Vanderhoof gathered his belongings, wife, and children and left town, three hundred and something miles from the town of his birth to the north central Missouri town of Boonville. Traveling with him were his wife and their three minor children, Vanderholt, Over Mers, and Van Dirk. As soon as he was gone, his brother had peace, innermost peace, while his business continued to flourish now into a juggernaut. Two years after they left town, Vanderhoof had another son, and he named him deJohn.

deJohn grew up different. He asked very few questions. He minded his own business. He had a mind of his own. He paid attention to every detail and seemed to acquiesce to every counsel only to do whatever he wanted going forward. He caused no trouble to his parents and bothered no one. But his father was in mortal fear of him due to his seemingly nonconformist attitude. He seemed not to believe anything his father held dear. That bothered his father. He had no interest in pedantry. Rather he loved to meddle with all kinds of stuff. As early as when he was nine years old he had shown such technical ability that it was almost obvious he was going to be an artisan, a journeyman. Unharnessed he could be a jack of all trades, and mastered none. But if harnessed, he could end up a top-notch scientist. Eventually, but surprisingly, it took him time to settle down and build a home. However, as soon as he got married it was not long before he began to churn out his own heirs and descendants.

When Turnkey was born he was unrecognizable. He could fit into a palm and comfortably so. His eyes seemed to have been buried inside his little skull. His brows were minuscule, and his nasal bridge converged thinly to form a deep concave. His nose seemed to have been sculpted that he seemed to have a feline pedigree. His mouth was small and pouted. He was so small. He was fragile to handle. But when he began to unravel his physique, no one could believe that he was that little boy that could have been appropriate if his mother had put up a sign reading, "fragile, handle with care"!

As he was growing up, he was a joy to behold. He was loved by all and sundry. Like his father, he bothered no one. He knew no colors until his uncle moved into his life and began to remind him of what he was and not what he thought he ought to be. As Atinga fled that evening he bit his fingers that the little African boy had slipped through them. While Turnkey bothered no one or even inadvertently sought anyone's palaver, he never forgot any slight of behavior. Dare to point a finger at him, and he would point two at the person who sought his umbrage. Dare to make a fist at him and he would throw a punch in your face. Dare throw him a punch and he would hammer his assailants as if they were an anvil. Turnkey was the last child anyone of his peers would seek his palaver because he craved to get even and an additional. He was vengeful.

He was a perfect urchin. His mother had learned not to keep an eye off him. He had the ability to wander off without a trace. He had learned to mix that with some pranks. It was not unusual for Turnkey to find very unusual place to confuse the issues and other people's minds. He had an allure to those areas and situations that could be repugnant to the next-door neighbor. He had once buried himself under a mound of animal dung and was never bothered by the stench. He was an animal lover. He loved to wag the tail of his puppy sometimes to the annoyance of his pet, and he was never alone without his dog. He loved to pull the ears of his neighbor's horses sometimes to the chagrin of those creatures that stood feet above his head. He had no fear for any animal, or he just thought he could play and mess with any of them. In one narrow escape, he was caressing the horn of a young bull left in its stall with the gates ajar. All of a sudden, the young calf, without warning, charged at him and hoisted him in the air. Only the clever and alert intervention of his mother saved his stomach from being gorged. Hollering and shouting she was on hand to see her child dropped into her waiting hands. Prancing and galloping the young bull gingerly went back into his stall. The guess was the calf used Turnkey for a test run, as he did not charge back at him again and again. Perhaps, he was trying to show the world that though young he, too, was a chip off the old block. But true to kind, Turnkey dusted himself up, but his mother went home a relieved woman.

He also owned a cat. The feline was his indoor pet and the canine, the outdoor. However, the three had shared a bed, and to keep them at bay from each other he had imposed himself in their middle. The trouble was just that the dog never stopped groaning and the cat never stopped whining. Turnkey had managed the affair such that none had beaten off the ear of the other. They can only complain by whining and groaning. But there was peace.

Peace he had craved, however, the few occasions he had strayed into unchartered territories were supposedly innocuous. Either out of childish exuberance or that of pure stupidity. As in. One afternoon under the blaze of a sweltering sun, Turnkey allowed his dog named Lass to lead the way. Prancing and sniffing the corners and turns and leaves and grasses, with no definite place in mind, they came under the McPherson bridge closed to downtown Boonville, loitering as Lass continued to lead and sniff the environment as if she was looking for a lost treasure, while Turnkey trudged on. Then Lass came to a stop at the foot of a heap of unknown stuff covered with a ragged rug of a blanket under the bridge. She dug her head under the blanket, and pulling away she uncovered a cage-like box. The cage had no keys. Rather clumsily tucked inside were torn carton parts used to shield the content from the prying eyes of inquisitive passersby. Also included inside were torn scrap papers. The environment was dingy and a little dark, but close to the base of the bridge was an ensconce that held a candle. There was an extinguished candle left on it which was used to give light to the inhabitant of this dingy abode at nighttime and during dark shades of the day. Turnkey touched the cage, and it seemed to have held firm. He touched it again, and there was no shift in position. He shook a little hard, and it still held firm. He shook it a little more, much harder, and the cage crackled where it was attached to the ground. Over the years, the owner of the cage, John Frankenstein, and who had laid claim over the territory under the bridge, had painstakingly dug a hole in the concrete ground with some screwdriver. Little by little, over many, many months, he had dug enough hole in the concrete that he had gotten it to the state where he wanted to have it. Having done that he had gotten a piece of iron, and with stone and hammer he had bent the iron to his will and into a shape that he wanted. Having achieved that he proceeded to buy cement from the flea market. Having already improvised a cage he designed from scrap metal. Since John Frankenstein had convinced himself that that was a permanent dwelling place, he might, as well, go ahead and make it as comfortable as a home could be.

As Turnkey shook harder the cage, from nowhere, out of the corner of the bridge came the languid figure of John Frankenstein. What he was witnessing bewildered him. He pounced on Turnkey. Turnkey scampered, turned, transfixed! More bewildered!

"How dare you touch my baby?" railed John Frankenstein. "Do not move! If you move an inch consider yourself a dead boy," he warned.

At this time Lass wanted to lunge forward, but seeing the iron cudgel John Frankenstein had in hand and ready to unleash it she stopped short and bayed at this rugged man who wanted to assail his friend and buddy.

"Is that how you wanted to end your young life and break your mama's heart?"

For the first time in his life, fear gripped Turnkey in an unspeakable degree. Actually, for a brief moment, he had thought himself a dead chap.

"If you do not wanna break your mama's heart, if you do not want for your mama to see an obituary in the papers of a young boy whose life was ended by a homeowner under the bridge then do not mess with my baby, do not mess with my territory, and do not mess with me. I'm a gentleman, but I can kill you laughing," he growled at him with his two hands clasping his shoulders and almost lifting him off the ground, his eyes bloodshot and menacing. And in the distance Lass continued to bay at the man, afraid of her own life.

Turnkey uttered no word and relieved that at last the man was going to let him go home in peace.

John Frankenstein had lived under this bridge ever since it was constructed eleven years ago. He was a beggar by trade, and his specialty was layabout but would hate to be called homeless. Before he found out that he could make a living begging he was used to work odd jobs. He was not among the laziest of workers, but he was always among the most unfortunate. Each time there was a downturn in activities and there was need to fire some folks, as if by lot he was always among the first crop of workers to get the pink slip and booted out. Unable to make ends meet he decided that he was going to be paid for doing nothing. He was going to make a living using other people's money. He braced up himself. The first day he found out that the collective empathy of the people was immeasurably immense. It was not like every other business where the first day or the first two years could be arduous. Help was instant and the dividend immense. On that first day, he found that he could make more money than a dishwasher's pay and tip put together. He learned quicker that in this business he had to play his cards very cleverly. Do your best to capture the empathy of this indifferent world, and everything else would be added onto you. To hell with their employment! To hell with the inconveniencies of shame!

Under this bridge John Frankenstein had all his life essentials. He owned a small dog that was dwarfed all his life. This dog never barked one bit, but it was always throwing a furtive look at everybody he encountered. Sometimes it did groan, but it was always muted, ominously, generally speaking.

John Frankenstein also owned some guns, which he had always kept in his cage under lock and key. It was those guns that he was in mortal fear that the urchin was messing with. They were his babies. When he left his last place of abode, he had sold off all his property except his guns. But even then as a beggar he could still have been able to purchase a gun because it was his inalienable right to have one when he had chosen. And as a beggar it was always a concern for him how to retain his babies. Then one day as providence would have it he stumbled upon a homeless dog. As frustrated as the dog was it needed care, care no matter how much shortcoming it may present. This dog had strayed to where John Frankenstein had pitched his tent under that bridge. Any kind of care would do for this canine. John Frankenstein was handy. With food inducement, the dog tarried. It did not desert him the first night. It hung around all day the following day. It would not leave the second night. And lingered around all day the following day. John understood and decided to fete the dog and really treated it nicely. They were off to a symbiotic relationship. During the day when John sauntered about for greener pasture, this dog named Redblood became the vanguard of John's environment and territory and measured belongings. Redblood bothered no one. His groan was muted. Each time he always lain on his front hinds, perhaps thinking what a blow life had dealt it! Typical of those canines that never barked, it was like an adder, dangerous and no one ever wanted to find out! And on this fateful day as John felt like he wanted to hew Turnkey, Redblood stood dutifully by his side while Lass was in the distance howling and baying, his neck veered toward his master in captivity.

Turnkey was a very, very lucky chap. If by clairvoyance John had found out that his father loathed beggars, abhorred loafers, and hated layabouts, he would have been a goner. His only witness of what might have happened to him would have been Lass who was so scared. All he had seen would have been forgotten as quickly as they had made an impression on him. Redblood would have had no story to tell, more especially against a man who had pulled him out of the dungeon of hell to the dungeon of the living.

CHAPTER 20

Turnkey did not have anything to do with Atinga for a very long, long time. As he began to add days and months to his youthful life he began to acquire the rubrics of sensing who was an albino, who was a mulatto, and who was colored even from afar. Diction and intonation were enough to place someone in the dark even without setting an eye on the fellow. Turnkey was growing up naughty by choice. Innately vengeful and unforgiving. Yet concomitantly kind when his feathers were not ruffled. One could say that he was merciful in his way, the way he wanted to go. He had become a segregationist by association.

But he was born tough. When he was delivered, to the consternation of all the nurses and doctors, he had a pair of two teeth honed like chisel on his lower jaw. He uttered no shrill or even a whimper as all newborns were wont to. It was not until Ms. Wagner, the triage nurse, pinched him so hard that he gave hail of wailing. Then he was inconsolable. But the nurses, hardened by experience, let him enjoy himself. Because his birth was a torrid experience for his mother, for some inexplicable reasons even though he was small, she did not know what was going on. When eventually she came to herself she still did not realize that the shrill was of her child. She had not beheld his face. As soon as he was brought to his mother his quaking cry died momentarily. His mother held him up and looked at his face. He was a beautiful, beautiful, beautiful, handsome boy! And she was happy. She kissed him profusely. She lifted him and held him up gangly to her face. He was adorable. She placed him on her heaving breasts. He was cute! When she lifted him up again he was wearing a smile on his face. And then the mother saw! Unbelievable! Momentarily, she could have dropped him, but she held tight. Fear overcame her. Mother's love overcame her fright. She cuddled him tight, tighter than tight, for his age. But the sight of his newborn set of teeth jagged at her. Intuitively she was resolving that she was not going to breastfeed her newborn. Her mind was racing to everywhere but nowhere in particular. She feared she could lose her nipple. It was self-preservation. In far-off lands, in older times, but not too long ago, her child would not have been fit for expiation of ancestral and kindred ills; his blood would not have been good enough for libation. He would have been dropped in broad daylight in the thickest of forests to be scavenged by the vultures and the elements.

But in this clime and time he was born to defy the odds. There were no qualms the way he was ushered to the world. Borne tough, he had grown strong. He had an uncanny instinct about him. This child who would have been unfit for the gods was a tough nut to crack. He was not of a tremendously great stature. He was not imposing in physique. He had a little more than an average height. His gait was measured. But he tended to dig on his heels to the ground as he walked. Perhaps a measure of his strength. The thing about this child and his strength was difficult to explain. He had flat buttocks growing up. There was no muscle mass on his behind. A cursory look at him from the back had a young chap framed on a straight pole.

Despite his frame and height, he had an imposing feeling of himself. The image he had of himself was an all-conquering mystique. Growing up he saw himself as a colossus. He tried effortlessly to live out that persona. He had seen his peers walk through his huge legs, and he had obliged them. At nineteen years of age he had no inkling that any homo sapiens was taller than him or would do anything he could not do or even surpass. He had a wardrobe full of armory. He made no fuss about his acquisition. He was used to owning guns that they seemed nothing to him. Yet he cherished them most fervently. Nothing came between him and his possession. Yet he had never been called upon to use any of them except in some hunting expeditions. Yet he could not stop asking and accumulating more. If he were to be called upon to use them in a moment of momentary crises, he would be encumbered by his own weapons of war. Weapons of war that had given him a sense of good security. He had not acquired these weapons to amuse himself with dates in the wild running with the beasts. He had acquired them over the years to defend himself against marauders and miscreants but had not been called upon to exercise his firepower. He had smoldered neither a deer nor a hog. Yet he would stop at nothing to amass more and more of his lethal weapons.

Nothing compared to it. The heavens were carved open with thunder and lightning. It was difficult to see beyond the bridges of the nose. Hail rained on the earth with immense fury, and with it came unimaginable thunderclaps. As the lightning tore apart the ceiling of the earth the image of Michelangelo trying to meet the outstretched hand of the almighty in sure futility could be seen in real time. Horrendous and dreadful, Turnkey, who seldom feared anything in his whole life, was perturbed and petrified. He turned to his left, and there were chasms of converging deluge. He turned to his right, and there was this dreadful gate to the Pacific. Whichever turn he made there was dread greater than dreadful. Then the downpour was unabated. Bedraggled and drenched, drenched and bedraggled, Turnkey found no solace in living. And death was not nigh enough. The eagle of the jungle could fly no more. As he made to jump a strip of creeks and riverine he found himself face-to-face with the king of the jungle.

The lion was ferocious and menacing, severely hungry and ready to pounce. It was one of those situations where no option was good enough for an avenging death or exchange to ameliorate the situation. Turnkey made to run, but the lion galloped teasingly about him. He knew anyway he could not make it beyond a foot. Just then he remembered his armory of arsenals. He turned to his right, and handily he grabbed his best shotgun. As always loaded, he uncorked the safety latch. He took an aim. The lion made no effort to avert the danger coming to him. He knew that this misery could have long been ended if he had remembered himself. He would not have been involved in this unending agony. As he crutched himself to shoot, the lion roared, on his hinds rocking back and forth as if to pounce on his prey. As he made to shoot the lion narrowed their proximity, lunging back and forth still on its hinds. He had no options. He could hear the sound of his own machine gun. Boom! Fire. Boom! Boom! Fire. But there was no fury. The gun was firing ferociously, but the lion did not bat an eye or feel the pang of the shots. Rather it was still inching closer and closer. This young man who had prided his collection of the best guns that were ever made now could not effectively use the weapon to save himself when it really mattered most. The futility of it all was dawned on him. Yet he was not going to sacrifice himself to the beast of this jungle. He turned to his right and grabbed hold of his cudgel. If his best-known effective gun in short distance could not deter this carnivore then a cudgel would be useless in saving his life. Without let the lion began to lunge closer and closer, rocking back and forth on its hinds. Threatening to make a mincemeat of him. By then Turnkey really feared for his young life. With the cudgel in one hand, he grabbed her ears and threw it at the lion who wasted no time in having it down its throat in a twinkle. It tasted good and it wanted more. The lion had tasted blood and now it wanted more and fast too. Turnkey cut off the other ear and threw in the direction of the now leering beast. Then it was the right hand. Then it was the right arm. The left hand and left arm followed suit. Then it was the right foot. Then it was the right leg. Then the left foot and the left leg followed suit. Then it was the torso. Then he handed everything. Turnkey knew that he had no margin for error. He had no bargaining chip left. He knew that he had failed. And there was a pool of blood, and he was soaked in it. He had just sacrificed his wife to save his own skin. He was beleaguered. The rain had stopped pounding the earth. The lion was walking away bellyful, smacking its tongue, licking the splatter of blood by the corners of its mouth, kind of giggling its body like an elk under the full weight of his archenemy, human being.

As soon as he turned on the other side of himself, he once again fell asleep. It was a night of a thousand nightmares. Then there was a knock on his entrance door. He did not respond to the knock that suddenly had grown in its intensity. He reached for his gun, but no matter how much he tried it was in another world. Then the knocking gradually petered out. In the place of the knocking were footsteps of someone sauntering toward his bedroom. He went for his armory again but found himself in the toilet for no reason. The intruder came inside his bedroom, but Turnkey was not there. When Turnkey sensed some danger, he muscled and muscled, but it appeared as if he was constipated. It was not quite awhile since he was there but a few hours ago. As danger loomed he kept trying to push the limits of his sphincter. Then a pebble of bolus of shit thumped inside the commode. Its sound was *Clute*, the name of that south Texas town that myth had it that it derived its name from the falling pebbles of feces into the water when folks perched on that log above the stream to help themselves. And a splatter. And then a splash of more poo. The intruder seemed to be loitering about his wardrobe. A little of the splash and splatter seemed to have pointed the way toward the toilet for the intruder, but instinctively Turnkey hurriedly cleaned after himself. Rather than flush his mess Turnkey dug his hand in his own excrement. That was his last defense. Anything could do. He did not need to do anything to invite the marauder inside the toilet. Turnkey waited. The intruder yanked the door open with a kick and his weapon drawn. To the surprise of the intruder, big and imposing, standing there with a hand soiled with excrement, and full with shit, was a little man ready to paint his assailant with skunk shit. Instantly the thief lost his nerve, dropped his gun, and Turnkey took advantage, picked up his gun, and gave a chase. Gun in one hand and shit in the other. The man who had nowhere to run to become incapacitated. Surrender was his only option. Flat on his back, a boundless fear gripped him. He was not as much pleading for his life. He was pleading to Turnkey to spare him being painted or fed the shit. Not sooner the siren of the police came piercing the early morning hours.

Turnkey heaved his body to the other side, and to his chagrin, it was a miasma.

"Damn it!" he shouted to himself. Instinctively he smelled his hand and to his relief there was nothing, not a specter of shit.

"Damn it!" he said again.

He got up from his bed. He was a little bit sweaty. He went to the window. He peered through the blinds. There was no torrential rain. There was no deluge. It was still some night ahead of him. It was still a long way to go before dawn. He went and sat on the edge of his bed. Then he lay down and momentarily felt ashamed of himself. Could he really have sacrificed anyone or let alone his wife for that matter to a hungry lion to save his own life? But then he had no wife. He tried to wish what he had just encountered away, but it would not go away.

Could life come to a point where one needed bullshit as a bulwark of defense? He knew that he was prepared to do anything to survive, but it never occurred to him that his own excrement was good enough to disarm a full-fledged man and make him to take to his heels and even head over heels. There was still plenty of time before dawn. And there still were rumblings of an inclement weather outside.

Then the sight of some lightning without thunder pierced the dense darkness of the night as they peeped through his blinds. Then there were some mighty thunderclaps. With it came a swirling of lightning as if two live naked wires were making contact in the horizon yet penetrating through the crevices of his window curtains and blinds. Everything he saw was just about to come except perhaps the menacing lion and the lily-livered intruder. Gradually and slowly the rain began to fall again. The pit-a-pat rhythm of the downpour like a lullaby finally soothed him to sleep.

That morning Turnkey dusted himself and decided to drive down to the junkyard for some spare part for his rickety jalopy spattering junk of a car, a 1960 Ford Marquis. Poor boy! The car was good for one thing, only one thing: taking him to work. But Turnkey had harbored this feeling that somehow he would be able to patch up the car, prolong its life/death sentence, and be able to see him through college. He had no good options. He was determined to fix anything that reared its head to continue to have this vehicle on the road. By his own estimation, by the time he was done with fixing the car, the only thing that would be considered original with the car would probably be the ignition. From the doors to the bumper to the hood, they had all been replaced either by Turnkey or one of the previous owners. This vehicle had seen better days. But it was not as if the vehicle had been too old. There were millions of older vehicles out there still plying the roads. It was just that this very vehicle was just an unlucky breed. Turnkey was prepared to hang on to it defiantly. He could not afford saving enough money to look forward to buying a better car. So he was determined to do everything in his powers to keep it on the road. So far it had delivered. As long as it was able to take him around then there were not much of qualms.

Wiggling its way down the farm road, Turnkey was focused on getting to work as timely as possible. Knowing the limitation of speed and his penchant to always be at work on time, he started out earlier enough for the eighteen miles' drive to work. The road was zagging between valleys and hills and zigging between hills and valleys. It was treacherous on normal days. But since it rained last night and was drizzling a few hours ago it had become even more treacherous. Much of the road was often lonely. It was the cross-link to the other bigger town. On the right of the road there were prairies, and on the left side of this road traveling south was a horizon of marsh lands. Hither and thither there were trees that oftentimes helped to stem the tide of a cascading erosion that had haunted the area for a long time. He knew this terrain. He had been plying it for upward of nine months. As he came to one of the zags, a daredevil squirrel just crept out of the woods and wanted to make a dash across the road to the other side. Not too certain it was going to make it safely, the squirrel seemed to have changed its mind, vacillated, and stopped in its track. Paused and undecided in the middle of the road, then it wanted to turn back all at the same time. There and then came Turnkey's Marquis trundling on. In the immediacy, trying as hard and as best as he could to save the life of the wretched creature he applied his brakes, and the confused and out-of- breath squirrel was safely bestridden in between the wheels. But then came the splashing sound of a rasping noise. What he saw in a flash was his bumper flying off and right on top of his front windshield. The force veered his vehicle off the road entirely. Right at the tip of the valley that could descend twenty to thirty feet down the hill.

Turnkey was a very lucky young man. His lucky stars bordered on limitless possibilities. Very often his friends referred to him as the cat. Because they believed that he had nine lives. The truth was that he had more than nine lives, a boy born with a pair of teeth chiseled in his lower jaw. Very often he had gotten out of very dicey, dangerous situations unscathed. Whenever it was thought that he could be getting into some unsavory situation he had come out unaffected. Growing up his friends never emulated him, copied him in some ways because he ventured to do something. That had its undoing. But Turnkey never took living and dying for granted. He knew his background enmeshed in continuous want and poverty stricken. Since he was fourteen, he had kept some kind of a job, cutting neighbors' yards for a pittance, and washing plates in every restaurant that gave him a chance. And at every opportunity among his equals he had always wanted to be the first, the head boy. In his job mobility, he did not mind a lower pay as long as among the taskmasters he was at the helm wielding some power over his peers, even ceremonial powers. All along he had angled for a position of leadership. As time went he changed works at the slightest whim. Not so much as for the pay but because he had an eye at upward mobility. If the opportunity was not there he was out of the place before anyone could say anything to dissuade him, especially if he saw an opportunity where the sky could be his limit. He was a calculating young man, astute and daring, unafraid of taking risks. He had driven this road for nine months because it offered him what he was looking for: some form of having to boss some other fellows. Yet, he had his eyes fixed on moving up. He was ready to jump ship if he had sensed that the opportunity, for him to move up or for him to be in some kind of leadership, was not there. While he had kept some kind of job since he was fourteen, this was the longest he had been on any of them.

Turnkey got out of his car as quickly and composed as he could. And standing before him was an apologetic Mr. Sledgehammer. And beside him was his sixteen-year-old daughter who disembarked from the front seat of the passenger's side of their glittering brand-new Cadillac sedan. Mr. Sledgehammer, a shrewd beneficence well-known in the community and surrounding locales. His great-great-grandfather was a slave owner, who made so much money holding and lending out slaves. The money made in the slave business had been handed down generation to generation. Much of the money had been invested in landholding, speculation, and real estate. He held large swaths of land in the community and its environs. And even out of state. In collusion with local authorities he always had foreknowledge of phases of land property developments. With that foreknowledge, he would expand his land acquisition to areas mapped for the next phase of development, down the line, twenty, thirty years hence. As development began to creep toward the area, he had already positioned himself to cash in on his investment. Even when government claimed eminent domain to acquire pieces of land for certain developmental project, he had already placed himself to cash in on the huge compensation that would arise from government largesse. It was always a win-win for him. And some of the lands he had developed into living quarters.

Mr. Sledgehammer did nothing else for a living. His investment worked for him. He could afford to while away all day and still got dividends to fend for himself and his modest family of five. Despite his immense wealth he was affable, approachable, and simple. He could immerse himself in a crowd and still be undistinguishable. The main thing that distinguished him was his willingness to give to different causes. That also he did without pomp. Very few people knew him facially. His works spoke for themselves. His charity-driven life was partly for the atonement of the sins of his forefathers. Most of his giving geared toward the welfare and needs of the black folks in any community his huge instinctive heart lured him toward.

"I'm sorry, young man, my name's James Sledgehammer," began Mr. Sledgehammer. Turnkey was nonplussed. Once again, he introduced himself to Turnkey.

"I'm James Sledgehammer. If you leave this to me I'm gonna make amends, and all of us would come out happier for it," he continued.

Still, Turnkey uttered no words. He hated clocking late at work. He hated excuses. He was not so much so worried about his rickety old Marquis. If he had done nothing right one thing he was religious about was to have his jalopy covered by some kind of insurance. And in this case, since from the look of things the gentleman that rammed into him just lost control of his vehicle despite the squirrel, he knew that if the man had no insurance of his own, assuming, at least, his would kick in to give him some cover. Again, he was not so much worried about his old Marquis. He was offended because in no uncertain way he was bound to be late to work for the first time since he got into this job.

"What's your name, sir, if I may ask?" Mr. Sledgehammer asked.

"My name's Turnkey."

"Again, I'm sorry for having done this to your car. And as I said before, if you leave this to me I will not only fix your car, but I will make amends. By the way you must be going to work, are you?"

"Yes, I'm going to work and about five miles away. And now I'm running late," said Turnkey regrettably.

"Young man, it was all my fault, but if you believe me then everything will work out fine, in your favor." There was a ring of sincerity in every word that he uttered, and Turnkey was hanging on to it. But he was also wandering how this could eventually work out in his favor, except that the man's insurance would repair his jalopy and put his misery back on the road again.

"Please, meet my sixteen-year-old daughter, Emelie. She's my youngest child," said Mr. Sledgehammer.

"Hi, Turnkey," said Emelie, waving her parochial hand at Turnkey, who stood about seven feet away from her.

"Hi, Emelie," said Turnkey.

"Emelie has just turned sixteen. She cannot drive on her own without an adult sitting at the passenger's seat beside her," Mr. Sledgehammer began to explain.

"I'm sure that the police would soon be here. Now, this is where Emelie comes in. You are gonna do me a huge favor, boy." Turnkey listened in rapt silence.

"When they come as I'm sure they will, I will tell the officer that Emelie was the driver and I was the passenger. The rest of the responsibility would be mine. Just do me this favor and everything else would be fine," he said with unequivocal assurance in his tone and demeanor.

Right on the mark, behind them came the flashing light of a galloping police Chevy Tahoe, the newest set of patrol vehicles issued to the police force statewide.

Mr. Sledgehammer had good reasons to make an honest deal with Turnkey and really meant it. Despite his philanthropy he was a man bedeviled by twin vices of drunkenness and smoking. And they had haunted his every move. He had no will and mental bearing to overcome them. All his efforts had yielded temporary results and permanent problems. All his skirmishes with the law had been as a result of his lack of control over his urges to drink and immerse himself as bees love honey. He had been on parole and freed of it. He was on a two-year suspended sentence for drunk driving. He was only ten days away from freeing himself of violation and avoiding serving time in the local jail in spite of his immense riches. There would be no ceremonies about it. They just have to haul him into jail without recourse to further hearing. And on this day, he had just had his fill, clear-eyed but enough to get him into trouble and some time in the local jailhouse.

As Officer D. Wolfgang alighted from his vehicle, his twenty-two years of service experience just told him whose vehicle was at fault. Everything else he had to do was for the records and to put some officialdom to the body of evidence in the case.

"Who was the driver of the Cadillac?" asked Officer Wolfgang.

"I am," said Emelie, waving her right hand right up to eye level.

"How old are you? Can I see your ID card or driver's license or permit, ma'am?" demanded D. Wolfgang politely.

"I'm sixteen years going to seventeen," said Emelie, handing the officer her driving permit.

"And you had your father, Mr. Sledgehammer, by your side, uhh?"

"Yes, sir," said Emelie timidly.

If D. Wolfgang suspected any foul play he did not show it. In fact, he had no reason to think otherwise. He knew Mr. Sledgehammer for his worthy causes and not his recalcitrant misjudgments. Since he was not the driver as his daughter had attested there was no further reason to do instant research on his person, or profile his character any further.

"Ma'am, can you tell me what happened?" said Officer Wolfgang so that he could note that in his report.

"It was an accident," began Emelie as Turnkey and Mr. Sledgehammer looked on. "The guy, the vehicle ahead of me, was trying to avoid running a deer over and suddenly applied the brakes. Before I could say jack, I drove my vehicle right onto the back of his car."

"Were you going over the speed limit?" asked D. Wolfgang.

"No, sir," said Emelie.

"Then, you just failed to control your speed. You failed to control your vehicle," said the officer.

She said nothing in return. And the officer turned to Turnkey.

"Sir, can you tell me briefly what happened?" said the police officer.

"I was driving to work. And all of sudden, this squirrel dashed out from nowhere. Not knowing whether or not it would continue its onward dash across the road, it vacillated and I slammed on my brakes to save it and what followed next was a bang on my rear side and yanked me off the road…"

Turnkey was still trying to explain his side of the story when a silent cracking noise began to emanate near under the right front wheel of his own vehicle. Gradually, a small tree, the height of a mustard tree that was like a wedge, began to bend over. The soil under it was giving in. Without further notice the ground completely caved in, and in a twinkle the car tumbled over down the pit of a valley.

"Whoa, whoa, whoa," gasped the officer as he tried to make a futile effort to stop the vehicle from descending below. It was all too late. The old Marquis had fallen thirty feet down the valley into an alley. Turnkey was believing his gut that Mr. Sledgehammer would live up to his promise. This was not foreseen prior to their gentleman's understanding. What that promise was he did not know. He entertained no doubt in his mind. His old Marquis had finally found a resting place in the valley.

"Does any of you have a need for the EMS or some medical attention?" asked the police officer dutifully.

"No, no," came back the reply in unison.

"Young man, are you sure you don't have need for some care right now?"

"No, I don't have any need for EMS right now."

"Oftentimes hits like this never show any pain, they come later. Watch out for yourself, okay," said Officer D. Wolfgang.

Officer D. Wolfgang's job was cut short. In his summary note, he had noted the testimonies of the parties. Ms. Sledgehammer had accepted responsibility that she badged into the old Marquis. In the traffic ticket note that was given to her the officer had stated she failed to control her vehicle. Pretty standard traffic note! He had also given insurance information of the Sledgehammers' to Turnkey so that he could pursue some kind of restitution. Actually, Mr. Sledgehammer had proffered his insurance to Turnkey prior. Without means to go to work or even go home, Mr. Sledgehammer offered to drop off Turnkey at his place of work. But the officer intervened. He insisted on dropping off Turnkey to work five miles away. He felt that that was the right thing to do to guarantee his safety.

With a wink and a nod, Mr. Sledgehammer looked at Turnkey as he got into the officer's truck. He wholeheartedly believed that he had struck a deal with the young man and that the young man would remain quiet. And as soon as he got home he called his vehicle insurance company and they took care of the rest of the paperwork. The traffic ticket note gave his daughter thirty days to appear in the municipal court to plead her case. They intended to send one of their lawyers to clear the records. Of course, she was a minor, so it would not count for much against her.

Four days after the incident, Turnkey received a letter in the mail. He was profusely appreciated by Mr. Sledgehammer. Tucked underneath the letter was a check of $18,711.11.

Benevolence begot benevolence. One good turn deserves another.

CHAPTER 21

For some unknown reasons, they seemed to be running into each other at every turn and bend. Ever since Chance pulled her aside and dressed her down, Candie had comported herself more affably. She had kept her dentition in her mouth whenever she came across him. Rather than flash them at him to buy herself some safe passage. But what Chance had not stopped was to take his eyes off her whether furtively or abashedly. He had always rained his gaze as long and as much the corner of his eyes could go. However, on this sunny summer day, it was excruciatingly hot and the humidity compounded its burning effects on the skin. If there was no need to venture outside a building then no need, but if one must be outside, haste must be the gait. Chance got it! He had never seen anything like that heat of a weather before, not even in his native Biafra.

There were dotted gardens of refuge littered all over the campus. On this day Chance had chosen the shades that lie between the art and science buildings to while away his time while waiting for the next class. Dotting the shades were cement and wooden benches to just sit and relax and savor the sweet breeze the trees and shades had hidden. Walking toward his favorite spot, Chance could see the posture of a damsel bent over her book. Because he was approaching the figure from the back, moreover, she was bent over, Chance could not tell who the maiden was. Nevertheless, he went over and made himself comfortable on one of the benches opposite her about eight feet apart.

The cracking noise of dried-up leaves trampled under his feet had alerted her to raise her face and see who wanted to pair her company. As their eyes interlocked there was a grin on her face while Chance was almost smiling from molar to molar urging. This was the right place and the right time, very auspicious to make a move. His heart momentarily pit-a-patted, but true to self, Chance gathered himself before she could tell.

"Hey, girl!" was his gambit. Candie looked up blandly.

"You seem to know beforehand where I was going to be," continued Chance, just to get the ball rolling. Candie looked at him now wearing a muffled grin on the corners of her sensuous lips.

"I was here before you," said Candie quietly. "I would say that you have been stalking me. Aren't you, my African young man," she added.

"Well, I'm first and foremost a Biafran before I become an African," he told her politely. "And me stalking you! Why would I? If I had anything to tell you I would go ahead and let you know. You are a beautiful girl. Aren't you? How about that?" he asked rhetorically in quick succession, and added, "If I had anything more than that to tell you, I will go ahead and tell you so. The earth I am standing ain't gonna cave in and swallow me," said Chance with unbeknownst nostalgia. Not long ago a colored boy talking to a white girl could make the young boy disappear from the face of the earth without a trace. The world was changing.

"I see," said Candie. "You will do yourself a favor if you stopped following me," counseled Candie.

"I've no intentions of following you, girl. There is something about you that keeps making us cross each other's path…"

"The something is about you, not me," protested Candie.

"Anything you say," said Chance resignedly. "But you are Candie…"

"And so what…?"

"I was about to ask you," said Chance.

"What?" snapped Candie.

"You do not want me to ask you."

"Why not?" queried Candie again.

"Do not be out with me," said Chance.

"What? What do you mean? Why? Are you now afraid of me, my Biafran boy," retorted Candie.

"Afraid of who? You? Never! Ever!" Chance snapped back in quick succession. "You have a beautiful name," he continued.

"What about that? Thank you, though! But I thought you were going to ask a question."

"You are Candie," said Chance again. "Are you chewable, lickable, suckable, or munchable?"

Candie's face lit up. Good-nurtured young girl that knew no wrong with a welcoming spirit that attracted friendship and love as honey was to bees. Make her happy, and she would laugh with abandon. Slowly and quiet was her speech, and guffaw was her laughter. One could hardly hear her voice, but she could be heard from afar by the reverberation of her laughter. And for days it could still be ringing like a sweet din.

"That's a good question," she said as chuckle came all over her face. "I'm more than a mouthful. I'm not munchable," she said emphatically. "You can't cram enough of me to be able to munch me to smithereens to swallow me. You can choke on me. And I'm not chewable either. And looking at you, you don't look like someone with strong enough jaws to grab a chunk of me," she said, throwing her face to the other side of the lawn.

"I see," said Chance, as his jaws really dropped. That challenge took him really unaware. It was completely unexpected, and he was caught off guard, more than he had bargained for. Sometimes, some quest for additional knowledge could be labyrinthine.

"You know," she began again as she turned to face him squarely, "most girls are suckable. I think that it is natural." She paused. By this time Chance was beginning to fill his head with things that could be and things that would never be. He looked up, and their eyes locked again in charming engagement.

"But, I'm gonna speak for myself." Now Chance was all ears. "I'm a little bit different. All of us are! I like it lickable, I'm lickable," she told him.

"I see," said Chance again, "and why?" He wanted to know.

"I want it to last for a very, very long time," she said and proceeded to school him. "If it were munchable or chewable, you run the risk of exhausting it before you knew it. If it were suckable you run the risk of having your tongue cleaved to your palate. But if it were lickable, you only have to worry how it would ever finish. I am lickable, guy," she said with so much fanfare.

"I see," said Chance again, dumbfounded.

Immediately, Joann, her bosom friend, appeared clutching some books. Without tarrying Candie and her friend left Chance like in the dust, without a goodbye. As he darted his eyes in their direction he could see them, heads bent toward each other, talking and giggling and enjoying themselves. He knew that they were talking about him and laughing at him, at his raw, naive Africanness. But the only laughter he seemed to have heard was that from Candie and it was really loud. He bent his head down toward his knees trying to keep his adrenaline in check. The more he stayed there the more his thoughts deepened. How can such a young girl be that much blunt? He was mesmerized. No doubt! He knew it. He had been in America for almost a year now. But there on his mind that day was etched as in an epithet: welcome to America.

What Chance learnt in a twinkle that day was that one should never underrate, or underestimate, what an American was capable of doing at any given time, even her littlest.

CHAPTER 22

If greener pasture was going abroad to acquire some wealth, then he did not need it. His pasture was already green. He had come to broaden his horizon at the behest of his mother, somehow, against the will of his father. They were rich and very comfortable, and that was long established. He had come to further improve himself. Studying abroad was one of those things. There was something ingratiating about "I was a London-trained economist or a Harvardtrained purist." What that meant! When a rich child sought to be London trained it was all about status symbol. For a poor chap, it can only be by dint of holy scholastic invitation. Hard-earned, purpose driven, gripping, and tenacious. The poor bagger had earned himself a stool to rub shoulders with the exclusives. All that never preoccupied Chance. He knew very much that he was never constituted among the poor. Being whom he was he was determined to do well. Failure was not an option. Coming to America was a pledge to do well. He must accomplish everything he set his eyes with flying colors before his father set his eyes on him. However, success in America was not his last resort. Having escaped the damning patch of poverty that swung around the head of a whole lot of folks he knew and would not go away, no matter how hard they had tried. Knowing that he had outrun poverty, knowing that a whole lot of folks he knew, no matter how much they tried, they were unable to snap the constant clinging hold of poverty. Knowing all that. And not having the excruciating burden of poverty hover over his head gave him some swagger in his gait. Exuberant and uppish, bordering on caring not much of a hoot. He had never been cowed and never wanted to cower to anything. He had a lot going on in his favor. For one he did not have to dodge the crushing blows of poverty or the opprobrium of its constant humiliation. Having known all that he had also come to realize that it was not always the case that the wielder of ultimate power commanded the uppermost strength. What his father had not taught him he tried to make up as in life lessons. Day after day in America he was confronted with the vagaries of the unknown. As his father had always told him, suddenness challenges a strong man, but a strong man also was known for his ability to surmount suddenness. So, while still focused on the tasks ahead of him and the vagaries that accompanied them, he had always exuded the aura of a son that had nothing to lose.

Chance had had a few not so happy encounters with Turnkey in the past. And the irony of it was that they always crossed each other's path. They seemed to have affinity to attract each other but for the wrong reasons. This day, Turnkey, not decidedly shaded his old habit was at his element, and on the prowl. He had just come inside the restroom, and what he saw did not please his sight, and the culprit must be he who was found near the scene of the nuisance. It was self-evident, the principle of last seen.

There were two urine commodes on the wall of the restroom. Severally, Chance had made it a point of duty to flush the two urine pits each time he came inside the restroom, whether they were flushed or not, before he used any of them. But on this day, he had committed a cardinal sin, either that it escaped his attention or that he did not care a hoot. He had eased himself and flushed after himself. The other pit was left not flushed. Then the unexpected happened. While he was washing his hand, Turnkey sauntered in, tired with his backpack straddled behind his shoulders.

"Hey, man," said Turnkey, turning to Chance. Chance just completely ignored him. "This restroom is not your father's latrine. The simplest thing you can do is to flush it. Don't you have to clean your mess behind you where you came from in goddamn Africa?"

Chance was determined to let go and just move on.

"You just wanted to ignore me. That is disrespectful, you black mother...pip-squeak."

Chance could have left. But he knew that he had a chance to put this little white boy in his place.

In a jiffy he snatched at his neck and pinned him to the wall of the restroom.

"How dare you talk to me like that! How do you want to die? You want me to spill your blood hewing you with my bare hands, and make a carcass of your old self or skinning you alive, and wash my hands with your blood? Choose one and choose it fast!" he shouted at Turnkey.

Turnkey tried to extricate himself from his grip on the wall to no avail.

"Leave me alone," Turnkey struggled to find his voice. "Take your coarse African hand off me, or I'm going to blow off your head," said Turnkey as Chance let him of the hook.

That was Chance's Moses's moment. No one had still shown up in the restroom.

"Leave me alone," said Chance. "Take your eyes off my business. You may not be that much lucky next time," he warned Turnkey.

"You gotta be kidding yourself. Never you try placing your hand on me next time, unless you wanted to disappear from the face of the earth without a trace," said Turnkey.

"We shall see," said Chance as he opened the restroom door and walked away.

"There is a lot to see and a lot to learn," hollered Turnkey at him.

Chance had a reason to want to put Turnkey in his place. What he taught would be a final solution to his continued spoiling for a fight. A few days back in the same restroom and at the same economic building Turnkey had accosted him. Chance had gone to pass out urine. Turnkey had gone to pass out feces. When Turnkey walked out he found Chance urinating. Turnkey began to make some derogatory noises, complaining about the stinking, poor, and uncivilized African boy. To compound the irony of the situation, he grabbed some napkins and began to clean his unwashed hands. What a way to show civility for a man who just had used the toilet to do the number two. Chance was about taking the law into his own hands when a young guy who was later identified as Jason walked into the restroom. Chance took his time to wash his hands trying to buy time in case Jason would step out before them. To his disappointment, Turnkey began to lambast Chance, telling Jason how unworthy and undeserving Chance was to enjoy all the privileges America had to offer. It was an exercise in futility as Jason was a willing listener, all ears. Frustrated, Chance bit his lips and left the restroom. But not without throwing a look at Turnkey, a telling look, enough to zap one off his feet. He was sure that the opportunity to address this incessant degradation will come.

Three weeks after Candie had welcomed him to America, within those three weeks he had discovered that they had two elective courses together. That in itself would make them to always come across each other. A seed of some rapport had been planted. Time and again it had started to germinate. And Chance had started to appreciate that rapport, the occasions she had darted a glance toward his way, and the occasion she was just seeking his attention. Whatever the case they all carried some risks. His tormentor in chief happened to be her brother. Somehow Chance understood that. Although that had not officially been made known to him. But the aura of having this elegant damsel talking to him was like a badge of honor. Deep down his consciousness he was bragging to himself having to enjoy the company of one of the most beautiful ladies on campus not until Turnkey found out what might be going on.

Actually, nothing was going on. It was all wishful thinking. The last thing Chance wanted was to get himself embroiled in a society where one could get hurt just for keeping one's mouth shut. He was doing his best. But, he had just been encountering Turnkey, enduring him. Turnkey, never had time to understand this kid he had taken pleasure in checkmating. And he, Turnkey, did not want to know anything about the peasant African boy. He had not forgotten how he was pinned to the wall. Always, he did not want to remember that he had threatened to skin him alive. And now he was hovering around his sweet sister trying to exert a relationship even if it was platonic.

They had just finished one of their classes and were walking leisurely to the other building where they would be having the next class. Leisurely since the group had some time to while away. In the company was Candie, Joann, Jason, and Chance. Then from nowhere came Turnkey charging at Chance. He had been longing for some revenge of some sort. The force of the push made Chance stagger and lose control of his books as they went flying all over the place. With no time for a second thought he charged at Turnkey, wanting to hoist him up in the air. But he was mistaken this time around. In spite of his supposedly small frame, Turnkey was difficult to be lifted off the ground. He had dug his legs to the ground. With enough time for a second thought, he pushed Turnkey away from himself. Turnkey then charged again at him.

"What's going on here, Turnkey?" asked Candie as she threw herself in between the two foes.

"He was going to skin me alive, and I'm going to blow off his big empty head before he had a chance to scratch me," said Turnkey.

"He has been stalking me. But if stalking was his only problem, I would not have minded…"

"Or you've been stalking…," began Turnkey.

"I mean, he needs to mind his own business," said Chance tamely.

"You're the one that needed minding your business," countered Turnkey.

"I'm minding my business," said Chance.

"No, you're not."

"Yes, I am. And until I get you skinned, you would not leave me alone," cautioned Chance.

"That's your undoing. If you do not take your eyes off my sister, then consider yourself a dead man walking."

"Is that your problem? You should be thanking me for doing you a favor. I'm relieving you of something you cannot eat. Or you think you can. Or you want to…," said Chance.

That got Turnkey riled the more. He once again tried to charge at Chance. But Chance had really readied himself to slam him on the ground. And then Candie was again the wedge.

"Just keep away from her," said Turnkey.

"I will not," Chance taunted him.

"Then you have got a lot to learn, and you need to learn them too fast before it would be too late," warned Turnkey.

"Turnkey, you need to let this guy be. You need to let this African boy get on with his life, get used to living in America," said Candie. As she spoke trying to quieten her brother, Jason, Joann, and Chance made a turn to the left and walked inside the economics building.

"He was going to skin me alive."

"That's what you know." She paused. "But, what you do not know." She paused again.

"What's that?" Her brother wanted to know.

"You do not wanna know," said Candie.

"Then he should get out of my business."

"What's this, your business? This guy is not the peasant you think he is. I thought you told me that you had given up your old ways, that you had turned a new leaf."

"Yes, I have! But he drives me crazy."

"Wait a minute! Before you drove yourself nuts, I want you to understand that this African boy is comfortable inside his skin and outside. He could pay your school fees and would not feel it. If you had known him about three months ago, he could have changed your rickety old Marquis without having to almost kill yourself in it. He could have paid your pittance of a wage before you drove yourself crazy and before the good Samaritan smiled on you." She paused.

"Is that all you have got to say?" asked Turnkey.

"No, not all I've got to say and not all you've got to learn. You just have got to turn a new leaf and I've got much to say and you've much to learn…" She was still speaking when they came to the threshold of the entrance of the economics building, and Turnkey turned the corner, and she went inside the building and unto her class.

CHAPTER 23

It was another summer, the next summer. Last summer foray into Biafra was memorable. Everyone thoroughly enjoyed themselves. Even Jewel. Turnkey had never-to-be-forgotten experiences the year before. The good had outlived the bad. While he still remembered all he went through two years ago, he had cherished more the beautiful memories of the Biafran people the year after. If last two years was to be forgotten in a jiffy, last year's visit was a makeup. And this year was going to be an encore. Visiting Biafra had become like a pilgrimage, and every member of his company was enjoying it. This year Jewel was not in the company, so also Dusty and Jason. On board were Joann, Turnkey's new girlfriend. And as usual, Candie and, of course, Chance. It was a smaller party so to speak, but the enthusiasm was not diminished.

Gradually, Biafra was coming back to life. Corruption was still rife. The vestiges of Nigeria had not been shaken off. It would take a long time to get rid of the entrenched habits of thievery, pen robbery, engineered commotion, monumental corruption, bad governance, general lawlessness, especially coming from those at the helms of affairs, whose whole bodies were still inhabited by the demons of the defunct Nigeria's DNA. This country was wrestled from the Nigerians and the British, whose master in trade was divide and rule. They two peoples function at best in the midst of confusion. When they created the confusion, a blind spot, they diverted the attention of even the most alert of peoples, and in that instance, they would start to throw spanners in the works. Their lackeys in Biafra were working assiduously to make sure that they would not remove their monkey hand in Biafra's business. But this year, the country was agog. The excitement was pervading, for it permeated the life of the nation. This was made most certain by the entrant of Dim of Biafra into the presidential race. By the peace treaty that ended the war he was to stay away from politics and governance for so long. And this year he had fulfilled those provisions. He did not waste time to indicate his willingness to contest the election. His entrance had brought so much excitement to the campaign. And he was a sure bet to win. What was denied him at the battlefield would be his for the asking, and even on a platter of gold. He was beloved.

Charismatic and measured in his speech, Oxford trained. Giving the chance he could hold a mammoth crowd spellbound for hours on end. No one came close to him. He really had the power of speech, and people paid attention to whatever he was about to say and not what he had said. He could say the same things another eloquent speaker had said and got rousing applause, yet this other speaker's eloquence was in vain even though they both had said the same things nevertheless in variant forms. This other speaker may have calmed the crowd but lacked the knack and panache to wow their audience and got no recognition for all their effort. Dim could sway the grass with his oratory. He could make the cattle, sheep, and goats cud again the packed nuisance still held in their guts. If anyone could make the greyhound stop in their hunt for that helpless antelope, he was he. When he went to Aburi, he used his power of speech to wow his counterpart that all his Nigerian counterpart did was to nod in agreement. He underlined his own power of eloquence with confirmative repetitiveness as if to say he was making assurance doubly sure. It was when they came back that his Nigerian counterpart had a reawakening. Everything they agreed on in Aburi was unraveling before his eyes. He swore that none of the things agreed on and listed in the communiqué were ever discussed with the Biafran general. That was the beginning of the demise of the Aburi accord. And that was the beginning of the atrocious hostilities and the completion of the attendant genocide.

His opponents hated him as unicorn hated trees. Those who loved him and there were millions of Biafrans, loved him with a passion. They held on to his every word like a bloodline. In those millions, chief among them was Ogidigi. Ogidigi had believed in this man. He held him in no fault. He could do anything for him just for the asking. He was ready to work for him in any capacity. And he would be ready to lead the chorus for his canonization after his exeunt from this life if need be. If men could be something more than saints and angels, he was ready in making an apotheosis of him.

On this day, the crowd was sizable and still growing. Some burrowed through the mammoth crowd, some wiggled forward in a surge as they tried to get as close as possible, and the littles ones meandered still forward as they sought a vantage spot from where they would tell their tales. A whole lot of young people just wanted to come and see this great man in person. He was like a fable to a whole lot them. There was a story to be told seeing him alive. And older folks did not need to bother themselves because they felt it in their bones that he was victory bound.

Ogidigi had taken his place among the dignitaries behind the podium. His frame towering above everybody else. The noise was loud, and in the din the voice of the Biafran war leader reverberated in all the corners of the field.

His message was clear.

"We must chart a new direction and a new course of action. Our direction must have purpose. For too long we have gyrated without purpose or direction. A ship must wrestle its way forward using some kind of compass, or it would be lost at sea. We are on the precipice to wrestle our country from agelong despoliation, total pillage. For too long we have allowed ourselves to be cajoled into believing things that have kept us in motion without movement. This nation, her people, you and me, must take our place in the comity of nations, not to make up the numbers but to also be purveyor of knowledge using the instrument of science and technology made possible by the endeavors and blessing of other peoples before us. The wheels are already invented. We are not inventing the wheels anymore. It's in our powers to find a way to make it sturdier to serve our purpose as a nation. The ship of this nation is not sailing to the east or to the west. We are charting our own course. Since we're not reinventing the wheels, we would take that which is good from the east and that which is good from the west and merge them into a Biafran fusion." His speech was interrupted with hollering from the crowd every now and then.

"The task ahead of us is more than the Augean table. We need a Hercules and all the Hercules we can find. If we succeed in cleaning the Augean table, it would block the flow of the river Niger. Yet we will not allow ourselves to be deterred. Even river Niger we will also dredge. We are capable. We can do it. We are Biafrans." He paused to a roar of applause.

The crowd had gathered for a leader, and not just a leader, but one that can lead them out of the morass they were in, a leader who would ginger them to do more than they did during the genocide.

"Lend me your ears. We are going to have an economy that caters to the needs of the people, the common man, an economy that works for the ordinary folks. Mark my words, we'll not have an economy that takes the Biafran people prisoners. We're not going to have an economy that makes any one of us Biafrans gnash their teeth. The people, the Biafran people, the common man are the engine that drives the economy. Anyone who tells you otherwise is trying to hoodwink you. That's voodoo economist. If you drove this economy or any economy, then you should not be toiling under its weight. The rich do no create or grow the economy. It's the poor people like you that grow the economy that the rich had had a stranglehold on. But my assurance to you on this day is that I'll not allow them to make you prisoner in this economy that depends on you, the people of Biafra. You grow this economy, and then the economy turns around and takes you prisoner. We'll never allow it. We'll never allow a winner-take-all economy while you, my people still have me at the wheels. We will be a great nation, but we will never give a dud check to the poor of this nation.

"Today, I would not be running if they had taken you hostage politically and leave you to have some good life. Today, the trouble with these people was that taking you hostage politically was not enough. They want to keep you in economic quagmire in perpetuity. No! We cannot continue to operate an economy of *monkey dey work, baboon dey chop*. Take it from me, give me your vote, and the era of baboon economy would be consigned onto the ashes of history…

"Hark! Harken to me!" he bellowed. His cadence falling and rising, pitch perfect. "Biafra has suffered a lot, greatly in the hands of people of all shades, black and white. First, it was the British. Then the avengers. Then the marauders. Then the whippersnappers. Then the charlatans. And then the neo-potentates. Everyone has had a field day in Biafra. Now, it's your turn. But, do not do it for me. Do it for yourselves. They've made you the rubbles of the earth. They've robbed your land. You've become peasants when you should be living in comfort. And they've become comfortable when they should be living in peasantry. Hark!" His cadence edged lower again and then veered off nostalgically. "Tell the world that Ironsi did not die in vain. Tell the world that Amadi did not die in vain. Tell the world that Theo, oh young Theo, did not die in vain. Tell the world that Tim did not die in vain. Tell the world that Egirigi did not die in vain. Tell the world that Nwafor and Nwofor did not die in vain. Tell them that Etuk did not die in vain. Tell them that Blackman did not die in vain. Tell them. Tell them. Tell the world that too many of your own, too numerous to mention did not die in vain. Tell them that this is Biafra land. Tell them that Biafra is Africa. Guard it! But, tell them also that Africa is not Biafra. Know that! And remember that! So we cannot allow them to scramble Biafra like the scramble for Africa. Tell them that the time has come to reclaim your land. Do-not-let-them-partition-Biafra" he reeled off the last sentence segmentally emphatically, punctuating every of its words as if they were complete sentences in themselves.

Like a demagogue he was not and like a rabble-rouser he could have been, he paused to allow the crowd to absorb the full import of his every word. And then he continued offering them not a single bight. However, the crowd was not looking for promises, they just believed. They had gathered to hear out the man who they believed had the oratory power and immense personality to lead them to the promised land. Ending the war was important, but what was most important now was what the people had gathered here to bear witness to.

"The days are numbered when you, the people, are held hostage by corrupt careerist criminal politicians at high and low places. The day would be gone when some servants of the people will in broad daylight commandeer the bights that belong to you into their own personal earning and deny you the chance to have good roads and steady water and power supply, beggarly hospital system that's not good for the pigs and their families. The days are gone when people would sit behind their desks and become millionaires and billionaires. The days are here when government jobs will have no attraction and people will run away from being appointed to serve the people. The days we've built prisons for small men but big men found their way out of the dragnet are long gone. The day of the net hauling the big fish is here. They've made thieves out of young men and the rest of us. While our young men languish in jailhouses for paltry infractions, people, whose acts of larceny had created these unfortunate young men, walk free like colossus before our eyes. The day when every day is a heyday for a government employee to come to work to make money from public coffer was long gone. Careerist economic criminals in political offices who have turned innocent people to criminals would have to swap places. And those days are here!" More applauses.

"Perhaps, Bazooka would not have been a criminal if Obiagu had not coveted the resources meant for the good of the people to himself and his family. Obiagu is a bigger criminal than Bazooka, but Bazooka was hunted down and Obiagu is a free man made relevant by the community he made wretched. This man who created Bazooka and today Bazooka is no more, but Obiagu is a chieftain in his community. Nwamesia and his ilk created Tondo and his ilk. Today, Tondo is nowhere, caught down by the angst of his community, but Nwamesia who made himself a millionaire on the back of our people is a titled man and respected by you. Even some of us who made the war more arduous at great loss of lives of your children and neighbors' children are walking free because the letters of the end of the hostilities prohibited bringing them to book. Now they are respected members of your communities, their atrocities forgotten," he said to the murmurs and whimpers from every section of the crowd. The crowd knew that only Dim would have the boldness to address the taboos in the land. Only he could be brazen to say aloud some thoughts a whole lot of people had been murmuring in whispers.

"Listen to me, my people. It's only in Africa. It's only in Biafra land that foreigners just walk into the mainland and start digging for silver and gold and diamond. It's only in Biafra land that foreigners dig up oil and scoop it with buckets and basins and move on with it and no questions are asked. I'm running because I want to put a stop to it. That was why we went to the trenches, but on the cusp of our victory they forced negotiated peace so that they would continue to have it life as usual…"

At cross sections of the crowd some folks were having a go.

"This man has got some guts," said Ochonma.

"I know. But they won't let him win," said Obioma.

"He will win hands down, but they won't let him do his job," said Agaracha.

"Why won't they let him win? And who are they, by the way? Look, my friend, I have my two eyes open even when I am sleeping. No one should try that hanky-panky thing again in this election and in Biafra land. We are watching," said Ochonma.

"If he won they would try to stop him or even kill him…," began Obioma.

"Who's this their they?" asked Ochonma.

"Foreign enemies and local collaborators, your brothers," said Obioma.

"We will get to them before they get to him. We will form a wall around him. They would have to get to us before they get to him. We will defend him with our blood…," began Ochonma.

"Listen up, my people," the voice of the war leader came back in full force, "since the Portuguese set their feet on these shores the African landscape has never been the same. Africa has become a no-man's-land. But remember that they could never have achieved the monstrous accomplishments without the connivance of your own people. Look at Obikolo. He has gotten a passage because the end-of-the-war terms have given him certain protections. People like him are in our midst, and yet there is no atonement for their sins, no restitutions. Biafra must act like a free nation," he warned tacitly.

"But we have got a lot of work to do," he continued. "We have got a great work ahead of us. You must be bold to confront those who had sworn an oath to punish you with poverty while making hay for themselves and their children. There must not be sacred cows, and please, my people, do not make me an exception. Hold my own feet to the fire. Have no pity, and remember, what we can't do is to wallow in self-pity. The oars are in our hands now. We can oar it fast and slow as we want but headed toward safety, with the catch still intact. We can no longer blame anyone else. We have got ourselves to blame for any resemblance of failure. To avoid having to blame others, your chance is here. Take it or leave. I stand here today asking you all to take it. Be counted. Do not be left out. Do not let me down. I need every one of your votes. I'm asking you all as you supported my leadership in the past, give me your votes, vote for me now. We must come together. As the Americans are wont to say 'ain't.' Biafra ain't free yet. Biafra must be free. Yes, Biafra must..."

A section of the crowd was rumbustious, and every one of his sentences was punctuated with "We stand with you." And then at the other section, a young man slipped onto the podium and whispered to Ogidigi something to the effect of a police raid at one of his protégé's kiosk. It was his beloved son, so to speak.

Among the small group of people gathered to watch what the police had up their sleeve were Chance and Turnkey. They had come to town to pick up a few items to put their blind in order. It was a spectacle already. It was pretty good business for the police to raid and ransack small business owners in that part of the city, most of the time on flimsy excuses and under trumped-up charges of theft or dealing in stolen goods. Such police raid had become rampant, and the traders' complaints had fallen on deaf ears. The traders had been helpless, and the police had taken their situation for granted. The police were still exercising their show of impunity when Ogidigi waded into the crowd, a man of great heights. The police, armed with batons, with the exception of one who had a revolver pistol attached to the holster on the hips, were busy tearing down the young man's wares looking for only-God-knows-what. They numbered about seven. As he continued to push his way through, all the onlookers knew him. Unmistakable! But, unaware of his presence until he began to survey the ranks of the policemen he came across first. He was disappointed to know that they were all without ranks. His dismay was dispelled when he noticed that one of them had the rank of a sergeant and others were mere recruits. The sergeant was the only one with a gun that probably had just one or two bullets, at most three. He walked up to the police officer and lifted his hand, delivering a slap to the man's face with force enough to make the policeman stagger. In the immediacy, the recruits rushed forward with their batons to stamp their authority on the environment and situation. But the cool head of the sergeant prevailed. He held back his men with a hollering command. If this man could pick him out and give him a dirty slap, he must be a man of immense capability and connection. Actually, the sergeant had been at his post for barely six weeks. He was not used to the town and did not know much about the man who just gave him a public assault and opprobrium. He pushed back on his men and asked them to lay down their arms if that was what their batons were meant to stand for. It was a botched operation!

The raid was brought to an abrupt end. And then there was little commotion brewing as the crowd began to fill up the environment with people who just left the rally adding to the numbers. As a face-saving measure the sergeant decided that Ogidigi would accompany them to their station. Having done what he did, the sergeant reasoned that the man that slapped him must be a respected member of his community. So instead of having Ogidigi ride at the back of the open pickup truck, he offered him a seat at the front. Secondly, he reasoned that if this man was to be a very important personality in this town, putting him at the back guarded by his men would be an act of very bad publicity. But Ogidigi would not take that for an answer. Either the police would let him go and let his boy do his legitimate business, or he would go to the police station at the back of the truck. Ogidigi never played to the gallery just for the sake of it. If one wagered with him, he would go as far as he who went furthest. But the sergeant had a job to do. Above that he had the image of the force to protect. How can a bloody civilian rubbish him in plain sight? That was one operation if he had known in hindsight he would want to avoid a thousand times. He could not force Ogidigi to ride with him in the front seat. He risked bringing a riot to the city. Anyway, Ogidigi was not someone that could be pushed around physically or psychologically. Weighing the options before him, he felt that this man must somehow explain his action at the police post. So he obliged Ogidigi to ride at the back of the police pickup truck.

That very act at that very moment made Ogidigi's path to freedom a whole lot easier, and the police job a whole lot more difficult. What followed was mere chaos unintended. The road to the police post about two miles was full of throng of people. Before the truck. Beside the truck. And behind the truck, young men and boys, some of whom had experienced police raids and brutality and high-handedness, followed and chanted their songs of war. It was like a crawl, the journey of the tortoise and the crowd swelled. To make matters worse, Ogidigi refused to sit down. It was a like a guard of honor. Hell was about to lose itself upon the land. The police had messed with the wrong guy!

At the police post the crowd milled around, waiting for Ogidigi. He was asked to render a statement. As the crowd became highly unruly, the police superintendent had to act fast to diffuse the tension. As soon as Ogidigi finished with his terse statement of nothing, he was let go, and on hand to pick him up was Chance and Turnkey. He was asked to report to the police post in three days' time, but everyone knew that that was the end of the story.

When Ogidigi and the throng of people had all gone away, the superintendent took the sergeant inside his office and dressed him down. It was short of a reprimand. But in the sergeant's personal file the superintendent left the words "spoken to about not disturbing the peace," without expatiating. A reoccurrence of such operation that would endanger the peace and tranquility of the community would warrant a more serious warning. The police were to maintain peace and order of the community and not to disturb it. A compilation of such indiscretion would earn the sergeant a full reprimand and other disciplinary actions.

Having witnessed the proceeding a horde of butterfly flew out of Turnkey's head. He had hoped that Joann and Candie had come with them to see people's power in action. He knew that that would never happen in his country where policemen geared themselves as if their place of work was a theater of war or that they were at war with the citizenry they were sworn to an oath to protect. Such exuberance of any man might be just an invitation for an untimely and summary death sentence. The police officer would have the backing of his superior because in the hidden and not so hidden codes they operate they seemed to have been licensed to act on their own and out of order with impunity.

At home Joann had busied herself with *Tom and Jerry* show on television. They had been her favorite show growing up and was glad to see it on television in this far-off land. It was a great treat for her. And on the dining table Candie had found some adoring companions.

In Igbo land, it was those who had excess wealth that rear dogs and cats. It was an axiom. And the Ogidigis were truly endowed. Because material things were none of their headache, they could afford to breed some dogs. And the grandma dog in the house loved to give birth to puppies. When a she-dog gives birth every now and then, her backside is never a good thing to behold. And Musket, the grandma dog, loved to have an affair, and was exemplary in giving birth very often and having a backside not good enough to the eyes. One may erroneously conclude that since she was legendary in having babies often and leaving her with some ugly backside, that her kids would be ugly. That was not the case. She had always had beautiful soulmates, belonging to their next-door neighbors. Her offspring were exceptionally beautiful. And as soon as Chance and his company came back, and as soon as Candie set her eyes on those beautiful puppies, she knew that she had some companions even in the presence of those who loved her dearly.

Alone! All alone she lured one of the three-week-old puppies to herself. She lifted it up to the dining table and began to toy with it. She cuddled it. She caressed it. Then grabbed it. With her hand under the front legs she lifted it up to her face, then to her forehead. The puppy licked her cheekbones and then her eyes. It tickled her, and she moved the puppy to her other eye. The puppy was enjoying it and she obliged it. Then the puppy was all over her face and began to lick her nose and her mouth. Candie stuck out her tongue, and the puppy licked it. She kissed the puppy on its nose and brought it to her bosom as a mother would cuddle a child. It was mother and child huddling together.

And then Dorothy sauntered into the annex. And there was Candie with one of the nameless puppies for no name had been given to it yet. She did not see her kissing the puppy or the puppy licking her face. Rather she saw her holding the puppy to her face, talking to it and seemingly asking it questions. It was too close to her face and was very suggestive of all the things she had heard of, of the mad relationship between man and dog in the western world. To say that she was bewildered was an understatement. She was speechless. There was no hiding that fact. She stopped short what she had come to the annex to do. She grabbed a seat and sat down right in front of Candie on the opposite side of the table.

"Young woman," she began, staring her in the face. "Did you say that your name is Candy?" she asked calmly.

"Yes, ma'am, my name is Candie," she acknowledged.

"Hmmmm," Dorothy demurred. "What a name!" she said quietly. "Are you a edible? Are you eatable?" she asked.

"Hmmmm," murmured Candie. "You sound very much like Chance," she added.

"Yes, that's my child," Dorothy reiterated. "And why are you cuddling and hugging and caressing and kissing my puppies?" asked Chance's mother.

"Oh, they're my babies, I love them," said Candie, mimicking cuddles and breastfeeding a baby.

"Who's your baby?" asked Dorothy incredulously.

"It's my baby," repeated Candie, pointing at the puppy she was clutching.

"You must be out of your mind. Puppy, your baby! If you want baby, Osai can give you babies…"

"No, I don't want those. I don't want those kinds of babies. I hate two-legged kiddos. I like four-legged kind of babies. I love them. I love them," cried Candie.

"Why? Has Osai lost his nuts? Or is there no juice in those nuts of his?" Chance's mother fired back.

"I don't know. Ask him. But I don't want babies," she cried again.

"And you want puppies for babies?"

"Yes, I love them, I love them more than babies. And can I go with one of them?" asked Candie.

"Goodness me! How do you love them more than babies? Are you out of your mind?" queried Chance's mother.

"No, I'm not. I love them. I can take care of them. I can't take care of babies. Can I go with them?" she cried again with her eyes now soaked with tears.

Dorothy got up from her chair. She thought to herself that the young lady she was talking to must be really deranged.

"You can't have any of them. You want to starve them," she said as she was walking out of the dining area.

"I'll not starve them, I'll take care of them. I'll feed them right. Please, allow me to take them along with me…" Dorothy could hear Candie's plea after her as she exited the annex, spitting in disgust and swearing *tufiakwa*, an exclamation of complete repulsion of knowledge of ugly and inordinate behavior or conduct.

No doubt Chance was livid. He knew that his mother could do anything, but it did not occur to him that his mother could provoke his guest to tears. When he inquired from Candie what the matter with her was, she could only tell him that his mother refused her taking home with her one of the puppies. That doused his temper. There was nothing in it. It was not enough to provoke a snivel let alone a tear. And it was never enough to provoke a vehement argument or a brawl with his mother. Were he mad, he had to show it with poise. Were he upset, he had to let his mother know in camera. Nevertheless, it was his mother who summoned him to the main annex of the building.

To have the building set up with an annex was her making. When she got married to Ogidigi initially, she learned fast. Despite his huge and imposing height, he had a very thin skin with things that had to do with affection. It was a riddle that needed to be solved and solved very quickly. If his manner were moans and groans that would have been a little kettle of fish. It was much more than that. Ogidigi was a swan when it came to copulation with his wife. He could sing and peck the wood at the same time. It was always a moment to lose one's comportment faculties. And he never learned to manage it! It was a put off, yet it was a necessary condiment of togetherness of a husband and a wife. Ogidigi could not be schooled on matters like that because it was beyond his control.

Ogidigi was on top of the pack of a handful of those men who lost their heads and promised their beaus heaven and earth when they were on top and their heads were no longer with the living. He never promised his wife that he was going to buy her a whole town when he got to a common material. No! He never did. Rather, he was a town crier.

Time and again she would cover his mouth, and time and again she would threaten to starve him of love. It was a distraction for her from enjoying the sweetness of copulation. She did not know whether to cover his mouth and quench his wailing or allow him to continue and earn the opprobrium of his kindred people. Covering his mouth with her hand limited her concentration, limited her joy, and made it very difficult for her to attain orgasm. They began to work on it. She was able to extract a promise from him.

"Mkpu oo, nma ntizi. Mkpu oo, nma ntizi." Wailing I would no longer indulge in.

It was a gentleman's agreement, needless putting pen to paper. He must work on not shouting when they copulated. But rather than keep quiet while they were on it, it became like a swan song. Instead of keeping a promise that he would no longer shout while they were making love, he always began to tell her in rote that he would no longer shout as soon as the beat was on:

"Mkpu oo, nma ntizi, Mkpu ooo, nma ntizi."

And the fact of the matter was that as he began to gain entry his shouts began to rise in low ebb. As he began to descend, his shouts began to ascend and gain momentum and more repetitive:

"Mkpu oooo, nma ntizi, Mkpu ooooo, nma ntizi, Mkpu oooooo, nma ntizi."

As he drove his manhood to the hilt his shouting rose to crescendo. When he had exhausted his sinew, his refrain began to fall. Like a deflated balloon his voice began to peter out still echoing the promise:

"Mkpu oooo, nma ntizi. Mkpu ooo, nma ntizi Mkpu oo, nma ntizi Mkpu o, nma ntizi."

Having emptied himself, he would lie there almost comatose and his wife on the other side as if she was coming from a semi asphyxiation. Copulation with her husband was always an epic. Having come down to earth he would lie beside her like the proverbial flaming fire that begot impotent ashes.

Getting Ogidigi to shut his mouth was an exercise in futility. Despite his agility. Despite his prowess. In spite of himself, he was still a man bedeviled by foibles he was incapable of overcoming.

No one ever asked her what was making her husband wail like that because they all knew that the noises that emanated from their bedroom especially at nights were the wailing of a grown man. Whether or not she was beating him was not a good story to tell. How could that happen to such an imposing man. There was one assumption. Few would begrudge her. It was her man. He was her man. But she never wanted to make a public fanfare of what went on in her bedroom. Or give out the impression that that huge man was getting beaten up by his wife. So to eliminate that public obloquy of what went inside their bedroom every night and day, without much ado she persuaded him that the house they were intending to erect was going to have an annex.

Chance did better to keep his nerves. It was a war he had not gotten enough artilleries to win. Eyeball to eyeball he demurred. He knew right away from the look on his mother's face that it was no time for polemics or inundation of the nonsensical. His mother's viewpoints were open secrets.

"Mom, why are you making that little girl cry?"

"You fool! She chose to cry on her own. By the way what's little about that old woman? I've had two pregnancies by the time I was her age. What's little about her? And do you not know that those who do not have the means do not rear cats and dogs? How hard is that for you to understand?"

"But, Mom, she could have one of these puppies for keeps. After all Musket is a serial birther. These people are in love with cats and dogs, it's a family thing for them. Cats and dogs are members of their families," said Chance.

"You really do not understand, Osai. She said that she wants a baby. How hard is that for you to understand? Cats and dogs members of the family? Sacrilege!" She scoffed and paused.

"No, she could not just be wanting one just like that, caressing, kissing, hugging, and cuddling like a baby just like that," said Dorothy.

"It's their culture to do all that. It does not mean a thing to them," said Osai.

"Did I not tell you that I do not want dog kissing, caressing, hugging, and cuddling individuals in my house. If you can't read between the lines, then you have not come of age. How old are those girls, Osai?" asked his mother.

"She would turn twenty-three in September, and her friend will turn twenty-one next summer," answered Osai.

"Twenty-three and you can't read the cue, Osai. Have you lost your balls? You father did not tell me when he castrated you."

"Mom, you are at it again…"

"How hard is that, Chance?" calling him by his nickname which she rarely used. "Just know it that when a lady woos you with her cues and you failed to grab it, it's a slight. When that urge is blunted you would be beating about the bush when you now think that you are ready. Your chance was gone, and she would be playing hard to catch. And really, she would be hard to catch. In these things, opportunity comes but once, Osai."

"Mom, you're at it again. I don't want to go into that business yet," said Osai.

"You don't want to go into that business. Let me ask you again, what happened to your balls? Are you a eunuch?"

"Hold it there, Mom! I do not know what you're talking about, Mom. She just wanna have one of your puppies for a baby, for a fond pet." His voice was rising.

"If you don't get what you want, you make do with what you have," said the mother.

"She just needed your puppies," said Osai.

"No, she just needed your babies," retorted his mother as Osai prepared to leave her presence.

But she was not done. She called him back as a mother would beckon his beloved son. Osai had been standing all along. Now she offered him a seat right opposite her on the dining table.

"You needed to be careful with your idolatrous friends. I can't stand any of these antics in the name of petty care and love for animals."

"There's nothing idolatrous about it. It's their culture, and when you deny her the puppies you cause her some emotional trauma, and that could be damaging till the rest of her life. And you don't wanna be mentioned in that story…"

"Hold your breath, young man. If talking to a child damages her self-esteem, you might want to stop bringing them to this land. This land is holy. We worship God in truth and in spirit and not what they've superimposed on the gullible. When you begin to adore cows and horses you begin to take away what belongs to God."

"That's not it, Mom. It's conditioning. For centuries, they've mastered the universe and conquered its inhabitants. With nowhere else to go they programmed animals to think and behave like human. They've brought them closer to their hearts and have made them house members with equal rights or even more rights in some instances. If you think of dogs, you ain't seen nothing yet. Cats are next in rank. They're multibillion industry, and you rather be humane with them…"

"Now, hold your peace. And even cat?"

"Yes, of course, it's always cats and dogs."

"Cats of all animals! You remember you grandmother, my mother. When she was alive, she would throw everything within her reach to any cat that came within her sight."

"Why? Remind me again," interjected Osai.

"She dreaded cats for some reasons. They're evil in their stealthiness. She would pursue them as far as she could, and she would haul anything within her reach at them so that they would go away with their evil omen as far as earth would not see them. For her, cats have two purposes, all which could be achieved without their help. They are predators of rodents, and secondly, they are harbingers of evil. When a cat comes to her threshold, my mother used to chase them as far away as possible because they bring death to the family. Chasing them away relieves the family of that calamity, and it will pass them by."

"That was a fable," said Osai to his mother.

"You think it's a fable? Have you seen a cat mauled down by a vehicle? You see dogs killed every now and then because they think that they are smart. But cats are like chimera. And they are only good for witchcraft. And that's why dog hates them. Because dogs see a lot more than the common eyes can see, because they see the witchery of cats, that's why they are always at loggerheads with cats."

"Mom, this sounds like tale by moonlight..."

"Goat," bleated his mother, "something that have been proven over the centuries has become a fable just because you went to the Americas. By the way, if cats and dogs are family members, your father's herd are family members too. And I tell you, you have a motley crowd for family members; you have a thousand and one family members. If your grandmother was still here she would just scratch your mouth on the rough edges of the ground. You think you would have outgrown her reproach to think that cats are family members."

"Mom, these people have overcome all that premonition that cats bring to their lives and have started to impact their lives positively."

"Sheep."

"You know what they say that before the second coming the gospel would be preached to the utmost ends of the earth. Before we get to that point, these cultures you're fighting against will permeate to the utmost ends of the earth. It will get there before the gospel, and then God would have had enough reasons to release the sword of Armageddon on his beautiful wonderful world."

"And you're trying to make it happen sooner than later. You have become the vector, you empty vessel."

"No, I'm just a spectator."

"I didn't ask your father to send you to America to be an onlooker. You were sent to learn and bring in the best."

"Yes, Mom, I'm bringing in the best."

"Please, I don't want her babies," she said as Osai finally left her presence.

When four days later and they were airborne on that Ethiopian Airways flight 349, Candie had in her company two puppies, one she named Pigeria and the other Bandit. And on that same flight, while everyone else slept, Chance picked up a copy of the *voodoo Lavaca Economist* right in the seat pocket in front of him, and sharing the front page was a picture of Dim addressing a mammoth crowd in Umudede. The main caption read, "The warmonger is back," With a subcaption, "We knew it," as a quote from a permanent secretary in the Foreign Office Ministry.

CHAPTER 24

How he had hoped that he could excise his father's spirit from himself. No, he could not. All's well! And money was not his problem on account of his father's accumulation. He had sustained himself on his father's largesse, furnished him ceaselessly. With that part taken care of, he had enough time to focus on his studies, and he was doing well academically. He had also kept in touch with his homeland and all the rumbling that was going and dug in tactic of the government. Nothing had changed. Corruption was rampant. What changed was the name, a new country, but the vestiges of the corrupt, defunct Nigerian system still held court. Coming to America convinced him that something must give way for him to have a country he could be proud of and to call his own. He knew that he would succeed and become his own man without the looming silhouette of his father all over him. He wanted to carve a niche for himself. And he was determined to. Yet he still recognized that he had a huge problem of unknown magnitude before him. He was an illegal immigrant student. He had come into the country through a crack in the back door. He had beaten the system. A whole lot of people come into America and blend into the system without a trace until one was caught in the web of a colossal wrongdoing. Bucknor had navigated that part. He had no business to engage in anything that would put him at loggerheads with the law of the land. And as long as he comported himself he would remain under the radar and he would be fine.

He had little or no distractions. His routine was go to class and go to the gym to keep in shape and retire to his apartments, while away a little bit of his time, and read his books and get ready for class the following day. Coming and going and going and coming, he had seen a figure he thought he knew from somewhere, but he had rummaged his wildest imagination, yet he could not place where he had met her before. Then one fateful early evening, the sun was going down, and he was coming from the students' lounge. Descending the flights of stairs, he ran into that same figure again, and as he darted his head to the left their eyes were locked in a unifying convergence.

Bucknor did not know when he spurted, "I knew you from somewhere."

"I don't know you from Adams," said Juicy Lee without a second thought. "I don't think I've met you before," she added offhandedly.

"Your face looks familiar. I know that I know you from somewhere," Bucknor insisted.

"Well, it's a possibility. You know that it's a small world," said Ms. Juicy.

"Sure, it is! And I'm trying to remember," said Bucknor.

"What's your name? My name is Juicy," said Ms. Juicy, extending her hand of welcome.

"My name is Bucknor Obikolo," said Bucknor.

"Now, you got me! That name rings a bell," said Juicy.

"Which one? The first or the surname?" asked Bucknor.

"Both. But especially the last name," she answered him. Bucknor shrunk a little bit, his father's name looming all over him in spite of the thousands of miles and all efforts he was making to excise himself from his father. He then remembered what his father used to tell him that no matter how fast one ran, one never outruns his buttocks or outpaces his shadows.

"I see. Then you must have been to Biafra, the land of the rising sun," said Bucknor.

"Yes, you got it! Beautiful people," said Juicy nostalgically.

Ms. Lee just left the university at twenty-one, precocious and wanting to experiment with the world beyond the shores of America. She did not want to join the Navy that would afford her the chance to travel freely all over the world in defense of a rampant freedom. She chose to join the Peace Corps, an appendage of the State Department, engaged in all sorts of activities around the world. Most of those who joined ended up teaching in classrooms or helping out in asylum camps in the countries where they found themselves. They were also the eyes and ears of their home government, wittingly or unwittingly garnering information for their government. In Biafra, Ms. Lee found a spot in the fledgling university and with certificate as a graduate in liberal arts and a major in English language. She was employed to teach introductory literature for first-year students. It was her first job as a professor, and she was relishing the opportunity. Her class was fairly large, but she was not intimidated by the number of the students she had to deal with. There was no stand-out experience to recall. But the second semester was calamitous. She had given an assignment on creative writing. She was hoping for a blast. But what the students turned in did not impress her, and she let the class know about what she thought ought to be creative. Majority of the class got less than a passing grade. She enjoined the students to be really creative and imaginative. The students returned to the drawing table and went to work. What they turned in did not impress her either. A whole lot of them was like a personal caricature of her persona or someone else. Some of them were outright porn in prose. And she told them without mincing words.

"When I wanted you to be creative, I didn't mean that you should get me some pornography, girls flashing, boys frolicking, girls spreading themselves, and all that. Those are not creative. I want you to be creative!" she told the class. But she was wrong.

After admonishing the entire class and at the end of the class among friends in small groups, the questions was whodunit? It was like a communal inquest among the disciples of Christ in trying to decipher who among the twelve must be the Mr. Iscariot. No one owned up to it until Bucknor, in one of those groups, stepped forward and offered a profound Freudian slip.

"Did she not ask for a creative writing?" he asked to no one in particular. "She ain't seen nothing yet. She will see short story. She will read short story until she will be running with her tail in between her legs," he told the throng of boisterous classmates that were headed for the bus ride to their hostels. They had heard it from the horse's mouth. There was no need to look further for whodunit! When they came back at the beginning of next semester, they discovered that Ms. Juicy Lee was gone back whence she came from, the United States of America.

"You just left us like that," said Bucknor as he pulled her away from the area to allow access to passersby.

"You drove me crazy. But anyway, I needed to come back for my master's program," she told him.

"You should have done it in Biafra."

"No, I needed to come home and secure some student loan for the program."

"And now, what are you doing?" asked Bucknor.

"I'm done with that, and I'm into my PhD program. And what about you? You left your father's name and glory and wanted to carve a niche for yourself, eh?" Bucknor recoiled inside himself. Nothing would be concluded without reference to his father.

"Well, I'm here for a program in banking and finance. And I'm trying to combine it with management. After that I intend to go and do a master's in business administration."

"That's a good idea. It looks like you have a game plan to go back home and manage your father's largesse."

"No, not at all," said Bucknor, trying to hide his discomfort. "I would want to carve my own niche."

"It's difficult to do that, you just have got to try."

"Difficult to do what?"

"Difficult to extricate oneself from a famous dad."

"I see. I just got to try," said Bucknor as they bade each other bye.

Each had made a very good impression on the other. As they went their separate ways, Juicy began to think back about her experience in Biafra during her short sojourn in that land. She tried to place Bucknor in vivid cognizance, and that creative writing class came back flashing, and the student that went by the name Bucks came back to the center stage. He was him.

Their friendship was just like hitting the ground and running. They had been bumping into each other every now and then. And within weeks they had exchange visits and everything was fine. The only snag was when she paid recognition to his pedigree. He loathed that aspect of their discussion, but with time she had learned to circle that aspect of his life and he was fine.

At the nick of time he began to talk to her about the problem with his immigration papers. At first, he was reluctant to let her into that window of his stay in the United States. But as his confidence grew he opened up to her, and it was not a bad idea at all. He did not tell her that he came in with someone else's passport. He just told her that he came into the country illegally with no mention of a Mr. Ghoostte. She had understood his predicament. She was willing to help him fix his papers so that he could go about his business without fear. A lot of immigrant population went through that due process. On her part, she was transparent. She had nothing to hide. She was voluminous. All about her was like a front page of a gorgeous book. While she was forthcoming he held back. Though he took none of the cues of her effusive affection for granted. But one night she took him to task. She sat him on the edge of his bed.

"I don't understand the matter with you. While you stand nothing to gain, so to speak, by my own inference of your thinking, you stand nothing to lose. In fact, you've got all to gain," said Juicy. "You African men are dumb asses. You lack courage to make the first move. This thing ain't a game of lose and be held hostage and to be ransomed," she continued. And still Bucknor made no effort to interrupt her or ask what was she talking about.

"Don't be acting as if you don't know what I'm talking about," she began again.

"Lady, I'm waiting on you to finish and explain to me what you mean to say. You've to bring me into the loop."

"I need to spank you to explain all that to you. Or should I say that you needed spanking me for you to get in the know of what I am talking about. How come each night I come into your apartment you would choose to roll yourself up and attach yourself to the wall like a leech? Do you sense blood on that wall? I can't feel you, yet I see the blood rushing down your vein. The blood is on this side and not the wall. So why are you punishing yourself for nothing? I'm here for you. I'm all yours. What's the matter with you, African men?" charged Juicy.

"Oh please, it's none of those your thoughts," said Bucknor tamely.

"Then, tell me what's making you effeminate when I see manliness all over your body." She wanted to know.

"Juicy, honestly speaking, I don't want to break your heart. I'm not going to stay here for that much long."

"Then, why did you have to come here? And let me tell you something, my heart was long broken. You're not breaking my heart, you're now searing it."

"Not intentional, Juicy," said Bucknor feebly.

"It's ignorance 101, that's your problem. I don't need your commitment. I know what you're thinking. I've a handful in two baby boys that I don't want or need any more. I don't want a manboy added to the mix. And for your information, I'm an American. Wherever the wheels come off that jalopy is its burial ground, and we move on. Let me tell you something you don't know but which I know would gladden your wretched mind," she said repositioning herself. "This stomach you see," she said, pointing at her belly, "it's like a rock, and no water sticks on a rock if it were still a rock. It's been turned upside down and inside out if that would assuage your nerves," she told him.

"I know what you mean, my sweetheart," Bucknor mustered to say.

"Do not sweetheart me! If you knew, why are you punishing yourself? You African people like to pretend. When you made up your mind, you will be all over the whole show. And I'll be pleading with you to come down and take a deep breath." Bucknor tried to suppress a chuckle.

"I tell you something, my African young boy. You got a chance tomorrow. If you don't play balls. I'm gonna crack those nuts, and you ain't gonna see me again. You don't even have to ask for it. It's given, just do it. Don't tell me that you don't know how to do it. It's never taught by your mama; it's natural, it's innate. Just do it! And live without fear." she snarled him.

They both slept soundly that night, and nothing happened. It gave Bucknor ample time to think about himself not taking a love offered on a platter. There was no way for him to collaborate her story, but one thing was certain and that was that he needed her presence to navigate his tricky waters of securing a travel paper to visit home. But she did not show up the following night and the night after and the night afterward, and he began to worry. It gave him still ample time to think about her again and again. It gave him ample time to also think about what he stood to lose. It was the fourth night afterward that she showed up and he was ready. As she rightly predicted he was all over her, and he emptied all he had in his barrel inside her.

"There are some springs in your agility. You were just rattling all the corners and perimeters inside of me," she told him when both had come down from their highs, thrusting her right forefinger inside the dimple in the left side of his cheeks. "It had seemed like you were trying to just put me in my place," she added.

"It's all good. Seeing is believing, and sometimes experiencing it is the only proof," he told her somehow triumphantly.

"This will last me for forty days and forty nights and will be remembered for eternity."

"That's not my intention. I'm looking forward to the sequelae," said Bucknor.

"Yep! No, no, no. I don't wanna melt my head in the heat of exhilaration. I've gotten to the edges of the melting point. This is it," she said while nodding and shaking her head at the same time, and moments later, she fell asleep and slept like a baby.

She was renewed, and when she looked back, in a long time that was the best sex she could remember she had ever had.

CHAPTER 25

The metamorphosis of Turnkey was truly remarkable. After Candie had spoken to him on their way to class about Chance, he did not have to think long and hard. There was no reason to be antagonizing this fella, Chance. And then, come to think about it, it was not actually his nature. Over the years, he was conditioned to believe in erroneous dogma and flirtations. Time and again he had been in and out of one philosophy or the other. So he had been swayed this way and that way as the breeze would sway the alfalfa. They had all stuck, but none had stuck for a long time. But the genesis of his flirtation with hate was sown by his uncle who saw a void to fill. He did not just fill the void. He shook and pressed it down. Now he had come of age and can decide what philosophy he had to hold dear. Shrewd and calculating as he was he had come to realize that he stood to gain much more from accepting this guy and that he stood to lose much more if he kept antagonizing him rather than becoming his natural self, open up to the world around him.

It was not long afterward, at that same rendezvous where Candie had a face-to-face, one-on-one with Chance for the first time, Chance was walking down to one of the slabs for benches when Turnkey just came from behind and gave him a nudge with his right shoulder and walk past him. Chance was surprised to know that his nemesis was at it again. And then he turned and was looking at Chance right in the face, eyeball-to-eyeball.

"Hey, my African young boy…," began Turnkey, trying to muffle a smile.

"Hold it there!" said Chance. "I'm not a boy, and secondly, I'm not an African boy. I'm Biafran before I'm an African. Africa was a creation of the white man. It's a creation of your uncles and forefathers. But Biafra is natural." He proceeded to school him.

"Now, give me your hand." Turnkey seemed to sound commandeering, extending his hand for a handshake. And reluctantly Chance offered his.

"As I know that you're aware, my name is Turnkey Golan Ghoostte," said Turnkey.

"Well, my name is Chance Ogidigi." As the old enemies began to walk side by side.

"You said that you're not African. And that you're Biafran. Being Biafran, does that make you wild?" asked Turnkey.

"I didn't say that I'm not African. I'm first a Biafran before I'm an African. I don't want us to confuse the issues here. And I'm not wilder than you, old chap," said Chance condescendingly.

"And what now?" asked Turnkey.

"Eh?" asked Chance.

"What did you just say?" Turnkey wanted him to clarify himself.

"I'm Biafran first and then African. And I'm not wilder than you, old chap," repeated Chance.

"It sounds like you are so full of yourself," said Turnkey.

"No, that's who I am. That's who we are," said Chance.

"Then you must be proud, you're a proud people."

"That's what people say, and tomorrow you yourself might say that I'm arrogant or pompous because you hate my gut," said Chance.

"I'll not. But I see you as someone who is uncouth, yet full of uppitiness."

"I was going to ask you if your 'I will not' is that you'll not say that I'm arrogant or you hate my gut. But anyway, tomorrow has not even come yet, and you are already saying those things that may not be true and will not be true about me or about my people, or the Biafran people."

"It may not be true, but you have to disprove it."

"I've nothing to disprove. It's like saying that you're guilty until you've proven your innocence, old chap," said Chance, trying to belittle him a little bit more.

Now they have reached the slabs of benches, and they sat down opposite each other. And then Turnkey continued.

"When you said that you were going to skin me alive and spill my blood, I found that very, very disconcerting, and that was the wildest thing I've ever heard in my whole life," said Turnkey.

"You'd bothered me a lot. I may not skin you alive, but I was going to really, really hurt you, I wanted you to know that."

"You are full of verbosity."

"You might say that. My father had told me that intimidation is better than harassment. You were the one harassing and stalking and wanting to pick a fight with me. I was just trying to keep you at bay. You were the wilder one. I just wanted to be left alone. And to be left alone, you must, at least, have the capacity to scare people away, or else you would be a dead man before your time," said Chance.

"That sounds like a plan," said Turnkey.

"It's a very good plan, and it works," said Chance as both got up and finally gave each other a firm, warm handshake as they departed.

"We would have to continue this discussion some other time," said Turnkey.

It was a relief for both men that they had thawed the iceberg. Turnkey, who had allowed this ice to form in the first place, was the one who had made the gambit to begin to bring it to a melting point. His morphing was complete. When a slumber became deep and consuming the snoring became rhythmic in its refrain. It was not the case in this relationship. It was like they hit the ground running. The two somehow had been longing for each other's friendship. When next they had met they were freely discussing about their classes and what the future held for them. Turnkey was studying to be an equine massage therapist.

"What's that?" shouted Chance.

"It's a nurturing program for horses…," began Turnkey.

"Is that animal husbandry?" Chance interrupted him.

"And what's that?" asked Turnkey.

"Then never mind me," said Chance.

"Equine massage therapy involves taking care of horses, understanding their traits, and helping them develop those traits. It also involves understanding how horses learn and follow instructions. Like humans, horses and other animals have emotions. Being a massage therapist, you try to recognize those traits and anything else that make them live healthier lives. A relaxed horse is a better performer. When people have strained muscles or even feeling they tend to underperform, so also with horses. A massage therapist prepares a horse for the big events. A happy and well-conditioned horse can outpace a cheetah," he told Chance who was now in confused attention and who could not understand why one would spend upward of two years trying to learn how to teach a horse to talk and react or trying to understand a horse whose knuckles were tightened up.

"And after that, what's next?" he asked.

"Oh, the job is there for the asking," said Turnkey. "There are thousands and thousands of horses and very few therapists, you literarily walk into a job as soon as you're out with a certificate."

"And what's next?"

"You can go on for further studies. You can be a manager in a large farm, in rodeo events, and in time you can own your own horses."

"And what's next?" asked Chance again.

"Chance, you are asking too many questions. What's next? Whatever life throws at you," said Turnkey.

"Oh no! I was trying to understand how you came about this weird course that would consume your life for more than two years," said Chance.

"As a fourteen-year-old peasant boy growing up in rural Boonville, I got a part-time job at a local ranch earning a pittance. That really got me interested in horses and other animals."

"That you started little doesn't mean that you can't think big. Else you gonna end up toiling for the rich all your life and they would begrudge you paying you that pittance. You see, my father had his hands involved in so many ventures and anything that he could make money off. Timber and logging, quarrying and selling gravels, and then grazing and raising dairies. And growing up at about fourteen years of age I was in charge of the cattle and herder of sheep and goats and anything in between, and anything life threw at me. And I hated it. To take my revenge, I'll keep those goats hungry for hours on end. Then my mother would come after me. They would be so hungry and bleated endlessly for hours that when I eventually got them the food they would not let me set it down and up for them. They would surround me and munch away while I still had the fronds on my head. Goats ate the fronds on my head. It was not one of those things that I thought I would do for life."

"I know what you mean," came in Turnkey.

"That I was raised among cows and horses, sheep and goats, geese and gander, turkeys and peacocks, hens and cocks, and that useless he-goat, did not mean that I was going to live among them."

"Why do you refer that as a useless he-goat?" asked Turnkey.

"It kept sniffing at the mother's backside. It's a bloody mother…"

"I see," said Turnkey with a chuckle on his face.

"You could do better with your life. You can think big and make it big. Do not get me wrong. Equine massage therapy is as good as anything else that is lofty and sovereign. It is like the old Orwellian Freudian slip that all animals are equal. But, some are more equal than others. Equine massage therapy or what have you will not take you to the pinnacles of power and influence no matter how big you intend it to be. You have to think outside the box and maximize your opportunities. What I'm doing right now will take me to Wall Street or Broad Street. I do not intend to have anything to do with cows and horses and geese and gander anymore. I don't want to restrict my opportunities, without a chance of breaking out of the jail. I want to make it big with less efforts. The amount of time a rich man invests to be rich is a thousand times less than what a poor man invested in poverty captivity."

"It makes sense," said Turnkey.

"It's all about the right choice. And life's about choices. Always about choices. Good choices. Bad choices. If you have a panoramic view of the horizon ahead of you then you may not need any compass. If not you will be grappling with your compass to find the right direction to the good things of life. Remember that when the rich advise you, most of the time they don't want you to be rich like them and rub shoulders with them. They want to keep you at bay so that if you were lucky, your offspring will tend to theirs and life goes on. In fact, your offspring, Turnkey, will tend to their geese and turkeys," said Chance to his friend.

When the two friends departed Turnkey's mind was set agog. He realized that there was something he had to fix about his course and the direction he was hedging toward. It was not too bad a direction. It was just that it was not too rosy a direction in the long run. The next morning, without intimating his friend, he was at the course advisor's office. After examining and exhausting the choices before him, he resolved that he was going to continue his program in equine message therapy as a minor and pick a major in banking. It was going to be long and arduous, but he was determined to veer off a little bit. He would have to do a whole new course to be able to fit in. It was a journey he was prepared to make and a sacrifice he was prepared to undertake.

CHAPTER 26

Bucknor was more relaxed dealing with Juicy ever since he became convinced that she was not setting him up for a long-term relationship. He could go in and out of her at will without minding any repercussion, and she was savoring it because he made her feel like a woman again. But his major concern still remained. He could not travel to Biafra to see his folks. Though efforts were in the works. By the fact of the marriage Juicy was helping to get him a green card that would allow him to leave the United States and still have access coming in again, having made it dubiously in the first place. He was making progress in his classes. And the flow of money into his account was assured. But his joy was not complete. He needed to travel home even if it were for a couple of days. That was the only thing that divided and sapped his concentration.

In the library one Wednesday afternoon, bent over his books, someone tapped his left shoulder. As he turned to look, standing before him was a look of a ghost beyond his wildest imagination. It was the ubiquitous Jorge Santana. Bucknor's heart sank into his stomach. Life could not be crueler than this. Jorge had become his albatross. Bucknor was unable to hide his disappointment at seeing the man whose image had haunted him ever since he left Buenos Aires.

"Calm down," said Jorge as he gesticulated to his kinsman to relax. "How have you been?" he asked.

"You are the last person I was expecting to meet here," said Bucknor, skipping the question as his mind was not coordinated.

"I know. But you have been doing okay?"

"You can tell I'm doing fairly okay."

"That's good to hear! I know. Life ain't that much fair. Do you hear from your people back at home? How's your father doing? And your mother? And your siblings?"

"They're doing fairly okay. It's my father who has been sick and I really would want to go and see him, but I can't."

"What's wrong with him?" asked Jorge.

"I was told that he had stroke and one side of his body was almost paralyzed. I was told that he had acute myocardial infarction. He was hanging on a thread. He barely made it and is doing much better as we speak."

"That's bad," said Jorge, feigning ignorance. "How's your babe?"

As soon as he said that goose bumps fell all over Bucknor. This man would not stop amazing him.

"Eh?" he muttered incredulously.

"I thought she was working to secure for you some traveling papers."

"Eh, now you're joking. How did you know?" asked Bucknor fearfully and at the same time trying to gather himself.

"I know. It's the way it is. I expect that you'll be doing so. If you were not doing so, working on getting your card, then you're too slow. And I don't think that you're that slow. I'm gonna leave for now. I'll suggest that we meet tomorrow at the William Aiken's Park, you know the garden outside Jefferson building, that's between Jefferson and Washington buildings," said Jorge.

"And *whata* are you doing here?" asked Bucknor as he nodded.

"I'm a student like you."

"And what're you studying?" He recognized that his "whata" was a slip of the tongue.

"You've forgotten that you don't have to ask too many questions. But you can ask me that tomorrow. What time is convenient for you? Is three PM okay for you?"

"Am I gonna get into trouble?" asked Bucknor fearfully again.

"No, not at all. I'll never betray my kinsman no matter what. If I did I would be like those I hold in low esteem," assured Jorge.

When Bucknor got home that evening Juicy was on hand to welcome him. But his body language was understandably different. He tried to brighten up, but his mind kept veering off toward his strange kinsman that seemed to be stalking him. He was not making connection with Juicy unlike him. In between their discussions his mind would veer toward the mystery man. He began to doubt whether or not he would keep the appointment tomorrow and try to avoid this man. But his best instinct kept telling him not to play any pranks with this dangerous man. Mr. Santana did not look like a man interested in any hanky-panky business. He knew that he had no place to hide away from this man that seemed to have a dossier on him. Without thinking further about what the repercussion of his going or not going would be he was resolved that it was in his own best interest to honor the appointment. Having come to that conclusion, he went to his small liquor bar, fetched himself a cognac bottle, poured out a shot for himself and another for Juicy and brightened up.

It was after his last class on that Thursday, and as expected Mr. Santana was already seated on one of the brick benches that littered the garden.

"Hello, Mr. Ghoostte," Jorge teased him. Bucknor looked about himself and smiled wryly. "You're here on my invitation, and I would want to go straight to the point. Do you have another class or an appointment to attend to?" asked Jorge, and Bucknor indicated that he had no engagement. He was more relaxed. He had resigned himself to the fact that if he could do the worst of the worse he would just take a one-way ticket to Biafra and harness all that life would throw at him. That feeling gave him more valve. He was ready to look at this man in the face and ask him to go to hell as long as he did not haul him into jail in this foreign land.

"Apart from the fact that you could not travel to see your folks, I imagine that life has been good to you," began Jorge.

"I've no complaints," said Bucknor.

"That's good. When you look around you, you must like what you see. The buildings, the parks, the grasses, the pavements, the streets. They look exquisite, aren't they?"

Bucknor nodded his agreement.

"By the way, how's your green card application going?" asked Jorge.

"It's going. It's like the journey of the crab and chameleon. It's slow, clumsy, and looking like it's going nowhere," said Bucknor.

"You see all these beautiful things here. We can have them in Biafra with far less effort and with cheaper labor and none on credit cards and all would be proud. But we don't tend to love our own. We're too misguided. We live like a people under a spell. People who say that they love their country yet they stash away the best parts of the country they love in another man's country. Does it make sense? Where's that love for country they professed? Nonexistent. Lip service. But I got good news for you. Freedom is about to come to Biafra."

"In what shape and fashion?" asked Bucknor.

"Just hold your breath!" said Jorge. "This is the eleventh hour for the rebirth of Biafra. Elections are in the offing in Biafra, and if things go as planned then Biafra would be free at last."

"What do you mean?" Bucknor came in again.

"Remember that you can ask questions but not too many questions and especially not any personal questions. Anyway that's not why I've invited you," he continued. "I know that you love your father, and I also know that you're the most ardent critic of your father, though not openly, but almost borders on the verge of loathsomeness. I know all that. That's courage. That's principle. That's manly. I pray you don't go beyond that because I know that no matter what, he's your father. Son can disown father. You can disown him, but he'll always remain your father. But, I crave you indulgence, permit me to say that he's highly misguided, and I'm sorry to say that. But, I say it with the highest sense of responsibility. When I said that some people don't love their country or don't understand what loving their country means, your father stands at the apogee of that group of people, permit me to say that." He paused. "Sorry that I'm this blunt against your father before you. But I tell you, if I don't understand the way you feel or see things I'll not be talking to you. Yet, I would rather say everything before you than say something behind you."

"No, I understand what you're saying, and make no mistake I've nothing against you for stating the obvious," said Bucknor.

"I've called you here today to speak to you earnestly about what I think we needed to start doing. You see this whole place, we can make it our own in Biafra land," he said, waving his right forefinger around and gyrating his eyes.

"How?" asked Bucknor.

"Good! Good question. And my own question to you is this: do you know how much your father's worth?" asked Jorge.

"No, I don't know, but I know that he has some sizable chunk of money stashed out there," said Bucknor.

"Well, you may know what he has in Biafra land some of which he transferred from defunct Nigeria. But what you can never know is what he had lodged in European banks, from Santacrista to Bogey Town, from Potomaca to Potokiri, from Potokiri to LaMesa to Pontiaca to Chimera Land to Chimera Sea. And if you knew it you would curse the day someone like him was born. And now the crux of the matter's that he'll never be able to repatriate the monies, not in a million years. And these banks and their managers like to hear when someone like your father's sick and dying. If your father kicked the bucket today, his deposits would be designated 'ghost accounts' and would be a windfall for them and their families and their countries. And you and I and all Biafrans would be poorer for it. You know why?" he asked Bucknor. He was all ears and engrossed in the revelation that he did not know that the question was meant for him.

"Because, these monies were lodged in these banks without next of kin relationship. Since these banks knew that these monies were stolen from the coffers of the general populace or obtained through dubious means and passed through multiple channels to get to them. They knew that they stand to gain from their duplicities. They asked the depositor flimsy questions if any at all. I can assure you that neither you nor your mom nor any of your siblings is next of kin or beneficiaries to any of these accounts. The onus is now on you and me to find ways to wrestle these monies from their grip either by hook or by crook."

"By crook? Now, what can we do?" asked Bucknor.

"Yes, by hook or by crook," repeated the spymaster.

"Yes, by hook," said Bucknor like someone who was confused.

"Good! Good question again. And that's where you and I would have to work as a team to deprive these Europeans the joy of their lives. They'd raped the continent of Africa, and they have brazenly continued to give us the middle-finger salute. And they would turn around and say that Africa is an accursed land. If I told you what your father has in Stockholm you will take out the branches of these trees with your head," said Jorge, waving a hand over their heads. "We're misguided, and worse still, on our own volition. We're under no duress. The Europeans knew that it was a given. They no longer demand of us to be corrupted. They just got it because we've dunderheads as leaders. But they've aided and abetted the cancer that had eaten into the fabric of what has remained of desolate Africa."

"Now, how do we go about it?" asked Bucknor, now sounding very eagerly like a foot soldier ready to do whatever it takes.

"Good question again. But tough question indeed. Nevertheless, let me tell you," pressed on Jorge, "what your father has stashed abroad can replicate everything you see in this institution and have remainder for investiture into endowment funds and chairs of scholarships. And listen up, there're over hundreds of such people like your father in Biafra land that had monies lodged abroad and yielding little dividend to the depositors like your father. And in the defunct Nigeria there are over a thousand of such people jostling and pleading with Europe to be a custodian of their loot. It's like a race of who will be the most adept of looters and thieves."

"How do you know?" Bucknor wondered aloud.

"I know because I've to know, and remember, not a lot of personal inquiries."

"What shall we do?" asked Bucknor again.

"Again, good question, nothing personal. Are you ready for what we can do to wrestle away these monies from the European usurpers and armless thieves?"

"Yes, go ahead," said Bucknor eagerly.

"You must travel home and have a word with him. You must be resolute. He may want to resist your entreaties. It's for you to convince him to do it. Do it! Now, you do it for yourself and you do it for the Biafran people."

"But, I don't have a traveling paper to go and still come back into the United States," said Bucknor.

"Tell him that you must do this for yourself, your mother, and your siblings, and most importantly for the people of Biafra. He must transfer beneficiary and next of kin to you or your mother, and since it's most likely that your mother may not want to fly that far, then it has to be you," continued Jorge, deliberately ignoring him.

"It's not going to work without having a green card unless we can wait for about another thirteen months when I would be due for an interview for my green card…"

"Biafra's more important than you. Biafra can't wait! Biafra first. The way it's now, we must spare nothing to make it work. You must be ready to sacrifice something, even everything to deny these people keeping that trophy of corruption."

"Really…"

"Yes. No, we can't wait for that long. But let us suspend this discussion and plan till by this time tomorrow, same place," he told Bucknor.

The evening made its way fast yielding to dusk before the watching world as usual. And morning passed as swiftly as night before it as Bucknor waited eagerly for the appointed time. Overnight he had wrestled about the possibility of abandoning his life's ambition just to help his country. All the efforts, having to steal someone's else passport, stepping into America walking incognito. He remembered that day he opened his big mouth to make mockery of an innocent man that led him to knowing this man. He thought even harder. The fish would not have gotten into trouble if it had kept its mouth under lock and key. He thought hard, and as he kept going, one thing was certain, one thing he had learned was to take Mr. Santana very seriously.

And he was already seated before Bucknor could get there.

"Now, you had time to think about what we discussed last night? We're gonna strike a deal. But before I tell you what the deal would be I want you to understand what's at stake here. You must not fail and I must not fail. That's not the deal. I want you to understand that the people you're dealing with are as wise as the serpent. And you know what else the wise are good at? The wise are very clever. Wisdom and clever are two different things. And what else? The wise will not easily give up your place, your own place, no matter your prior friendship. You understand that? And what else? The wise will trick you to no end. And you know what else? The wise will not give something for nothing. I want you to understand all that. You must be as wise as and as clever as the serpent." Jorge paused, having answered all his rhetorical question himself.

"I want you to understand that whatever your father has in those banks were deposited in cash in what is called cash flight away from Africa. But listen up. The people you're dealing with like cash flight from Africa to Europe. But they hate cash flight from Europe to Africa even when the money came to them in cash. Remember, the British came to Africa empty-handed, not with a shilling, but they left stashing their bulging pockets with money and goods they confiscated from Africa, in the name of their civilization. Civilization, my foot! If you want to take solid money from Europe to Biafra, they would want you to have it in durable goods so that they still kept your money and sell you some junk you may not need, most of the time weapons of war. Never mind! This time we're not going to be beguiled into taking anything that's to our detriment. We're spending those monies on durable equipment and materials, name it, caterpillars, forklifts, tractors, boulder machines, and perhaps airplanes, which we can donate to the Biafran government that's to come," Jorge told his listener.

"What do you mean?" asked Bucknor who was thinking that he had missed the deal.

"Elections are coming to Biafra and Biafra emancipation is here, and I'm convinced that the leader who will restore the pride of the Biafran people is come to be elected." He was digressing, and he understood it and did not want to divert the captured attention of the son of Barnes Obikolo. The longer he would keep him in suspense, the longer whatever he wanted to implant into his subconsciousness will dwell in his mind.

"And now the deal: you have to travel to talk to your father…"

"But, I still don't have the green card that would enable me to travel and be back," complained Bucknor.

"You'll talk to your father and convince him to travel with you to Europe and fix his financial holdings. How you will travel, just leave that to me. I'm going to provide you the paper that you can travel with and still make your reentry into the United States without any hassles," assured Jorge. And as he said that Bucknor's heart rate that had flew up began to deflate much more quicker than it went up.

"Really!" Bucknor inhaled.

"Just leave the rest to me. I assure you that you'll be fine," said Jorge.

Bucknor, who never trusted this man, tilted his head forward as he began to wander what this man had up his sleeve. Was he eventually trying to take a revenge on his father through him? He has been in the United States three years. The only thing he had to worry about was those years he had spent here studying. If anything went wrong all these years would be like an interregnum in his life, wasted, empty. His assurance would be nothing. Where would he find him? Even when he found him, he could still not do anything. He had distanced himself from his father, and his father had left the force he built to his own image, corrupt, greedy, and unabashedly unprofessional. And since his father had lost relevance, most of his protégés had decided to leave him in the lurch. And even if he would be able to convince one of them to do something, this man may be too powerful and even dangerous for anyone to try to be an impediment before him.

"You need not to think about it." And that jolted Bucknor.

"No, you must swear an oath for me," said Bucknor, feeling some energy in his spirit to throw a challenge at Jorge for the first time.

"No, we need no oath. We're not an oath-swearing people like that. It was hardly in our culture, as a people. I say to you if I don't bring you back to the States, just break my testicles and drink its water," said Jorge offhandedly. "You just have to deliver on your part. My own part is assured. Your own hard work is just to convince your father to play balls. And when you succeed, what that success would mean is that we can build our own citadel of learning in Biafra that would be the envy of the world around us. You'll have no need for Yale, Columbia, and Cambridge, Harvard, Princeton, and Dartmouth wasting money in raw cash flight. You've to understand that some of these hallowed institutions of highest learning were built with inglorious Dark Age dealings of unsavory nature, of the exploitation of your father's and my father's kinsmen and women. Your father owned no slaves, but he's made slaves out of us all. He had no industry, but the amount he has in bight and pound can give us Yale and Cornell and some change to institute scholarship chairs that would finance themselves down the road with interests they would yield year after year." He paused, and Bucknor still said nothing.

"You don't have to think about it," Jorge continued, "just do it for yourself, do it for me. But most importantly do it for the Biafran people."

"I'll do it," said Bucknor firmly. "You needn't urge me any further. If my father had enough that would deliver this magnificent place to the Biafran people, are we not worse than senseless things? Our land has been wronged long enough that we needed not look any further to find why it has stymied. Each and every one of us needed to lose something that we hold dear," concluded Bucknor. Jorge was happy having to realize that this young man was ready to sacrifice everything for the good of all.

"And the good news is that your father has amassed large expanse of land to house the biggest university in the world. And you know that this hallowed institution was founded in the name of one who made himself and his descendants comfortable with proceeds from slaves' pity. Who cares! When that big plan would be named after him, fifty years down the road, very few people will remember that he climbed to fame and wealth on the back of the suffering people he met along the way. Well, not to belabor the matter, check your mail a week from today and get your traveling papers and bring it here for me to take a look. Tuesday, one week from today, I'll be here to see you," he told Bucknor.

As he left the man's presence, Bucknor wondered how this man whose slight limp had gradually vanished over the years was going to pull this trick off his magic hat. But he had learned to ask no further questions.

All of a sudden, Tuesday was there and he got no mail. Not to allow any doubt to permeate their relationship, he still got up and went to see the man as was the agreement. But he waited in vain for two hours, and Jorge did not show up. When it was Wednesday, nothing came in the mail. Not leaving any room for suspicion on his part, he still went to see if he could see the man anyway. Since last week he had been salivating at the opportunity to travel and see his folks he had not seen in three years. Now his hope looked to have been dashed into pieces. Again, the man did not show up. Doubt had started to rear up its ugly head. But on Thursday, it was not just an ordinary traveling paper. It was the hallowed green card in his name. He wasted no time and went to the rendezvous. However, surprisingly, Jorge was already sitting when he got there.

"Are you still in any doubt of what we can do?" he asked. And Bucknor began to wonder who are "we" in the statement he just made. He was about to ask who really was he actually. But he remembered that this man had cautioned him not to ask too many questions, and especially those that were personal to him. If he could provide for him a green card in such a mind-boggling fashion, he could as well take away his breath at a moment notice, that was if he felt godly to warn him. He was without speech, so he could not thank him openly because his head was swirling.

"Go and do your bit and come back and see me."

"Where and when?" asked Bucknor.

"Come right here the day after you returned from your trip," said Jorge.

"How?" asked Bucknor.

"Just come here," he said as he made his move to depart, and turning he said to Bucknor, "I wish you Godspeed."

Bucknor buried his face in his palms. His legs felt like rooted to the ground. When he lifted one up he was too weak to move. Nevertheless he did make a move and leisurely left the place.

Now he had a promise to keep. The man had also handed him an envelope which he did not realize that he did not open to see the content. It was when he got to his apartment that he opened it, and to his consternation tucked inside the envelope were two tickets, one a return ticket back to the United States. He was bemused to say the least. The other ticket had a flight date of four days from that day, and that return ticket had a six weeks' interval. It was summer. He might as well take a long summer break and can even change the date to come back if he was done with his assignment earlier than expected. But he realized that the date the flight was to depart from the United States meant that there was cognizant of some urgency in the matter at hand. He did not need to be further explained the import of that date.

The following day Juicy showed up, and they relaxed and chatted. He did not bring up the stuff that had gladdened him most these few days or his impending travel plans. But she had noticed that he was vivacious than usual. When she left after two days she had no inkling of what he intended to do. However, she was happy for him for having been more cheerful than usual.

That day Bucknor went out to the grocery store and bought so much groceries than he had ever bought before. To add more elements of mystery to his impending disappearance he also purchased a luggage box, instead of using the one Juicy had always seen in his apartment. That evening he hailed a taxi and was driven to the airport for his first visit to his homeland after three years of sojourn in the Americas.

As he was stepping inside the taxi here came Juicy but he was gone. First it was every two days and then every three days and then every four days and then every seven days, but Bucknor was nowhere to be found. When she eventually got frustrated enough and convinced that he was gone for good her frustration boiled over, and she began to call him names and curse him out.

"This uncultured African bushman had disappeared without a trace. What does he think I am? A fucking sex tool to be used and dumped. I'm going to bite off his dick when I got hold of him. Who's he to think that he could leave me in the cold and scram about like a cur. I'm not his little baby mama he thinks I'm…" All the time she had come in his absence, she had always gone straight to the refrigerator, poured herself some good wine, turned on the television, and flipped through the channels. On the third week, she did what she had not done these past weeks. She went and intuitively sat on the edges of his bed, and inadvertently she knocked down one of the pillows and came flying out was a handwritten scribble: "Baby, I shall return!"

"What a heck!" she exclaimed. "Look at this pip-squeak fucking… uncouth untrainable African man."

Bucknor had disappeared from his father's after the eleventh-hour revelation that he had his papers to travel out to America. He just wanted to vamoose and away from his presence. He was never home or always home late. By that time his children had retired for the evening. So when Bucknor unceremoniously left for America belatedly with his father's knowledge and he was distraught although he never showed it openly. Life was not about providing for your wife and children but also your presence, winning their hearts, minds, and souls. On that front, he was a complete failure. And he knew it. Part of his job as a policeman involved running around looking for pecks, pecks that had put him on the pinnacle of wealth and influence. And being the chief he was accountable to very few superiors. And his superiors did not demand professional accountability from him. Sharing extorted shillings and bights with them gave him additional latitude to run around to make him raise his knack for more extortion to the next degree.

Now, he had suffered some debilitating stroke, and life had become painfully difficult. He was nearly paralyzed in his left side, and his whole hand seemed to be dangling on his body. He could hardly move his left hand that seemed to be begging for a lift. Once a great figure now laid waste and beleaguered.

Unannounced and suddenly here came in Bucknor. He was driven in by his sister, Amarachi, who was the only one with an inkling of his coming, who had made it possible for him to have a very good life while running away from the influence and notoriety of his father.

He had heard about his father's illness and had spoken to him over the phone. But he was dying to see him faceto-face. Behold alive and in person, the moment he set his eyes on his father his spirit caved in and tears rolled down his cheeks. His father, bouncing at fifty-nine when he left the shores of Biafra, had completely been transformed by illness and heartache. His first son, supposedly heir apparent, did not want to identify with him. That alone seared his heart. Now, looking at that very son after three years, joy came to his soul and, with that, some speckle of tears of his own. But something remarkable happened. Amarachi had noticed that as her father held his son in a warm embrace, he had shown more agility than he had never shown in a very long time. Again when they let go of the embrace, as he was holding his son in a very warm handshake and staring him in the face, his left hand had shown some unusual strength and vigor. Perhaps, he was going into the far recesses of the reservoir of his manliness to muster that which would make him what he used to be but what he was no longer in the eyes of his son. Or perhaps, the healing feeling of having his son around him soothed his nerves. It was with great effort, and it was not lost on Bucks.

What he saw of his father convinced him that his journey and promise to deliver was worth it. Though he could not afford to fail he had to help his father come off his deplorable situation. His condition was that bad. He had seen the western world and how things worked seamlessly. Biafra could do as well if she did not have leadership misguided as if they were under a spell and his dear father was part of that leadership. No denying the fact! In any case, one had to drive away the kite before one would come back and admonish those chickens that they have wandered off too far. That night he called on his mother and explained to her how alarmed he was due to the conditions he found his father in. He talked her into the necessity of taking her husband, his father, for some medical checkup abroad. The rickety medical service in his homeland was nothing to write home about. He did not have to do much of explaining or cajoling his mother into agreeing to let her husband make that trip. Having secured her permission, everyone else in the family expressed no objection. Armed with a green card that would allow him entry without a visa into every European country except perhaps one, he was ready to go. His father, on personal recognition, was able to secure European Union visa in a matter of days. In the next few days following his return, he worked the phone to secure an appointment with one of the best hospitals in Lapland. Money was not the problem. One week after his return to Biafra land, he was airborne with his father to Beggars Hospital in Laramie Sea, Berber, Lapland.

The efforts he made to bring his father to Laramie Sea endeared him to his father despite years of unspoken disagreement. The cracks in their relationship seemed to have been repaired overnight. His father's illness did not bring him home. The desire to pry away the largesse his father stashed overseas was the major factor in having the opportunity to visit with him. That assured him the green card unexpectedly. He now appreciated that chance. Still focused on his father's well-being he did not take his eyes off the promise. Both were achievable. It was like killing two birds with one stone.

His intention was to spend three weeks during their trip. He had budgeted two weeks for his father to have a thorough medical examination and recuperation and in between those periods exploit the chance to quietly talk to him about the whereabouts of his extorted millions. There was time for everything.

First the hospital staff placed him on all sorts of examination and laboratory tests. With the outcome of those tests, his treatment began in earnest. And seven days in the hospital his mobility began to improve tremendously, and the doctors and nursing staff did not deem it necessary to keep him on hospital bed any longer. He was let go out of the hospital and to come back to the hospital every two days for routine checks and therapies. Obikolo was doing well and retired to his hotel room to recuperate.

Having adjudged his father healthy enough to engage in some level of interactions Bucks decided to make his move.

"Father, I'm sorry I had to steal away without much of your knowledge or blessing. Whatever you gave me is something you could not just afford not to give, willy-nilly, almost against your will. But I was doing it for our own good. You had a very sensitive job to do, and that made it easy for you to cultivate so many enemies. Armed bandits were marauding the communities, and political thugs were having a field day.

Your job was a very difficult one, and I was afraid we could get in the cross fire of it all. There was never an absolute certainty, but what was a sure certainty was that the air three years ago was eerily disconcerting, too disconcerting for my liking," said Bucknor to his father.

The former police chief sat down at his corner, listening. His jaw dropped to his chest, all ears.

"You're my son. I understand you like the back of my hand. You said that what you did was for the good of us all. That good cost us all a lot. Look at me. But I still prayed for your good wherever you were. I'm glad you are back and that you are making progress. I hope that your coming back will bring recovery to our frayed nerves. At a point, it took the wind off my sail," said Obikolo, seemingly suggesting that his son's absence had contributed in no small measure to his failing health.

"But I'm glad we're here. What I could do for you yesteryears I can do for you today. I've labored long enough. I've toiled under the weight of my conscience to provide for my family. The world out there is not what you see on the surface," continued Obikolo.

"Dad, we appreciate all you've provided for us growing up and now. It had made life a whole lot easier for us but a whole lot of the time disconcerting…"

"You did not have to and do not have to," came in his father slowly. "The world we live in is as merciless as it is unfathomable. And the job I took up and cherished is a miasma. And the countries we lived in, first Nigeria and now Biafra, are even more complicated than miasma. There was nothing straightforward about the force, and strangely enough more complicated is the country that was bequeathed to us," said Obikolo.

"Does that explain why there seemed to be no rules?" asked Bucks, trying to slow his father down.

"What about rules? What about laws?" began Obikolo. "I'm a law officer, and I know about rules. But both rules and laws are designed by the powerful for the weak. Laws and rules are not absolutes. They are not encompassing. The British left for us systems designed to fail. Because it was crooked it was labyrinthine. Things come in twos. So also rules. There are rules for the poor and rules for the rich. You end up in life what you have chosen to be. If you followed the rules of the poor you might end up a pauper, and if you followed the rules of the rich, then the skies become your limits. The rich we trust. My son," called Obikolo, trying to get his son to stay focused.

"My son," he called out again, like a man who was weighed down by a recalcitrant burden that would never go away.

"Yes, Papa." answered Bucks quietly with some of his own nostalgia.

"I've worked too hard to provide for my family, to provide for your mom, you, and your siblings," said Obikolo.

"You've provided more than enough, Dad," said Bucks like in a pun.

"Sometimes the weight I put on my shoulders seemed to tear me apart," said Obikolo.

"You didn't have to work that hard," said his son.

"You didn't have to work that hard but you have to. Most of the time your professionalism counted for nothing. Your superiors sometimes never judged you because you are a stickler to laid-down rules but how much you can provide when they call upon you to deliver. Sometimes it became a burden on your conscience if you had any, my son," he said again. "It's hard out there. If you didn't do it, someone out there will. And if care was not taken, you would be out of work, pounding the pavements for another job. That was the corrupt system the Brits left behind to us, and that was the system we perfected. It was a free fall…"

"But you didn't have to…"

"You had to," returned Obikolo energized, "because everybody was doing it. Do you not know that public nakedness is the preserve of the mad? When you go to a place and everybody got rid of their clothes. You'll do well to also get rid of your own apparel because when everybody is naked and you are the one clothed, the paradigm of madness has been reversed. You, the clothed wise man, have become the mad one in the eyes of the people."

"But, Dad, you don't have to. You could have set a precedence for..."

"A precedence? In that land?" asked the elder Obikolo.

"Yes, a precedence! Yes, in this land!" affirmed Bucknor.

"That would mean going through life gnashing your teeth."

"No, Dad. That would mean living within our means."

"Look at your head. Living within your means would only leave you bony head, distended belly, and empty skeleton."

"Perhaps not. And sure, it'll buy us some virtue," said Bucknor, still recognizing the personal shame he went through going and coming from the American consulate, and yet having to steal an innocent man's passport in the most vile of ways, which was not necessarily in public domain, but which he thought that he incurred for himself shame and dishonor because of whose son he was.

"Virtue! Are you going to eat virtue? Look, all virtuous people are poor." said the diminutive elder Obikolo, for he had turned a man of not too great in stature yet wielding a larger-than-life confiscated influence and power.

"No! Not necessarily, Dad. We'll not swallow precedence, but at the end of the day, we'll have honor and virtue, and set a precedence for all to point at and for others to follow. In time immemorial, people will point the way and say that Obikolo led the way of virtue. That that signpost of virtue was Obikolo's."

"Son, I don't want virtue on an empty stomach. What if there were no tomorrow?"

"Dad, there'll always be tomorrow."

"No, you don't understand. I don't mean that tomorrow you're conceiving in your big head. I mean the tomorrow of opportunity."

"Well, it's not bad to live within your means, or even to live poor, and buy yourself a virtue," said Bucknor.

"No! Don't even think about it, young man. If I had chosen to live your virtue, hunger would have made your head all bones, *isi okotoko*. I would have failed as a father, and you would have been a walking skeleton. Nonsense! You must find a way to snap free and dash away from poverty, or else its clasping hands will hold you down from age to age, up to the fourth generation."

"And then we'll go through eternity without virtue and without honor."

"Son, you're just talking this your virtue and honor. You've not seen those poverty dealt a small blow. They never had a good sleep, and they wake up cursing their God and pointing, not a finger, but all fingers at poverty, 'you again.'"

"Dad, those who made it virtuously wake up thanking their stars and walking tall and not worrying about anyone looking in their direction as if they were looking for something in their possession," said Bucknor, invariably telling his father that he had acquired his wealth dubiously.

Brave son! Walking a tight rope. Yet, he understood that his father's best days were long gone behind him. He was mainly clinging to old hopes and not new lives. There was much less a man could do at the point he was in his inglorious life. Still, Bucknor did not want to stretch his luck beyond breaking point. He realized that he was on a mission and failure was not an option. He needed treading softly, or else all his efforts would fall apart, amount to nothing, if the wily old police officer could dig deep inside the recesses of his almost-exhausted sinew and lash out at him for daring. While his father rested his chin on his chest without looking up, absorbing the underlying insinuation of his oldest son, and as he mentioned those words of bony, distended, and empty, Bucknor could notice his father's lower lip quivered, like someone left stranded in a cold, chilly, and breezy winter day in the heart of the Windy City of Chicago. It was his collaboration with the enemy that accentuated the menace of kwashiorkor in the lives of hapless children of Biafra and reduced them to fried skeletal heaps. Obikolo was among the breed of African men that were averse to leading a worthy legacy for the next generation. They lived like there was no tomorrow. They had no focal compass for any legacy of virtue that was beyond their wretched souls. If men were God, they would gather and bottle up every available air that they would never ever need just to asphyxiate the rest of mankind!

"What are you implying, son? You're not listening. You don't understand," said Obikolo as he wiped with a napkin some streak of saliva coming out of the left side of his mouth. "If I didn't have to, lived on your virtues, how could I have provided for you all and still be able to come here for this kind of treatment?" said Obikolo.

"That's the nitty-gritty of what we're talking about," said Bucks, as he saw some resilience in his father and his own confidence starting to grow.

"Listen, son," said Obikolo, as he lifted his chin off his chest. "Nigeria was a country of the devil-knows-what, and there are no saints in hell. If you didn't do it, someone else will. And the greatest blunder you would make was to stand in the way of those who wanted it at all cost. Then you stand a lofty chance of losing your job or crippling your career. You've got a family to fend for. You may even lose your life. It may not sound noble, but the alternatives are grim."

"You're right, Dad," said Bucks. "They're not noble, and the alternatives were grim, but now we have alternatives and they're very, very noble."

"What's it?" asked Obikolo, his chin dropping to his chest again.

"Dad, it looks like you're tired. I'll leave you to get some nap. When you wake up we'll go out for a walk. And then we can talk. We've all the time in the world to make up lost ground," said Bucks.

"That's fine," muttered inaudibly Obikolo who was already snoring.

Bucknor had gotten his father where he wanted. But he wanted to make sure that he was fully engaged and aware of their discussion moving forward. He did not want to task his conscience to get his father to say something he did not think through. With that nap and a short walk that was part of his therapy, he would be rejuvenated. It was also time enough for him to rehash his game plan.

"Dad, you remember where we stopped," said Bucknor, trying to make sure that he and his father were on the same page.

"Yes, of course," snapped back Obikolo. "You think that I've turned vegetable already," said Obikolo.

"No, I was just making sure," replied Bucknor.

"Making sure that I've not gone to the vegetables or that I've not lost my mind," said Obikolo with a small smile on his face.

"None of those, none at all," he repeated. "You said that some of the things happening at the force were not noble and the alternatives were grim. And I was going to tell you that in this time and climate, we've alternatives that are noble," said Bucknor.

"Yes, I remember all that. And now what do you have?" asked Obikolo. "Now, what's that noble alternative you've got up your sleeve?" he asked, trying to reassure his child that though he was sick that he was not completely damaged.

"You made us comfortable by toiling for us. You provided more than enough for us. And we know that you're very rich by any standard," said Bucknor.

"How do you know?" asked Obikolo, lifting his chin off his chest. He was getting more alert. The discussion was taking a turn to his money.

"I just know."

"You can't just know," said Obikolo. "Are you into espionage? And whom are you working for?" he asked. These were some of the questions Mr. Santana never gave him, Bucknor, any chance to frontally ask him.

"I'm not into anything like that. I just know."

"Son, you can't just know," repeated his father, with searching tone of a veteran police officer.

"I'm not into espionage. I'm studying to be a number cruncher. But that aside, Mom told me some three years ago that you've got a lot of money."

"I see. And now, what do you want to talk about noble alternatives," said the senior Obikolo.

"Father, you have to give me time to explain myself."

"You've all the time in the whole world to talk to me, son." His tone of voice gave Bucknor a boost and an opening to exploit for the promise given that must be accomplished.

"Earlier in the day," began Bucknor, "you said that putting your money in foreign places like here made it possible for us to come here for treatment. While I think that you're right I can completely debunk that in its entirety. I'm going to make haste to say if we put our house in order, create an environment that allows us to thrive, we can have all these in our backyard and with enough to spare."

"Not in Nigeria as it were and not in Biafra as it is," said Obikolo.

"Well, we can say that of Nigeria but not of Biafra. Biafra is a new nation. If we set the parameters right we can move in the right direction, away from the wretched compass Nigeria loaned to us. And with the new election coming and the possibility of the general winning the election, we would be on a sound footing."

As soon as he mentioned the general, Obikolo recoiled and his skin tightened. He knew that life would never be the same if Dim and his band of vengeful nationalists won the upcoming elections. The part people like him played during the war was what prolonged the war and made victory on the battlefield unattainable.

"If we have stuff like this in Biafra land, we would not travel this far to get treatment. Mommy would have taken you down the road before I was back. Now, we never had that chance, and your condition seemed to have deteriorated. We'll not spend much, and those we made poor, the less privileged will have access to better things for less a hassle."

"I heard you, and for your information, my son, I didn't make anyone poor. I know that you've become a been-to and have begun to have this utopian outlook to living and dying. That place you want to be like ours have had a strong foundation, and they have followed laid-down principles over the years. And it has worked for them. Not so with us. Nigeria was designed to fail by the British," said Obikolo to his son.

"I know all that, Dad. Nigeria was designed to fail. But Nigeria has not designed Biafra to fail. Or if they did, it's in our powers to change it! What we make out as utopian culture has survived on laid-down principles that brooded no work of the fifth columnist," said Bucknor, skipping telling his father that in what he called utopian outlook, people like him would be cooling their feet in the dungeon of a prison cell until they returned the last farthing.

"Yes, Dad, we can do better," he continued. "We can have these things at our fingertip in our own backyards without having to fly and spend an enormous amount of money in an economy that is well-off already. We put money in their banks that we may never need, that we may never use, and that we may never see," said Bucknor, choosing his words carefully.

"Dad, you've been to the western world, and I, too, have. I'm studying at one of the best universities in the world. That institution, like most of the other hallowed universities, were built with free labor of slaves and money made out of unsavory dealings. Today, they've their pride of place in institutions of higher learning. Today, no one remembered or cared about their checkered history. All's forgotten, buried in that mammoth dustbin of lies and forgotten history."

"That's true," said Obikolo.

It was then that Bucknor realized that his father was actually imbibing his every word and that he was actually making an impression on him. He did not want that opportunity to slip by, so he pressed on.

"We can borrow a leaf from them. Dad, you've money abroad like here in Laramie Sea." His father looked up quizzically at him.

"You must be into some espionage," he accused his son again.

"No, I'm not."

"Then, how did you know?"

"Because, Mommy told me."

"Hmmmmmm," hummed his father.

"And I just imagined that there's no next of kin or beneficiaries in all the businesses you've got abroad."

"Hmmmmmm," murmured his father again.

"And she has said that you've eight to ten bank accounts in Europe…"

"Hmmmmmm, I think she had seen too much. She has known too much. She had divulged too much to you and you've now known too much, as well. What else did she tell you?" His voice was rising a little bit.

"That they run into millions of pounds sterling or millions of Biafran bights," he told his flabbergasted father.

"Hmmmmmm."

"If we've all you have abroad repatriated to Biafra, we can build a university in your name, and a hospital in your name, set up a scholarship in your name, a whole lot of things in your name, and those who disagreed with you will begin to see things differently"

"Easier said than done," chirped his father. "The trouble is not giving a monkey a cup of water, it is the difficulty in retrieving the empty cup from him. Retrieving your deposits from the Europeans is like the camel passing through the eye of a needle, son."

"Well, we have to try. The Americans have an antidote for every poison, there's always a solution to every problem."

"So, what's your solution?"

"First things first, Dad," he began. "We're praying for your full recovery, for your longevity of life. I want you to see my children, your grandchildren. And maybe, great-grandchildren. But no one knows where the paraffin light bundle will cease to aflame. Wherever the flame goes out, there the paraffin bundle would be dropped," he started again gingerly.

"Not long ago, Mr. Nkemjika suddenly passed away in his sleep. He had houses in Potomaca and Pontiaca. But he didn't put his house in order. There were no next of kin in his holdings and no beneficiaries. Automatically, all he left behind in those places were bequeathed to those countries, and they did with them what they will. It was like reaping what one never sowed! No one has, not even in his family or his children, any locus standi to make a claim. Because nobody else's names were on the papers. They were windfall for Potomaca and Pontiaca, so also his bank accounts. I can give you more instances. It was ignoble! Mr. Nkemjika lived in infamy and he died in infamy." His father kept rocking his head as in a nod. Whether he was nodding in agreement or full realization of what his son was trying to let him understand, no one could tell. But one thing was certain: he still had his faculties intact. He was paying attention to what was unfolding inside his ears and mind.

Again, Bucknor has gotten his father where he wanted him to be. He now had to gradually wean him off any erroneous notion he may have had. He kept strategizing. They had been in Laramie Sea for about ten days, and his father had made tremendous improvement and had started to endear his son. His coming and his sharp savvy to bring him here for treatment was something he would cherish till the end of his life. Gradually, he had disentangled the mind of his father. Night after evening Obikolo and his son would sit down and talk freely. During the intervening days, out of his own realization, senior Obikolo constituted a tribunal of conscience in his heart to really query his own sanity to have hidden so much in far-off lands, depriving his compatriots goodies for a good life and feeding those who actually never needed any of the things he had placed in their custody, which only they had accepted to hold on account of that egregious avarice which was at the head of man's wretched faculties. As Obikolo became freer with his son, his son's confidence before his father began to multiply in bounds. At every turn and opportunity, he would pounce on it and told his father that he stood to lose all he had invested in if he did not get the documents right. Out of his volition he told his son how most trips he took while serving as a police chief were to open a foreign bank account to deposit some wayward money of shady acquisition. In the course of his career, he had made fourteen trips and had opened eight different bank accounts. And none had a beneficiary or next of kin assigned on paper to any one of them. To allay his fears or any misgiving, he had encouraged him to get the name of his mother attached to those bank accounts instead of his. Having understood the necessity of doing that, he, as a matter of fact, decided to conquer all misgiving he may have had about his son. He had decided that his first son also would have a huge part to play if he were no more.

One Wednesday morning, both boarded a flight to the Pontoon capital of Pontiaca. The one-hour flight from Laramie Sea was like a bat of an eye. Before Obikolo could retire to a snore they were ready to alight. A few miles from the airport took them to the bowl of the imposing *La Premiere Banque Transatlantic*. A private bank with strong focus on serving expatriates and international civil servants and specializing in wealth management. Bank! For international civil servants?

When the father and the son walked in and filled out the form indicating their intention to see a banker they were indicated to make themselves comfortable in any of the posh chairs in the lobby. It was not long when Monsieur Beauregard came out to usher the duo into his office. Monsieur Folquet Beauregard had grown in the bank to become an insider after more than seventeen years in this very branch. He used to be a teller, but over the years, he had risen in rank and had become a senior banker and financial adviser with a little office. So he knew Obikolo senior to some extent.

"Bienvenue, messieurs," said Folquet in his assimilated French language, introducing himself meaning "welcome gentlemen."

"Thank you," said the Obikolos in unison, and senior Obikolo quickly added, "I'm Chief Obikolo, and here's my son, Bucknor."

"Bonjour, Bucknor," said Folquet.

"Hello," said Bucknor.

"Now, how can I help you, messieurs?" said the Pontoonman.

With some tremor in his voice Obikolo senior began to explain the reason they were in the Pontoon capital and the need to have a next of kin documented in his bank account. As he was fighting to make himself clearer, Monsieur Beauregard betrayed his emotion as his face crimsoned.

"Y a-t-il une raison pour laquelle vous voulez faire cela maintenant?" Meaning: is there a reason why you want to do this now?

"Excuse me..."

"Je vous souhaite de limiter notre conversation à l'anglais s'il vous plait," said Bucknor, who had some passing knowledge of Pontoon, having taken some classes in Pontoon when he was in an elite high school in Obigbo, the heart(land) of the Igbo people. Bucknor had just told the Pontoonman that: I wish you limit our conversation to English please.

"Oh, tu es bon en francais. Oh, I'm sorry. But you're good in Pontoon," said Folquet, translating himself, and had appeared knocked off his strides having heard a seldom request from one once stupid international African civil servant.

"No, I just have a passing knowledge of your language I picked up in high school," said Bucknor.

"Je vois—I see," said Folquet.

"Dad, he was asking you the reason why you would want to put anybody else's name on your account," Bucknor tried to bring his father into the loop again.

"But do I have to explain to anybody why I'm doing this?" said Obikolo.

"No, you don't have to, but such minor details may be necessaire in case, par exemple, you're doing it against your will, you're being forced to do it," said Folquet awkwardly. "The decision is yours, but we have to do our homework. The money is yours, but we have to protect it."

"No one is forcing me to do anything. Young man, do what I asked you to do," said Obikolo, clearly and finding his word much more easily.

"Desole pour ca. Je ne veux pas dire que. Excusez-moi. I'll be back," said Folquet as he got up and disappeared into the adjacent room, after apologizing saying: Sorry about that. I do not mean that. Excuse me.

Now it had become a zero-sum game. Folquet had gone to consult with his superior. The dice was cast. In actual sense, there was no need to consult any oracle. But in this unprecedented move when one klutz African civil servant had made an unheard-of request, it was not stupid for a dedicated employee to verify with his superior. Coming back and wearing a clenched-toothed grin, he offered his apologies and proceeded to accede to their request without further ado. It dawned on him bitterly that the useful fool was about to have a great escape. The whole exercise took less than an hour to accomplish.

"Au revoir," said Folquet, with voice tinged with utter disappointment.

"Goodbye," said the Obikolos.

When they stepped out of the bank, Obikolo was the happiest man alive. He had unburdened his heart with one deft move. He saw it as a triumph. He was rejuvenated. And since he had one other bank account in the heart of Pontiaca, they hailed a taxi, and in the next twenty-five minutes, they were knocking at the entrance of the bank doors. The second port of call was like a quick walk in the park.

It was still morning. The Obikolos decided that they would fly to Potomaca having made a last-minute decision of calling one of the airlines and discovering that they could still be accommodated to make the fifty-five minutes' flight from Pompey Airport to Potomaca Lust Airport which was about thirty-six miles from the heart of Potomaca.

Barnes Obikolo felt at home at this bank. He was well-known inside its corridors. It was not quite six months ago when he visited Potomaca and as usual was receiving pleasantries from almost all the employees. He was that well-known. Bank of Union Promissory Notes was situated in a nondescript building about two miles away from the heart of Pillage Circle in the tenement of Potomac, Central Potomaca. Pillage Circle was alluring in its beauty and cleanness. For that or for some other reasons, nations small and big loved to hoist symbol of their presence in and around the Circle. Different nations' banks going by their names, dotted the Circle and its environs: Bank of India, Bank of the Philippines, Bank of China, and even Bank of Bangladesh. The odd thing about Bank of Union Promissory Notes was that though it was hidden, it still was holding huge financial capital investment more than most of these other banks. And the funny thing about this bank, although its name smelled Orient, those who established it were not Orient. Bank of Union Promissory Notes was set up, established, and owned by international rogues and many nations' bandits, civil servants of their nations who commandeered their nations' money, siphoned it abroad, and felt secured investing it on foreign soil. Chief among them were citizens of defunct Nigeria, and one of them was Barnes Obikolo. Now, a Biafran citizen.

Even though the Bank of Union Promissory Notes was established by rogue expatriates it had Orientals as fronts, from the tellers to the bankers to lower functionaries were populated by sons and daughters who had become major beneficiaries but who were not major financiers in its establishment. This bank with just five other branches was rich by every standard. While it received deposits from stolen funds from rogue government officials and dubious business peddlers from erstwhile colonial potentates, it had turned around to dish out loans with incredible success. Some of the businessmen who could not secure loans to prop up their businesses in their home countries got it easily in Potomaca at cutthroat interest rates. It was ironical a case of taking possession of someone else's stuff and loaning it to the person at a price, and that idiot turning around and thanking the other for helping out.

When Obikolo was ushered into the manager's office the cordiality and respect was self-evident. He was a stalwart of a customer, but his condition was also self-evident, and Mr. Conman took notice of it.

"Hello, Barnes," welcomed the banker, in his acquired quaint English language

"Hello," said Obikolo.

"How's life treating you, my friend?" Then he paused and offered them chairs. "Needless asking. You've gone through some life-changing experience in the past few months."

"I'm hanging in there. As you can see I'm here in person," said Obikolo as he used his handkerchief to dab the small drool that was about to come out of the side of his mouth. The two short flights he had taken had begun to tell on him, but he was ready to push on.

"What happened?" asked Mr. Conman, evidently very much unsettled.

"It's one of those things. No condition is permanent, you know, Mr. Conman. Meanwhile, meet my son, Bucknor," said Obikolo.

"Hello, Bucknor, my name is Iscariot Conman," said Mr. Conman, extending a hand of friendship.

"Hello, Iscariot."

"Are you enjoying yourself? You know Potomaca is the center of the Pontus weather. You don't know when it's going to rain or when there's going to be sunshine," said the banker. It was midsummer day, but for the past three days it had been a constant drizzle. And with it came an unusual chill for a summer day but not quite unexpected of Pontus weather near the channels.

"I'm doing fine in all ramifications but the health condition of my father," said Bucknor.

"Oh, never to worry. I'm sure he'll overcome this setback. More especially now that he's in the right hemisphere. Give him time. It's a matter of time and right medical attention which understandably he could not get, neither in the new nation Biafra or in defunct Nigeria."

"I'm sure of that, his recovery. He's improved a lot. He's constantly on the mend," said the young Obikolo.

"That's what I'm seeing," said Iscariot and turned to Barnes. "Mr. Obikolo, what brought you to my office today in spite of yourself and in spite of the intemperate and unpredictable Orient weather?"

"Never mind the weather and never mind me. I'm in good spirits," said Obikolo, finding some new gallops of energy. "I've been in Laramie Sea for a few weeks now to receive some medical attention owing to my debilitating stroke of about six months. Actually, two months after I left here I was struck down unannounced. Anyway, that's by the way, the thief would not succeed if it made a hail of noises. It always lurked, but I must say that it's beautiful to have such a place to get medical attention." He paused.

"Well, while in Lapland, I was decided that I needed to iron out my bank papers. We were in Pontiaca this morning before coming over here. We've two other places to visit while in Potomaca. Anyway, when we were coming here I was thinking making my wife a beneficiary to my accounts. However, I've changed my mind. Instead of her I'm going to use my son as the chief beneficiary or next of kin to my accounts here and everywhere else." He paused as he dabbed the trickle of drivel that perched on the corner of the left side of his mouth.

"Is he the heir apparent?" asked Iscariot.

"No, he's my beloved son, he's my beloved child," said Obikolo firmly.

When those people who surreptitiously wanted to undo one burrow under anyone's skin and siphon the carcass of anybody, they made the person feel like higher than a baron or a mogul and place that person on where everyone else knew that it was a make-believe. Holding their noses, kowtowing, and condescending, they fleece till their fill. They could even place one on a rubbish nickname or bestow an imbecilic title to make the one feel good while underneath, they kept burrowing and left the person an empty vessel. Now and then, it was business as usual: wrongdoers helping wrongdoers, thieves assisting thieves, one acknowledging his past and present and dying to make amends. The other not knowing so, unrepentant, not knowing having been born a thief, raised a thief, and thievery welded in his composition. It became his nature and saw no ills in his makeup, gaits, and laughter because he felt himself human, so also his kindred people from time immemorial.

"I see," said the banker.

"He's my first son and he's living up to the billing. He just came down from the United States where he heard that I wasn't doing well. He rushed down home to save my life. We've been in Lapland for weeks now, and we're coming from Pontiaca," gushed the ex-police officer with the exuberance of the aged who wanted to showcase the fact that he still had his memory intact. "We've two more ports of call in the Orient isle before heading to Liebigland and to Santacrista and then back to Lapland."

"Are you doing this because of your present condition or...," began the banker.

"No, no, no! It's the right thing to do. I was an imbecile to have done this in the first place. It's a shame. Shame on me. I should not have been here to receive common medical checks if I had invested my hard-earned money in my country's economy," said Obikolo. "I'm a man of no virtue in my country," he added.

Mr. Conman had a mental inundation of thoughts unimagined. If this man was thinking anew then a lot was in the offing. That new awakening was pernicious to the welfare of the Orient people. With no further con plan, he did not have much he could do but to accede to his beloved client's request. He got the paperwork ready, and the changes were effected. It was eighteen minutes past two in the afternoon when the pair left the bank. Bucknor, having noticed that his father had done most of the talking and felt really exhausted, decided that they must check into a hotel and continue their assignment the following day.

Against his father's remonstrations, he stuck to his guns. His complaints were that he was still in good spirit and that he could still handle the rigor required for the remainder of their assignment in Potomaca without a break. He was loudly vehement about it, and his grouses were that he was being treated like a child when he was still as fit as a fiddle.

Later that evening they took a walk around Pillage Circle, and as they loitered about Obikolo could not stop chastising himself. When a grown man chastised himself before his children it was the highest level of remorsefulness and atonement. Bucknor did nothing to stop his father but only listened just to allow him to continue to unburden himself. But, realizing that engaging his father would assuage his feeling of guilt and pain a lot, he began tentatively.

"You don't have to be hard on yourself. Life has been hard on you already," said his son.

"Yes, it's not been cruel enough. I've been cruel on a whole lot of people, children deprived of their daily bread because I stashed their money abroad, women deprived of good hospitals to cultivate their babies, children starved to death. No! No, this isn't karma enough. No karma is enough for what I've put my people through," Barnes Obikolo wailed.

Realizing his stupidity over the years and reckoning that he had acquired much of his wealth by crook far beyond what he was entitled to as a careerist civil servant he truly had a fitful night. As a police officer, exercising power and influence was his huge fringe benefit and spoil. All he had to gain from them was his guiding light. If he was not going to be given the hugest part of the spoils, police Chief Obikolo was sure to throw a monkey wrench in the works; he became a very infuriated bull in a china shop, knocking down his mirror images, and ultimately, a dog in a manger. But, before that! Growing up he had shown all the hallmarks of duplicitousness; deceitfully argumentative, wise guy-smart aleck, quarrelsome, fire-eyed, untrustworthy, always in denial, clever by half and had lived up to fill the bill and come full circle because he never spun off the rails of his original orbit. The plight of a man at war with himself. A man unequivocally facing his own constituted tribunal of conscience.

The following day they were up and running. After breakfast, they were airborne to Liebigland where surprisingly the paperwork was smoother and swift. Banking and hiding stolen wealth was their business and a major source of their hallowed wealth. They took no offense at the request, no ado. They were cocksure that the money was going nowhere. It was one of those things. As long as the dimes remained in their vaults, no qualms! But they did not foresee what was about to hit their pockets! By early afternoon hours they were back to Laramie Sea, where he took care of his Lapland account. Still complaining, but, this time not for being treated like a child but for him acting foolishly more than a child over the years in holding down his countrymen and women and denying them good life. Again, Bucknor offered him some succor urging that restitution would assuage his self-vilification and the opprobrium of his countrymen and women. That restitution would bring his atonement full circle. Whether his country would accept his change of heart was yet to be determined, for his sabotage was monumental and costly.

While his wife, Bucknor's mother, was listed on the bank accounts in Pontiaca as next of kin, Bucknor was listed as beneficiary and next of kin on all other accounts. For four whole days, father and son crisscrossed five European cities to effect those changes. Five days later they were airborne back to Biafra. Once in a long time Obikolo was healthier and happier, despite being beside himself for what he had done to his countrymen and women. For once he was prouder than proud of his first son.

Bucknor had another five days left before he would go back to the United States. Within those days, he had taken time to give his father a pictorial panoramic view of the investment he could apply his largesse to in the new Biafra that was to come. His joy knew no bounds, and in that spirit he had told his son that he would donate a large expanse of land to whatever he was planning. For the first time in a long time, he saw his father really, really happy, and willing to face his challenges with some stoic forbearance of indefatigable spirit. On the very day Bucknor was to fly back to the United States he noticed that there was less of a tremor on the left hand that seemed to have been affected most by his ailment. And he was happy. And standing right in front of his father he could see him shed real tears. Man conquered by emotion. It was reconciliation come full circle. And Bucknor, having promised himself long time ago that he would never cry in public, but as much as he tried to suppress his, he gave his father a bear hug, some warm handshake, a stare into nothingness, and then turned his face away from his father as he sobbed off to both surprise and admiration of his mother and sister. And now if that promise was a code, he had broken it twice in a space of weeks.

CHAPTER 27

Chance had completed his program and immediately applied and gotten admission into a master's program in business administration and financing. Turnkey, on the other hand, was in his final year of his major. Already he had pocketed a diploma certificate in equine massage therapy. Because he had veered off a little bit he was doing a catchup race with time. But even at then he had secured an intern job with Kaspar and Kaspersky Investment Inc., a hedge fund company dealing with stocks and bonds, IPOs, shares, and blue-collar investment counseling. It was while doing his internship that he noticed and realized how money made a merry-go-round. Busy and engaging. He had started to salivate about the prospect of securing a job with Kaspar and Kaspersky. And they did offer him a conditional job opportunity, mouthwatering and promising. All he needed to do was to complete his internship, present his bachelor's certificate, and all would be his for the asking. But right now, he was making a stipend as an intern, and what he was making as an intern was way lot greater than what he would make working full-time as an equine massage therapist. While a whole lot of kids would be contented with securing a job that quickly with Kaspar and Kaspersky, he was already in his mind plotting his way up the ladder.

Ever since he accepted Chance as a friend there was no going back. They had become so close that Chance had become his foremost confidante. In fact, Chance had displaced his mother as his foremost confidante. They shared the same apartment complex, so reach of each other was not a distance. No day passed without a chance to meet. All days on the lookout for the welfare of each other. And their intimate relationship was of no concern to anyone, least of them Turnkey's mother. Turnkey had completely moved away from their family home.

But he had always paid a visit to his family house in the company of his best friend. Chance was always welcome to the home. He had become a family friend, well regarded and accorded some liking and respect. The doors were open to him as they would to a family member. An honor it was just because he was friend of their son, Turnkey.

Then one late Wednesday morning, Turnkey had felt lethargic and decided to skip class for the very first time in his academic career as far as he could reckon. Chance had no class of his own. Being in the master's program he was allowed some latitude of time and choice. He had come to visit as usual, for as they were wont to, whenever they had spare time to while they spent it together. On this day, Chance had just made it into his friend's apartment when there was a knock on the door. Turnkey made to open the door, but Chance was there before him. And standing outside the door was a huge man, whose breath Chance could feel as soon as he opened the door. He was a massively built man whose weight was crushing, and that could explain why he was breathing so heavily. He wore a little smile on his concave face. He had a briefcase in his left hand. He wore a dress shirt and a red tie to complement it. But for his weight he was smartly comported in his dress. He was looking like someone with some kind of business proposal. Not as a sales agent but as a business tycoon.

"Hello, hello," the man and Chance said to each other simultaneously.

"I'm looking for Golan. I mean Mr. Ghoostte," said the man.

"I'm here, come on in," shouted Turnkey from inside where he was reclining on the couch, and then sprang up from the couch. Chance opened the door wider as the man made his entry.

"My name's George Skeleton," said the visitor, extending his hand for a handshake.

"And my name's Turnkey Ghoostte," said Turnkey, offering Mr. Skeleton his own hand. "And meet my friend, Chance."

"Hi, Chance. Hi, Mr. Skeleton," both said almost simultaneously again.

"What a name!" said George. "Of course, as you can see that there's nothing skeletal about me. Ain't that ironic?" asked Mr. Skeleton.

"Oh, my name's Herk," said Chance.

"It's all okay." And turning to Turnkey, he added. "I've come to see you, Mr. Ghoostte," said George and dipping his thumb and forefinger inside his breast pocket, he brought out his business card from Chase Manhattan.

"Is everything okay?" asked Turnkey matter-of-factly and offered him a seat.

"You've no record, everything's okay, my friend," said George. "Can Chance excuse us for a little while?" he asked.

"You said that everything's okay, then why do you want him to excuse us?"

"Everything's okay, and we know Chance. It's just that this is a business matter, and I crave your indulgence. It has to be accorded all the privacy it deserves until such a time its confidentiality was no longer warranted," said George.

"He doesn't have to leave. He's privy to everything I do," said Turnkey.

"We all know that and you can bring him into the loop when I'm gone. That's up to you."

Chance gave a pretentious whimsical salute and left the room.

"He can stay outside if you feared for your life, but you don't have to. I'm harmless," Mr. Skeleton tried to reassure Turnkey.

"But by the way, who are these people you kept referring to as 'we' and what do they know about my friend, and not about me?" asked Turnkey.

"I'll tell you in a short while. We know you first and foremost, and we know all your friends and close confidantes. Last year, when you went to Kasper and Kaspersky to fill out some forms you had him as a reference who could attest for you. How that could help you no one could tell. He was understood to be a very good friend of yours. Every year for the past five years and counting you had traveled with him to his homeland in Biafra. We all know all that, Mr. Ghoostte. If you lend me a little bit of your time I'll explain to you why I'm here today. And it's all good and you should not worry or allow your mind to wander to empty horizon." Turnkey remained quiet, still casting a suspicious look at the man six times his weight.

"Now, Mr. Skeleton, you're beginning to get on my nerves, what do you have up your sleeve? You're keeping a dossier on me, infringing on my privacy, eh?"

"You seem to have a pretty large family, scattered all over continental United States, involved in all sort business from iron bending to shipping magnet, to household products manufacturing to retail stores."

Turnkey was all ears.

"And they've made a success of all they do in that tenacious American spirit. Do you know the Ghoostte family in Indiana?"

"No, I don't know about them but I've heard about them."

"Well, there's something about them that your father has not told you or your grandfather is yet to let you know about them," said Mr. Skeleton.

Turnkey had been bogged down by poverty and privations to begin to worry himself about who his distant relations were. When his grandfather, Vanderhoof, left the town of his birth he had wanted to move to a place where no one could find him, no one would know him. Boonville provided such an amazing hiding place. And he had pitched his tent, raising family and shielding them from their roots. While he had shielded them, he did not shield them from poverty. It had ravaged them. deJohn had toiled to extricate himself from its fangs. But poverty loved to entrench itself wherever it found a sturdier ground to berth. With Vanderhoof, deJohn, and Turnkey it had found a conducive harbor to anchor its huge ropes. Hard work could sometimes keep it at bay, but it never made it go away. Sheer willpower never bruised it to make it shift base on its own. In most cases it would take the pretty hand of lady luck to disentangle its clasping hold of tethers for it to begin to move and find a new haven for a resting place. In Turnkey's turn, it would be said that he had fared much better than his father and grandfather. He had been lucky. Perhaps, there was something about him that poverty itself recognized that it never placed a stranglehold on him. Perhaps, it was his inclination to be angling for the top. Perhaps, poverty had looked at its crystal balls and recognized that this boy had a rebellious spirit and was ready to oppose it as long as it took him to be standing up. If he was lucky before, now, he was about to be very, very lucky.

"As I was saying your grandfather was a blood brother to Vander Sar, the scion of the Ghoostte family in Indiana. This man had made a fortune for himself in retail business. He had huge retail stores in the whole of Indiana and all the Sunbelt region of America. The details we don't know, but what we know is that he had left a magnificent fortune in your name. Why you and how you, we don't know. We do not think that he even knows you. Because he died just a little over twenty-four years ago. He died a young man, so to speak. So it was possible he didn't know that you were born. But he was crafty enough to leave you some piece of his fortune…"

"Now, what are you talking about, Mr. Skeleton," came in Turnkey. "You're, this is a rigmarole, and I don't get it."

"Yes, that's what I'm saying. It's mind-boggling, but this is no April fool, my friend," said George emphatically. "When I'm gone you can talk to your father and mother, who we understand are still alive." He paused.

"Your granduncle, we understand didn't want to pass on a part of his fortune to your grandfather or your father for reasons best known to him, but in his will he had left a small chunk of the percentage of his fortune to you. How he came about the permutation was best known to him as well. And no one can ask him now. But the letters of his will were clear for all to see. He left no ambiguities. Are you following me?"

"No, I don't understand," said Turnkey.

"Do not worry, I'm coming to explain it to you. Just hang in there with me. I'm but a messenger. Do not take me, take the message Chase Manhattan Bank, the custodian of the fortune, your granduncle had left for you, wanted me to deliver to you."

"Mr. Skeleton, I'm listening but it's boring."

"This man, your granduncle, left some percentages of what he thought was good for himself to you. He bypassed your grandfather, bypassed your father, and bequeathed that to you, which over the years

347

had grown into an enormous amount of money and wealth." He paused. "Now, I've come here to pass across this message to you. If you don't believe it I'm in complete agreement with you. For only fools would not doubt the inheritance of such humongous fortune."

"Are you done, Mr. Skeleton?"

"No, I'm not done," said George, as he took another sip of the water Turnkey presented to him. "I was sent to deliver this message and ask you to come to the Chase Bank on 5737 Liverpool Avenue on Wednesday, a week from today so that you can open an account with Chase and begin the simple process of transferring that money from Chase Trust into your own personal account. And that process would likely take less than an hour, and that would be what it would take for you to join the billionaire club," said Mr. Skeleton, as he unzipped his folder and brought out an envelope addressed to Turnkey Golan Ghoostte.

"George, you really wanna get me into trouble, contrary to your promise. Now, you want to lure me into a sinkhole. You ga-ra-go. Or I'm gonna blow your chicken George head off."

George threw his notebook and a pen on the little table between them and with a tone unusually loud but tinged with feigned sarcasm, said, "Write down your own will here, bequeathing all your estate, known and unknown, to my two little girls. When you are convicted of capital murder, after the state minimum statutory period of eight years for soul searching and double checking concrete and incontrovertible proofs that you quenched my life in cold blood, you'd be gallowed, and my girls who are no doubters will inherit your estates, and live large afterward on account of your unbelief. You poor child of some doubters!"

"You've got to leave. I want no troubles," repeated Turnkey.

"No, not at all, my friend. You've a week to ask questions. And you're right to be weary though. I'm just a messenger. And take it from me, this is real. Again, think about it, why would I elect to bring you a monumental hoodwink. I never knew you from Adam. I could tell how you feel, but know it that once in a while things like this happen. In our society of nowadays with the system currently in place, it's harder and harder for young men to join the millionaire club. A whole lot of the nouveau riche you see in the towns and hear about across the nation either made it big winning a lawsuit, winning a lotto, or bequeathal of some kind. So you're not different. What made yours different is the largeness of your bequeathal." He took another sip of water and then continued. "I tell you most solemnly, my friend, what you've got coming your way is enough to buy you a fiefdom or a chunk of a country. I've seen it, it's enough to compete with annual budget of some countries, some banana republic."

"The question, George, is why me?" asked Turnkey.

"I'm stupid to tell you that I can't try answering a question and that is one I can remember in living memory. But as a matter of fact, your granduncle's brother, your grandfather's still with us, he would be in a better position to throw light on that inquest. I'm just a messenger," he told him for the umpteenth time.

"Now, I may have to add, which is not why I'm here. I'm an investment banker, specialized in growing wealth. I also know that you have been offered a somewhat lucrative job at Kaspar and Kaspersky Investment Inc., which pales to nothing but which I suggest that you take in the meantime. I know that those guys at the firm are eagle-eyed and ravenous. They would want to co-opt your fortune unto their stable. But I tell ya something, when wealth becomes concentrated at a place its growth becomes labored, especially, very humongous wealth. I'll let you call the shots, but from an experienced standpoint, if you were not buying a chunk of country in far-off lands, I'll suggest that you split your fortunes into different portfolios. I'm going to tell you upfront, I'll be honored to be allowed to take hold of a chunk of your fortune and let it grow. I'm ready to quit my chicken job at Chase right whenever I'm tapped to come on board," said Mr. Skeleton.

"I hear you, George. Let me digest the import of your coming."

"Oh, take your time. You've a week to keep your appointment. Yet, even if you didn't show up, we still can't do anything about it. Chase Manhattan can't will it away. And you can't wish it away. It's all yours when you're ready."

"And if I didn't come by next Wednesday, am I out of the game?" asked Turnkey like one who was beginning to see the light and that which was remotely possible.

"No, not at all. This is yours for keeps. It's going to be yours forever and ever, until you're pronounced dead, somehow. And lest I forgot, I would advise you to keep the lawyers away from this. They confuse the issues and come back to say that they had fixed it to prove their relevance. You would need a lawyer if there were a duel about this. But since this was signed, sealed, and delivered you have no business with a lawyer. Going forward after, you might need the service of one, but right now, you're good," he said as he lifted himself off the couch to leave. "You've my card. When you come in next week, I may not be there, but you can holler at me. And for convenience, you've my cell phone number which is on the business card I gave you, as well," said Mr. Skeleton, who was among the first private individuals in the whole Chase bank to own and possess a cell phone in those days. As he heaved himself out of the door he met Chance who had positioned himself outside all along in case of any eventual whimper of chaos from inside his friend's abode.

"Bye, Mr. Skeleton," offered Chance.

"You know that there's nothing skeletal about me," teased George as he ambled gracefully toward his car.

When Chance came in, as soon as he sat down, Turnkey threw the envelope on his lap.

"You open it and tell me what's in there. That man was a joke or a conman."

"What did he tell you? Why must he choose you for his pranks. He looks a decent man with a decent job. There was no reason, to the best of my knowledge, for him to be pranking you…"

"Then, open the goddamn letter," said Turnkey, more relaxed.

"Now, listen up," said Chance as he began to rip the edges of the letter apart. "Now, listen up," said Chance again.

After the customary greeting of "Dear Mr. Ghoostte," the letter read in parts:

"This is to inform you that you have come of age, and based on the letters and provisions set by Mr. Vander Sar Ghoostte in his will, you've earned an inheritance of nothing less than four billion US dollars, transferable in cash and depositable into any bank of your choice.

"The maturity for you," the letter continued, "to be in possession of your earned bequeathal was when you turned twenty-four. That was one limiting factor in this journey. The other limiting factor was that you do not have any mental retardation. You met that mark on August tenth nineteen hundred and ninety-eight. Congratulations, as you made it to that landmark and as you are welcome into the exclusive billionaire club.

"We are at your service. We have a team of financial luminaries that are ready to help you chart a course of financial sustainability. Their track record speaks for itself. Where you go from here. What you do with your largesse is your call. It is your business. However, we would like to be involved in shepherding your wealth. We have a proven record over the years as top-notch financial planners and wealth builders. We would appreciate it if you would let Chase Manhattan Bank house your largesse. That is our hope. But, whatever you decide to do going forward is your call, we are here at your beck.

"We are inviting you to our office a week from the date on this letter to our Andrew Jackson branch to complete the paperwork. If you were constrained to come, let us know and we will find an auspicious time for you to come and effect the transfer.

"Once again, congratulations." The letter was signed by Mr. Foolproof Counterwit, chairman, Chase Manhattan Bank of New York.

Chance was not sure what he was reading was actually in the letter he was holding. Turnkey was not sure what he was hearing was right. It was hard to digest and was even harder to comprehend. Never in the history of the world was it known that such a humongous wealth was bequeathed. Turnkey was not sold on it yet. Rather, he was decided that he was going to go to his grandfather who lived on the other side of town, about four miles away. He most certainly would be the only one capable of unraveling the riddle.

He rarely saw his grandfather. In the company of his best friend, Chance, he met his father's father walking his dog named Lioness. Lioness had a queer perception of herself. She seemed to hate her name, Lioness. She seemed to prefer to be called Lion. Each time she was referred to as Lioness, she always growled, as if she was disappointed. But each time she was referred to as Lion, she would wag her tail. She was a spoiled brat. She had enjoyed so much conviviality with her owner that she now believed that she was the king of the domestic jungle.

"Hey, Grandpa, I'm here to see you. Are you doing okay?"

"Everything's okay, so also Lioness." Lioness groaned at the mention of her name. "Have not seen you all months, everything okay?" asked the octogenarian.

"Everything's a'right," yapped Turnkey.

"It must be something crucial that brought you here, what's up, son?" asked Vanderhoof.

"It's all good. But we need to sit down. It may task you to do some recollection," said Turnkey as they walked back into Vanderhoof's sitting room.

"I hear you," said Vanderhoof, reclining on his favorite sofa while Turnkey and Chance took the three-seater opposite him.

"Tell me, Grandpa, tell me about Vander Sar, Vander Sar Ghoostte."

"Has he come back to life?" Vanderhoof asked with a sense of foreboding.

"No, that was your brother, my granduncle as well?"

"Yes, he was my brother. We grew up in Fort Wayne in the Rust Belt, near the outskirts of Ohio," said Vanderhoof nostalgically.

"And…"

"And he was a spoiled child."

"And…"

"And, he was so shrewd he could con a cat."

"And…"

"Hold it, son! Where are your all these 'and' coming from?"

"I just want to know a little more about him and why you never mentioned him to me."

"Oh, we never agreed on anything except guns. It's a long story." He paused.

"And then he went away…"

"No, I went away. We could not see eye to eye, so I left on self-imposed exile. It's a long story." He paused again. "Let me ask you, why do you want to know all that now? You've been with me all these years," said Vanderhoof.

"Yes, Grandpa. It has just been brought to my attention that you had a brother and that that brother of yours was a very, very affluent man."

"Oh yes! He was absolutely rich in every sense of it, and that was one of my troubles with him."

"Troubles with him? How could that be a problem?" asked Turnkey.

"First, he caught my hands in the cookie jar. And he didn't like it."

"What do you mean?"

"You're asking too many questions."

"Too many questions but a chance for some introspection, Grandpa."

"Yes, still too many questions."

"You know, Grandpa, by asking questions, you gain more knowledge, and knowledge is power. And by talking, one unburdens oneself. Sometimes for sober reflection, sometimes to walk back, sometimes for penitence, and perhaps, an opportunity for redemption…"

"That's true! Growing up, I was what the French called an *enfant terrible*. Dutch people call it enfant *verschrikkelijk*. And my Jewish people call it *shreklekh pitsl kind*. The closest thing to it in the American lexicon was a rascal. I was all that and more. In those days, it was white-privilege right, and you could exercise it with impunity. In those days, there were very, very few relationships like you are having with this your friend. I overplayed my hand, and as they say, no condition is permanent except kicking the bucket. I'm a changed man. Growing up I could not stand someone like your friend. Young man," he said, referring to Chance, "I'm sorry, young man, but I could not stand more colored people like him. Colored people were Lilliputian to me."

"Grandpa, some other people would see you as colored, based on our family lineage of Dutch—Jewry," said Turnkey.

"But, they didn't see me as colored," said Vanderhoof.

"Those who knew and would not want to tolerate anything they erroneously labeled imperfect would smell you from afar and do you harm."

"I know and that's the way of the world," and he quickly added, "and I still remember you, son. You, too, are a changed person. Those that stand against change are always swept away by its torrential cascades, especially, for those things that are not immutable. Growing up, I got myself entangled in opposition to change even when I claimed what I was not. I was all bravura and no brain. No one has control over change. But, I found myself fighting it, and in the end I was caught doing it."

"Doing what?" asked Turnkey.

"Growing up, it was a status symbol to do wrong and get away with it. It was normal to oppress those who were unfortunate not to be as colored as you are or as white as the next white folk, or lower than you," he said reminiscently. "As for your question, son, that would be another story for another day. But, what caught his ire most was that I was his most vociferous critic. He got this small loan and started this little retail business. Overnight he was opening businesses in the Rust Belt and beyond, and I felt that at the speed he was going, there must be some duplicity about his rise in wealth. I felt it must be robbing Peter to pay Paul."

"But, Grandpa, that's how our system works. It's full of holes, and you've to be smart enough to exploit it without qualms even if you're vicious in your quest to exploit it. At that point, it was no one's business. The loopholes in the system are on your side and are deliberately left there by lawmakers."

"Son, that would be your thinking. But, I was looking and thinking that my brother was milking the people dry. A system that makes you a billionaire in a twinkle of an eye was stinking of official corruption. If any state is allowing it that would be a state-sponsored corruption," said Vanderhoof bluntly.

"But, Grandpa…"

"Don't get me wrong, young man, people got awarded millions in grievance lawsuits, other people through class action lawsuit got billions of dollars, some other people got billions through inheritance, and others bequeathal wills. But, I felt like my brother was dipping his hands into the pockets of the generality of the people and emptying them into his, a majority of them poor people. I was vehemently opposed to that kind of avarice in the name of business."

"Grandpa, that's why I'm here…"

"Are you here vehemently opposed to that kind of avarice, or are you here emptying other people's money into your own?" Vanderhoof wanted to know.

"None of those. I'm here because your brother left a will and in that will, he has reportedly left some handsome amount of money in my name. I'm here to find a correlation of that will to me and why me?"

"The correlation has been established, but why you, I can only guess," said the old man.

His only brother, Vander Sar. Ever since they knew that they could relate, they had opposed each other. Before their parents could arrest their downward opposition to each other it had negated all the laws and affection of consanguinity. And they had carried it over. Of the two, Vander Sar was the shrewder. And true to that purpose of the shrewdest, he became really tightfisted. He saved every penny he could lay hands on, even the ones he picked up from the ground in the streets. They did not have much going for them, but while Vanderhoof busied himself with hatred for colored people his brother was plotting to evade poverty at all cost. While the little he saved would not make him rich, but he had learned to save anyway. When he secured his first loan to start his first business, he did not secure the loan because he had some saving. It was paltry. But, when lady luck smiled at him, he never looked back. When his own brother began to query his rise to wealth and power, he detested it. It was not difficult for him to arrive at what he would do. As simple as it was, it was still difficult to understand how he came up with such labyrinthine way of making a point. In his will, he had directly excluded his brother from benefiting even a little of his immense wealth. According to the will, he had decided to bequeath 7 percent of his total wealth to whom would be last male child of the last male child of his brother. By so doing he had figured out that it would have to be the grandson of his brother. The child would have the money released to him a day after his twenty-fourth birthday. As soon as the will was deposited with the law office of Charlemagne and George with Chase Manhattan as the trustee, Vanderhoof had been followed wherever he had pitched his tent with his household. Whenever he dropped a baby, the surveillance team was handy to take note without causing anyone to lift an eyebrow in a pig's eye as they dutifully sentinelled the genealogy of Vanderhoof. When deJohn was born and no other child followed after him, male or female, the surveillance team turned their focus on little deJohn. As deJohn was growing all unseen eyes were on him. When he had a job as a truck driver, crisscrossing the grasslands of Kentucky all the way to the tunnels of New York and Newark he had a security detail, Mr. Hunt, on his trail. Mr. Hunt was paid to do a job, and he applied every due diligence to it. He had a few escapades in the course of his life as a truck driver, but Mr. Hunt did not take his eyes off his balls. At one time to make his job a whole lot easier he had seemed to befriend deJohn. He was his detail, but why he was detailed to account for his every moves, Mr. Hunt had no clue. During his wedding day, Charlemagne and George sent in their men. On that occasion, a well-attired middle-aged man with a boyish gait from nowhere, supposedly among the attendees, came up to him and with a warm handshake and a smile on his face, asked him how many offsprings he planned having. Not knowing the import of the inquiry but between a chuckle and wry smile his short answer was "you never can tell." When he churned out Candie and before Turnkey, a man he never knew, to the best of his recollection teased him about going to churn out more babies. He swore with his life that baby Turnkey was his last. That was not to be. After Charlemagne and George thought that they had gotten their man, four years later, deJohn's wife became pregnant again. However, it came out a girl who was named Mermaid. It looked like at last that they would settle with Turnkey, and then the waiting game began for the young man to turn to maturity.

Vander Sar died in his early sixties. If he was thinking that if he stretched out his goodwill period before Vanderhoof would benefit and invariably his brother, then he got it all wrong. In his mid to late eighties, Vanderhoof was as fit as a fiddle. He walked with no canes or any other support. His gait was sturdy. He wore no glasses and had no difficulties with his sight. His eyes had a twenty-twenty performance. He had a full dentition with no wiggles or holes. His hands were full and full strength, no shaky. His handshakes were warm and his grips were firmer. He looked every bit a man ready to weather all that life may throw at him even for the next twenty years. In fact, he had readied himself to kick the can of old age down the road to a century mark and even beyond. He was not in the initial calculus. But, right now he was in its midst. Never say die. If his brother's purpose was assuming that he, Vanderhoof, was not going to have a longevity of life, then he got it all wrong.

When Turnkey and company left his grandpa, he was certain that Vander Sar was his granduncle. In fact, speaking with his grandfather was more of a validation than the letter he received from the banker. And he had gone to his business as usual. He had trepidation but it was muffled. On Wednesday, the upper week he had taken leave of absence for one day and gone to the bank with his friend, Chance. All eyes were on him and his friend as they walked into the bank, for a few who were privy to his story and those who were not aware of the mystery surrounding him nowadays. He was ushered into Mr. Skeleton's office who had charge of his file, while Chance waited at the lobby. The papers he had to deal with were laid bare before him. As Mr. Skeleton began to explain to him things he had to know about the system that had given him this opportunity, the smell of methanobrevibacter smithii that oozed from his breath was palpable and permeated the space between him and the young billionaire. Turnkey felt he was being fed some overdose of methane.

"I know that you still have doubts about your largesse. Did you have time to talk to your grandfather?" Mr. Skeleton wanted to know.

"Yeah, I spoke to him, and he said that he had a brother that was getting rich by the hour…No, you don't wanna know."

"He was getting rich in leaps and bounds, and a percentage of it he had given to you, bypassing his brother, your grandfather, his nephew, your father, and on to you. Lucky you! But that is by the way. I got papers for you to sign," he told him, guiding him as he began to append his signature to the papers. One for Uncle Sam, showing that he had received his money. Another form showing that he had paid his taxes which were factored in the percentage before it was released to him, which could have made his estate even bigger. Then there were the other papers he had to append his signature signifying that he had opened a personal account with Chase Manhattan Bank. Then he had to sign the indemnity release form which would absolve Chase of any responsibility in the event the bank happened to go bankrupt the day after tomorrow and he lost all his money. A few other signatures followed, and he was done.

Mr. Skeleton went ahead and explained to him that since they were dealing with a large sum of money, it would take a whole lot more days to completely effect the whole transfer.

"You know that you can't put all your eggs in one basket. When you completely have this money transferred to your account, it's my humble opinion, it's not an advice because at this stage I'm not qualified to advise you on your wealth. I'm just saying. My unsolicited opinion here is fiduciary with no price tag and yet not legal opinion, either. It's my humble opinion that you decentralize the money, so that in the event of a catastrophic downturn, you will be safer.

"Check out your statement next month and see how much interest it has yielded to your account. That alone may be enough to last you a lifetime. Having said that, Mr. Ghoostte, you have my business card and my cell phone number. I'm at your services any time, twenty-four seven," said Mr. Skeleton as he extended a handshake, handing over to Turnkey a huge folder stashed with lots of paper. Included in the folder was a copy of the will and its provision to understand how the Chase Bank of Manhattan arrived at the figure they released in Turnkey's name.

"It's been a pleasure talking with you and knowing you," said Turnkey as he exited the banker's office.

When he came out to the lobby, he found Chance reading a book he picked on the lobby shelf titled *Who Moved My Chicken Dice?*

Turnkey and Chance went home as if nothing had taken place when in essence one of the biggest bequeathals in history had just taken place. The following day both were in their respective classes, and later Turnkey was in the office of Kaspar and Kaspersky. And it was business as usual.

CHAPTER 28

J orge was already sitting when Bucknor made it to the rendezvous the day after he returned to the States.

"Were you able to deliver?" asked Jorge.

Smiling, Bucknor nodded in acquiesce.

"Problem solved! Promise kept!" said Jorge.

"But the problem is that I was not able to get myself be the principal beneficiary in one Paris account, my mother is. Though I got in as the contingent beneficiary. Elsewhere, I'm the next of kin, as the principal beneficiary."

"Still problem solved, mission certainly accomplished. All we needed was to have next of kin attached to the accounts so that in the event that your father was no more, the monies could be salvaged. You did a marvelous job, my friend."

"The other good news was that I sold the idea of a monumental investment in his name and his eyes sparkled. I could see it. He bought into that idea and has offered to provide a large expanse of his landholding for any project I may want to embark on."

"Good!" quacked the linguist. "Now, I would suggest that you go back to your class. Take a deep breath. I would also suggest that you take a master's program in management. You've to arm yourself for the role ahead of you. You'll need that knowledge that would guide you in the hands-on part of the life ahead of you. We would be working closely from now onward. There would be need for us to draw a master plan. There would be need for us to have a blueprint. We would have something greater than this in Biafra land…"

"Hey, Mullah, Mr. Hardwood!" howled a voice from afar. Mullah, a name fondly bestowed on him by his co-workers on account of his ever-growing bushy beards.

Jorge turned to look in the direction of the voice, and Bucknor turned to look behind himself.

"How's it going over there?" asked Beckman.

"I'm having a blast here," said Jorge.

"Well, not to bother you, I'll talk to you later," said Beckman, as he continued his onward journey past the pair.

Bucknor was once again startled. He was about to ask his countryman something when Jorge continued.

"For your information, intelligence reaching us indicates that the general is going to have a landslide victory in the upcoming election. The western world don't want this happening, but that's what the people of Biafra want. When the people insist on something and mean it, then everyone would have to stand down. The west understands that. They'll throw sand into your garri if you were stupid, and they understood most African leaders and peoples are deaf and dumb. It's rebirth of a nation nobody can stop at this moment. And as soon as that's confirmed through the election and he's inaugurated I'll table my resignation, and given the chance I'll run where no American can ever find me, you know what I mean! My work here would be done, and a new one would be started in the land of the risen sun. I did not mean rising sun! Do you get what I am talking about?" asked Jorge.

"Yes, I do," answered Bucknor.

"I'll counsel you to be in constant touch with your father. He has the yam and the knife. You can't alienate yourself from him anymore."

"We've mended fences," said Bucknor.

"I hope it's solid. I hope it's permanent," said Jorge.

"It's permanent. It's solid. My father gave me his word of honor. It's a bulwark in honor. It's a sure banker."

"I'm taking it to the bank," said Hardwood as he bade his young protégé good evening.

When Bucknor got to his apartment that evening he found a seething Juicy waiting. That was their first encounter since he came back yesterday.

"You think you can appear and disappear at your whims, young man? Bye the way, where did you disappear to? I hope you didn't go to your goddamn Africa. If you traveled to your goddamn Biafra, where did you get your traveling papers from?"

Bucknor uttered no word.

"Now, you can't talk. You've not become deaf as well. You didn't even have the courtesy of telling me that you were going nowhere. Now, you don't have the courtesy of saying anything to me. That's disrespectful. Do not tell me that you went to Kinston because you still gonna need some traveling documents to leave these shores and still make reentry without your big black ass being shipped back to Africa."

"I went to Tallahassee," said Bucknor tamely.

"Liar! Tallahassee, my foot! You gotta tell me about your baby mama in Florida. Let me know who that tramp is and I'll crush your balls and deny her your juicy stuff. Liar!", she repeated. "Do they not have the damn telephone to make a simple call over there? And you gonna spend fucking six weeks out there and couldn't reach out. Your mama did not send you to school well to learn how to tell a lie."

"Baby, you need to chill…"

"Chill for what? You're freezing me here, and you still want me to chill. Perhaps, you do not want or need your green card anymore. If you still do need or want it you gonna be ready to play balls with me. Don't mess with me, understand that!" she cautioned her ceremonial husband.

"Please, I don't just need the card, I need you as well," he tried to reassure her half-heartedly.

"If you need me then you just got to get it together."

"I got it, baby."

"No, you don't get it. The way you're acting, one day I'm gonna close my eyes, and the next thing you've disappeared into thin air and the next thing you're in your godforsaken Africa."

"You're right," punned Bucknor teasingly.

"Again, don't mess with me. Don't try anything funny with me, or before you disappear I'll make sure that they ship your black ass back to Africa."

That night all efforts to pry from his mouth where he disappeared to for six weeks proved abortive. Bucknor stuck to his guns. Notwithstanding that fruitless effort they still thoroughly enjoyed their reunion that night in two passionate rounds of love tango.

CHAPTER 29

Turnkey came to believe that he had some wealth at his command when he got in the mail a bank statement showing some interest yield on his account. That dispelled all the doubts that were still lingering on his mind. Yet he went about his daily business as if he was still that ordinary peasant boy of Boonville. And in actual fact, it was not until the second month that he brought his mother into the light of his newfound fame. Between his mother and father, his mother was his best chum. First, he asked her of her bank account number, and a few days later, one million dollars was lodged into her account. When she found out that raised an eyebrow and she began to ask questions. Turnkey was not forthcoming with the details of his sudden wealth. He only told her that his only granduncle had left him some money in his will. His mother never kept quiet when she had not found answers to anything bothering her. If her son could lodge that much amount of money into her account overnight then there was a whole lot of money involved. There was more to it. Turnkey would not provide her with further details. So she went digging.

There was a functionary of the bank who had been her friend since they moved down into this area of Boonville. Mrs. Higginbottom, an unassumingly quiet individual at work but slightly cantankerous off duty, liked to sniff around for other people's business. She had no access to the provisions of the will, but she had overheard Mr. Skeleton talk about enormous amount of money involved in the will and the two limiting parameters that could have posed some problem for Turnkey. Wanting to know the details of the windfall for her son, Splendor began to sniff and dig to find more about the much bequeathed to her son. She urged her friend to find more details especially about the two limiting factors. Those were not hard because it became an open secret in the bank circle. So when she made an appointment to see Mr. Skeleton, she had all her facts intact.

Welcoming her into his office, he was smiling from molar to molar.

"Mrs. Ghoostte, I understand that you're here to see me for a very important matter, is everything okay?"

"Everything's okay, Mr. Skeleton," began Splendor. "I understand that my son landed on a monumental piece of fortune, which has been shrouded in secrecy and handed over to him secretly by your office," she paused.

"I'm listening," said Mr. Skeleton, as he lay back on his swivel chair, staring directly into Turnkey's mother's face.

"Mr. Vander Sar, his granduncle, had left a will and in that will had left a certain percentage of his wealth to my son."

"If that was why you're here, I think that should be a family matter, between you and your son. I was just a messenger. And this bank was a trustee and guarantor, but no more. However, if you wanted to discuss the issue of the will, I'm not qualified to discuss that with you. I'm going to refer you to our legal department. They're in a better position to entertain any question you might have about Mr. Vander Sar's will or any other will for that matter. As you rightly stated, wills are shrouded in secrecy. So you might not get anything out of it unless that which is already in public domain. And more especially, since there was no reference to you in that document," said Mr. Skeleton, as he tried to cut her off and from delving into the privacy of his client.

"Couldn't it have been nice if I were in the picture?" asked Splendor.

"You might wanna go and talk to your great-uncle, I mean, your husband's great-uncle. And by the way, why will it be nice to have you in the picture? As what, Mrs. Ghoostte?" asked Mr. Skeleton.

"As the mother."

"It wasn't called for. I see! I guess that was why the benefactor structured the provisions of the will the way they are. Perhaps, he designed it so that he would come of age so that old folks wouldn't lord it over him. Your son met requirements enshrined in the will, and the bank's hands were tied to do otherwise."

"I weaned him. He's still my baby. I know him. He's not acting normal. Did the will not make it clear that he must be mentally competent to handle fame?"

"Ma'am, you're veering into the realm of classified information. As I've told you, you can direct further inquiry on this matter to your son or to the bank's legal department, and they're in the best position to address your concerns. This office has done its due diligence…"

"Your due diligence didn't alert you that my son may have some hidden mental issues."

"That's news to me, ma'am," said Mr. Skeleton.

"That means that you haven't done your homework well enough."

"What do you mean, ma'am?"

"Is it not said that by their fruit we shall know them. Can we not decipher one's mental acuity by the company or friendship they keep?"

"Ma'am, you're speaking in parables," said the banker.

"My son doesn't get it. He's surrounded himself with people of color. He hasn't one friend among his people."

"I see."

"As I said earlier, that means that you didn't do your homework well enough."

"We did. But you don't have to know the details of our operation, and we followed the letters of the will. But just for your information, based on the provisions of the will, we scoured the databases for information that would dent his chance of getting hold of his possession. Your child has a clean medical record, has not been to a hospital for admission for anything. Your child is as fit as a fiddle. He's not coughed to the best of our knowledge and investigation. You're the mother, please, if you had any information that was worth being on his record, you should have put it out there. Now it's too late. Do not do anything rash. Get to our legal department. Get a lawyer! Remember, it's not an advice. I'm just running my mouth. I'm ahead of myself here. That's my humble opinion. But be careful so that you don't get yourself into a very wild goose chase. I do understand that he's already allotted a truly huge sum of money to you. Take a holiday. Spoil yourself a little.

"But before you do anything, find out what it takes to lose. You can gamble with a judge or jury, I'm just saying. Remember that all it takes would be for the judge to raise his gavel and hit on his or her deck and that's final. Or for the jury to take a stand. I'm still just saying. And it would be hard to find jurors who would be on your side because of your big myopic eyes. I don't mean that way, Mrs. Ghoostte. Actually, you get a counsel before you get a lawyer. Lawyers like polemics and create a rigmarole to try to confuse issues and convince the gullible and not so gullible to see reason in the confusion. If they convinced you, you're a goner. If they confused you, you're still a goner.

"Now, I'm giving you a free counsel, and that's why you needed a counselor if you felt like. Find out what it takes to lose. In the event that you lost the proceeding against your son for whatever reason, you need to find out first if he could recall his gift to you because you have made a bad call. Not all lawyers will take time to tell you all that you needed to know. They are trained to argue to convince or confuse to win. What am I even saying?" said Mr. Skeleton, trying to pull himself away from digging into a matter he should not have a dog in the fight.

"In the meantime, it's not a crime to have a black folk or person of color as your best friend and confidante especially at the tail end of the twentieth century. The will was blind on that account, and we can't control or change it. To have a confidante in a black or colored person doesn't equal to mental problem."

"It does," fired back Turnkey's mother.

"Ma'am, you want to get me fired if I kept giving you this free counsel which I'm not qualified to do, and I think, ma'am, that you're getting yourself worked up. You're losing your mind over nothing, over something that would not have made you lose an iota of sleep. What you have in your kitty is enough to make you quit your job. I'm a number cruncher. If you decide that you gonna be spending an average of two hundred dollars a day without working you can live into your hundreds and still have enough for your funeral. Or if you wanted to be a little extravagant, take a risk: squander your money and come back and ask for some more. That would be a better risk worth taking than get yourself in a legal tussle and duel you've no chance of winning. Don't get yourself into a quagmire and lose everything in the bargain.

"Another free advice from me is for you to go home and think through what you stand to lose and not what you stand to gain. Ma'am, I wish you the best of luck."

When Turnkey's mother left the banker, she was convinced she had everything to lose. She never had an issue with her son having a black man as his confidante. In fact, she had always welcomed Chance to their home warmly and have had a good regard for the African young man. She knew that it was Chance who got her son to change his major to something that was more fulfilling. She was aware that Chance had taken her son on a yearly pilgrimage to Biafra land in each of the past five years or even more, and they had all been eventful except the first one that he was robbed of his passport and given a black eye in the aftermath. She had made no complaints. She had cherished every artifact that they had brought back as souvenirs. In fact, she had spoken of her wish to sometime have the opportunity to visit Africa.

That evening she invited her son over to their house, and as always, he had Chance as company. Turnkey had no idea where his mother was earlier and the sudden opinion she was having about his friend. She had to take Turnkey to the visitor's room.

"Son, I know that your mind is a one-way traffic, but time has come for you to reconsider your relationship with your colored friend." She went straight to the point.

"Mom, is that why you've invited me over?"

"Yep," was her short reply.

"There you go again, Mom. First, Mom, my friend is not a colored person. He's black. In fact, black is a misnomer for him and his kinsmen. It would be apt to say that he's brown, or best to say that he's chocolate. Black is derogatory. They are melanoid people, the beautiful one you hate to admit."

"Turnkey, say whatever you want to say about him. Define him any way you want to, but don't stretch the issue."

"Listen up, Mom, what else do you have to tell me? You've seen me with this guy all these years and you never made a whimper, and suddenly you've woken from your slumber and discovered something that was wrong in him and that was wrong with him since man had an Adam's apple. There must be something else that you've invited me over, Mom."

"There's nothing huger than this, Turnkey."

"Then you've gotten nothing for us to talk about. You should have something else, or I'm out of here."

"There's nothing else worthier for us to talk about. Time has come for you to realign yourself before you become colored yourself," she said, her voice rising.

"Really! Mom! You married my father not minding that he's colored somehow," fired back Turnkey.

"Your father's different."

"How is he different?" asked Turnkey.

"He's different, he's not colored enough."

"Goodness me! I guess I'm not white enough, Mom."

"You are. It's just that you've got to draw a line. You're my child, and I know that you've a mind of your own. But, don't do this. Don't pack your belongings and move down to Africa because you can afford it."

"Mom, you've given me some food for thought. My father was not colored enough and I'm not white enough, and if I moved down to Africa I might necessarily become colored, become black, or nicely become chocolate."

"I didn't say that, others might," said Splendor apologetically.

"You know, Mom, I never thought about it, but I'm starting to think about it now."

"Think about what?"

"Think about moving to Africa as you suggested," said Turnkey.

"I didn't suggest that. I was just thinking aloud. But if you wanna go and live among the jackals and the hyenas and the leopards and baboons and chimps and what have you that's your cup of tea."

"Mom, I don't know where you get your erroneously archaic orthodox philosophy from. I've been going to stay among these people for the past six years, I've never seen a squeaking squirrel on their doorsteps, not heard the roar of a tiger, the moof of cow dog, the howl of a jackal, the scream of hyena, the rasping yowls of a leopard, the groan of a lion, the yelp of coyotes, or even the gibber or whoop of a monkey, and you are here, Mom, still believing in old orthodoxy held by your forefathers. It's a shame, Mom."

"You can shame me all you want."

"Yes, Mom, this is more than a gibber of chimp. You're hooked up to fantasies you have no clue about."

"Moron, you can call me names. But as your mom I'm gonna tell ya if you wanna go to hell please don't go to hell as a minority group or else the majority inhabitants of hell would just conspire and throw you inside the hottest part of hell fire. You understand me, fool?"

"You know what, Mom, I'm gonna leave you since you have nothing else to tell me."

"You can leave if you choose. When you don't work hard to earn a thing, you don't tend to appreciate it."

"Mom, you would not stop."

"Yes, I'm not gonna stop. I don't want you to end up a pauper you started out with. I don't want you to invest in an environment that would swallow you up and everything you put into it."

"I don't care."

"I do care," said his mother. "Give it to me."

"But, you won't appreciate because you didn't work hard to earn it."

"I do care," said Splendor again.

"I don't care, Mom. Before this I was on my way up. You're just leading me to what I should do. If these people needed help I can contribute to that and you should not lose sleep over it. You should concern yourself how you fare and not how the next person whom you're better off is taken care of. That would not be your business, Mom. Now,

I've enough to last me a hundred lifetimes. How many lives do I have to live?"

"You're a cat. You've many lives, more than nine. But, you're just thinking like a poor man, who has one wretched life to waste away."

"I know. I was born into poverty, and you made me poorer. Now, leave me to my own devices."

"No, I would not. You needed to be saved from yourself."

"No, Mom. You don't need to. You're the one who needed turning a new leaf."

"Son, you've not finished reading this page," said his mother.

"I may never finish it because it'll take an eternity."

"Son, I know why you're hell-bent on wanting to throw away your goodies. You did not work for it. That's why you are planning to throw it away like that."

"Yes, that's why I should give it away. I don't need it as much, Mom. I was on my way to big things, to making it big without granduncle magnanimity. I gotta leave, Mom. But, remember, you were here before I bumped into this young man you're having pleasure denigrating. You didn't point the right path forward for me. I found myself. You raised me hollow, not to know who I am, the tradition of my people, even when to wash my hands. But, he reminded me! He not only changed my course work, he changed my life's course. He offered me a new compass. But for him, I might still be frolicking in the dung of horses and stallions. I got it, Mom, and leave it to me."

"Do whatever you want...," said Splendor as Turnkey made his way down the flight of staircase to meet his friend.

CHAPTER 30

The election in Biafra had gone as was expected. The former general that led an insurrection against godforsaken Nigeria was back on the saddle. Everyone saw it coming, and the excitement was pervasive. His coming was a rebirth of a nation. The nation that was in existence and was surreptitiously swept under the carpet could breathe again, and the joy of the people was lucre, and the ululation was limitless.

The joy was effervescent. People took to the streets to celebrate and exercise their bottled-up free weal as was in the days of the thieves and bandits of old. Mob justice of a different kind was afoot. Sensing a clear and present danger, high Chief Omeke, in the ministry of urban development, a well-known usurper and confiscator of official unofficial pedigree, was in flight before those he was holding their stuff could reach him. He was headed for Europe, the headquarters and safe haven for those who brought ruination to their countries in Africa. But his family home in his village of Umuoshi was razed to the ground. However, Nwankenke was pulled by the irate mob from the bowel of the aircraft ready to zoom him out of Biafra and given a beating of his life before being rescued by the security forces. Other with soiled hands and of guilty conscience who had not disappeared before the results held their breath and sweated. Again, the day of reckoning of a different kind was here. If a people did not make a concerted effort in unison and booed and shamed elephantiasis of the scrotum when they had a chance, it never vacated a family, or a community, it had found a fertile ground to anchor it huge balls. That was what the country folks had just started to underline. There were no gawkers or onlookers, cowards or traitors. The license to hunt down the civil careerist criminals was evident in the massive, tacit, and loud support of the generality of the nonparticipants, save the marauders, whose actions had brought the people down to their knees. Now, the people had their mojo back and were in a fight for a new beginning until the last dog was hung.

His election reverberated around the world. The British were served a notice and that they would not be that great again. The ex-soldier trained in their culture understood them well enough. The British did not just understand him. They knew him indeed. As a sixteen-year-old at Eagle High, he wrote an essay that caught the eyes of the Home Office that forced the office to forward that very essay to the Foreign Office in Lagos.

In the essay, he had assailed the colonial rule in his homeland. He had argued that conscience was a subjective scepter. It was a parchment of sores on the soul and mind of man. If it did not trouble you then no worries. And at a point it would never matter. Yet, at some point it will trouble you even when you are feigning, stoutly enduring its crushing weight. The old quip that said that the end justifies the means was what mattered. It was the mantra of the British conquistadors. He excoriated the British for the exploitation of the African continent and jabbed at their arrogant assertion that they were great. There was nothing great about their greatness. He queried and cajoled the foundation of their greatness. He had opined that if you had people under the gun and forced them to pay taxes without accountability and siphoned the tax proceeds to your home country, that even if you were a moronic minnow, you were bound to be guiltily great. He had argued that the source of their greatness must be enunciated for all to see. He had also queried the essence of their civilization. How can a people so civilized be a purveyor of slavish concept old and new? How can a people claiming to be great and rich be caught with a soiled hand of theft, no matter under what guise or nomenclature it went on with? The woes of much of Africa can only be traced to the unholy doorsteps of the British government and her people. Civilization, he told his audience, was subjective. Reason was subjective. Proven facts were the only objective analysis. A palm wine tapper was knowledgeable and civilized on the rudiments of wine tapping, which a doctor who knew how alcohol could be a danger to the health of the individual may not know. Nigeria, he told his listeners, was bound to fail and that the British knew about it in advance. Because, he told his audience, its foundation was anchored on false premise, lies, and not on the needs of the people but on the convenience of the British people, not on the good of the indigenous people they sought to civilize. Christianity, he told his audience, was a yeoman's service used to conquer the attention of the people. How can a people who preached Christ be engaged in heinous crime against the people of God they had come to save? Christianity was at the heart of the ruination of the African man, the evisceration of the African landscape. That the black man, he finally told his attentive audience, was wallowing in his mighty conundrum largely because of religion, and at the heart of that religion is the Son of man.

The angle of his speech was like treatise, and his listening audience was spellbound, and his class teacher took note. When he finished there was no applause, rather a deafening silence. How can a sixteen-year-old enunciate such truths that beggared the minds of those who had thought that they knew much better? Even though the points he had noted were not organized in the real sense of it, but the plot of his argument was clear for all to see and appreciate.

Dim was the brightest chap in his class by miles. He was precocious. He needed no pedantry to understand the curves yet for anything that challenged him to no end he fought to master it. In spite of all that, he was always raising his hands and asking questions sometimes to the discomfort of his tutors. He wanted to understand it at the moment. He never wanted to relearn a thing when he had the opportunity to grasp it the very first time.

He made no fuss about it. He had openly claimed that he knew what to do with power. Now, once again he had all the levers of power to bend this young nation to his iron will. During his inauguration as the civilian president of Biafra he had called on his countrymen to close ranks. He had espoused them to ask questions of their leaders including himself. He had urged his countrymen and women to call out on members of his administration who they may adjudge to be doing something for which they were not paid to do. To the listening audience among some who were poised to be members of his administration, he had urged them to live within the confines of the law and be ready to prove their innocence or disprove their guilt as they stood accused in the eyes of the people. Innocence should be earned and never to be taken for granted. That inquisition of the people would be the most lethal bulwark to stem the tide of the erosion of our constitutional state. The British, he told them, had made corruption a craft, and an art. If they did the right thing, they would stop it from festering, but if they ignored it, then it would eat into the fabric of the life of the nation. No nation founded on corruption and false premise would ever make it out of infancy. When it managed to make it out of infancy, it would have a stunted growth. Like a man if it were to have offspring the genealogy would be ranked like those children begotten of vagabonds.

"Defunct Nigeria was the devil's vineyard, Lucifer's workshop! The devil needed no incentives to do his heinous job, but the Nigerian state kept giving the devil something he could not resist. Even when the demons in the devil kept resisting, the people of Nigeria went on their knees to plead their case before Lucifer. These people bribed the devil to double his strength and unleashing his whirlwind thirst for wickedness on innocent Biafran people.

"My people, we cannot be what we abhor in others. Nigeria was a bad example to the African peoples. To whom much was given much was expected. Much was given to Nigeria and much was expected of her, but all it had was frittered away. Because she was limited in what she could do to harness all that was endowed on her. When a mediocre was charged with setting the limits of human endeavors all the rest of the people would be dwarfed by his limitation and the potentials of those who wanted to move beyond the benchmark would be thwarted. Defunct Nigeria was an accursed people."

His country, he reminded his countrymen and women, had been awash with the blood of the innocent. United in one long checkered history, he enjoined his people to say, enough was enough, never again.

"We must be vigilant. We must abhor the ill of the failed Nigerian state at all cost. In fact, a problem is half solved if we knew what the issues involved were. The nightmare that was Nigeria we shall experience no more. The foundation of our success would be to learn from our experience in the defunct Nigeria. People maketh a nation and not the other way around. The love for country would be our mantra. But the love of country must not be lip service. It must be concrete and crystal. We must not borrow a leaf from godforsaken looting Nigeria. That would be tantamount to self-inflicted injury, a thoroughfare to perdition. That would be quintessential self-destruct, my countrymen. Nigeria was a heinous crime; an interregnum in the lives of too many a wasted life for the longest period of time. Nigeria, old or new was man's inhumanity to man!

"We are open to business people of every kind, both communist and capitalist. But whatever your interests are it must be geared toward the uplifting of the common man. Our economy is not for those who were already lifted. It is for helping those who are steeped in the deep to come ashore alive, not washed ashore. We want investment into our system. What we do not want is exploitative investment. That is investing in the self. That we do not want. As I said on our campaign trail, this country cannot afford to have a baboon economy. Our detractors would be surprised how resolute we are moving this country forward."

At this point, the ambassador of a minnow state, who was sitting next to the ambassador of another minnow state, muttered to each other, "What's he talking about?"

And then the ambassador of another minnow state added on his own, "This man would drive away foreign investors and would wreck his young economy."

Then they continued to listen almost willy-nilly. Were it not for diplomatic coolheadedness and niceties, they would have broken protocol and walked away.

"We're nonaligned. We're not going to be anybody's ping-pong. We welcome the Bolshevik salutes and clenched fists as well as the capitalist paradigm and handshakes. All our efforts first and foremost would be for the betterment of our people and peace at large. This land had seen its unfair share of ruination, some of it self-inflicted but largely through foreign manipulation. Biafra wants a peaceful coexistence with her neighbors. We're determined in the defense of our territorial integrity. We don't seek to conquer the east or the west. We don't need to be hoodwinked by the lackeys and bootlickers among our own people, stooges they have employed to beguile our way forward. And as I've always said we're ready to defend this land with the last drop of our blood and even to the last man.

"For twenty-two years Biafra had pretended to be free and independent and in our own hands, but for twenty-two years we've witnessed that the so-called our own leaders are nothing but fronts and misguided by parochial interests that never represented your own interest. Biafra must be revamped from its foundation for it to be sure-footed. This is imperative because all your past so-called leaders have shown that they are worse than senseless things.

"Biafra had been bullied for a long time by petty tyrants of the west and satraps of the local north. We've passed a crossroads to put a stop to it. We need the cooperation of all peace-loving people of the world. Nevertheless, we want to be masters of our own destinies. We ask for no reparation because if Europa, for instance, were to pay back all that they had siphoned then there would be no money left in the House of Brussels to take care of the royals. Rather, we're asking for repatriation of the missing billions both in bights and bonds. We can make a fuss about it because it's rightly ours. When you hold up a thing belonging to a baby and the baby could see his thing within sight, it's natural for the baby to keep crying while pointing at the thing and rightly would never stop until he gets his thing back…"

"This man is bent on destroying the Orient economy. If he achieved one-tenth of what he's just enumerated the Orient economy will yearly suffer tens of billions of pound sterling and a lot of people will be out of welfare. And if he were allowed to remain in office for a whole term he might sell these whole ideas to these banana republics in this west African coast. And if this new paradigm he's toying with caught fire, and I'm sure they'll catch fire, then the great Orient holdings as we know it is finished," said the ambassador of a minnow state.

"Why?" interjected the ambassador of another minnow state, who was having his first posting as his country's top diplomat.

"There'll be peace in the subregion, and invariably there'll be no more wars," said Mr. Catapult, the ambassador of a minnow state.

"Really, that ain't gonna happen," said the ambassador of another minnow state with some congruent naiveté.

"Watch it! It's about to happen. And your country's about to take a beating," quickly added the veteran ambassador of a minnow state.

"Really, not under my watch," said the ambassador of another minnow state lowering his voice as he continued. "While my government's technically opposed to anything untoward to governments, I know my countrymen, those vulture capitalists, I mean to say, those venture capitalists," said the ambassador of another minnow state, trying to correct his Freudian slip, "will do everything within their reach to make sure that there's free flow of business between the hemispheres."

While there was no "diplomatese" or finesse in this young diplomat from another minnow state, he was just saying the obvious without any iota of subtlety. Many a times western and European governments had looked the other way while their citizens had subverted and wrecked governments and peoples in Africa. And in some cases, these governments had been the ones that engineered the subversion of these small governments and their economies while feigning innocent ignorance. The young ambassador from another minnow state, Mr. Slingshot Ursprache, was being diplomatically uncouth because he was talking to his country's diplomatic closest confidante and comrade in diplomatic malfeasance.

"You better figure out what to do and figure it out fast. I'm looking at the whole thing and saying to myself, 'If this man succeeds, Africa would be on the mend.'"

"Well, his success does not depend on him or his people. It depends on you and I. It depends on us," said Mr. Slingshot Ursprache.

"Intelligence report I have says that the man is on a mission: he wants to decolonize the African continent, but he wants to start with de-indoctrinating the minds of his own people. We tried to stop his election, but it fell short. His support was too laudable that he could not be rigged out. It would have been like a broad-daylight robbery. We could do it in the old order, in defunct Nigeria, but here we were checkmated."

"You should have rigged it anyway, and we'll suppress the riots in its aftermath, using as always, their useful fools and our unseen backdoor maneuver. Nevertheless, he now has a mountain to climb. And we've an arduous task on our hands. This ominously looks like a beacon in the labyrinth. The African landscape and horizon never had a pantheon or constellation of the greats. This could be it. That said. This could be our last stand and our last bastion of expropriation, exploitation, neo-colonization, and imperialism. My friend, all said and done, this is Africa unbound. Every script written by man must have an end. But my worst fear is that their arc is bent toward the total sovietization of their fiefdom," said Mr. Slingshot Ursprache.

At this point Mr. Slingshot Ursprache's contribution had become shorter. He had started thinking to himself, *How could Phoenix have allowed this to happen?* Now they had made his job more arduous. As an ambassador, he was sent to protect the interest of his country by all means necessary, by hook or by crook. His failure would mean that his country will take a beating as his minnow state counterpart had just said some while ago. He could ill afford that. More so, it will touch him personally. He had family members who were mining gold and diamond in neighboring countries without proper clearance from those governments. They just moved inside the hinterlands, and with connivance of useful idiots, useless and senseless local whipper-snapper leaders who had no inkling what they were up against, they just started digging and carting away what they could not do elsewhere except in Africa they had desolated. He also had friends who were in the business of disturbing the peace and stirring up conflicts. They pounced on the slightest misgiving among peoples and made it snowball into a shooting brawl. They surreptitiously fed the embers. As the nations burned they became the propagandists of articles of brotherly hate, supplying catapults and slingshots, *uta*, bows and arrows, created more confusion, and sold more articles of bloodletting. The land was withered with weapons of lock horns. The people's naturals were pillaged and plundered while their imbroglios raged on. And in conferences it was the job of liars like Mr. Slingshot Ursprache and Mr. Catapult to engage in diplomatic sophistry and subterfuge, confuse the issues involved, and in straight face tell the world that they had no hand in the making of the cauldron bedeviling Africa. But the inevitability of change was what they were up against.

As they chattered without paying attention they did not know when the new president rounded off his speech to the applause and standing ovation of everyone except the pair. It was their Panamanian counterpart that alerted them, and they jumped to their feet, almost falling over, but helped each other to regain their steadiness.

Dim was master of the art of speaking. As he spoke his cadence ebbed and rose, and truly the people listened. Among those in the VIP lounge on special invitation were also Ogidigi. And sitting close to Ogidigi was Amadike Ahulele. Ahulele was specifically invited by the general, and he had placed a special request that he was coming in the company of Bucknor Obikolo. The name did not just ring a bell. It was well-known. It was a household name. That name evoked all the cruel animosity toward everything that had the imprimatur of Nigeria. By the power of his own persuasion and after thorough vetting he was given permission to bring in an Obikolo. It was a common adage that when a child thoroughly washed his hands he would dine with the shakers and movers and kingmakers of his time. That was what Bucknor had done through his association with Amadike and the assurance to repatriate the loot.

Even before his inauguration, in fact, ever since after the hostility that brought an end to the genocidal war, he had worked under the scene to draw a master plan of what he intended to do for his country when the opportunity came calling. Soon after his inauguration as president and commander in chief, he had instituted a flurry of programs. He had commissioned a whole of body of works, some under the direct supervision of his office. One of those works was the field of known soldiers and corridors and theater of peace.

Before Dim was a soldier, he was a civilian. But growing up his whole life had had the hallmark of a soldier. Sometimes, he felt he was born a soldier. When he joined the army, it was a fulfillment brought ashore. He relished it. He ended up cherishing it. He had been to a peace mission in Congo. He came back unscathed. It was a peace effort. But the genocidal war on the Biafran people was heart-wrenching. The leadership of the moment was entrusted upon him by an unseen hand of fate. He could not abdicate it. That would be dereliction of duty. It was steaming hot, and he had no place to turn to. All his peace efforts were spurned by those who stood to wash their hands with the blood of the innocent. As the situation spiraled out of hand, he watched his countrymen slaughtered in cold blood like in blood sport. He could take it no more. When he corralled his people into a homeland, then they became bayed about and hunted. Haunted by what was unfolding before his eyes and the eyes of the world he issued a battle cry in defense of his people entrusted under his care as governor. And for thirty months Biafra land was a theater in experiment in starvation and massacre. When peace came it was a relief, but it did not bring solace to the dead. And long after that there was no remembrance for the fallen. No monument for the brave people of Biafra. Day after day he agonized, no posthumous insignia for the brave that lost their lives. But he could erect a memorial in their honor. That was the least we could do for the heroes of Biafra's road to emancipation.

On the day the construction of the field of the known soldiers and corridors and theater of peace was set afoot, he was sober and his mien was solemn. Haunted, all around him were oceans of blood, cries of babies gorged out of their mother's wombs, bones of children left to wither in a plentiful world, their mouths begging to be fed, as they dropped in skeletal heaps in a cruel world. Haunted daily, daily haunted. And today he had a plan! He did not have much to say. And six months later, the field was ready for the people of Biafra to pay the ephemeral homage to those who fought to defend others and those who were slaughtered in cold bloodletting for nothing. In attendance again was Lieutenant Ahulele, retired. Also in attendance was Ogidigi. And surprisingly among the crowd of onlookers were Chance and Turnkey and Candie and Joann and Jason and Jewel.

The field was littered with tombstones of the fallen with glittering brass crosses buried at the apex of each of the tombstones and two feet apart. The field spanned five acres of land, manicured and beautiful with some water fountains that were symbolic in cooling the unsettled roaming spirits of the dead that would never return to earth but whose presence would dwell with those who knew them for years to come till kingdom come.

"We are here today to honor and preserve the names and memories of those who paid the ultimate sacrifice in defense of all of us," began the president in his first commissioning of an official monument. "We have no unknown soldiers or unknown civilian," he continued. "Every one of our sons and daughters are human and known to us, some of them my comrades in arms, some of them your kinsmen and women." He continued to move solemnly. Then he came to the apex of phalanges of rows and columns of crosses and tombstones.

"Here lies the bones of Tom, the general of generals. Here lies the bones of he who beguiled death in so many battlefronts only to be betrayed by his comrades in arms. He was the lion of the treacherous seas who weathered the tempest of storms by his sheer will and doggedness. The crab, at the point of death in that small pot, sighed with clenched teeth. It has swum all big and small oceans and seas only to find its waterloo inside the ugly, tiny pot of an old housekeeper. Tom was not the first Biafran to dash his life for nothing Nigeria, but he gave his life to wicked nothing. He's my general through and through. Tom was the proverbial crustacean that swam all seas and oceans only to find a waterloo in the soup pot of the old housekeeper. His only crime was that he was bent on preventing bloodshed. If Tom had listened to his better angels, he would have allowed more bloodletting and defunct Nigeria would have been better for it. But he didn't and he paid ultimately, and devilish Nigeria paid dearly and Biafra was worse for it. But today you've a resting place, Tom, a rightful place in our hearts. This is your eternal place, among your people. We interred you with full honors. The carcass of your bones we picked in the streets of bloody Nigeria. But today, your soul had wandered back to us, and we have you in our heaving hearts and our warmest embrace. Brave soul! Adieu, at last."

This president, this ex-warlord as the west would want the rest of the world to behold him, was a believer in the old philosophy that good steps at the right time would always lead to immeasurable fortunes, but when missed the voyage of life "is bound in shallow and in miseries." While he was not intent on disparaging his general whom he had looked up to while aspiring for a life in the military service, he knew now in hindsight that if he was ruthless as those who murdered him and set Nigeria on the path to perfidy, the blood of the Biafran people would not have been poured on the altar of nonsense Nigeria. In private, he had scoffed at him. In private, among his confidants, he had assailed him as the straw man. He was the last straw, yet, he was the last bulwark, when breached, then, defeat was assured. He, that very last dice to save his people led to the slaughter by others before him, failed them woefully. Every drop of blood of a Biafran that dropped, everyone, young and old whose body was withered by hunger, everyone who suffered a heart attack and gave up the ghost, every life that was martyred, he laid it all at the feet of this general who abandoned the ruthlessness of a soldier to don the garb mundane pity of a bloody civilian. In private he never stopped accusing him of turning victory into an almost pyrrhic defeat. The president had laid the death of millions of his people squarely at his feet.

Then he moved two tombstones to his right. For the first time in his public speaking exercises, his voice quaked. It was the tombstone of Phil.

"Interred here are the bones of the most dependable soldier. True brother, true comrade in arms. On occasions, he had loaned me his life and lived without breath. He once told me that he was ashamed to live when he saw women and children, the weak and the old, die for the cause he was a champion. He was conceived on the day tigers mated. He was born when lions were littered. And at his death and exeunt, comets appeared in the firmament. He was knighted for the cause of freedom, conferred on him by Chukwu Okike Abiama. Willingly, he gave his soul. Willingly, he died for Biafra." Laying a wreath and stepping backward, he gave a bow longer than any other bow, and a salute he held longer than any other salute.

As he laid the wreath down he stepped back and stood sturdily erect and threw a firm salute of honor. Then he moved a few tombstones to his right and came to Tim. Tim was his classmate at Royal Military Academy on Owlsmoor Road at Sandhurst, and they had as well shared a room together. He knew Tim and Tim knew him.

"Countrymen," he said, turning back to face the throng of ministers and functionaries standing a few yards away, "Tim was the bravest of all men I've ever met. Braver than me, I must confess. He had no recourse to look over his shoulders. He lived his name to the fullest. He feared no death. Tim stood inches taller than death. He once told me that he was like a rock never inundated by water. Water on him was like splashing breeze, water on a rock, never gotten soaked by it. People who wanted to do him harm understood that and had given second thoughts to all their diabolic inclinations. His gallantry was evident and death understood that. Today, here lies his bones and value of his valor. Countrymen," the president repeated, "one death for Tim was like a whispering breeze. Tim was not killed by one death. He was overcome by legions of deaths. Rest in peace, my brother!" said the president as his voice ebbed while he turned to face the tombstone again, bent down to lay the wreath and then a firm salute.

He then passed the tombstone of Colonel Orok, the tombstone of Colonel Njoku, the tombstone of young brave Lieutenant Nwafor, the tombstones of Brigadier Kubo and Captain Edet, and Colonel Egirigi. Each of them he laid a wreath and stout salute. Each of them he had some kind words to say about them, every one of them something new to say about him and his sacrifice for the people of Biafra.

"There are soldiers and there are soldiers," said the president as he came to the tombstone of Lieutenant Nze. "'The valiant never taste of death but once,'" there was no terrain difficult for him to navigate. He had the spirit of the Spartans, imbued with stoic forbearance of hardship and privation. There was no assignment too challenging for him to demur. My people, he, whose his kinsmen sent to steal, knocks down the door with his jackboot and with noisy fanfare. Oblige him run, and he would go much more farther than he who thought he was running furthest. We had our differences, but he was purposeful in candor. This man whose bones are laid to rest here would never wander the netherworld again looking for a resting place. Today, his own people appreciated what he stood for and died. This man who knew no tribe but every tongue would know that his own people knew that he did not die in vain. If I had to choose a soldier I would like to fight side by side and die side by side, he's him. He's the quintessential comrade in arms, he's the quintessential soldier. You shall die no more. Your spirit shall roam no more. You'll live in our hearts forever." He laid down a wreath for him and then a vigorous salute.

Then he came to the tombstone of one of the leading lights for the agitation of independence from the British. He gave one of the best eulogies of all times. After that he laid his wreath.

He passed a few more tombstones and came to another. It was the tombstone of eighteen-year-old Theo. Theo was a baby when Nigeria levied what they called a twenty-four-hour police operation on Biafra. He was plucked from the laps of his mother and thrust into violence. His mother did not object, and his father was enthusiastic about his participation in the war. They had already sent two of their eldest sons to the battlefield, and reports reaching them suggested that they were doing well and still safe. He understood the danger. Because he had already given two kids to fight recruiters were not pressing on him to hand over his sixteen-year-old. But due to the dire need of infantrymen, as soon as he turned seventeen the urge to shield him from the wars was gone. So when the recruiters came asking for his son to enlist he still did not object. The emancipation of Biafra meant emancipation of his sons and daughters. He blessed him. For a man to give up his three children, put them in harm's way for a cause showed how much they agreed with the purpose of the struggle.

Theo fought alongside Ahulele. At the Abagana sector they held their ground and he was barely seventeen. He followed instructions and did all his superiors wanted him to do. He learned quickly and was dutiful. He dared. He trusted his gut and had the will and in abundance. Because of his discipline more than this bravery he was made a leader of a small band of youthful soldiers that went out to survey the terrains before another advance force was sent to repel the enemy. He belonged to the reconnoiter unit, and two months into his eighteenth birthday the unexpected happened. He was cut down by enemy fire. Before medical help could come he bled and died in the distraught hands of Ahulele. Until that shrapnel cut through his entrails he was magnificent in battle.

"Countrymen and women, here lies the body and soul of the child soldier. Theo did everything right. He was born to lead, but his life was cut short. He was martyred. He died in the belief for the freedom of his Biafran people. He would have been here with us today if Nigeria had let us be. If genocidal Nigeria had taken the provisions of Aburi to heart and letters. The joy of this family would have been complete if this chap had made it home. His parents believed in what our struggle was all about that they sent three of their boys to fight and defend the Biafra in you and the Biafra in me. He was enthusiastic of living as he was enthusiastic of wanting to be free. We know that his mother was inconsolable, but today we want the family to know that this is a grateful nation because this young man laid his life for the good of us all. I want to say to his parents and to all Biafran families that this country would always live to protect that which he gave up his young life for." He turned, and a few meters behind him were the family of Duru, mother and father of Theo, his brothers who fought in the war, and six other brothers and sisters. "Mazi Duru and Lolo Okwerekediyakara, the Biafran people asked me to give this medal of honor to your child posthumously for his willingness to serve and his bravery and martyrdom. We remember him now and we will remember him forever," said the president as he handed to Mazi Duru a box with shining plates at the four corners. On the top of that little box was etched the insignia of a lieutenant which was the elevation of rank he earned posthumously. To his parents, he said, "Your son paid the ultimate sacrifice. He did not die in vain. He will live in our memories till kingdom come," then he turned and laid down the wreath that was handed over to him by one of the courtiers, took a step back, and saluted, saying, "Adieu! Young soul. Adieu! Lieutenant Theo Duru." When he turned to face the Durus, his mother was dousing her eyes with a piece of one white handkerchief and his father's eyes were soaked with restrained tears. Man vanquished by grief, and a disaster that was avoidable. By their side was the clumsy frame of Amadike Ahulele, his own eyes red but without tears.

As they remembered Theo that day, it was not lost on his parents that when their child was cut down on the battlefield, it was Ahulele, in true comrade in arms esprit de corps, who hoisted him on one shoulder, gathered their rifles and kits on the other, and trudged for miles. Imbued with the spirit of the young lad, he walked for seven miles without weary where he met his follow Biafran soldiers who were making merry, having driven the beastly enemy soldiers away, abandoning their guns, caches of ammunition, as they took to their heels. Without wasting much of a time, a makeshift burial rite was organized for Theo and his bones were interred with a sporadic gunshots salute, luxuriously made possible by the seizure they made from fleeing enemy soldiers. About a tenth of a mile away from where Theo was buried, stood a towering iroko tree and as Ahulele contemplated the wears and tears and traumas of war he knew that that iroko tree was a landmark where the remains of his brother and compatriot was led to rest, and that was about seventy-two miles northeast of the city of Umunwuruogu, his hometown. When the fogs of war were extinguished and its dust settled it was Ahulele who led the way and his body was exhumed and final internment was organized in his honor. He endeared himself to the Duru's family and they were grateful for his dedication to duty and comradeship.

A few tombstones away from Theo's was that of also a young chap by all indications, the Cupid in all of us that love souls.

"Cupid's eyes shed blood instead of tears," began again the president. "With the world under his feet he threw all those chances arrayed before him and told the world that he could take it no more. Before the world that was united in hypocrisy, before the very building of the United Nations whose founding charter had stated 'never again' after the deafening silence to allow the Holocaust to have happened in the first place, before that very building beside a statue that bore a biblical inscription "Let us beat our swords into plowshares," before the guards and sentinels, this young man martyred himself for the millions of Biafrans that were plowed down in cold blood. Before the charter of the United Nations that was not worth the ink with which it was etched, this young Jewish son laid down his life, set himself ablaze for the children of Biafra. Found on the placard he was carrying before he lost his balance was written, 'Peace is where there is an absence of fear of any kind.' This young man knew in his heart of hearts that the children of Biafra had put aside all fears so that the rising sun, their flag will fly in the firmament that needed a new soul." When he had said all these, he laid his wreath, and took two steps back, and instead of a salute, he bowed his head.

Then he made it to the other side of the wall, and etched on the glittering marble was "Conundrum of blood and bones." Here, Dim clenched his teeth as he struggled to say, "Here, the bones and blood of millions of our children who had longed for my coming to save them are interred. They waited in vain. They longed for me to get them water. They longed for me to get them food. And they longed in vain. And before our eyes, beyond our reach they withered and wasted. Slowly and painfully, they did not count among the living. For the first time, the lexicographers in Webster were happy to popularize the ghoulish Ghanaian word *kwashiorkor* to their array of words to describe our slow death. We left them bones in a plentiful world. The world left us bones." Ashamed, his mind began to wander then he continued. "And the question was why? Because Aburi Accord was starved of food and suffered its kwashiorkor. Those who never wanted peace in the first place made Aburi mere skeleton and bones. My people died because they killed Aburi. These, my people, would have lived if our detractors had allowed Aburi to live. They did not mean to go for peace in the first place. And for us it was a wild goose chase. Painful as it were, we'll always remember. Today, this conundrum of blood and bones would be a constant reminder that we'll never forget. This is a constant reminder that we must not let our guards down. As a person or as a people. This is a constant reminder that we must be vigilant. This is our own wailing wall. This is our own Auschwitz monument. This is our never again."

As he said this, he stepped a few steps back and bowed and turned to his retinue of functionaries.

That was the last rite of honor for the day. When he got to the podium set up at the foot of the gallery of the known soldiers and known civilians as it had come to be known, he lowered his voice to address the nation.

"Today, we honor the life and death of those who pointed the way for us to live, who showed us that there's valor in demise. We pay tribute to those who fought against newfangled impositions and oppression. Much more, we pay tribute to those who were needlessly martyred for their opposition to new hegemony and old hatred. Life should not be how long you've lived but how that life was well spent. The people we honor today, soldiers and civilians, are hallowed. There was no monument too great for them and their sacrifices. All we did by this monument was not to say that we had done enough, nothing would be enough for their souls. All we are doing was to say that we did do something in remembrance of their efforts that we might live…We owe these men and women immense gratitude. All we are doing today is to assuage their spirits. We want them to be happy and to know that we are doing everything to safeguard all they worked for and for which millions of us perished. In dying they have enjoined us to be vigilant. Vigilance is not frightfulness. Yes, we must be vigilant. Sleeping with one of your eyes open is not good enough. We must safeguard our vicinity assuredly to have a good slumber with our two eyes shut. We must avoid the mistakes of the past. We must never trust our enemies, foreign or local. Do thou never lose your sight again. Do thou never take your world for granted. We must saddle the horse and never allow the horse to bestride us. We are a people of unlimited capabilities…

"We must always remember the toils and work of varied charitable organizations who, at the risk of the lives of their personnel, still were hell-bent to salvage the children of Biafra. We remember pilots and airmen, doctors and nurses, who saw in life nothing but sacrifice for the helpless. In the end, it was not futile because we recognize that some of us were spared starvation and extermination by their noble efforts. We remember them, we remember.

"And we must always remember the sacrifice of those who never knew us. We remember those who organized protests in capitals around the world to drum our pangs of pain to the watching world. They just saw the untold hardship of the Biafran children and truly queried the conscience of the world. We must not forget that young and vibrant university student, who saw such man's inhumanity to man in starving Biafran children and queried the existence of the most high God who tolerated such heinous crime meted against defenseless children and looked away when he still had the sword of Armageddon to again remind a deaf world his omnipotence. Such indifference of the almighty made him say to himself that he was done with God. He was an American and true to that American spirit, and ethos. Today, we salute him not for abandoning God, but for asking why God abandoned the helpless children of Biafra, his own people, a people that christen themselves, Chukwu, his own very hallowed name. We salute him for feeling our pain in a world he was incapacitated by bloodthirsty wickedness. He who felt our pain left God, but we the children of Chukwu Okike, the most high, still have no other recourse.

"This is the land of the rising sun. Our sun has come full circle, blossoming and hoisted in the African skylines for all to see. Our task is not too difficult if we believed in ourselves. Anyone who tells you otherwise is trying to sap your energy. Trying to understand and know how we got hung and framed on that despicable wall of history is important. So that history does not repeat itself before your eyes. Dwelling on it is misery and a waste of your mental resources because it's unfathomable. Just unbound yourselves. De-indoctrinating events predating *anno domini* with devious and brutal conditioning is a tall order, but it's your niche to carve. There's nothing wrong with you, black man or woman out there. Combat your doubts! Whack them away. Do not believe what anyone says about you or your capabilities, as long as your cause is noble and just. Do believe in what you know of yourself and what you can do. I say to you, my countrymen and women, young and old, do not be fainthearted. Rather, be stouthearted. Shout out to yourselves: eureka! Biafra is that jigsaw puzzle of Africa's woes, that loose nut when found all our mechanics are aligned. Above all, hold it in your hearts, see it on your skin as a scar, and may that scar you behold on your flesh and in your spirit ginger you all the time to say, never again!"

As he left the podium the solemnity of the occasion had turned to some kind of animation. The spirits of those who had lost loved ones in the war were lifted from their doldrums. This was a painful reminder of the price they had to pay. Nevertheless, it was assuaging. When suffering was collective and pervasive pain was shared. When pain was shared that everyone got a little chunk of it then its woes were dissipated that the wailings and sniveling became muted in their collective forbearance. There was no Biafran family that did not lose a man or woman, a boy or a girl, an arm or a leg in that war. Not everyone had a tombstone erected in their memorial, but the war memorial commission set up to account for those who really perished as a result of the war was working to identify and verify every name submitted. Not everyone would get a tombstone, but every name identified would be etched on one of so many monuments of the fallen built or being built across the country for all to see and remember.

During the campaign, everyone knew where he was headed, but no one knew how far he could go. Dim was not a man of half measures. So far, his young government had become a beehive of activities. There was no dull moment. Yet nothing was scripted for the gallery. He meant business from the moment he was sworn in as president. He had come from the dungeon of the pit of the trenches of transient power to the gantry-like mystique of permanent prowess on whose rails and guard power the people had found a passage to new-fangled hope, belief, life, and existence. His first proclamation was to issue a restricted ban on all government ministers and functionaries of the previous governments from traveling abroad. To guarantee its effectiveness entrance and exit points were reinforced. Then foreign tongues began to wag that dictatorship was afoot. He had moved swiftly to appoint his ministers. He had worked feverishly to have them endorsed by the national assembly. For those who had doubts how far he was heading the caliber of people he had in his cabinet was a testament of his resolve to move his country to a different direction.

His minister of justice was none other than the combative legal luminary, Mr. Guzo, and the chief of national security agencies was none other than retired lieutenant Amadike Ahulele. Mr. Guzo was well-known and his work spoke for itself. Mr. Ahulele, on the other hand, had been shadowy since after the war. But the president had known him for a long time even during the war as a man of uncompromising character, a man he could vouch for, a purveyor of attention to details even over minute matters, a stickler of a different kind. He brooded no nonsense. A man given to no hanky-panky. If there was a man given to security it was Amadike, the linguist and spymaster. His foray into the American spy agency had even imbued him with unparalleled dexterity and guile. Why on that beat, he had stealthily collected and built dossiers on his own Biafran people which he knew he was going to put into use in due time. And now the time had come.

However, he understood that his paramount task was the security and safety of his comrade in arms and commander in chief in the past and at the present. He had diligently gone about and scouted and recruited the best minds who had no shred of doubt in their allegiance and who were willing to lay down their lives in the defense of their country and protecting their president. And the justice minister had given him all the tools he needed to succeed. He had also been of immense help to the justice department in providing them hard-core information. The justice minister, on his own part, had gone about with the help of the security chief and his agencies recruiting the best minds, accountants and lawyers, economists and researchers. There was no dearth in the pool of people to bring to clean the Aegean table. And one of the brightest minds Mr. Guzo tapped to join him in his effort to hunt down Biafra's stolen billions of bight was a dashing young man, Atinga.

Atinga left Biafra for the United States and United States to British London School of Economics. He had obtained a bachelor's in economics and a master's in accounting and another master's in information technology. In fact, when the use of computers became rampant he was among the first set of computer aficionados. He embraced it without knowing that its vistas were panoramic with endless possibilities. He had perfected it. In the labyrinthine nature of computers, he could never be found wanting or lost. He could flip it like a gymnast will flip and turn in midair, hit the ice deck running, and still find his way on the slippery slopes. Atinga was a master in the art of computing and a number cruncher, and he was employed to do just that in the justice ministry.

In an effort to stem the tide of corruption, a presidential proclamation had given sweeping powers to the justice ministry to pursue corruption and every ill-gotten wealth to the utmost ends of the earth. With dossiers already in hand, building cases was easy. And one of the people who was not under the radar was Mr. Sansom who had risen to be the police commissioner. He was swiftly placed on compulsory retirement as soon as the new government took the reins of power, and his movement was severely restricted. On this day, he was invited to the ministry of justice annex building of what in the invitation letter was considered an informal invitation.

Seated around the oblong-shaped table was Atinga, flanked by a team of young lawyers thirsting for opinions and briefs, petitions and summons. On his immediate right was Mr. Aririguzo. On his immediate left was Mr. Okosun. On his far left was the reclusive Mr. Akpan, and on his far right was Mr. Okon. And without wasting anyone's time he introduced his team members to Mr. Sansom and went straight to the point.

"Mr. Sansom, you've done well," said Atinga. At twenty-nine years of age, he had the world under his feet, young, elegant. That was who Biafra was thirsting for. Though he was summarily retired he still gave himself some wishful thinking, that it was a mistake, that he was being singled out for some belated accolade, so he strengthened himself.

"You've done well to have come," he said again while Mr. Sansom looked on.

"You've done well for yourself and for your family, and I don't say it lightly," said Atinga once again, and once again the ex-police chief uttered no words. "But to the detriment of the generality of the Biafran people," he added.

When he was prematurely retired he knew that the government was coming in to undo a whole lot of stuff, and when they began to dish out proclamation after proclamation, he knew that the game was up. Why he still gave himself a chance of redemption bordered on blind, senseless hubris. He was living in the olden days. In defunct Nigeria, it was utter foolishness to do the right thing. So, he had done nothing wrong! But, then when he was informed that his own nemesis was heading the justice department it dawned on him that the new government was coming for everybody's jugular.

"You've made yourself so rich while the people whittled," said Atinga.

"You're also a rich boy," said Sansom, trying to lighten the atmosphere a little bit and at the same time trying to put the young man in his place.

"That's not what I'm talking about. And for your information, I'm not rich," said the economist.

"You are, no denying the fact. You studied in Britain and the United States."

"No denying the fact that I went to school in those places, but that alone doesn't make me rich. I rode my way to those places on the back of my father. If that made me to be rich I beg to differ. It was my father who's rich, no denying that fact. And as you know he had a checkered history. He was an apprentice. Then he was a petty trader. Then he was a petty businessman. Then he was a petty industrialist, and then he became rich to be able to afford sending me to study abroad," said Atinga.

"And so," said the ex-police officer, sensing trouble. Mr. Sansom had been used to giving orders, and on occasions he expected orders to be carried out without having to raise a brow. He was just understood. Yet, he understood that it was a changing time and a new order.

"But, you're a rich man with no industry and neither no stall, no shop, and nor even a kiosk. You're rich by turning a blind eye and not following the law. You're rich by arrogating to yourself more powers, including ultra vires powers, breeding master thieves and budding criminal elements," said Atinga.

"I've worked hard for my earnings…"

"Bazooka had worked hard for his earning too," said Atinga sarcastically, and quickly added, "I don't mean to insinuate anything or impugned your character or disparage your person."

"I hope you've not brought me here to assassinate my character. I would say, gentlemen, before you assassinate my character, I would advise that you sever the head from my person before you got to that."

"No, Chief," said Atinga flippantly, "the justice department with the powers vested in it has invited you here to inform you that this government has taken stock of your financial dealings and has found some inordinate wheeling and dealing, and has slated me to inform you that you've some explanation to give to the Biafran people."

"Some explanation? I've served this country diligently and to the best of my ability," the ex-police chief began to lash out.

"Your diligence and best of ability has fallen way too short. Your personal evaluation here is inconsequential. The government has decided that you've a case to answer. You're a lawyer by training. I'm not a lawyer by any stretch, but on my flanks are legal minds I've deepest respects for," said Atinga, as he opened the folder before him and brought out an envelope. He placed it in the space between him and the ex-police chief.

"I was asked by the justice minister himself to pass this on to you. You're a lawyer. Go through it and come up with a response," Atinga told him.

"What're you talking about, young man?" asked Mr. Samson condescendingly.

"Go through this," said Atinga as he lifted the envelope and handed it over to the ex-police chief. "The government had concluded their investigation into your stewardship and had determined what you're worth from day one of your employment to the day you were retired…"

"What're they talking about?"

"The papers you have in there tell it all. You're richer beyond your means. You're a lawyer, you can disagree with their finding, and you can seek redress in the appropriate quarters."

"That's nonsense."

"That's not, Chief. There's a house in your name in Annandale, a suburb of Washington, DC, but in northeast Virginia. There's another one in Essex, southeast of England, that's registered under your name. These two houses are worth millions of Biafran bight. You've a few other holdings and plots of land both in Nigeria and Biafra that are of interest to the government of Biafra."

For a moment, the ex-police chief felt some inertia and deflated.

"To give you heads-up," came in Aririguzo. The lawyers had allowed the economist to do the talking all along. "When the government throws the book at you they mean business, especially if they had the fact against you. I'm not going to tell you what to do. But, I'll advise you to go home and take an incisive look at their finding and the offer they're making to you and see if they're something you can live with. You can unceremoniously decide to relinquish what in their finding they've considered loot and abuse of power or contest those findings. In any case you've to prove that those properties aren't yours. As I speak to you now plans are in the offing to reclaim those investments for the Biafran people. The government is just asking for your cooperation." He paused.

"You're a lawyer. I'm a lawyer, and so are these other guys here with us," continued Barrister Aririguzo, waving his index finger around the other team members sitting with them at the ornate table. "The government has prima facie evidence to want to reclaim those properties from you. If you want to fight the government in court that would open a cankerworm box with unintended consequences. As a matter of fact, if you pursued a legal duel, the government would eventually pray the court for some time in prison if they could prove a case against you. I think those are enunciated inside the package before you."

"So the ultimate consequence of serving one's country with all your heart is a threat of life in prison or even life imprisonment?"

"They're as a result of the choices you made," said Atinga. "As you know, I studied abroad. And as I know, all your five kids studied abroad or studying abroad as we speak. You own a house in the United States you use once in a long while. I went abroad to study not because my father wanted to waste his money but because conditions were not made right for me and your children to study here. It costs enormous amount of money to study abroad. If we had a Cambridge here there would be no need to travel to Cambridgeshire. The money we used to buy property we don't need in all these foreign places could be put to good use to build our own Yale and our own Princeton. They could improve our roads and hospitals. They would have made me stay here and study and so, too, your children. The choices we chose make me think that we are worse than senseless things. I'm not going to belabor the choices before you now. You're talking to a number cruncher. If you brought yourself to court these lawyers will flay you alive and you'll leave their presence a walking corpse..."

"So I've become the fall guy of the Biafra state."

"If you thought so, you put yourself in the quagmire. The Biafran people were the fall guys for you for a long time," said Atinga

"The stakes are high," said Aririguzo. "You should consider yourself lucky. You can't bargain this any further. It's in your own best interest to cooperate with this government. Those who have a case to answer but hell-bent to engage the government in legal abracadabra and waste taxpayers' money may discover that they would be cooling their feet behind bars for a long time to come."

"You're not alone on this matter," said Atinga. "This is not a witch hunt. It's a recovery crusade, a corrective measure. There're no sacred cows. Dim's administration is unlike anything anyone has ever seen. For your information, your mentor, and boss, Obikolo, has relinquished his holding at home and abroad to his child and to the Biafran people and the construction of a landmark citadel of learning comparable to Brown university is underway…"

"So, this is what my patriotism has fetched me?" griped Mr. Sansom to no one in particular.

"This has nothing to do with patriotism," said Barrister Okon. On the day of "boy oye" demonstration, young Okon was among the throng of people that had pledged to continue to lay siege at the police post until Mr. Guzo intervened. "It was under your watch that armed robbers could walk the streets in broad daylight brandishing their instruments of terror. It was under your gaze that police guns could be recovered from armed robbers' hideouts…"

"Please, don't impugn on my character or cast aspersion on my personality. I've done well. As a police officer, I literally laid down my life for the peace and security of the people and areas I had had the honor to serve," said Mr. Sansom.

"You've done well, but you refused to control the people that were supposed to be under your command. You had looked the other way because they paid you with the spoils of the war against the people you were supposed to protect," came Barrister Akpan.

"That explains why you've become so rich, rich beyond your means and rich beyond all measures. That explains why you think that you've done well," said Okosun, whose brother was a petty businessman and who had fallen prey to bands of thieves severally that he had considered himself a lucky man that no attempt had been made on his life, in spite of his losses.

"You should consider yourself a lucky man because the poor man is created a benevolent animal," continued the barrister. "In spite of your deprivation of their best lives they still accord you access of passage in the desolate dungeon your actions have thrown them in. But not to worry inversely, 'a Daniel come to judgment,' sir," said Okosun.

"Mr. Daniel is looking for judgment at the wrong corner, at the wrong person," said the ex-police chief.

"The Biafran people are looking for their own stuff, and they're looking at you and seeing you clutching their things," said Okosun.

"I don't have anybody's stuff. All I have I had earned. The rest are gifts from well-wishers and friends."

"All you've earned are gifts from friends and well-wishers? You're not talking like a lawyer, Mr. Sansom," said Aririguzo. "I guess you had forgotten the statutory provisions of section 420 penal code, subsection 14C pertaining to public officers, officials, and personnel accountability. Or you were thinking that the free fall that was in crooked Nigeria would subsist in the state of Biafra. Mr. Sansom, do you still remember that penal code and what constituted statutory illegality and what you are entitled to take in rare cases as gifts and what constituted an itching palm or bribery that would make you do your work differently?"

"I know what you are talking about, but I don't have access to the treasury. All I have you might term otherwise are gifts from the people who appreciated my services to the towns and communities I had been posted..."

"Mr. Sansom, that means you don't understand. You're still living in the nonsense Nigeria world. But Nigeria was defunct some twentysomething years ago. Welcome to Biafra!" Barrister Aririguzo told him.

"Left to me, Chief, a whole lot of us are good for the gallows," said Atinga.

"What did you say?" asked the ex-police chief.

"What you heard. Some of us are worse than senseless things. Too boneheaded. Not good enough brain to share a life with the living," said Atinga, as he paused before he moved on.

"Go through the papers before you and think through your next steps of action. But before you leave I want you to know that patriotism was never a lip service thing or gospel of the white sepulcher. You made your money here, either by hook or by crook, and decided to stash it in some far-off lands, doesn't make you patriotic. What anyone who does that sort of thing had achieved was to take what should have circulated among the people who needed it most and gave it away to presumably those who don't need it. First, that was unconscionable. And secondly, that was idiocy of the first order.

"Let me tell you, the British came to Africa to exploit us as English people, but when they left they had become Great Britain. Take away all they siphoned from Africa and are dredging from Africa and you would have laid them bare to nothing.

"And now, I tell you what's patriotism. During the Nigerian war on Biafra, my father was a millionaire and is still one today. When you heard about *Ogbunigwe*, it was conceptualized by a group of young engineers hungry for patriotism. There wasn't enough money in the Biafran coffer to bring their work to test and eventually to the war effort. My father laid bare his vault and provided millions of Biafran bights to the Biafran government so that those engineers would stay focused and accomplish their work because they understood that we were in a life-and-death conflagration. Their families were supported so that they didn't have to worry about their welfare.

"I tell you what's patriotism. When starvation became a weapon of war to starve to death millions of Biafran children at the behest of the evil genius from western Nigeria, when food aid blockage was a great good policy for the west, my father laid bare his wealth of funds to do anything within his powers to save the starving children of Biafra. Patriotism isn't perfunctory. It's not what you stand to gain but what you stand to give and selflessly, too, and at a cost to you.

"Based on the records we have, you had started making gains off your people even during the war. When the poor had cried you had taken advantage. When hordes of thieves were on rampage they had counted on your force to give them cover and protection, and in many cases, your rank and file had provided them machine guns to accomplish their nefarious mandates. When pen robber politicians succeeded in their gobbling escapades they had paid you off so that they would remain sacred cows when the full weight of the law was to descend on them.

"You presided over a force where fish dragnet only caught little bits and allowed the very big and large fishes to find their way out of the dragnet. The poor of this young country would want to see you poor, indeed.

"You've done really well, Mr. Sansom. While your dereliction of duty had deprived millions of Biafran people their livelihood, you've gotten yourself and your family in an unassailable pedestal. You've gotten your children through the best universities there are in the world. Now, they can support you. Not many people of this generation are that lucky. Rather, a lot had perished because of your dereliction and complete abuse of power. For your information, the justice department, as we speak with you, is pushing a piece of legislation through the national assembly that would require beneficiaries of all hues to pay back to the Biafran government anything earned by proxy. So it may affect your children paying back what would be estimated that you spend on them through college which by your legitimate earning there was no way you could have afforded them that. What that meant was that the poor of this nation had sponsored their training, and that would be a debt they had to pay back to the Biafran people. If by any chance you were a beneficiary of looting menace you've got something to give back to the people. It was neither a privilege nor a right coveted by any means. As beneficiaries of crooked malfeasance, they already had gotten ahead and gained an advantage over other young people. If they had to pay back, they already gained an advantage that no one could take away from them. This administration was not joking. It meant business, and you might want to think about that, my friend. Children of the poor must not toil to take care of the children of the rich, and yet they're still told to kiss their asses. It's no longer going to happen in our time, and we are here to stop it even happening in the future. This country is moving in a different direction, and for it to succeed it must be cured of all vestiges of the criminal enterprise of defunct Nigeria. When that becomes law kids like yours still stand to gain because their acquisition of knowledge had been paid for by others who were not given as much of a chance but whose collective deprivation had afforded yours the chance to stand and make it in life and just do restitution for a pittance. Once again, when that piece of legislation becomes law your children will not be free until the pay the last coin. If they fled abroad or exile themselves, we'll pursue them to the utmost ends of the earth and they'll sleep with one of their eyes open. Planet earth will not hide them. They can run but they can't hide!

"Take what you have been offered. Take it! But if you want to test this government's resolve, these guys would lead the charge against you, and I'll be there to provide them with the damning numbers," said the economist.

As they stood up to leave with the ex-police chief still glued to his seat, Atinga went on the final offensive.

"I tell you most solemnly, it's in your own best interest to alert this government what else you've stashed out there by other proxies. It's the intention of this administration and subsequent ones to monitor you and your ilk. You can no longer live above your means. You've no assets out there we don't know. Nevertheless bring to our attention what we don't know. If we made the discovery on our own, this government would take away every concession granted to you and make sure that you spend the rest of your life living in penury like the rest of the people you made poor."

When the former police chief left the justice ministry building, he had cold chills all over his body. He tried hard to steady his head. That was the easiest thing to do. Because, looking at the bigger picture, he had lost his mind. He knew that power was transient but not in his wildest imagination that he would find himself in such a mess. He who had the power to set bandits free by refusing to bring charges against them even when it was public knowledge that something needed to be done to so-and-so persons. He who had looked the other way while criminals had a field day, he who had given sanctuary to murderers by allowing them to slip through the net until there was a public outcry for something to be done, had found himself haunted by his past. There was a great unwillingness for him to do his job. Now, the day of reckoning was here.

He presided over a police force that could not answer a phone call placed on their 911 call system. There was an expatriate who came to see the minister of interior. Since the visitor was no government official from his country, his visit was personal. The minister decided to provide the guest lodging at one of his private homes. He also made sure that the police chief was aware where the visitor was staying. In fact, the minister personally introduced his visitor to the police boss and urged him to guarantee his safety as long as he was around. The police boss, recognizing the enormity of the task, had decided to add an extra layer of assurance to the visitor. He asked the expatriate to call 911 in the event of any need such as burglary break-in. He also counseled the expatriate to call first a personal number he gave to him. It was the earliest age of cell phones. The use of mobile walkie-talkie was no longer tenable. Three days into the expatriate's stay, in the thick of the night there was a severe attempted break-in. The expatriate decided to do the right and logical thing by dialing 911, the official emergency number recognized worldwide. He was savvy enough to do the next reasonable thing. As he was dialing in one hand the official emergency number, he was also dialing the private number given to him by the police boss in the other hand. Dialing the official emergency number was like calling on Baal. It rang off the hook. The private cell phone line did the job! In a twinkle of an eye a band of police officers were on hand, and the burglars were in flight before they could be apprehended.

He knew that if this administration could descend so heavily on him, then no one was spared. If he had thought that the young men of the justice ministry had read to him the riot act, the details in the letter they had given him kept his mouth agape for a long time.

They had identified his business interests at home and abroad. All his bank accounts at home were frozen. His foreign bank accounts and propertied holding abroad were identified and their market values estimated. The letter had urged him to transfer the ownership of those property to the Biafran government without ado. The letter had urged him to cooperate in making a smooth transfer of ownership. It had also urged him to transfer the money he had stashed abroad to the Biafran government to boast her foreign reserve. It had also provided in vivid tabulation his total earning as a civil servant for thirty-six years of service as a government employee. The letter had cautioned against unnecessary litigation against the government in which case the government would have no other recourse but to employ all the legal instruments it could muster to press for criminal proceeding for corruption, theft, embezzlement of public funds, coercion to defraud, collusion with criminals, gun running with criminal gangs, running of criminal enterprise with thieves and miscreants, and causing death by brazen dereliction of duty. All these individually and collectively when proven against him would be enough to make him spend the rest of his life behind the iron bars. The mountain of evidence was preponderance.

But there was a silver lining in the letter. It assured the ex-police chief that his pension and gratuities are still intact on the condition that he did not have to initiate a legal duel with the government. In the event that he took that legal high road, then all bets would be off. Then the government lawyers would seek a lengthy prison sentence and if he were to be found guilty he may spend the rest of his life in prison and forfeit his pension and gratuities to the Biafran people. When he made it out, if he would ever, he would have to live off his so-called people that gifted him while serving as a policeman, or off his children. He dreaded the thought of it. This man was a lawyer, and he knew the body of evidence against him. He did not seek the counsel of a lawyer. Rather he sought the candid advice of his wife and children who recognized that there was a new dispensation in the land that wanted to bring sanity to the system no matter whose ox was gored. His pension was enough to take care of his needs year in, year out. They urged him to stay clear of any legal tussle with the government. If push came to shove he would become their own responsibility. He was stripped of all the trappings of affluence, all the trappings of his unconscionable soul that he decided that he was going to leave the metropolitan city. A few months later he moved to his hometown of Okomoi, on the outskirts of the ancient city of Opobo.

Seven market weeks after he retired to his hometown, his circle of friend had dwindled. He no longer held courts to lackeys and bootlickers who had floundered at his presence whenever he rode into town. News of his being brought to ordinariness of the man in the streets was national. A man of immense power, now fallen from grace, and flummoxed deep below the level of some of those who had cowered before him. Bedeviled by newly found indulgence into drinking where he found solace and spiraled down, one late morning, he brought out a keg of palm wine and grabbed his calabash cup, the very cup that brought the real taste of the brew to taste buds. He poured a cupful and gulped it down in one fell swoop. He did that a couple more times before he paused. Since he was unceremoniously retired, he had floundered himself. His children were all abroad. His wife had fallen also like him, dejected, and like a defaced picture in the eyes of the townsfolks, she chose to stay indoors, having lost all the fringe benefits of confiscated power.

As the afternoon began to draw nigh and as he continued to gulp the tasty brew all by himself, he had begun to feel full, yet he continued to push beyond his limits. Not drunk but really sober. This brew had suddenly become the aphrodisiac of his own mental excitement to query and to ponder and to reason. All of a sudden, without warning, he threw the remnant of the drink inside the cup on the floor a few meters away from himself, outside his *obi*, every family courthouse, and got up from his recliner, pointing and cursing at the place where he had poured away the drink. The hallmark of his soliloquy and curses at the brew was that how could he be pushed around by something he had complete power over like palm wine or its keg. He had always seen life from the prism of power and control.

Sansom was among those African men, and there was a legion of them, who had no willpower to think straight and substantively until they were made sober by some aphrodisiacs. They sharpened the thinking faculty and made them rediscover who they ought to be or what they should have understood from the outset. He began to think about defunct Nigeria that gave him fame and the trappings of good life and power and the new Biafra that had taken all those away from him and shared them among the people. Sobered as he began to have a panoramic view of the past and the present sans the future for he was incapable of imagining tomorrow.

In clearer terms, with the aid of his little tipsiness, he saw defunct Nigeria as a metaphor for nonsense. But upon further reflection and in total sobriety, he saw that defunct Nigeria was not just a metaphor for depravity—that defunct Nigeria was depravity itself! And since some men think clearer when they were a little bit pushed by the external aphrodisiac that was not in their innate makeup, like a turncoat, it suddenly dawned on him that the contraption that had brought him so much glamor and life fanfare was a metaphor for stupidity and no tomorrow. In hindsight, he saw that defunct Nigeria was the metaphor why other nations, big and small, outside of Africa, had taken Africa for a ride. He was a police general, and it was under his watch that a bloody civilian would meander through the rank and file of his men to find an officer with a rank or the highest rank and delivered a blow of a slap to his face in plain sight in one moment of public letdown and nothing happened to the civilian who had the boldness to do such unheard-of thing. So, it was similarly meted on Africa! So, it was done to defunct Nigeria! So, it was such that Biafra was called upon to put a stop to. If small nations could rubbish the bogus claimant giant of Africa, there was no hope for the rest of the minnows. And Africa, as a whole, floundered into inert doldrums, holding not even a straw.

When defunct Nigeria was a poster boy why Africa was denigrated and despised and pillaged and raped, Sansom and his ilk were the reasons defunct Nigeria then and part of Biafra now were in tatters. These men were the proverbial constituted multitude that could not catch a calf, either because they were wired differently or their heads were mere tabula rasa, empty. Either because of their imbecility or that they were innately bereft. Yet, they were not bereft scavenging the African landscape with "bloodstained monument" of deprivation of their kinsfolk. Walking tall and feeling good, when they were beholden frontally, they resemble humans. Turn them around, and behold their head—it was filled with *manihot esculenta* pulps, mere starch, mere animals, mere beasts, mere curs, mere hatchet men— and their minds were nothing but tabula rasa. If that could be said of their minds, that could be said of their brain, blank, empty, worse than a baby. That could explain their lack of knowledge, and that innate gift: common sense. Common sense had suddenly become not so common. A rear commodity in the constituent makeup of so many a man. They just did not have. But, under self-oath and more oaths, they touted their relevance, patriotism, and humanity, ill-defined as taking care of their families on the backs of the masses, whose long-suffering had inebriated their faculties to think less and to lose reason. Yet, these men, regrettably these men, when they looked at the firmament and see the constellation of the greats, they thought that they also should be there, and rudely realizing not, they bemoaned their missing among the pantheons of the hallowed.

It was a misnomer to call them men! These were creatures; creatures without courage, without dignity, without empathy, without honor, without integrity, without virtue, without trust, and without conscience. Even when there was courage among buffalos, dignity among deers, empathy among orangutans, honor among dogs, integrity among eagles, virtue among rabbits, trust among dolphins, conscience among whales, these creatures just irredeemably outsmarted raccoons in banditry. They were pit bulls against humans. Sometimes, wild cats walk away from their preys and let them make it, but not these packs of wolves, brood of vipers, no, these earths worsts drew no lines in the sand. These Biafra's bogey men, excusez, these Africa's creatures were more vicious than the black mambas, and it was easier to teach a goat, a pig, or coyotes to think aright and reason than these spineless caricatures of many a man. They scythed the world right around them, wielding scutch instrument of power over hapless humans, unconscionably destroying the world right about themselves.

Sansom and his ilk were the epitome of rot in olden Nigeria and nascent Biafra. These creatures of men, and man had never been further from the beast. The thing to note was that man was wilier and just got himself separated from lesser beasts, which he cared no hoot about. Man is the biggest beast. That explained Sansom and his capricious outlook to life, conquering and wanting more. As if that was all to life, he kept going, pushing his limits, and then consumed by that ailment of the affluent and the powerful: greed for it all; unbridled greed, that when examined in the context of its fullness and reason, was akin to kleptomania. That was Sansom and his kind that made

Africa a marshland where elephants continuously fought on and the grasses suffered. Now, he was by himself, lonely and lately facing the imponderables of life, and he thought to himself that he could take it no more.

Though feeling drenched and bedraggled, he started again to pour himself one more cupful of the palm wine. Then two. Then three cupfuls and some more. He had started to saturate himself again and was not aware when his chin fell on his chest as he fell into a trance.

On the other side of his world, he could see nascent Biafran flags fluttering in the wind among the comity of nations. There in that pantheon of a building housing the flags, he could see a throng of Biafran men and women, and children drenched in colorful blood, beatified, and some of them canonized greats of the Biafran people. Of all the pantheons of the Biafran greats, he was missing. Rather, he saw a people beaming with limitless enthusiasm and optimism. Biafra had become a metaphor for all that Africa was looking for since time immemorial. A light ensconced under a bushel must emit its rays. And from that the floundering steps of never-do-wells, now Africa would falter no more.

It was creeping evening, and no one had ventured inside his world. In trance and out of trance, he got up and gathered his waist wrapper, girded his loins, and gathered another wrapper that bestrode his shoulders. He gingerly moved to his enormous backyard. He had no yam barn, that olden and golden benchmark and measure of greatness in the community, because until he was unceremoniously let go of his post, he had always lived in the big cities. Rather, he was greeted by a brood of creeping chicks that pecked on his sandals. In the shed for his herd of goats, three of the remaining goats sprang to their feet and momentarily stopped their cud and moped blankly in absent-minded awe. At another corner of the backyard near the main building stood an outhouse kitchen mainly for big occasions. Inside the outhouse were three gridirons, one huge, one not-so huge, and a very small one. On top of each gridiron were cooking pots of different sizes. One huge and gigantic for communal events and rarely used. The other, not as huge for clan event, and also seldom used. And the small one for the family and always in use. On this day, under the small gridiron smoldered the embers of a dying flames as Sansom came to pass. Sensing trouble, his Alsatian, a German shepherd dog, followed at a distance as he waded his not-too-steady gaits out of the compound through the small back gate.

Further from that gate was a groove of guava, *ube*, and orange trees whose branches sort of interlocked but not engrafted. The orange trees were delight to behold, especially during the fruitful seasons. Each of their branches held tufts of oranges hanging on them, like a bunch of dumbbells, almost touching the ground. Children of some age played around them. And some climbed on the branches with penknives and peeled and enjoyed and made merry like in the Garden of Eden. Gone were those days. All those things that made their world the apple of God's eyes were lost to modernity's miasmic new-fangled life in bigger cities and towns. And that *ube* tree—it was of a semisterile kind. But it had lived for a purpose. Since it had come of age, it barely accounted for any pear. Hardly! But it was on one of its fairly big horizontal branches that Sansom anchored his noose. That which was already reserved!

When Sansom started to make his efforts to get his head in the noose, his dog was stupefied. When it was clear to Viking, for that was the name of the dog, it howled and hollered. And for something uncharacteristic for a dog, somehow, it ran with the determination of a cat up unto the branch and struggled momentarily to untie the knot and crashed woefully to the ground and bayed on top of its voice. The cosmos heard it. Surely, there was something amiss. The now-dry-throated barks attracted Sansom's missus to venture outside the backyard. Gripped by fear, she pondered in hysterical outbursts of her husband's whereabouts. But, right behind her was next-door neighbor Mazi Ibiam, who trailed the dog's howls. When they got to the scene, there was not much they could do. Sansom had stopped kicking! Even when he could help, he could not do it alone until the boy-men left to hold the home fort came around. There was not a whole lot of able-bodied men around; the trickle of elders that heard the call knew that they had an emergency in their hands.

Before complete dusk, Sansom's body was taken down. The elders would not let him continue to desecrate the land in plain view. His burial would be before sunrise, for what he had reduced himself to, and then, *and then* the spiritualists would start to cleanse the land, for what he had done was abhorred by the gods of the land. It used to be done differently, left to rot in the thicket and scavenged by the vultures and the elements, but in these parts of the lands, he would get a shallow grave away from his home, his high-profile life reduced to low-key memorial that would follow at a later date. A man given to astronomical chances, now reduced to less than human, with his children, part of the raison d'être of his depravity, nowhere near to witness his ignoble end.

Suddenly, it became a beehive of activities with neighbors' hands held intertwined on their chests or around their torsos, dazed by the turn of events of the day. Coming and going that evening, Ibiam, a man of impeccable character, poor and bent over by its impact but highly respected by the community, led the charge of the internment of Sansom, his nephew, the only son of his oldest brother, now driven to his death by the burden he placed upon himself and conquered by its huge impact.

Ever since vile men lost conscience or completely lack of it and had known depravity, Africa had been at the center of it all, and Biafra was the largest chunk of that wholesome denigration and dirty slapping. Africa had brought the beast out of the all humanities since time immemorial, be it the marauders, to the barbarians, to the neo-potentates, and to the newest savages, the human rustlers, the *untamables*. Africa has seen it all! And surprisingly, depraved men had never been in short supply. It was from the genealogy of the depraved men that Sansom sprouted from. They were those who meted out unspeakable ills against others. But more surprising, Africa and Biafra had remained a breeding ground for a tidal force of supposedly Homo sapiens who seemed to love to be oppressed and dehumanized. They had cultivated a culture of people enjoying their painful laughter, mired in suffering without knowing that there ever existed an alternative to suffering. That could explain their proclivity to accepting oppression and their subservient obeisance. Deceased Sansom and his ilk had held and raised the torch of destitution and wanting to hand it over to a chosen few willing to continue the business of making depraved men out of Biafra.

His remains were still oozing hot when tongues started to wag that he died shamefully for the expiation of his sins. That was the pedestrian thoughts of many, which gave credence to the fact that men were never God since no one could, for certainty, say what God thought about this man and the ills he heaped on his own people for they were monumental and could not be explained right away like that.

If he thought himself unlucky for which he had no mental fiber to manage, he needed to hear what had happened to the ex-customs chief. In the eyes of his people he was a criminal in defunct Nigeria, and he remained a criminal in the eyes of the people of Biafra. He ran the Biafran customs as his own personal property. He made himself a billionaire that exposed him very much that his case was easy to prove. He accounted to no one. So when Amadike began to privately track him as soon as the war was over, he knew that he had enough information that would put the buffoon in jail and have the jailhouse key smitten to dust.

This man had no industry, had no business, had no stall, and had no kiosk. But he had made himself stinkingly rich. His moneymaking machine was his office as chief executive of the department of customs and excise duties. And he had run it like his own business. He was not doing anything different in Biafra. He had carried on in Biafra where he left off when Nigeria was buried in the ashes of forgotten history. When the president spoke about revamping Biafra from its foundation, it was people like the ex-customs chief, Mr. Akirika, that he had in mind.

Mr. Akirika was larger than life. When the current dispensation was inaugurated their first task of caution was to restrict movement of people especially traveling out of the country. When armed robbers were counted he was counted a variation because he was never armed literally. However, everyone, even himself, knew what a rogue he was with reckless impunity. He had owned some colossal money that spanned outside the shores of Biafra, and those held the gaze of the incoming administration.

There was a gentleman's understanding between the general and the lieutenant. While the general did little to win the acceptance of his countrymen, they avouched for him on personal recognition. The former army combatant turned spymaster had worked assiduously to collate as much information on spare time as he could, and that had earned him the respect of his people, as well. And with unparalleled dexterity, he had amassed so huge an information base on individuals he was focused on. The administration had so much on him that there was no need to bargain with him. He did take more than enough to catch the eye of the owners. As the investigators zeroed in on him, he had no wiggle room to negotiate. Whatever leeway that was given to him was dashed to him just to make him to cooperate with the recovery units. Whether he was going to spend a lot of years in prison was a forgone conclusion. What weighed on those who had been keeping a tab on him was how long he would have to spend in the prison he had built for the low-level smugglers he had confiscated their goods and cornered them to himself, denying the rightful owners their sweat and depriving the public what should have been theirs in the alternative. From the loot he had commandeered to himself, he had built two five-star hotels overseas. That left those who knew how much he was worth to wonder if he were patriotic, why ship your country's hard-earned money abroad to develop places that needed no additional injection of investment, especially when your own country would be worse for it. Such raised the ire of the people following his money that as soon as they got hold of his investment knowledge they had immediately gone for the papers. As soon as they had gotten all they needed to have they knew that they had him on the scrotum, squeezing and tightening. He was adamant and headed for the courts, but having no longer financial muscles to mount a challenge against the government the fight was over before it even begun and Mr. Akirika was headed for life in prison for twenty-five years. Add that to his sixty-three years, he was going to be an octogenarian before he could smell the breath of fresh air. And since President Dim had a mandate of one term of six years, for Mr. Akirika an earlier release from jail could only come by fiat of presidential pardon, he knew that he was in for the long haul. His Appian Way of getting out of jail was as long as it was of old. From the day he was taken into custody, he had resolved that if he ever came out alive, he was going to retire to his country home in Umuburushi, twenty-seven miles southeast of Umukabia and two miles outside the city of Umuoba.

CHAPTER 31

Turnkey had not missed work in eighteen months since he became a full-time employee of Kasper and Kaspersky Investment Inc. He had lived life like he was still an ordinary person. One who could rub shoulders with the rich and the powerful should be able to assume his place at the high table of the society no matter where that society was. But he was unassuming and carried himself as of old. Before that year's Thanksgiving holiday, he had requested for an additional day off. Before that he had scoured the newspapers for information on some of the leading architects in the country. That quest for information led him to the office of Dang and Tang Architectures and Designs. It was a fairly huge office with a tastily decorated front outlay. In the lobby were some of the works produced by the company. A tall glittering office complex in the heart of Hong Kong. Seemingly looping towers in the shores of Singapore. The ocean liner shaped like the one in Chengdu New Century Global Center. This building with its shoreline location gave a blue whale tantalizing visage. On the other side of the front office was another one of China's tallest architectural designs of Dezhou, resembling a sundial structure. Dang and Tang Architectures and Designs had concentrated their work in Hong Kong, mainland China, and Singapore. They were trying to break into the American architectural and building design. Their business plan, as it pertained to grabbing a chunk of market in this hemisphere, was to establish a base in the United States with the overall game plan being a focal pivot to neighboring markets of Mexico, Canada, Brazil, and other big satellite markets. And they were showcasing their work for all to see. If outlays were anything to go by then Turnkey had found what he was looking for.

Dressed in a shining white long-sleeve shirt that was rolled up midway between the wrist and elbows, he looked svelte and tasteful in his attire. He wore a tie that was loosely donned. His hair was cropped up with a chunk that was combed to one side of the hairline. As he got out of the car that misfortune smiled at him with, his hair flustered in the air, covering a little bit of his view as he pushed it back away from his face. Even though he could change his car a million times, he had cherished his Chevy as one would behold and cherish the undying feeling of one's first love long consummated and filed away on the shelf of old accomplishments. His stature was not great, so he had nothing to alleviate his ordinariness.

As the doors of Dang and Tang Architectures and Designs office swung open, he was welcomed by the smiling face of receptionist, Ms. Savivanh.

"Welcome to Dang and Tang Architectures and Designs, how can I help you?" said Savivanh in oriental-accented smattering English.

Ms. Savivanh was born in Laos, and found herself in Vietnam during the displacements of people, young and old, by the communist government in Vientiane. It was moving from frying pan to fire. However, her own fire turned out to be cooler than ice. When the Americans were evacuating thousands of Vietnamese kids fleeing persecution by the Vietcong army, Savivanh happened to be at the right place at the right time. She was counted as a Vietnamese and flown to Kentucky.

"I want to take a look at your gallery…"

"Sure, sure, sure," said Savivanh, as she pounced on the man's words before he could finish what he wanted to say, leading him inside the exhibition.

The place was cool, cold, and serene like a graveyard when the ghosts had gone sleeping and the angels were singing hosanna in the highest.

"Do you have anyone I can talk to about your…"

"Sure, sure, sure! Uhhhhm, none is around now. But you can leave your phone number, and they'll call you when he is back."

"So they're not always here…"

"They usually are, but they have gone out to a meeting," said Savivanh. "Mr. Chang. They will call you when he is back," she added, unknowingly highlighting her inadequate mastery of the English language.

"Who's Chang?" asked Turnkey.

"He is the president?"

"I see," said Turnkey as he leaned on his elbow on the deck of the receptionist, where on top lay business card holders for one Dang, Tang, Chang, and Xi. Turnkey ran his eyes on the cards before him, picking one card from each holder.

"Who's Xi?" asked Turnkey.

"He is the president," said Savivanh.

"Who's Tang?"

"He is the president," came the same answer.

"And who's Dang?"

"He is the president," said Savivanh, as Turnkey echoed that in unison with her.

"I see. All of them are presidents. My question to you is who's the boss among all of them?"

"Chang."

"And after Chang, who's his president?"

"He is not here," she said.

"So where's him if I wanted to talk to him…"

"You do not have to talk to him, Chang is here."

Turnkey paused.

"You do not have to. Chang will take care of you."

"Chang may not. And you know why I'm asking to know all about your company?"

"No, I do not know, sir," said Savivanh.

"I just want to be aware of the hierarchy of your organization. Salesmen and women are fond of wooing you for your business for as long as it takes to secure the business. Soon after they would be sending your calls to the answering machine and sometimes giving you the middle finger," said Turnkey, knowing full well that the lady before him would not in eternity bother that he had crossed the line of making a point and sounding chauvinistically rude.

"I see what you mean. But we are not American. This is a China company. If you want to talk to the top, top president, you will have to go to China," Savivanh tried to remind him.

"That's what I'm saying! And that's what I'm trying to avoid," Turnkey quickly added, as the front office door swung open and in came Xi.

Chang may call the shots in this office. But Xi was the whiz kid among all the design personnel in the whole of the American satellite office. Flat-faced and flattened buttocks, he had an uncanny knack for drawing and designing mind-boggling edifices. As he strode in, he offered Turnkey a handshake, warm and collected, assured of his knowledge of the art of architectures and designs. Still wearing his arcane smile, he ushered Turnkey inside his office.

"You are here to see me, I guess," said Xi as he motioned Turnkey to have a seat in front of him on the other side of the ornate desk.

"I guess, you can say that," said Turnkey.

"How can I help you?" asked Xi.

"I wanted to take a cursory look at what you do, a look at you works."

"What are you looking for? A high-rise? A skyscraper? An office complex? An apartment complex? Or a small individual building?"

"It could be any or all of the above," said Turnkey.

"Then, you are at the right place," said Xi as he added, "What company are you working for?"

"I have no company, but one is in the works," said Turnkey.

"I see," drawled the Chinese. "Well, we are here for business, big or small, anything to do with design and building."

As a salesman and as someone who was not a native speaker of a language he was eager, forthcoming, and seemed more voluminous as he tried to pitch his trade and showcase his dexterity with someone else's mother tongue. Intuitively, he just wanted to impress his visitor with his command of the language.

"If I may ask, are you in the business of building houses?" asked Xi.

"No, I'm in the hedge fund business," said Turnkey.

"Ahh, I see! You must have a lot of money then."

"Not necessarily," said the young billionaire.

"That is okay! Money is your business, design, building, and build is our forte. And if I may ask, are you looking to build in this state or another state? Or even in another country?" asked Xi. "As you know, our reach is worldwide," he added.

"Does it really matter?" asked Turnkey in reply.

"It does matter," said Xi, trying to impress with his mastery of the English language again. "Different states have different codes and ordinances. In some states, you have to specify the nailhead for each wood and how tight the juncture have to be, and some other states have it different, and these minute variations have to be specified before the blueprints. But in some countries, there are no fast and hard rules. As I said, our reach is worldwide. For instance, in Nigeria you as the builder can do a whole lot differently even as when the building itself starts. But here in some states asking for a nail change is like going back to the drawing board. You tell me where you want it and leave the rest of the worries to us."

"Can I take a look at your catalog?" asked Turnkey.

"Oh yah," said Xi as he sat up and placed a huge catalog full of building pictures of every kind before Turnkey.

As Turnkey flipped through the pages, Xi reached for his drawer and brought a smaller catalog and placed it before him.

"You can take this one home. Take a look at it and tell me what you wanna do. I can help you with anything you want to do building-wise. Of course, you should know that we are competitive. And we design and build to your specifications and taste. We are Chinese. We give you what you want and how you want it. We may be one of the biggest architectural companies on planet earth, but no job is too little or too small for us. And in this new age of architectural designs no one beats us in design, style, and aesthetics. For some companies, their design approach is linear, but we use integrative steps to come to reach the ultimate art and beauty," Xi reeled off.

As Turnkey got to his feet, Xi sprang to his as well. And reaching inside his breast pocket he got out a business card and offered it to Turnkey.

"Give me a call whenever you are ready to do something," said Xi.

"I sure will," said Turnkey.

When they got to the front desk, Ms. Savivanh clasped her hands together and bent her height from the hips in farewell greetings to the young billionaire as the sliding door swung open and Turnkey and Xi exchanged final handshakes as he exited the office.

CHAPTER 32

C hance had traveled down to Biafra. For the first time in many years, he had been to his homeland without the company of Turnkey. However, he was scheduled to join him in what had become a second home for him. It had been eighteen months since Turnkey got hold of his largesse. And for eighteen months, he had worked his beat as if nothing had happened to change his life. As he boarded his flight for Biafra he had with him the catalog he got from Dang and Tang's office. It kept him busy in flight as he perused the catalog. Without being schooled, he could see in their presentation dynamic white lighting mimicking daylighting. The sample houses had a mixture of oriental architectural masterpieces. But since this catalog was packaged for the American western market and taste, it had the cute of Queen Anne veneer and was redesigned and reshaped to meet the modern mind frame, from château-esque mansions to dingbat, from defined cottages to Californian bungalows with concrete foundations. The samples were really innovative and built with care and with unparalleled superior craftsmanship that was packaged to deliver an enduring value for money spent. The exterior walls were exclusively bricks and stones from end to end covered with stucco for durability of the life of the finished products. The interiors were a combination of alder and oak woods, mahogany, maple, and hickory hardwoods and cherry sapwood combined with deep reddish-brown heartwood. The floors were ceramic and porcelain tiles, and the countertops were natural stones of the finest qualities. Presented in such alluring colors Turnkey thoroughly immersed himself in appreciating the package and presentation that he needed no further explanation or persuading to think otherwise.

Biafra was changing, and he did not just feel it. He saw it. Chance was on hand to welcome him. In over many, many months he had not taken an extended vacation. However, this time around he was prepared to have one. He was dedicated to his job and duties. But this was a man who had nothing to lose. If he had decided to walk away from his job with no call, no show he would still be insulated from the reprimand of poverty and want.

This time he was traveling alone. And as he settled down for the evening, he brought out the catalog that the Chinese architect had given to him.

"Chance," he began, "I think we gonna go into real estate management," said Turnkey as he pushed the catalog toward Chance.

"If you provided me the land I'm ready to throw in half of that bequeathal into the plough," he continued.

"Are you serious?" asked Chance in stupendous bewilderment.

"I'm dead serious. It's of no use gathering dust in the banks."

"No, it was doing pressing down and push-ups," teased his friend.

"I'm dead serious," asserted Turnkey.

"When did you come about this conclusion? Have you spoken to your girlfriend?"

"I've no friend worthier than you to tell or to know first. I've spoken to no one, and I've been thinking about it ever since Mr. Skeleton broke the news to me. Real estate is the biggest market by miles and it's still growing in leaps and bounds. The first time we met with him and he spoke to me about possessing a largesse I had wished I had a million dollars and what I can accomplish with so huge a million. And now look at that. A common wish for a million had turned into reality of billions of dollars that I don't even know what to do with it."

"That's a whole lot food for thought for me," said Chance.

"When the money was turned over to me, I felt nothing different. But in the past few months, I've had some fitful nights."

"But why Biafra, or you meant if I found a piece of land in the hills and valleys of San Francisco?"

"If I want a piece of land in Kentucky I'll go looking for it myself. The people of San Francisco had no needs for more investments. My spirit is urging me to do it where it's mostly needed, and the Biafran people I've encountered in over six years I've made my pilgrimage here are people of immense talent and drive."

"I appreciate it, my friend. You hit the nail on the head. But have you broached your mum and your dad?" asked Chance.

"My dad, as you know, doesn't care about living and dying. He's just doped up on retirement. And that doesn't mean he wants to die. If it does give me joy his blessing was a given. He wants to be left alone. My mum, as you know, will always be on board when her bottom line is taken care of, when she gets her manicure. Ever since she understood that I'm the one in the driving seat on this matter, she's left me to control the wheels. She's fine if I guarantee her bloodline of money supply. Forget all her shenanigans. She is fine. Yet, in any case, while I'll appreciate their blessing I don't need their consent," said Turnkey.

"This young nation has great lot of an empty stomach to absorb more food. A billion dollars would be massive, and two billions of dollars would surely change a great portion of this country. And the truth about it is that whatever you bought in America could be gotten here half the price and still accomplish the same end product and perhaps of better quality, using less both in materials and labor. You've found it in good stead here. If that's what you wanted to do I'm going to put the clout of my parents to bear. You gonna save a lot of money without breaking the law, without circumventing its perimeters. Of course, we all understand that itching palm is a thing of the past in this new Biafra. But, we gonna need a bunch of people with myriad of expertise, bankers and accountants, financial planners and business developers, lawyers and gawkers. And I'll put it this way, my mother's a lawyer, but I think that you would need accountants more than you will need lawyers. It would be a massive undertaking."

"I don't see it as would be a small thing! It's a massive undertaking. Get me the land and I'll provide the funds. How hard is that?" asked Turnkey.

"It's not hard. How much land are we talking about here?"

"A large expanse of land, enough to contain hundred units of homes, a supermarket as in Uptown Mart, a recreation center, five swimming pools, and about five restaurants…"

"Then we gonna need a massive stretch of land. We gonna need city town planners to come in. We're looking to build a new town in a town."

"If we can find a place we'll build it."

"And who would live in those houses?" asked Chance.

"You want to tell me that we can't find hundred people who would want to buy houses in a well-lit corrugated neighborhood, secured, alluring, and safe? Well, if we could not find those interested here we'll put them up in foreign market. If we did it well I know that Americans would love to have a place peaceful and alluring to spend time and vacation twice a year. If security is assured some may move down and settle here for good." He paused.

"I've brought this catalog so that we, you and I, can start making some decisions and fast too," he said.

"That's more food for thought. Then we can transform these structures and pictures and designs to meet local sensibilities. We'll need local planners and designers, structural engineers and developers. We're looking to build a town," opined Chance.

"Whatever it takes," said his friend.

"Surely, we'll need local architects who understand city's ordinances and specifications, from bolts and nuts to screws and nails. Biafra has already developed a universal building code system, and there're no shortcuts."

"That's even better! That's what I was looking forward to. As long as we get the job done! Whatever it takes," said Turnkey again.

That evening Chance went over to the main annex. Since Dim came to power Ogidigi had been more active, playing court to a cross section of the people. He still had the ears of the president, but there was little or nothing he could do to change the course of national proceedings. The days of unbridled corruption had long been dumped in the wretched dustbin of forgotten history. One could influence certain things as in what's to come, but one could not be seen to be greasing an official's palms or be accused in the public eyes of itching palms. There was a nongovernmental watchdog that was scouring the Biafran sphere looking for elements of corrupt practices. That watchdog had another watchdog watching them. And another watchdog watching those who were watching them. There was no breathing space to think ill or want to do wrong or engage in any hanky-panky business. They were empowered by the national consultative legislature, the highest lawmaking body in the land. They have no prosecutorial mandates, but if they recommend to the justice department for an investigation to ensue or certain action be taken against an individual or an entity, then it would be warranted that the justice ministry should take some kind of investigative, corrective, or prosecutorial actions. So everyone was forewarned. But in this instance, Biafra had nothing to lose but everything to gain.

A group of young men had just left his house when Osai walked in and made himself comfortable in the sofa left of his father's.

"My friend has the biggest plan in the whole wide world. It's a great idea, and to top it up he has the means to back it up."

"And what's that plan you want to kill me with suspense, making you to lose your breathe?" asked his father.

"He wants to build hundred units of houses, five restaurants, five swimming pools, a huge supermarket, a recreation center, two lawn tennis courts, a hospital, and so on and so forth. And he has the means to back it up, Dad."

"You didn't hear him right," said his father.

"I did, and I know that he had more than enough to back it up."

"How much are we talking about here?"

"He has at least three billion to back it up," said Chance.

"You must be joking," intoned Ogidigi.

"That's what I'll say if I didn't know," said Chance.

"How did he make all that money?"

"He had a bequeathal from an unexpected quarters."

"I know," said Ogidigi offhandedly. "Only in America! In America you can also be stupendously rich like that only through bequeathal of wealth, winning a lotto, judicial judgment, or some Ponzi schemes using other people's money."

"And now we have a decision to make. We need a land…"

"You need a massive expanse of land to have all that in place, and that would cost a lot of money. Anyway, the whole of Biafra land would be hard-pressed to find a land large enough to accommodate all in one gigantic pool."

"That's where you come in, Dad."

"I see, but I don't have it," said Ogidigi.

"You must use your good offices to work the phones and get us a deal without breaking the law. Someone doesn't have to pay you to dump some goodies on you. You're looking at new streets, new amenities, thousands of jobs that would take miscreants off the streets and provide gainful employment for others for a long time to come. You're looking for a new lease of life for a whole lot of people." He paused.

"We'll be developing a brand-new town in town. It could be called Ghost Town."

"What!" exclaimed Ogidigi.

"Ghoostte Town," repeated his son.

"Find something else and call it."

"Why? It sounds ghoulish? What's in a name? Are your maternal people not called Umuagbara?"

"I see, and that would be getting government involved at the highest levels."

"I don't think you have to. I think it's a local thing," said Chance.

"Even if the local government would provide you that piece of land, when a massive injection of capital, liquid or otherwise, is involved, then the highest levels of government would have to be notified," Ogidigi told his son.

"Whatever it takes, Dad," said Chance.

That night, overwhelmed by the possibility of the truth in what his son told him, he placed a call to Amadike, the spy chief. He left a message on the answering machine when he did not pick up. It was a minute past midnight when he got a return call from his friend. They spoke at length about what was on the table. It was a wonderful prospect to give a thoughtful consideration by the spy chief as well, but he welcomed the development. He promised his friend that he would get the men in his chain of command to look into this personality. When everything was cleared, he would be glad to meet this young man and if need be eventually get the president's inner circle to know about the proposal. In the final analysis, it might be worth the president's time and honor to meet with this nouveau riche gentleman. Three billion dollars investment is worth heaven's attention.

The following morning after breakfast, Chance and his friend drove out of town fifty miles away to the office of Akalonu and Akamgba estate design, architecture, and engineering company. Well-known and ambitious in their design and presentation. All the new layout in the horizon had their imprimatur, and their works spoke for themselves. It was they who it was said mapped out the Woliwo new territory, Nkalagu Newfound Land Quarters, and the EndPoint Amalgam Layouts. When they did not do the topography of the layouts they got involved one way or the other in being awarded the construction of some of the units. It was no coincidence that it came to mind easily when a referral was needed.

Mr. Akalonu, the architect and chief engineer of the firm, sat behind a room of a desk in his spatial office. On top of the desk were model and prototype housing units. Prototype paved lawns, lush and green. Prototype streets and trees lining both sides like boulevards. It was complete retail marketing in one spot and at a glimpse. Even with all that littering the table there was still room for more sampling of what they could do for a prospective customer. But the table was so large that it was mightily impossible for a handshake across the reaches. So Mr. Akalonu had to go across to the other side to welcome his visitors with handshakes and a nod to sit down.

"I know I can do something for you, what's it that I can help you with, young men," teasingly began the architect. "You're welcome to the office of chief executive of Akalonu and Akamgba, and my name's

Architect Engineer Gabbi Akalonu," said the architect, who, over the years because of his numerous works building and supervising the construction of housing units, now thought himself an engineer as well.

"Hi, my name's Chance and meet my friend, Turnkey," he said.

"We're on a mission," said Chance. "We are looking for a good firm do some construction for us. We've heard about you and had decided to come to see you in person and see what you can offer."

"You're at the right place. And even though our works speak for themselves we still have to blow our own trumpet if we had to, and of course, we still do not consider any opportunity as too little. We're driven to be busy, and we're insatiable," said Architect Akalonu.

"Busy we have brought to your stable if you can guarantee your work anew. This guy you see here can make you a billionaire if you could add assurance to your claim," said Chance, skewing a finger toward Turnkey.

"I hear you, son! Which part of the world are you coming from, young man?" asked the architect, trying to absolve the audacity in Chance's candor.

"I'm from here, sir," said Chance.

"I know you are from here. But which part of Biafra land are you from? And from your accent you must be coming from upper United States or lower Canada, close to Ottawa."

"No, I'm from Umudede, and my friend is from Boonville in the southern state of Missouri, not far away from the Sunbelt states of Tennessee, Arkansas, Virginia," said Chance.

"You're all welcome," said the architect and quickly went on. "Over the years we've earned our business by trust, and we've earned the trust of our customers delivering what we proposed in any prospectus we give out as part of our commitment to do the best for our clients and straighten our reputation. Very few companies can match what we bring to the table in terms of quality, assurance, and actual delivery," said the architect, seemingly indifferent to the huge amount of money ascribed to the little white man seated next to the son of the soil, that seemed to know nothing to say.

"We've got our works by referral from those we guaranteed our jobs," he continued, still indifferent to the amount of money mentioned. "Well, what can I do for you? Are you looking to build a building, an annex, a duplex, or an estate? I know young men of nowadays seem to have a special taste, a quiet bungalow in a secluded area? I'm sure you're not looking for an estate. Are you?" reeled off the talkative architect.

"Let us see what you got," said Chance as he pulled from his small briefcase the catalog Turnkey got from Dang and Tang. He handed it over to the architect.

"We're looking for one who would replicate those structures or at least some of them without a fuss," said Chance.

Akalonu flipped the pages and nodded his head. He went behind the huge table and pulled out a drawer and brought out a catalog of his own. Beautiful and bigger in terms of density size and pagination.

"To replicate all these, you're talking about erecting an estate, a massive piece of land," said Akalonu.

"Yes, more than an estate. It's gonna have a huge supermarket, half a kilometer long. Some restaurants, recreation center, swimming pools…," said Chance.

"Then you're not talking of an estate, you're talking about a town, a town in a town, a city. You're looking at about three to five square kilometers of a virgin land. That would be the crux of the matter," said Akalonu.

Chance and Turnkey bent heads together in a tête-à-tête and seemed to appreciate what they saw in the catalog given to them by the architect, while Akalonu kept flipping through the one brought to him by Chance and his friend. While Akalonu's catalog had no prices attached to the houses on it, Dang and Tang had estimates on their catalog which had a caveat that they were subject to change based on location and market volatility. Everyone understood that as a rule of the thumb.

"The good thing about this is that I can offer to build these for you for a ten-to-sixteen percent discounts and still come up with a product more alluring and unsurpassed quality and unequal aesthetics."

"Really! You got to be kidding me," said Turnkey as his words seemed slightly to have emerged through his nose.

"Yes, I can," said Akalonu as he came over to the other side to demonstrate what he was talking about. "The American standards we know," he said, opening one of the pages and pointing. "These walls you see here are hollow walls covered with Sheetrock. But, our buildings are blocks and bricks and stones if that's what you preferred. In addition to ceramics we can throw in marble. But since it looks like it's going to be for commercial purpose, we may not have to apply every extra to every one of them.

"You see that house there," he said pointing at the first building on his own catalog. It was an annex. "That building there," he continued, "gave me my first break and ever since then I've busied myself ceaselessly."

"You mean this one here," said Chance, pointing at the same picture, "that looks like my father's house."

"Who's your father?" asked Akalonu.

"Ogidigi, Diokpa of Umudede," said Chance.

Akalonu's eyeballs became dilated.

"You do not mean it," he said.

"I do. I've no reason to disclaim my father and claim someone else's father if he were not mine," said Chance.

"I should have known that! I should have seen that in that bridge of your nose. It's a strange world. Children of nowadays have mind-bending stories. They claim to have millions on their persons when they are penniless."

"You may be right, but you're assuming a lot and some erroneously too," said Chance.

"You strike me as right. You look every bit of a chip off the old block except in one thing. He's no exaggeration. He's a mountain man but plain speaking. His creator exaggerated him already, so he had no need for additional elaboration or to embellish what he can do or what he's capable of, or what he is. By the way, how's he doing? And your mother? And your siblings? You've been long gone. And now you're bringing back the promises."

"What promises?" asked Chance.

"Now, you're bringing in some success and good fellows such as your friend."

"Chief, can you do this for us. This gentleman here with me wants to contribute his largesse to this town in the American spirit, and we're looking for a company that would not disappoint. We don't need to bring in a foreign company if we can find one here in Biafra," Chance informed him.

"Seriously speaking, I can construct anything for you," said the architect as he seemed to have noticed some exasperation and detachment from the son of his old friend. "I can build anything. I have men and personnel to design and build anything and on time too. You see that your family house, that was thirty-two years ago. There was nothing like it then. It was a quintessential poster boy. Because of it I've built thousands of individual homes. Because people were asking him, and in his magnanimity, he was referring them to me. Because of it I've made a kill over the years. Because of it I've moved on to the next level. And you know that house has a unique history about it."

As he kept talking something pricked him to believe that these young men before him could be bringing the biggest individual business to the Biafran nation, and he found the innermost reckoning and urging to press on and pitch for his own elevation. He saw in Chance and company his own chance.

"Take a trip to Umushishi New Territory. It was this company that designed the layout. Take a trip to Woliwo residential quarters. We didn't design the layout or its topography, but we built majority of the housing units in the area. I'm sure that you never lodged in a hotel since you came here," he said, referring to Turnkey, "because he who owns that kind of house like his father had no need to be looking for a guest house. But if you had been to Mazi Hotels and Inn, we did the architectural work and built it, you'll know what I'm talking about.

"I'm proud of what we do. Even when our works littered the whole landscape for all to see I needed blowing my own trumpet to drive home the points. Look about you, we've become the foremost construction company in the whole of Biafra land. You seem to have an enormous plan, and I'm throwing my hat in the ring for it," said the architect.

"You might wanna start putting your proposal and bid together," said Chance offishly.

"I would need to have details of what you plan to build and expanse of area you have so that I would be able to fit it in into my board and come up with a quote in no time."

"Of course, those pieces of information would be provided in no distant future time," said Chance.

"I hope, sir, you do understand that we would be comparing prices in this area before we can make a decision about who would help accomplish our plan here, whether in parts or in a whole," added Turnkey.

"Sure, I do understand that, but my point which is an assurance is that we live in a competitive world and I'm ready to slug it out with all comers. I just want to be given a chance to compete. This is not for the highest bidder. It's for the lowest bidder with some pedigree of success of getting the job done."

"All right," said Chance as he and his friend got up on their feet.

"I look forward to seeing you come back with details of what you have in mind," said Akalonu as he came around to the other side of the huge table and escorted the young men on their way out of his office.

CHAPTER 33

"You've never been able to explain your fascination with the heathen people of your second home, these your Biafran people," Splendor, his mother, confronted him on his return from Biafra.

"I don't have an explanation for you, Mom, or for anyone else. It's my decision and nobody else's. And moreover, I've nothing to lose."

"You've everything to lose and nothing to gain," shot back his mother, who had of late become evidently agitated and fastidious over minor stuff that may become detrimental to her wellbeing overtime.

"I've nothing to lose. You should worry about your own welfare and not what the next person stands to gain."

"When you don't work for some fortune you seem eager to fritter it away at the bat of an eyelid."

"Mom, this is like much ado about nothing," said Candie. Candie had been Turnkey's best ally by miles, especially since their mother started angling to be a spoilsport. As soon as he took hold of his largesse he had moved swiftly to take care of his favorite sis. She had done her business, quit her temporary job, and flew off with her beau to the Far East artificial island for a weeklong hiatus of relaxation and merrymaking. She was never such a huge fan of her mother, and in this matter, it was not difficult to decipher where her allegiance lay. Unlike her sister, Mermaid, she had always been vocal and sometimes opinionated to the chagrin of her mother, especially when she had always liked to annoyingly pull her tails. Hardly had she been on her side on any matter where family alliances were required to get by. Mermaid, on the other hand, of the siblings was less likely to provoke any argument on any matter. As long as she was left alone, she bothered no one and held no contrary opinion that would ruffle anyone's feeling. She was a jolly good fellow. Ever since her brother landed his fortune, she had gone about her business as if nothing had happened to affect her life. Yet, in the scheme of things she knew that her brother was not going to leave her in the lurch, and she was not. He had a chunk of money deposited in her account with promise that she would never walk alone, she would never lack, if she kept focused on what she had to do, and she needed help down the line she knew where her help cometh.

His father, deJohn, had kept his job religiously unmindful of the new status of his youngest son. He had driven from Albuquerque to the reaches of New York and then to moorlands of Alberta. From the fringes of New Orleans to the approaches of New England he had made fun of jobs and kept company of beaus on perennial basis as long as his job permitted him and as far as he could go. He had relished what his work had presented to him, a man of seemingly no fixed address as he hobbled through for some fun and livelihood. In thick snow and sweet sunshine, he had ploughed the terrains of North America in an unending commitment to duty and hard work. He had never missed a day of work and never missed a night of fun. Whenever he could not drive through the dusk he had made a home for himself wherever his options were exhausted. He had also found company in some easygoing, fun-loving damsels. One of them being Michelle. He was swept off his feet, against his nature. It was intense, it was rowdy, and it was hot. She would not let him go an inch without her. Virtually she lived with him in his 18-wheeler, cozy and roomy. She traveled with him to New Orleans. He drove with her to Albuquerque. It was a roller coaster. It was nonstop fun, and the result was self-evident. But she had no early morning sickness. No bedside spittle cup. It was not until the end of the second trimester that little Ehud began to move and kick. He was kicking so vigorously that both believed it was real. They had been together since the first night they met that whodunnit did not arise. When a child ate that which had kept him awake he would succumb to slumber. deJohn and Michelle needed to find a home. And he got her an apartment on the outskirts of Albuquerque metroplex. In no time, the baby came calling. It was a mixed feeling. Things were looking up

431

for him before, but right now he was not so sure. Albuquerque was far from home. Not a din could be heard. By Michelle, he sired a son. deJohn had spoken of his wife and child to Michelle, but in the heat of the moment she never cared a hoot. But forty-four days after Michelle's son, Splendor had given birth to another son, and deJohn was handy to welcome his second son to a troubled world.

When Turnkey was born, the surveillance crew took their eyes off Michelle's son. The occasional interest turned to him just in case if Turnkey would meet an untimely death. While at times Turnkey would cajole his mother about how lucky she was to have begotten him, unbeknownst to him he was the luckier of the two. Ever since he had control over his largesse, she had angled herself to know the full details of the Will. The full detail of the Will was never to be made public, the provisions of the letter of the Will had made it known that that son must be "the last son of a woman legally married" and "that son's authority over the will can never be usurped nor abridged." It had also enjoined the recipient to accommodate and take care of "all individuals related to that son directly by blood of consanguinity."

"Mom, I've made my decision, and it's set in stone, and we've gone through this time and again," said Turnkey. He didn't need to highlight this fact because everyone knew this.

"Here are your sisters, and these are all you got! Don't tell me. Tell them why you're fascinated with these people," said his mother.

"I'm not fascinated with any people. I just want to be an investor."

"You've the biggest market here, why do you want a smaller piece of the action?" asked his mother.

"I want to conquer new territories."

"You want to conquer the savages of old. You want to teach the unteachable. You want to tame the untamable. You're gonna lose everything in the bargain..."

"You got it all wrong. Mom, you're sitting on your hind here and making a generalized opinion of people you don't know."

"I know them! How're they different from the things we know about Africa?"

"They're different in a whole lot of ways. Given a chance they're a whole lot different. I've visited them these past six years. They're a wonderful people. They're a people set apart…"

"That's good to hear, Golan. As long as no one feeds me to the lions, take me along with you when you get to your kingdom," opined Mermaid.

"And me too," said Candie.

Turnkey had made an appointment to see Mr. Skeleton in the morning. He had decided that he wanted to know much about him from the horse's mouth. His gut feeling was that he would use him to spearhead a team that would help him navigate the terrains of investing millions if not billions of dollars at home and overseas. From review of his personal contribution at his work at Chase Manhattan he seemed to have a sterling résumé. A consummate analyst. A big thinker. His mind-set was as big as his huge frame. He believed in big businesses and big opportunities, and when he saw one he knew it from further afar.

But Mr. Skeleton had moved on. He had founded his own investment company called Beyond Borders Investment Inc. His company had touted their acumen and paradigm on wealth management, wealth growth, and wealth protection and preservation. These were the core principles on which their business model was anchored. They could help with start-up businesses or even help fine-tune existing ones. They had touted their unparalleled skills in doubling investment growth through insightful analysis of market behaviors and economic indices. It was the age of desktop computers. They had mastered using the algorithm of computer analysis to pursue trend in the market and made their moves. They had been adept in using the computer algorithm of stock market to take positions on investment. They did not wait on the market to open; they opened the market because they never slept. Someone had got to monitor and watch the features all night without batting an eye. Watching the features was like being in charge of prisoners. No guard took their eyes off an inmate. Their approach to business had paid off. In six months, he had seen great results and his customers were happy.

"Mr. Skeleton," said Turnkey, "the time has come to joggle the dominos a little bit and move the dice forward." Mr. Skeleton had an inkling why he was visited. It was all about investment. What he had no idea was the arc of the young billionaire's choices. Not wanting to jump at him he listened to him attentively. He knew that his guest had money however, he understood that having money was different and having money and anchoring it on a strong financial foundation was a different ball game altogether. But Mr. Skeleton understood that building a business in the financial world was as dicey as throwing the dominos down the table. He had hoped that his guest would be leaning toward being a shipping magnate or upstream real estate investor than a venture into the topsy-turvy financial industry world where the ripple of one loose coin reverberates around the world, and throws the stock markets world over into a tailspin, than the improbable happenstance of a sea juggernaut lost at deep sea.

"I've decided that having this money do push-ups and collect dust in the vault of Chase Manhattan does no one no good." He continued, "If one irreverent Ponzi guy decided to throw a monkey wrench into the works the financial market will come off its wheels and millions of us would be left scratching our heads. I've decided that I needed acting and acting sooner."

"Now, wait a minute, Mr. Ghoostte," said George. "Softly, softly! The world is not running away from us, and anyone touting that it's coming to end sooner is trying to bamboozle us," said George softly. It was ironic that such a huge man would speak with such a taciturn that he was almost verging on inaudibility.

"I'm elated to see you and wanting to trust us with some of your largesse. You've made a great choice in wanting to utilize our services and expertise. We like to tread softly. Our business model is anchored on wealth protection, wealth preservation, wealth management, and wealth growth. I'm glad to see you and wanting us to lead the charge in your investment forage into the future.

"Anyways, before I digress further, Mr. Ghoostte, have you decided what area of our economy you would like to throw down the gauntlet?" asked the former investment banker.

"You know ever since you implanted the idea that I can buy a fiefdom somewhere out there I've decided that I want to go into real estate…"

"In other words, it ain't gonna be in this country," cut in George.

"No, not here yet," said Turnkey.

"Where's the damnedest, godforsaken of a place that's about to get a face-lift? I guess it must be in your Biafra?" said George.

"You're right, Mr. Skeleton," said Turnkey.

"Lucky people! Why this place of all places and peoples?"

"I've been visiting there for the longest time, and they seem to be a people I can do business with."

"You know life ain't always the same as when you are in a courtship and having free and unholy copulation as when you tied the knots. That's when your differences seem to come off the seams, some that reared their ugly heads and were ignored, some that were erroneously thought would go away with time, some we thought we could deal and live with only to discover it was excruciatingly difficult to deal with afterward. Who're these people, and where are they located?" asked George, swirling about the global map on his table and bringing the African delineation to view.

"Mr. Skeleton, as I said, I've been traveling to these people for some time now, and on those visits, I've had the privilege of meeting some other people of other African nationalities. But these people are different. They fought a gruesome war some years ago, but today you can hardly notice any of the relics of the war. In fact, today they're better off than those whose intention was to decimate them, whose intention was to exterminate them. They're doing far better than their detractors. They're a people set apart, my friend."

"What made them this thick?" asked George.

"I don't know, but they have self-assuredness in their gait, confident in their strides, breathless in their pursuit, indefatigable in the face of adversity. They're resilient; irrepressible, never-say-die! They're like that candle ensconced on the hilltop. You know, Mr. Skeleton, you can light a lamp and put it in a bushel, yet, it will still glow and emit its shine for all to see. That's what I see of these people, exuberant, audacious without being arrogant, but arrogant for some reasons, daring without dillydallying on obstructive cost. Self-assured without doubting their own abilities."

"You must be speaking of the American people," said George.

"No. They just seem to exude the American will. They're go-getters. These people pride themselves as first among equals, played no second fiddle. Envied and at the same time despised by their neighbors. And they just keep pushing, mindless of the grunts of their detractors. That they are mindless rankled their envious neighbors most…"

"They are just like Americans…"

"And much more than that! I would not tell you that I've traveled the width and breadth of the African continent, but I've traveled the breadth and width of this young nation. I've seen poor people among them, but I've seen no beggars. They're ashamed to beg. They rather fight than bemoan their state. They're like the Spartans. In fact, they're Spartans. But not ashamed to dirty their hand and not tired of ploughing their land. I've seen artisans and journeymen. I've seen truck pushers and night soil men. Hmmmm, whatever it takes. They keep going, workaholics. They like to bulldoze their way through a minefield mindless of the danger inherent in a booby trap. Their quest for success was insatiable, always thirsting for some more even when they have more than enough. In that regard, I would say, I may be wrong, that they're perverse a people. Yes, I may be wrong. Yes, I've seen them. And I've seen and read enough of the African people, but there were no other people like the Biafran people.

"I was made to understand that they like to travel. They are like the Jews dispersed all over the world before their gathering back in the eternal city. It's said that anywhere you go and there are not these people in that habitat, then the place must be uninhabitable. They are restless. They hate an enclosure. They hate to be sequestrated. They hate to be limited. They want a free rein. They like to conquer other environments. They are all over United States, hell-bent on scaling any hurdle strewn on the path to success.

"And then think about it. They've no natural ills. They've got no tornadoes, they've got no hurricanes. They've got no whirlwinds and no typhoons. They've no mind-boggling floods. No tremor. No earthquakes. A land needing no dung, neither artificial manure nor fertilizer to nurse her crops and feed her people. Their bane was bad government and bad ways of doing things bequeathed to them by the British and subsequently by the defunct Nigerian governments. But, goodness me! They now have a government that's bent on cleaning the Augean table no matter the cost. They're at it vigorously and are brooding no opposition, and no nonsense. I'm sure you must have met them here." He paused.

"I know Africa's about tribes and clans and ethnic groups, which tribe are you talking about now?" asked George.

"There're many tribes and ethnic nationalities, but the most conspicuous among them are the Igbos, and their smaller bands of neighbors, sharing the same cultural melee and progeny. I'm sure you must have met one of them in this building…," said Turnkey.

"Oh, I've met a lot of them. They seem to be everywhere. And I've heard their story."

"Some interesting tale and not so good stories," chimed in Turnkey.

"I've engaged some of them. They're very astute. They look at you in the eyes as if they want to zap you from the face of the earth. But from their story they're a beleaguered people. And they tend not to have any stomach for vengeance. And until they learned it they may suffer another pogrom," said George.

"Oh! Never again!" exclaimed Turnkey.

"Never again, we have heard it time and again. Oh, there's one in this building. He comes down to grab some tea. He's loudly friendly, but he does mind his own business," said the hedge fund manager.

"But more importantly, they're no communists and have no Bolshevik inclinations. Their land itself is an untapped potential that needed to be harnessed," added Turnkey.

"Too good to be true," said George.

"Believe you me."

"Seeing is believing."

"What I'm here for, Mr. Skeleton, is to let you know that I've found a fiefdom that I can invest a great chunk of my money in," said Turnkey.

"It's a good thing that you've decided to invest your money so that you can make more monies. The core value of our company is asset protection. We may not succeed in making more money on your investment as much as you may hope for, but the most paramount and basic tenet of our existence is to make sure that you don't lose money on your investment. Rather than in an effort to make you gain money you lose it, we would pull back. Mr. Ghoostte, I know the huge amount of money at your disposal. And I know that you want to invest big. But we need to do a feasibility study to ascertain that the Biafran economy would be up to it to absorb the kind of money that would be thrown into it, and then come up with a business plan. You get my point?" asked George, just to make sure that the young billionaire was paying him attention.

"I'm with you, Mr. Skeleton. That has been taken care of. We've gone beyond that stage," said Turnkey as George nodded his head.

"I'll let you into all that. But right now, what I want you do is to raise a team so that we can get down to business. I don't want a team of lawyers. I want a lawyer and a team of accountants, business developers, architects, structural engineers, and perhaps some task masters.

"Without having to keep you in the dark, I've secured a five square miles' expanse of land. I want to put hundred units of residential homes in it with a large supermarket tailored to the like of Uptown Mart in Philadelphia and across much of the eastern corridor. The design has also a recreation center, and we are asking the local authorities to erect a police post. It's gonna be a brand-new town with all the trapping of a modern city. We intend to put the houses up for sale which could be a decent holiday resort for some folks thirsting to escape the drudgery of American city life," said Turnkey.

"This sounds so good, Mr. Ghoostte. But, how much do you plan to invest in this project?" asked George with a tinge of trepidation.

"As much as good for the goods," replied Turnkey.

"And my next question would be how much can you stomach to lose?" asked the former banker and quickly added, "You know it's a virgin land and the prospects are ill-defined to say the least" with some concern in his tone but on a second thought, with consternation at himself for venturing that far when he did not have the goose in the bag. He needed high-profile clients to add to his portfolio. Turnkey was not yet high profile, but he was the kind that would be bringing a whole lot of money to the table.

"I've not put a marker on that yet, and have not given it a thought," said Turnkey.

"I'm just thinking aloud. As an investor, we're always juggling between the ups and downs of market forces. Our thoughts are never in convergence. They are always running parallel but not parallel in the same direction but parallel in opposite directions. Well, they may come to some convergence, at some point. But, you know, it's always convoluted"

"I completely see what you mean. It's not something I want to lose one minute of sleep over. Where there's something to gain, there's much to lose. If that was your concern it's well-taken. I've come this far materially not by dint of hard work but by the good grace of providence. I've got nothing to lose."

"We'll help you to preserve your wealth, especially where we see opportunities, and for me, from experience, there're always opportunities in unchartered territories."

"I'm not offering you a deal yet. However, if you agreed to examine the challenge, I'm inviting you to travel with me to Biafra and see things for yourself. See the enormity of what I've envisaged and come up with a supervisory workforce needed to bring it to completion. You can add us to your portfolio, and as time goes by, I would be inclined to throw my hat in the ring of the American market.

"Mr. Skeleton," he continued, "if you accept my invitation, you can put a price tag on your remuneration and that of your team before you tried it out. We'll take a look at it and see if that's something that we can afford."

"Oh, you can afford us. We're a fledgling company. We want to be competitive at home and abroad."

"Come on, the ball is in your court...," said Turnkey.

"It sounds good. And it sounds like a plan. I might as well take a vacation on the back of that," said Mr. Skeleton.

CHAPTER 34

In company of Turnkey and Mr. Skeleton were Ms. Shipley, his girlfriend, Mr. Firewood, a ravenous corporate lawyer with an incisive mind and inquisitive eyes. This guy trusted no one, not even under an oath. He was on guard all the time, suspicious of the next move of his opponent. That in itself had become one of his shortcomings. Those who knew him as such tended not to trust him either. That was true of him than that which he held of others. He had become a loner in the skirmishes of corporate world. Mr. Skeleton had tapped him because of his incisive mind and knack to unearth hidden maneuvers. Young and dashing with a track record of considerable success in spite of his age. Mr. Firewood had a gaze that seemed like he was gawking instead of looking. He had a corrugated forehead. That made it difficult to tell whether he was browbeating or just assuming his usual self. His looks seemed to pierce the hidden thought of many. He had a look of many stares, querying and unrelenting. His was such that would make the feebleminded own up without persuasion.

The farthest place he had traveled from where he was born in his thirty-two years of age was to the University of Kentucky which was about fifty-five miles away and where he obtained a bachelor's in criminal law and a masters in corporate law, and about four hundred and twenty miles out of state for some corporate skirmishes. He understood corporate antics as he knew the back of his hand. He was an avid reader, inquisitive, and with a penchant for wanting to know more, itching to discover, un-mesmerized, undaunted by the challenges of new topography and terrains. Saying that he had not traveled much was an overstatement. He had not traveled at all. But that was not a drawback or an impediment. Swirling a table global map before him and with ease he could tell you where the beaches of Normandy lay and where the equator line transverse the world and the countries in its crossline from Congo to Sao Tome and Principe, from Kiribati to the corridors of Brazil and Maldives.

Also in their company were Mr. Fairbanks, an architect; Mr. Towers, a civil engineer of twenty-two years of experience; and Mr. Riverbank and Mr. Dooley, accountants, both with a combined nineteen years in corporate intrigues and interchanges. Besides Turnkey, all these gentlemen had one thing in common: they had not seen the African sky nor stepped foot in its humus soil and organic sand. And two of them had not stepped foot aside the shores of America.

The flight across the Atlantic to Charles de Gaulle airport was smooth sailing with very little turbulence for those who had had the privilege of flying long. But for Mr. Firewood it was a different ball game. Because Mr. Firewood had not flown in an aircraft before he could not understand why there were bumps in their flight as one would have if one was driving. The air was cleared for him when one of the air hostesses announced that they should buckle up, sit tight, and brace up for a round of turbulences. After that announcement, there were really some heavier turbulences that had seemed to make him clutch his heart in his hand as he could feel the flight seem to drop and rise again and hit a bump. He could hardly sleep as he relapsed into a doze off, on, and off. At last they made it to the French capital, and in a single file they began to crawl out of the belly of the aircraft. Then they had to wait to make the connecting flight to Biafra.

If the flight across the ocean was turbulent the one across the huge African continent was smooth with much less turbulences, despite the hot African air. A few hours later, as the plane heaved itself deep inside sub-Saharan Africa, one thing became absolutely noticeable: the air in the bowel of the aircraft became more humid. The drumbeat of the African sun began to permeate the entrails of the aircraft. Everyone could feel the change in temperature, and a few began to fan themselves. Turnkey had gotten used to the weather, but for his guests, it began to dawn on them that that could be the beginning of a new normal.

On hand to welcome Turnkey and his company were Chance and a cousin with a pedigree of family of petty businessmen. They were driven to a posh five-star hotel, newly constructed, and that presented the first shock to Mr. Firewood. He never envisaged that he was going to see such a beautiful inn to lodge. Nothing good had ever come out of Africa. The notion he was fed to believe had persisted and lived in the back of his mind hitherto. That false notion just instantly evaporated from the recesses of his imposing faculty. Now he had to do introspection of a different kind. He was going to sip their water. But now he was sold on taking a gulp without any reservation. A suspicious man by all measures. But in a twinkle, he had reason to clear his mind. He saw for himself people of supposedly from every nation milling around, Greeks and Turks, Arabs and Jews, Chinese and Japanese, Caucasians, British and even Americans, whites and not so white, and of course, blacks, local, and those that seemed to be of South and Central American descent.

For the first time in his coming and going to Biafra, Turnkey would not be lodging at the Ogidigis. He took a room on the third floor of the palatial hotel at the city center. The men with him had their reservation on the second floor. The following day Chance came around and gave him a detailed catalog of phalange of houses of different shapes and designs with layout for recreation centers and sites for other amenities that would be true for a layout of a modern town. It had the imprimatur of Akalonu estate and designs. While away in the United States, they had been under constant communication, and Chance had updated his friend on the goings-on. The project had been advertised in both local and national news outlets for bids. The interests to take advantage had come in howls and droves. It was competitive and it was vigorous. Akalonu's presentation had the blessing of the Ogidigis, but in itself it was top class. It spoke for itself.

Chance had also briefed his friend on the locale of a stretch of land he, with the help of his father's reach, had secured for the development projects. Finding a compact stretch of land intact for about five square miles was a huge task based on the area they were angling to institute the initial development projects. The closest they found were two swaths of land perpendicular to each other fifteen miles out of Umudede from the city center, two and a half miles traveling east of Umudede, and seven miles traveling westward. When Chance brought down the map for him, Turnkey was sold on it. He did not know much about the place, but he trusted his friend to truly help him navigate the terrains.

Chance also told his friend that based on the large sum of money earmarked for initial capital investment he had taken his case through his father's web of connections to the highest quarters that plans were in the offing to offer him that expanse of land for a pittance, for little or nothing. For little or nothing? Turnkey had thought to himself. Now, he had surrounded himself with experts, perhaps, not at the highest levels, but savvy enough in the entangled acts of reading between the lines of business intrigues and maneuvers.

Before Chance left the hotel's suites that afternoon, impressed with the energy he had channeled into their project, Turnkey gave him a prototype design of a supermarket he had envisaged for the new town, something akin to the layout of his granduncle's business that got his grandfather into perpetual estrangement of which he had become a benefactor of immense proportion. It was part of the initial plan. He wanted Chance to take it to the architect and have him deduce it to a local plan that would meet local ordinances and specifications to the barest requirements.

When Turnkey gathered his team inside his expansive suite and laid bare the details of his enterprise in Biafra, everyone had a chance to voice their observation and opinion. As he passed the details and summary around the table, everyone seemed to be in agreement with what they had before them. The architect among them openly expressed his admiration of the presentation and wondered aloud how apt it would be if the final product would be as good as it was presented.

"We're gonna hold their feet to the fire to make sure that all the nails were at the right places, and that's why we have you here, and if you do need more hands I'll be here to furnish you with additional help," said George.

"I'm ready for the grind. I'm all weather," said Mr. Fairbanks.

"We're here in supervisory capacity and armed to impose American excellence and ethics upon the whole deal," said George.

"I would suggest that we be given additional time and space to critically look at the financial summation of the works to be done and as tabulated in the presentation and present a concrete financial analysis of the works envisaged, not to undo anything but to enhance it," said Mr. Riverbanks.

"Because, what we see here looks good and sounds too good to be true," said Mr. Dooley, the other accountant. "They're budgeting to build to completion at seventy-five percent the cost to an American company, and at the end of the day they would be left with zero quad in the baggies. They would be put out and dry for nothing."

"You can't say that for sure. They would employ local labor at half the wages. They would burnish their image and advertise their know-how on a grandeur scale. But that would not be the concern of any of us here today. We just have a work to do, and our ultimate goal is to do it at the lowest of costs, save money for other investment interests, which was why Mr. Ghoostte wanted us to take another in-depth look at the layout," said George.

"What I wanted was for us to conquer new horizons, provide succor to newfound land people. America is on the cusp of stagnation. In due course, we'll be running in circles. The worst we can do would be to lose our paltriness, yet we stand a chance to be the progenitors of new colonies, new markets, and new dividends. My intention was to take the ideals of America to new havens," said Turnkey.

"Mr. Ghoostte," said the lawyer, "we can avoid all the pitfalls envisaged and imagined in this noble enterprise. As Mr. Dooley had rightly observed the whole outlay looks too good. Three things I'm looking at now, and would need to be addressed, are though our friends had provided paper and designs, but a piece of paper is as good as it can be when it's yet to be smeared. We would need the service of a realtor who would break down the letter of the estate agreement to a layman's language, even to a lawyer like me. Secondly, as Americans, we know that there's nothing like a free brunch. Someone's got to pick the tab. Somewhere down the road, in these lands and place, the government might fall, a dictator might emerge, the republic may become banana, and old promises may not hold sway. They must put a farthing to every piece of land and must be documented. So that in case of any eventuality we would know that there was a price tag. And when the American government throws her weight behind it they would be fighting for something. And finally, I'm a lawyer with a panoramic view of law. But no matter how much we hold lawyers responsible for the ills of the world, I would want to bring a local lawyer on board with no vested interest. I need that gentleman or woman for certain advisements with local statutes," concluded Mr. Firewood.

"Put some meat on the bone, Mr. Firewood," said Turnkey.

"We can't trust the locals in all that they promise especially when they don't have any pedigree. From a lawyer's point of view and based on the millions of dollars involved we would want us to get the service of a professional real estate company with proven track record. The Camdens, the Pelicans, or the Merchants. They would help us get a great deal of deals out of the whole deal in terms of land acquisition and values. That's what they're out for…"

"Their service would add to the overhead cost of the project, and that was what we're trying to avoid," said Turnkey.

"There's value for the money spent, and that's service, service anchored on experience, experience with a proven track record. It buys a lot and saves a lot," said the lawyer. "And my take on the free land deal is that it must be written in stone."

"What do you mean?" asked George.

"I want it to remain free now and when it appreciates. Is there a moratorium on the value now and not in the future? Is it free now and remains free twenty-four years down the road? I would rather have it on record that there is a moratorium on the value of the land for ten years, and the value after ten years must be stated in pen and paper now and not later. Our trust must be built on ironclad guarantees so that in the long run, at the end of the day, we're not left scratching our heads. If we're gonna invest this huge amount of money, we must have guarantees at the highest levels of their government and perhaps get the secretary of state office to take a look at it so that when push comes to shove, it would become a government-to-government engagement in our behalf."

"It doesn't have to come to that, Mr. Firewood," said Turnkey.

"It doesn't have to come to that, but we've to cover our bases in case the wheels go off the rails," said Mr. Dooley.

"It doesn't have to, but we need all those caveats so that we don't emasculate ourselves," said the lawyer.

"But I don't want government involvement…"

"Well, there's no how you'll invest huge American money overseas without the government's prying eyes hovering over it." said the accountants and George, a variation and almost simultaneously.

At the end of the discussion Mr. Firewood prevailed on the group on the need to have a price tag on the property. While he touted his own credentials as a lawyer he was able to convince Turnkey on the need to get the service of a local neutral lawyer to be co-opted for advisement on local statutes. On the other hand, Turnkey stoutly rejected the need to bring on board a high-profile international realtor. And having seen the layout and topography of the plan in blueprint, Turnkey was counseled on the necessity of each bidder to come forward and espouse on their presentation and be able to answer some questions to gauge and enunciate the level of confidence building needed to execute such a humongous contract, first of its kind in sub-Saharan Africa.

Everyone was eager to make their presentation. Everyone else was eager to listen. He whose father was Abraham never smelled the gates of hell. Akalonu was miles ahead of his competitors, and with his exquisite package he put himself further miles ahead. To top it off he addressed the Americans' concerns with such depth repertoire of knowledge that every one of his and his team's words became a din. He spoke by rote, offhandedly and with great panache. He left no doubt in anyone's mind that he was the right man for the job. He believed in his own performance that he was convinced that he was on the verge of securing a monumental, life-changing bargain. With the comfort that his friends, the Ogidigis, would chime in a word or two for him, he knew that he was home and dry. If he had any concern, it was the challenge of the Macadam Builders. However, his concern was allayed by the simple fact that the Macadam Builders had specialty in road construction. The other bidder that made the cut was a fledgling new company, the Extra Miles. Both the Macadams and the Extra Miles made a strong show of their own depth with deftness. However, they never enjoyed the connection the Akalonus had both in high and low places.

At end of the deliberation, it was resolved that each contractor would get a piece of the action but how much each would get was a conjecture for Turnkey, George, and Chance to resolve. There was no doubt that Akalonu and company had made the best eye-catching presentation, but George was not ready to have Turnkey put all his eggs in one basket. One hundred units of a story building which in American estate parlance would mean a two-floor, some one-and-ahalf story, and some bungalows, were not a whole lot for a typical American realtor mogul, but to the Akalonus, it was massive. By consensus of the three, it was resolved that they would construct twenty-five percent of the road and streets and lanes in the estate, and fifty to the Macadams, and the other twenty-five to the Extra Miles. In self-oath Chance had vouched for the Akalonus and still throwing the name and all the substances of his family he had sworn that the Akalonus would do a better job erecting the supermarket. With his family name on the line the right to award the other contracts to a company of his choice was ceded to him, and without hesitation, the Akalonus got them for the asking, except thirty-one percent of the housing units.

CHAPTER 35

The land of the Umuagbara was bordered on the east by the people of Okosie. On the approaches from west were the people of Umulihilihi, and to the north were the people of Umunkenke, and to the south was a patch of land that stretched for about three miles from Okosie to Umulihilihi and continuing southward for another three miles onward to the creeks. Beyond the creeks and about twenty miles out was the Atlantic Ocean. It was in these parts of Biafra land that Chance and his father had secured for the proposed investment for Turnkey.

When Turnkey and Mr. Skeleton were driven down this expanse of land, both were impressed with its location. But for the fact that it was being mapped out for housing and other commercial investment it was extremely good for some mechanized farming. The land was humus and arable, dense with grooves of thick forest on one side, and toward the end of the other was a seemingly flatland, interspersed with hills and valleys and minor trees, savannah, grassy and evergreen year in, year out. Adorable land from end to end. That this patch of land was juxtaposed among the creeks provided some aquatic expedition for Turnkey whose love for the waters was never to be overstated. The creeks led to vast stretches of moorlands in its outskirts. Mushroom-sized trees and shrubs, staggered and seemingly immobile stream of water, encumbered more by the heavily branched and dark fibrous water hyacinth. The water hyacinth was new to these waters and creeks and seemed to have migrated from far-off water away from these shores. The colors of the water hyacinth provided the creeks and its moorlands some very beautiful scenery, violet blue and yellow plumes. And some thirty miles yonder were the tributaries of the Bight of Biafra. And ninety miles beyond the ocean banks were the contiguous zones where conflict armada and armaments, and expropriation mercantile vessels were arrayed against the sea, the land, and against her people, who still went about the businesses unfazed. And as dusk began to bid farewell to early evening hours the croaks of frogs, the shrills of the birds, and the yelps of bats disturbed the peace of the evening as Chance and his guests made their way out of the marshland and creeks and valleys and hills into the savannah on their way out of their expedition.

The following day, Chance, through his father's connection to the corridors of power, had scheduled a meeting with second topmost guy in the department of foreign investment, who happened to be none other than the enigmatic London-trained economist, Atinga. Atinga had moved from his position in the justice ministry to a more advanced role. This coming investment into Biafra had gotten the ears of the people in top echelon of power. The spy chief and his people had done their homework and had nothing to pin on this young man. But it had fallen on the laps of Atinga to clear the air on any areas of gray patches.

The huge conference room in the ministry of economic development was spacious and tastefully decorated. There was a huge oval table at the center but still afforded much of a room for jockeying around it. It was so long and oval, yet no matter how diligent one was looking there was no telling where it was joined together. It was a masterpiece and boggled the mind how it made its way inside the conference room. Everything wood in the building was made of mahogany and cedar, cedar and oaks. So it had the best of the best.

Inside were Atinga and two of his lieutenants from the ministry, flanking him on each side. Turnkey led his team but was ushered in by Chance who introduced Turnkey and his entourage. Everyone that traveled with him to Biafra was there except one of the accountants, taciturn-talking Mr. Dooley, who last night came down with an explosive diarrhea. It was that kind of runny tummy that would make one a pariah and certainly grant some days off to any employee, even the most dutiful and indispensable of employees. He had some food poisoning after consuming a mound of local delicacy. Mr. Dooley was troubled by the watery stool that he had positioned the reading table chair in his hotel room only five short steps away from the commode. He was miserable for it, no doubt!

"Mr. Ghoostte," said Atinga, "my name is Atinga. Atinga Woma. Please, welcome to Biafra land."

"But, you can call me Golan," said Turnkey as both men had a warm handshake.

"No worries," said Atinga, as he urged the company to take their seats.

Turnkey was a man of great acuity. If bears and elephants could smell things farther than anyone else and bats could hear a pin drop in the cacophony of a din, Turnkey could see someone once and internalize the face for the longest time perhaps till the end of his life. He had known Atinga playing in the field of Boonville, and that was a long, long time ago. It was not the name he remembered most. It was the face. That gangling African little boy that called him names. He had no doubt some long memory. But beyond that he seemed to have some compound eyes and sharp boding of the eagle or a hawk or a buzzard. How he could have remembered that face was a thing to be queried. Because, Atinga had changed a lot. His hair was no longer those tiny, little bit dense crop of hairs that seemed not to grow a bit day in, day out. His hairs had grown thicker and beautifully manicured with a side parting on the left side above his eyebrow. But Atinga, in his wildest imagination, had no iota of a clue of who he was dealing with. As Turnkey introduced members of his team, Chance could not understand why his friend of old would suddenly choose his middle name as the official name for the commerce.

"My compatriot," began Atinga, referring to Chance, "you're the epitome of the citizenry we want. Without belittling your person and age, you know as I know that when a child killed a lion he drags it to his father. This young nation of you and me would be eternally grateful for the friendship you have cultivated." He paused.

"And to our friends from overseas," he continued, tilting his head with a nod in the direction of Turnkey and his group, "you're welcome to Biafra. You're the friendship we crave for. You've chosen Biafra as a signpost for your investment foray into Africa out of your own volition, we appreciate that. And we'll treat you right! We welcome you with open heart and mind, not unmindful of our checkered history eon ago where we became beleaguered and eventually orphaned ourselves on the altar of open mind and heart and our foolish goodness. That experience, foolish goodness, that history has become the bane of our long-suffering, untold hardship as a people. For too long we've moped while raw cash grew wings and flew out of this land and out of Africa," said Atinga whose diction and accent were perfect and in tone with the English spoken in and around the Buckingham Palace areas of England.

"My friends, I don't mean to bore you with our inglorious history and self-inflicted injuries. It's just part of my story I like to tell my friends and friends of Africa to get them situated and understand where we're coming from. Bear with me. And moving forward, since you took this giant leap, we're going to extend our hospitality to you so that your good intention would be made manifest. Because of the huge outlay of investment plan you've mapped out, the Biafran government has asked me to relay to you that you pay no farthing on the whole expanse of land for quarter of a century. After twenty-five years, you still own the land, but you pay a paltry sum at today's price, a token, no more, no less. This government has instructed me to tell you that you would receive every support you need. And my office has created a special hotline for investors like you so that you will have a seamless investment terrain to accomplish your aim at earliest possible time without crunchy bottleneck of officialdom. We want to create a most conducive environment to operate your business, and every other incentive to boot.

"We also expect that your business practice would be an investment in the people of Biafra. In us you have a workforce unafraid to work and eager to receive a good wage for their toils. In fact, it's a taboo to lay about here. While it's in our blood to work hard, we demand to partake in the spoils of labor. We as a government are here to protect labor against the vagaries of the rich and powerful. In defunct Nigeria and before the coming of this government, the economic paradigm was baboon economy."

"What's that?" asked Mr. Firewood.

"I'll get to that in a moment," said Atinga. "We don't want the denigration of labor or the despising of the worker where one big guy invests some money and soon starts to make and corners the dividend to himself like spoils of war, leaving the people who really made the wealth with nothing except a pittance. We're building a nation where everybody has a stake. If an employee happens to spend twelve months with your company, at the end of the financial calendar year he gets a bonus if those at the top feted themselves to bonuses. You cannot fire the worker in that twelfth-month period just, just because you don't want him to partake in the bonus dividend. If he's fired, just, then he's entitled to receive his due bonus in the mail. It's the worker who makes money and not the investor. We don't want to foster a system where the baboon toils all year round and lazy monkey corners the whole profit to himself, gentlemen."

"Wait a minute!" said Mr. Riverbank, the accountant. "Using your analogy here. The baboon invested no dime in the business."

"That's unfortunate. But it was on his back that the business has progressed to such an enviable height," said Atinga.

"The baboon invested nothing. If the business fails, he just walks away. He lost nothing," said Mr. Riverbank.

"No, he lost everything, a means of livelihood. He doesn't want it to fail. If it failed his family will be in serious want, serious peril. The fact that he gets something at the end of the years gives him an incentive to work harder and guard against anything that would pull his means of livelihood into jeopardy, my friends," continued Atinga.

"I've never seen anything like this before. It'll not work," said the civil engineer.

"Well, it's nothing new. That's the same system obtainable in western economies. The only difference is that we don't want a winner-take-all economic affair. Those who provided the initial investment capital and those who daily toil to see the money yield dividend must be rewarded at the end of the year. The government and this nation will never allow its people to be exploited just to assure the survival of market forces, daily giving ordinary folks a mountain to climb with no chance of changing their circumstances for good."

"Are you a capitalist, and do you believe in capitalist principles?" asked the accountant.

"We're all capitalists, all of us in this country," said Atinga.

"How about you, sir? Are you a capitalist, yourself?" asked the lawyer.

"I'm a bloody capitalist, trained in the western worldview of capitalism, and I believe in capitalist principles. I'm also an economist. And I understand how the numbers bandied about are arrived at. Look, gentlemen, I'm a number *cruncher*, and I know how to cook up the books. Sometimes, they are churned out to sustain manipulated pre-established conclusions. But we're here as a government to protect the people against the ravages of market forces. We, as a government, are here to make sure that market forces do not take control and destroy that which we hold dear. Market forces by itself are indices of greed designed by the rich to unconscionably justify the exploitation of the poor. If the translators of the original text of the holy books could tinker and muddle to bolster expected rigged outcome, then tinkering with market indices to continue to cheat unsuspecting masses would be a walk in the park. Allowing market forces to fester without checks in the life of the people is toying with their survival. When market forces collide, the poor suffer. My friends, the dignity of the laborer must be assured. This government is out to protect the people against the tyranny of a tiny minority, bellyful, yet still leering and salivating for more fleshing of the downtrodden that are already being held down," said Atinga.

"What you're saying doesn't provide the conducive environment for business to grow and flourish. It ain't gonna work. Most investors would think again and again to come up with a frame of mind ready to accept and invest in your economy. Your prescription would not attract investors into your economy which I'm aware you dearly desire and need," said the accountant.

"We're not doing anything different except that we want to curtail wholesome greed," said Atinga.

"Greed is the energizer of our world and development. It's the bedrock of the advancement in science and technology," said the lawyer.

"No," said Atinga confidently firmly. "The bedrock of the advancement in science and technology was fame. The quest for fame, to be known and to be remembered for years after we were gone, before greed superimposed itself in the melee of human endeavor with its insatiable covetousness. Greed is good, but wholesome greed is what we are up against. That worker who helped nurture the surplus must partake in sharing the bonuses, no matter how small…"

"And when the company packs up the investor will lose all his life savings and the monkey will just go home, back to the woods," said Mr. Firewood.

"No, Mr. Firewood, the worker is not happy going home because he's losing his livelihood. The company does not get liquidated because of the employee. The company is run aground by the rich and they turn around and falsely point an accusing finger on the employee. The worker only follows laid down rules established by the rich and powerful, the very owners of the means of production, and even the poor. And for your information, the book I have before me of which you will receive a copy today will tell you a lot how we intend to make you succeed," said Atinga. "This government wants every investor in Biafra to succeed. We guarantee every foreign investment if the company does everything right, follows led down guidelines…"

"Is that a communist manifesto?" asked Turnkey jokingly.

"No, it's not, Mr. Ghoostte, Golan," said Atinga, wearing a wry smile. "Every country has its own guide to trade, whether local or foreign. We want you to make as much money as you could. We also want you to enjoy the fruit of your labor here. Your great-grandfathers built many cities in America. Jamestown and Georgetown and numerous other cities. They built those cities with wealth they eked out of the lands they conquered and inhabited. They didn't build New York and uprooted it back to Yorkshire. Or repatriate the money they made to build the Thames of London. No! The Thames of London and Trafalgar Square were erected from wealth confiscated elsewhere around the world but America. And they lived in New York and made it a shining city on a hill. Mr. Ghoostte, you have a greater chance to build a Ghoostte Town here so that three hundred years hence, it'll be an ancient sprawling city that would be the envy of the whole world.

"We've nothing against foreign investors who are taking advantage of the cracks or loopholes in our system. It's all fair game. You can have this land if those cracks allow you to possess it for an inheritance. What we're looking for is partnerships to harness this land. The endowment is enormous. We can till this land on our own for ages but we can't eke out enough of the resources in its bowel without your help. We need you and we need you badly! This government is here to promote and protect old and new businesses. What we're up against, more especially, is local criminals, those fifty percenters, after all, it's the dubious house mouse that bandied about to the outside mouse that there's fish in the wicker basket. They're the folks we're up against; the never-do-wells who had by subterfuge positioned themselves at the sources of the people's means of livelihood, commandeered everything to themselves, filled their fat, big stomachs and still held the people to untold misery, left them with farts and excrements and still gave them the middle finger, having dazed them with the baseball bats of confiscated powers. You've nothing to lose but everything to gain. And be rest assured that this government wants to succeed with your help. Our guarantees are sure banker. Take them to the banker! And be rest assured!

"We're not communists. We're capitalists. But we abhor wholesome capitalism because it's rooted in unbridled greed. Wholesome capitalism is like the fight of two elephants where only the grasses suffer. Here the poor suffer. You've nothing to fear. You've gotten our guide to trade and investments. You also have our writ of acquisition of the land where you can pitch your investment tent. If you need more land we'll make it available to you. Don't hesitate to call my office anytime, or you can send words to this office through your good friend and my compatriot. Let it be on record that you have my word, if you require more land for expansion, we can extend your present delineation to the tributaries of the sea," concluded Atinga.

Space and time gave Turnkey and company an ample room for consideration. On arriving at their lodging rooms, he called them for a review of their meeting with the young technocrat. And everyone had an opinion. In variant opinions and assumptions, the arc of their views except Turnkey was bent toward distrust.

"I can bet you with my life that this piece of shit of a document means nothing to these people. It's full of promises they're not willing to deliver. It, in the long run, would not be worth the shit it was written on," said the accountant.

"You see, when I see these tiny countries and small economies and they've these different dos and don'ts and they begin to present them to you in booklets and pamphlets, it sounds to me like the Bolsheviks' manifestoes. They hide under pretentious assumptions and call their plans and ideas different nomenclatures, but they're communists herring," said Mr. Firewood who had never been to any country but had traveled to almost all countries based on somehow half-truths he had read on the faces of *Washington Teller* and *Tribune World Timer*.

"I don't think that any of us would have to lose a moment of sleep over this. Mr. Turnkey's an investor, and he had gathered us here to help him make it happen. I've not seen anything in what that gentleman passed across to us that was out of the ordinary. It's just who they are. It's just the way they understand living and dying, investment and opportunity. Mr. Turnkey has taken a business decision, and we have to help him achieve success. The questions and doubts we all have are all in order. They're part of due diligence. We have to give it a shot, a shot in the arm," rallied George.

"I'm afraid these natives can't be trusted. I'm looking at it and saying to myself, 'Too good to be true,' before, but now it's in plain English, buyer beware!" continued the attorney.

"At this juncture, gentlemen, I've something to say," began Turnkey. "My friend, Chance Ogidide, tells me that sometime ago when his grandfather was alive, if you came to him for a piece of farmland if you didn't have enough, he would take you to a thicket of bush and spreading his hands he would motion to you to signify that you could cultivate as much as you could. It was left to you to ambush the land as much as your strength could afford you. These people are still like that. They welcome you with open heart. When they say that they're dealing with you with open mind, open heart, they mean it, and more than that, they welcome you also with an open soul. I've a problem with that. And that was what got them into trouble eon of years ago and they haven't learned their lessons." He paused.

"When your forefathers came to these shores, these natives welcomed them with open hearts and open minds and open souls. They left themselves bare. Before you could say jack, our forbearers began to lord it over them, stole them, stole from them, and siphoned it away. It was the worst reversal of fate known in human history. They're yet to recover. In fact, in most places they still don't know what hit them. Before they knew your forefathers, these people were gentlemen. Their words were their bond. They had no time for some irreverent paperwork because they were not necessary.

"If you viewed them with some misgiving, it's not in them but in ourselves. If you doubted them it's not in them, it's in our makeup. Before our forbearers came to these shores, these people had no beggars. Woe unto to you to be begging. What a curse to be seen begging! They had no thieves. Woe betide you if you were caught stealing or coveting your neighbors' vine, and suddenly they've become thieves. They swore no oaths because their words are their bonds. Their openness had brought untold hardship on them, and we still doubt them because we're children of doubters. We're offspring of those whose business was to hunt but would never allow a child with a cudgel to go behind us. Now, we've taught them to doubt, but they still have the undying ethos of their kindred spirits, and those gone before them. If they didn't have thieves before our forbearers came, it's obvious that we taught them how to steal and lambast them, but we forgot who are the linchpins.

"I agree that the paper given to us today may be a worthless sheet of paper. They did it to satisfy us and for the convenience of this age and time. But for these people the witness of you and me was enough bond for them going forward. We ain't gonna live like that in this age and time, I understand that. But, it's a telling tale of some characters," said Turnkey.

"I'm just saying," began the attorney defensively, "they've a lot of restrictions on your way to maximize your opportunities and chances of

458

making money… I don't want us to later find out that these sheets had turned into one big bullshit of paper."

"Wait a minute, Mr. Firewood, capitalism is a ravenous enterprise. And capitalism laid bare without checks is a harbinger for the rape of the hoi polloi, the downtrodden, the common man. I'm going to tell you a story, part which only Mr. Skeleton can attest to." Turnkey paused.

"I'm a beneficiary of some generational wealth. My grandfather, who's still alive today, missed being a recipient of some largesse from a kind benefactor, and the gentleman being his blood brother, of the same father and the same mother. This is part of my story Mr. Skeleton was never going to be made aware. You all are aware of the fact that the Ghoostte family name is a household name in Indiana and much of the Sunbelt region of the United States. They made their name in the grocery and supermarket industry, and they made it rapidly. The fact was that my grandfather didn't fancy the race to the top of wealth ladder that my granduncle achieved almost in a jiffy, and my grandfather let him know about how he felt in no uncertain terms. Both men had their digs, and they seemed to disagree on almost everything. They were rivals and had a lot going in between them. Their rivalry later became unhealthy. My grandfather would have to leave town, or he would face some jail time. It got to a point they would not see eye to eye." He paused.

"Well, that would be a story for another day. Because of the way my grandfather castigated my granduncle there was so much animosity. He was stinkingly rich, wealth acquired in a short space of time. My grandfather was of the opinion that that huge earning of the rich is the combined aggregated pittance of the poor. When you get rich too quick too soon, you've taken too much from the poor. My granduncle had passed away. But when I spoke to my grandfather two years or so ago he was still adamant in his objection to his brother's rise to opulence. And my grandfather's brother before he died, he made a will, and in the will, he bequeathed what presumably he could have given to his brother, not to his children but to his children's children. The way he constructed his will it felled squarely on my lap. I would say that I stumbled upon richness by lot, or do you call it providence." He paused again to the rapt attention of others.

"Do I condemn my granduncle for taking advantage of the system? The answer is a resounding no! Do I join issues with my grandfather? The answer is ehhhhh, no! Perhaps, it's that kind of rise to opulence that formed the basic economic philosophy of these people…"

"Are they privy to your granduncle's disagreement with your grandfather?" asked the engineer.

"I don't think so, but they see the ravages of our system, the vagaries of capitalism, and the degradation of labor and had decided to tweak our system to suit their sensibilities. Theirs is still a free enterprise. Not where greed runs riot and leaves the common stampeded. I've no issues sharing profits with those who are in the front line of making profit for me from the smallest to the topmost. I've no issue with price control that's used to check the profit driving saga of today's businesses that has sapped our collective conscience and brought the beast in our humanity. Success must not be akin to man's inhumanity to man."

"You must have taken after your grandfather," said the lawyer like a kid listening flabbergasted by an adult tale by the moonlight.

"I don't think so. But my friend, Chance, tells me that anything begotten of a snake must have a long tail," said Turnkey.

"It would be hard to break even and make money in this economy," said the other accountant, Mr. Dooley, who had recovered from his medical condition of explosive bowel movement the other night.

"I don't think so, my friend. I'm from the tribe of Gad," said Turnkey as both Dooley and Riverbanks glanced at each other. "We don't throw in a shekel where we've no chance of retrieving it in worst-case scenarios. We don't put in a shekel in the plough and not reap it a hundredth fold. I think I know what I'm doing, gentlemen. We'll make a lot of money if you come with me…"

"Well, it's not what you think, my friend," said the lawyer. "These people exhibit the traits of the Bolsheviks. They walk like communists, they speak like communists, they smell communists. The economic doctrine they're espousing has Marxist undertone…"

"They don't seem to believe in free market economy, and if you don't have a free market place of economic ideas, then chances of growth would be seriously hampered," added the accountant, Mr. Riverbanks.

"You know, gentlemen, we Americans are a very clever people. We're schooled to place a badge of dishonor on other people, and then we run with it. When an economic doctrine doesn't cohere with ours, we're made to see it as akin to communism, and the mass of the people will run with it. These people can't stomach free market economy as ours because they'll be competing on an uneven ground. They have to tweak free market system as we know it to protect their economy," said Turnkey.

"Very smart people," muttered the engineer.

"We don't indoctrinate people. Our government just presents things to the people, and the people make their own conclusions out of their free will. It's the communists that are masters of the art of programming," said the lawyer boyishly.

"I see! Then, we're not paying close attention. There're no better people artful in the art of bending the mind of her people in the whole wide world than my country. If we don't see this, then it's understandable, that's love for our country. And I'd add that we're just quintessential patriotic, see nothing, hear nothing, and say nothing. That's a great love for country. However, I beg to differ. If any of us here thinks that some people out there do it better than us, that means that they've learned fast. It's unfortunate that we've been outsmarted in our own best game," said Turnkey. "But anyway, we've some business at hand, and I want all hands on deck. Mr. Firewood, take a more in-depth look at this document and let me know where your concerns are the greatest by evening tomorrow…But in the meantime, I would want to see you in my suite after dinner tonight."

"And someone here is not dry behind the ears. I've concerns right from the get-go," said the lawyer.

"We'll acquire that experience one day, and I tell you, you should not have any concern, not when you've not opened it," said Turnkey.

Immediately after dinner at about six forty-five, local time, Mr. Firewood walked into Turnkey's suite. Pacing up and down he offered his guest a couch, took a few more back-and-forth strides and sat right on the edge in the middle of the bed.

"You seem to have a misconception of what we're doing here," began Turnkey.

"Perhaps. Right, em…"

"But, you don't have to."

"I'm just afraid you don't understand how capitalism works," said the lawyer.

"I do, Mr. Firewood. I've held a job since I was fourteen. I've never been out of work. And on each I've aspired to get to the top so that I can have a firsthand idea of how the systems works and how decisions are arrived at. I never cared how low that job is, but among the lowest I've always angled to be first among equals, the guy at the top of the queue," said Turnkey.

"I know about all that, but there's something in this arrangement that's missing our spirit as Americans. While this may be a new terrain we have to look at the character of the people we're dealing with here. You can come here empty-handed and still make money. These people don't know or that they don't care, or when they know they don't just care. Look at their history. The British came here empty-handed and left their shores with their potentates in power after making themselves great off their riches. The children of Mao are coming, and they are gonna be smiling at them with clenched teeth…Anish, the Indian tycoon, came here and collected the waste of nuts and even the kernels and turned them into something else and made money, real money out of their waste," said Mr. Firewood.

"Well, that nut and kernel stuff wasn't in these parts of the world. You may be fantasizing about a different set of people in defunct Nigeria. These set of folks you see here are wiser than their parents and certainly much more wise than those folks that run their country aground," Turnkey tried to explain.

"They may be wiser than their parents, but they still have their blood flowing in their veins, and the point I'm making is that you can come with nothing and leave with some fortune."

"I'm virtually bringing in nothing, that's if you consider what I'm investing and what the finished product is coming out to be. What you take to build a foundation in America is what it'll take to erect a building here and still have some change left. And they're not complaining. It reminds me of my granduncle who took advantage of the loopholes in the system and became rich. He had broken no laws. There's always gonna be loopholes deliberately left in the law by law makers, and you'll be breaking no rules latching on them and improving your lot. And you know what, loopholes are man-made jokers. My friend, lawmakers are mystery people. They are a fun people anywhere in the world, creating Appian Way leeway that may impact them positively. They insert jokers in the laws, and jokers are anybody's to exploit to their advantage. My friends, success in any business is playing by the sides of the book but exploiting its loopholes, hidden in its recesses." He paused and sipped some water and continued, "They see the loopholes. They left the loopholes. They refused to rectify their mess. Why's that? Joyous people!"

"That's still whole lot…"

"Now, Mr. Firewood. If I may ask, if I triple or at least double your take home, will that make any difference in your helping me actualize my objectives here?" asked Turnkey, trying to tip him and to assuage whatever misgiving the lawyer may continue to harbor

"Well, that's not what I'm saying. I just want us to succeed in exploiting the land, and then maximal pay increase would not hurt."

"I wasn't even thinking along that line of exploiting the land. But I know that we'll make tons of money here, but whatever deal I offer you guys here, it's a done deal. Whether or not we make money I got your backs," said Turnkey.

The exchange of visions squared itself out. He walked out of that suite self-assured that however the wind buffeted that ship its oars were assured of some sweet sailing. He did not bring up the idea, yet he was not averse to broaching it when the time would call for it. Yet, it had come without him asking for it.

It was a few days later when Atinga stumbled unto Chance at a community event that attracted the crème de la crème of the community and its environs. Since the day they sat as compatriots with Turnkey and his crew, they had not met. There were some issues raised verbally by Atinga or implied to be in the package handed over to the billionaire and his band of crony capitalists that gave him some concerns.

"There is a likelihood that history seemed to be repeating itself here, my brother. Growing up with my grandfather I saw him assign lands to strangers without measure. It was the golden age. It was between a people that understood themselves with full knowledge that no one was going to be clever by half or take advantage of the other's blind spot. In that age, if you took a hocus-pocus advantage of your brother, you are just inviting Amadioha, the vindictive, hot-tempered God's angel of thunder to strike you dead. Boundaries were drawn by spoken words, not with a writ," began Chance.

"I know where you're going, my brother. And we know what we're doing here," said Atinga.

"How do you intend to achieve that?" asked Chance.

"Just leave that, that to me," said Atinga, with uncharacteristic sarcasm. "They have not read the fine prints in the documents. Take time and look at the fine prints. They'll understand that we've mastered their game and have become adept in it, as well."

"I'm just saying. Africa got into its mess by being open-minded and openhearted without clear-minded, and that was the beginning of our woes today. Open-minded was the beginning of our destruction, and not being clear-minded really eviscerated us the most. We must be guided by historical signposts. Those seemingly unseen handwritings on our historical wall have been ever present in our lives. Those warnings of history we've always ignored to our detriment. We cannot make the same mistakes of our fathers, and their fathers, and our great-grandfathers. We can't give these people a blank check, and they're too shrewd to let them have a field day. These people are smarter than we think. It isn't about giving the monkey a cup of water, it's outwitting her to retrieve it back," said Chance.

"My brother, you've nothing to fear. You've nothing to be worried about this government. We're not just clear-minded. We're fire-eyed. We're aware of the story of the devil and the long spoon. But we don't just have a long spoon. We've a long machete. The days when pigs fly are over. The days when these guys from overseas mesmerized our collective ignoramuses were long gone. We've really learned from our experience. It is the best teacher. But, it costs much! Our collective inexperience cost us much more than much. We can't afford those mistakes of our forefathers. Those days are gone…And look at he who is trying to draw your attention," said Atinga, as he pointed in the direction of a young man, motioning in the direction of Chance.

It was Chibuogu. Chibuogu participated in the initial "boy oye" demonstration that drove the gangs of marauding thieves, big- and small-time criminals, and miscreants out of Eureka. He now had a bustling law firm. Like Mr. Guzo, he was always at loggerheads with the authorities. But since the dispensation of Dim, he had seen a dwindling of fortune. There was a sea change in the polity. There was sanity in the system, and that had affected his fortune a lot. But, in any case, he was still doing well by all standards. He was like a friend of the Ogidigis and somehow a distant relation of Dorothy, Chance's mother.

CHAPTER 36

Work had begun in earnest at the site of Turnkey's real estate development. It was like the old descent of the locust. Men and women, old and young. Caterpillar of all kinds. Bulldozers and crawler dozers and crawler cranes, excavators and tractors, choppers and mulching machines. Dump truck equipment and trailers. Unique large equipment for special clearing, subsoiling stumps, and brush mowers made light and quick work of dense thickets of bush and swamps, of acres, of land. Within weeks the Akalonus, the Extra Miles, and the Macadams had made mincemeat of the estate. The perimeter of land acquired by Turnkey laid bare within view, from end to end and as far as the eyes could see. When Turnkey visited the site before he traveled back to the States, he was the happiest man on the face of planet earth. He was impressed with the work of the locals. In fact, it was deft on his part to insist on using local know-how and labor to do this project, and he was enjoying what he was seeing.

There was no problem. Chopping and clearing the bushland was also going on smoothly until it happened before his eyes. The previous day, he was an eyewitness as far as he could remember. A section of the estate was leveled to the ground for all trees big and small. But to the consternation of all the following morning, there was one lone tree standing in the midst of the ruins. It was conspicuous for all to see. The bushes around it stood down withering. Mr. Akalonu, having seen this phenomenon again and again, understood. A cursory look told him that the tree was a budding iroko tree. The iroko tree was the king of the forest trees. No matter how small it was in size, it dwarfed the rest of the trees and its stature was always hallowed. It was never brought low to the level of the minnows in the bush without ceremony. As in solemnity of tradition, Mr. Akalonu explained to Turnkey the solemn reverence attached to the iroko.

In a lighthearted mood, he intoned, "Give to Caesar what belongs to Caesar."

He got no further response from the architect. He knew what was to be done. He left the tree standing there for another week or so while work continued around it. Those days it stood there a loner, every night there would come a whispering sound from the direction of where the tree was standing. It was eerily and wrenching. It was about the thirteenth day that he invited the augurs and some priests of ancient spiritual worshippers who came and poured libation and a deluge of incantations. When the following day the iroko was chopped down, it was sans a whimper. But in the eyes of the locals the iroko was not chopped down. It was unrooted and taken to another location. That was the immense aura and awe in which the iroko tree was held among the people. Besides that, there was nothing remarkable obstructing the process. Day by day, the whole landscape began to change. Streets began to emerge. Housing shell began to spring up. The town of Ghoostte began to emerge. From one end to the other, it was like the old industrial revolution. People were coming and going, milling and engaging in all sorts of works, bricklayers and carpenters, plumbers and diggers, roofers and painters, and of course, urchins and miscreants.

Six months into the estate construction, a towering signpost was mounted on the two approaches to the estates. The signpost was covered so people could not see the inscription on it. However, as the days flew by the elements began to unfurl the cloth covering what was written on the signpost and part of it read, "Welcome to Ghoostte Town."

CHAPTER 37

The groundswell of opinion about the building of the institution and other outpouring of emotion was effervescent. As the foundations of the buildings went up, the whole area became a sort of some compass that held the nation in one hand and numerous gazes in the other. Every citizen who had had the chance of witnessing how the stones and bricks and boulders of the building juggled for space on one side and attention on the other was held spellbound by what was happening. The foundations were so thick, they looked like they were designed to withstand an earthquake even though in these parts of the world such things were unheard of. It was a taboo to think of it, and it was an abomination to imagine it. So why did Bucknor and his co-travelers conjure up such huge, imposing structures? The answers could only be found in the fact that that was what they saw and that was what they envisaged by association and appropriation for their young nation. But above all, the fact remained that there was enough money in the coffers to execute such a gigantic and ambitious project. The whole of this endeavor could not be described in one and not the other. It was both gigantic and ambitious. It was not a feat known to just Bucknor and Ahulele, but the whole nation knew it as well.

Today marked a momentous day that would live in the memory of the generality of the people. And its story would be tales to be told for years to come, perhaps centuries to come, perhaps eon hence, ad infinitum. It was colorful and boisterous. Boisterous and colorful for self-evident reasons. This country, much like the rest of Africa, had been raped to the point of debauchery. It had moved from one wanton destruction to the next with increased severity, and there were no letups. So what was being experienced today was akin to anything good coming out of Nazareth?

Everyone was seated. The dignitaries invited took their places at the high podium. The students were in high spirits, decked in their matriculation gowns and hats. There was a massive pomp. They were the first set of students to be inducted into Obikolo National University. Ensconced in a corner of the dignitary podium was the Obikolo family clan. At the other end of the podium was Atinga. Beside him was Chance, and in his company were Candie and Joann and Turnkey and a couple of his protégés. Between the left and right of the seating arrangement was a small elevated platform large enough to accommodate additional eight or so dignitaries.

Seated in this box was Obikolo himself. Seated beside him was his son, Bucknor, whose deft of purpose had made this occasion possible. He was made the provost of the new institution. While the school was under construction, he had gone back to school to acquire a doctorate in management. Also on the platform was the deputy vice chancellor of the new institution, a diminutive man of impeccable erudition, who would have the arduous task of assisting in shepherding the school from its infancy. Also among them was the vice chancellor, a veteran of the Biafran war, who left the weapons of war on the battlefield to go back to school and improved himself tremendously. Astute and enterprising, a young man of great eloquence, whose main forte was to rally an ebbing morale. No man was more qualified to fit into a shoe more than him. He was billed to give a keynote address at the occasion. And then there was the country's president who was scheduled to deliver a short speech to the new students. Every student looked forward to his speech, and he never disappointed. Rising and falling, reverberating in the horizon, he told the 13,907 matriculants, "This is a nation on a journey, and in the years to come when her story is told you would be among her forbearers. In this journey, we'll not let you walk alone. At every turn, at every stumble be rest assured that this nation will always be by your side to offer you a helping hand…

"Every artisan must show his craftsmanship. Every baker must know what a baker's dozen is. Every medical doctor of all facets must be ready to defend his calling. Every engineer, and all engineers from this citadel must prove that they passed through this hallowed place with proficiency in practical terms. No one leaves here with just a certificate. Everyone is called upon to defend their honors. It's part of the promise made and promise kept. This government, even before this institution opened its doors, has established several villages of practical experimentations. These places of practical experimentation are called villages because they are fashioned to be the bases of our scientific springboards. Show us what you can do, and we will help you bring it to the market. You're witnesses. Some of the twentieth century's best and enduring discoveries are founded by those who abandoned the four walls of a university to pursue a higher essence of audacity and vision. If you had what I'm talking about then this place is not for you…" As soon as he said those words, three young men, seated at the engineering department, sprang to their feet.

"Now, that's what I'm saying. For good fettle, that's what we need. But hold your peace," continued the president. "The director of these springboards will assign mentors to you shortly, and you'll show them your mettle, young men. But your enthusiasm is appreciated. Countrymen, this is what we need. If you got into this institution for masonry or carpentry, you're as appreciated as he who got in here for aeronautics. No discipline was elevated above the other. If your calling was palm wine tapping and you are adept in it, a medical doctor can't tell you how to do your bit or he may find himself crashing into the woods, pleading for his dear life. A stethoscope will never save him. So be as proud as you can be hewing the wood as the next person can be drawing the water…

"You are first among equals. Your pledge to your parents and to the Biafran people today is to know that the benchmark for your success is to remain second to none. You're Biafrans. There's no place for you to play the second fiddle. Challenge and compete with and among yourselves and be ready. When they bring kids from Dartmouth and Yale and Cambridge, show them that you've come of age, that you can compete and compete to win. What had hindered you was lack of opportunity. Now, the opportunity is here. The sky is your limit.

"Everyone has something to bring home: laurels, diadem, gold, silver, diamond, your good, your bad, your ugliness." He paused. "We can freshen them to make them the best we can. In the long run, it may not be bad after all. We aren't a people given to doing nothing. It's a tough strength of character to pause and do the right thing. The founder under whose sweat the institution was founded has shown us that he wasn't afraid to bring something home. And he had brought home something mighty and enduring. Speaking factually, he has brought to us the best launching pad. All great nations have great institutions like this. Institutions like this are desideratum for our own national greatness. We can build on it! Who among you has ever heard about Dartmouth or Princeton?" A few hands went up but it was rhetoric.

"Of course, you've heard of Cambridge! The British, by subterfuge and administrative brigandage, created royal charter for themselves and made so much money all over the whole world, in the orient, Asia Minor, and here in our backyard. They have made so much money off us to oil their University of Cambridge and others while we're left to carry the cans of nonsense.

"That and these other universities are of hallowed statures. They were founded in those days, whose foundations were made out of money generated through unsavory trade, built with slavery labor and, of course, unpaid for, to boot, under the harshest conditions. But today they're frontline citadels of learning. No one remembers their gory past. We only hear about how great an institution they are. Their gory past is embellished as a footnote in their history, if you found any mention of it. Today, I urge you to aspire to do the right thing. Credit to them nevertheless and credit to my compatriot, Chief Obikolo.

"What Chief Obikolo has done for us here is to give us a launchpad for our own greatness. We shall in one accord say no to the rush to go to Dartmouth, or Cambridge, or Princeton. Here's our own Dartmouth, here's our own Princeton, and here's our own Cambridge," said Dim as his voice echoed in the horizon.

He did not want to dwell on Obikolo or praise him for anything, but he could not help mentioning his name. That caused a lump of sputum to clog his esophagus, and he swallowed hard. He could not eschew to remember the bitterness and excruciating pain Obikolo caused him and the Biafran people during the genocidal war. So instead of castigating him for what he truly was, a traitor, he chewed on his own words, and for once he failed woefully on his own dictum: onto thyself be true.

"This is our Renaissance," he went on. "This is not a question of take it or leave. We've got no options. Our only option is to take it. Earlier I spoke about villages of practical experimentation. Yes, my government means business. As I've said time and again, we're not going to reinvent the wheel. The wheel will always remain round. But we can alter the number of spokes around it and it'll still run right. We're providing some brand-new automobiles to the villages. It's going to be fun, not fun as in driving it around. The directors of the villages will give instructions. There're about 11311 parts, screws, bolts, and nuts in an average vehicle. Our scheme would be to disassemble them, examine them, study them, sift the necessary from the unnecessary parts, and reduce the number of parts therein. If the directors, the engineers, and mentors decided that not all vehicles needed engine blocks, then we'll do away with it. We must be inventive. We must reduce the parts and still come up with our own design.

"When you ask bold questions, you're bound to elicit more questions, but you must be ready to confront them. They would be asking you about your intellectual right, as if you've no intellect of your own but you must be prepared to defend yourself and be willing to remind everyone that you've an inexhaustible dose of intellect given a free rein to enunciate yourself, and never forget to chip in about your natural resources that have been siphoned for centuries and still being siphoned, as we speak. Don't be afraid to confront your detractor with hard facts. It's our considered opinion that if we remain focused we'll get to where we're setting out to reach. And this government has created a road map that in ten years starting from today, importation of all manner of motor vehicles would be a thing of the past. As a matter of national policy, ten years from today, importation of motor vehicles would be banned." There was an uproar of approval from the crowd, before he quickly added, "If we failed to implement and achieve this, then we shall be ready to trek from Umudede to Timbuktu.

"Our next target will be to lift the aircraft off the ground and keep it in the air. This is not magic. If any people that trod the face of the earth would do it we'll do it. If it were magic then that's our turf and we'll be flying in no time, faster and safer. And we're going to make it impossible to fall out of the sky. If it meant fitting it with a baker's dozen engines we'll do that. Before all of the engines will give up, we'll fly it to safety and bring it down safely.

"Every moment has to be seized or lost. Life's always war by other means, and by proxy. Victory is never ceded. It's earned by dint of hard work and perseverance. But today we've in our midst a young man who had decided to cede something valuable to the general good of the Biafran people. Bucknor Obikolo's the driving force behind his father's vision and benevolence. Surprisingly, he's ceded this opportunity to us. It's left to every one of you to seize this moment and run with it where no world can stop you.

"I tell you this and I really mean it: we're cutting a new economic pathway for our country. We aren't going to let this fledgling nation be exposed to the vagaries of world economy. Some of the indices they churn out are figments of their own imagination that keep changing like the British weather, as well. If we left our economy to world model, we'll be competing on an unequal level. World economy is prescribed for the benefit of the rich nations, and we're not there yet. If we follow that paradigm we'll never get there and we'll never be rich. In fact, we'll remain in the woods. That's what they like and that's what we're up against. So as you begin this journey, so get yourselves ready for the tasks ahead. I'm instructing my ministries of economic development, trade and commerce, and finance, to come together and chart a new course for our economic advancement that will in the years to come offer something or some commonality with the world economies. Folks, the current doctrine of world economies aren't meant for us, and if we don't deviate from it we leave ourselves naked for molestation by a world mired in the survival of the wiliest. Our economy and survival can't be left to the vicissitudes orchestrated by the rich and powerful nations, whose stock in trade is to cause ripple in the water and reap handsomely from its crisis. We do that to our own perils. We're the little Davids, and for David to deal with Goliath he has to stay away from the giant. A David closer than an arm's length from the giant is a dead David. We've to understand that logic," the president said in one breath and in another he added, "We welcome foreign investment. But foreign investment must be on our terms. In that regard, there's a young man in our midst that's here to invest and grow with us without gouging our people. We welcome Mr. Ghoostte in our midst," said the president as he turned his gaze toward Turnkey and co, and to the students he continued, "and as you begin your journey today your focal point should be anchored on how to improve the quality of lives of the people who are sending you out today not at no cost.

"I must not leave you here today without this moment of truth. We must be self-reliant to fend for ourselves. We can't have the dignity to be respected if we live our lives wretched, expecting some handout from the supposedly godliness of others. When we begin to feed ourselves, the world will begin to accord us the respect we deserve because we earned it even if they accord it to us grudgingly and looking for ways to undermine it. We're the underdogs here, so we should be proud of ourselves. If we cannot feed ourselves and wallow in some form of self-pity, we open a window for those who give you nothing without an embedded price tag most of the time unforeseen. The agriculture ministry is charged and provided with everything they need to mechanize this land. We're the salt of the African earth. If anyone tells you otherwise pay them no heed," he echoed in one breath to a huge round of applause and in another he added, "Biafra is the breast milk from which the African continent will succor. We can't fail. If we failed, our detractors would tell to the mountain, 'I told you so.' We must not give them the chance to thumb their noses at us. If we succeed, as I'm cocksure that your crop of Biafrans are determined to succeed, we'll not just be admitted into the comity of top-performing nations. We'll take our place of pride in the comity of nations. And then we can say, 'Keep your halfhearted goodness and mercies to yourselves.'"

All along it was muted applause, but when Dim said those words, they elicited some thunderous applauses from the crowd. However, applauses could not explain the good feeling emanating from the crowd of visitors and students. Dim was a leader who had separated himself from the throng of African leaders. In two years of coming to power, he had distinguished himself from others. His words or actions did not speak to satisfy what the people wanted to hear or see. He spoke their minds as well. He was frank to his people, and they trusted him. If it came from him, it must be the truth. If he told them that it was doable, then it was doable. If he had told them to run, then they needed to gallop with their heels knocking the back of the pate. If he told them to stand, then they knew that they had a bulwark in their defense. That was the kind of leader standing stranded Africa needed. A man of immense charisma who the generality of the populace had come to believe that he had some knack of doing things no one else could. Of course, that feeling was not unfounded. The people could testify that things were beginning to change for good.

"We're on course with our government. But we must not do things because the west or the east are bent on it. The people of this land are Republicans. Our paradigm should be Republican democracy. It's in our pedigree and cultural melee. Before the white man came here we had a flourishing democracy. We were instituting a democracy as the Athenians of old, perhaps before Athens, a government of the people, by the people, and for the people. Our consultative assembly, the lawmaking body is crafting a law that would make it impossible to dislodge the people from their own governance. The assembly must craft a means whereby the commoners must take the reins of powers. They either have to cede it to you or yield it or you will have to seize it. Don't let them fool you again. You've been fooled for too long already. Bring it down! Seize it in the streets! Install your own man who sees your plight and shares your hopes and aspiration." And the audience liked it and applauded him then he continued. "The manner and detail of this scheme is being deliberated in the assembly. The import of this is to stop the pendulum from swinging back and forth or from the juggernauts to the lords or from the lords to the juggernauts," he told a crowd where half hardly understood what he was trying to make them to understand. But since it was coming from Dim they had reasons to believe that he knew what he was trying to make them to understand. Not understanding it that time was none of their concerns.

This president was not a rabble-rouser. But his oratory was akin to rabble-rousing, and that had become one of his flaws. He knew that he had the power of speech and could hold his audience spellbound hours on end. His father saw what he was capable of in his early years and decided that he would be a lawyer. When he was of age he did really send him to England to study law. But with no warning signs he ditched that prospect to the chagrin of his father and switched to study history. He wanted an in-depth understanding of his people's history and their place in the world. He had a burning feeling that the black man had been hugely mistreated and without honor. That the white man crawled inside his soul and exploited, and bent it, and completely ruined it. He knew growing up that history will always repeat itself. Nevertheless he wanted to guard against it and ameliorate its impact on the land that had been devastated and raped and made to feel worthless.

"I'll leave you with this: you've made me your president. Every day you allowed me to remain in office I'm going to put in my utmost best for you, my people. I say to you today as I'll say to you four years from hence, I'll not succeed myself. I seek no reelection. I've a one term, six years mandate. If I could not deliver my promises and the expectations of my people in six years I can't deliver them in donkey's years. That's the tenet of the bill that we're sponsoring through the consultative assembly. I seek no lifetime stake in office, and no one else would. I'm here to shepherd a new constitution, a constitution that'll live in the annals of this country. A proud constitution that would be representative of the will of the Biafran people. I'm your servant, we're servants of the people. And no servant is greater than his master. The master must keep his servants in check, in case they spin our wheels off the rails. If you see something say something. Lodge a protest, organize a rally against me and any member of my administration when there's a glaring undoing. Call your government to order! Make it a habit. Challenge members of this administration. Make it a habit. When it becomes a habit to see something and say something, over time it becomes a culture. When it becomes a culture, those you've employed to serve you would be on their toes.

"As I said at the beginning of my address, when we begin plying our roads and thoroughfares with the vehicles we made, all of you have collectively brought something home. It makes our country stronger. When we fly our own aircraft, think about how much money we would be saving. Don't be afraid to try. Be afraid of not trying, indeed! Go! Biafrans. Go!" he concluded as his booming voice echoed in the horizon.

The conclusion of his speech got everyone to their feet, heralding applause upon applauses. The president had thrown down the gauntlet, and it was anybody's to pick. The throng of the student body understood it, and from that moment every one of the matriculants felt challenged to do something for their young nation.

People began to gather in groups discussing the challenge of the day. Others milled around. And others began to disperse in different directions. Turnkey and his entourage lingered around in the company of Chance. They were talking about the speech of the president. They were also talking about the magnificence of the structures erected on the campus of Obikolo National University. It could rank among the best anywhere in the world. If the curriculum was right then the bent of the arc ceased to be unknown.

Chance and Turnkey were still talking when Atinga briskly came by with two of his protégés.

"How was the speech particularly and the ceremony generally speaking, Mr. Ghoostte?" asked Atinga as he came to Turnkey and his entourage. Turnkey had sought an auspicious avenue to take Atinga down memory lane ever since they met at the ministry building, and Atinga was welcoming him to the Biafran business world.

"I think it was a well-crafted speech and beautifully choreographed occasion, Mr. Culex," replied Turnkey awkwardly. Atinga did not quite hear him very clearly the last part of what he said as Turnkey pulled him aside away from their parties, but within earshot of Chance.

"I know that I had seen and known you from somewhere," continued Turnkey. It was a play on words.

"Yes, you were with me in the ministry annex a few weeks ago," said Atinga sincerely.

"Yes, that was recent. But I think that I had known you of old," said Turnkey.

"I don't think so," said Atinga self-assuredly.

"You don't intend to bet me on that, do you?" said Turnkey.

"I might," said Atinga.

"I see you losing your wager."

"I lose no bets, I lose no wager. I play to win."

"Let me save you some regrets", said Turnkey and quickly added, "Are you not Culex?"

"Culex?" queried Atinga.

"I put it to you, you're Culex and you know me."

"I don't know you from Adam except...," began Atinga.

"You weren't too young to forget, my friend. You once lived in Boonville with your mother. I'm Golan, whom you messed with, calling Culex on the soccer pitch. How dare you say that you don't remember, Culex?"

"Wait a minute! You've got to be kidding me!" echoed Atinga in complete consternation, as he stared into his eyes, offered him a handshake, and bear hug, and then both men clasped their left hand on each other's shoulders, eyeball to eyeball.

"You suddenly disappeared without a trace..."

"It was one of those life races," said Atinga.

"What happened?" asked Turnkey.

"America wasn't all there's to life. I found a greener pasture..."

"Playing soccer?" Turnkey cut in.

"No, not at all! Soccer was done and dusted when I moved to London. Like a good old soldier, I left everything on the battlefield."

"That was interesting. I thought you could make a living running after the round object..."

"I could have, but there're other ways to make a living...And how about you, you still want to blow up my head?" asked Atinga whimsically.

"Well, that was for the ages," said Turnkey, donning a smile.

"And I hope you didn't come with any of your arsenal?"

"No, not a musket. They're at the war front," said Turnkey.

"I hope so," said Atinga as he took a look toward the direction of his protégés.

"And I hope that I can get them over here."

"I don't know about that."

"Why not?" asked Turnkey.

"It's a process. And you may not need it here! And you may not have the tenacity of character to go through it."

"What do you mean?" asked Turnkey again.

"It might be easier for the proverbial camel to pass through the eye of a needle than for you to bring in a bayonet into Biafra or even own one."

"But I don't need a bayonet, I need a gun to protect myself and…"

"Protecting yourself is why we have the police, and that's why we've a government. We don't need a militia citizenry…"

"The police can't do everything, my friend," said Turnkey.

"You don't have to worry about that, Mr. Ghoostte. We're building a society without hoodlums. Before the white man came to these shores, there was not a single thief. When they came here they found not a single hoodlum. They brought thievery along with them, and we're trying to return our society to the good old days," Atinga told his friend.

"That was in those days. But now it's a shot at utopia. It ain't gonna work."

"While we can't reverse time. We've prepared ourselves to reverse a trend and chart a new course. How come Europe could place her jobless folks on welfare and dash them money monthly, year in year out with wealth stolen from Africa, but we whose land lay the golden eggs cannot dash a day worth of wages to our Europe-displaced people? Worst still, the mythical white man stealthily burrowed under the skin of the black man, tore his heart to pieces, violently joggled his mind, ruthlessly bent his soul, and completely destroyed him. Our work wouldn't be done until we de-indoctrinate our people to once again believe that they're humans. Two thousand years of mind-bending guile may take four thousand years to reverse a trend for the black man to rediscover and save himself. We won't be here to savor it but a journey of four thousand miles must always start, not with a giant leap, but with one sure-footed step. This is Biafra unbound. We're on a journey of Africa unbound, and the black man unbound. We must not worry our heads about how this beautiful and bright continent became dark. It's unfathomable! Perhaps, it's divine if you believed in the divine. That divinity turned the black man to self-destruct, perhaps. Perhaps, it's the white man's witchery or wizardry if you believed in chicanery or sorcery. Perhaps! We ain't gonna rehash old wounds here Golan, but we've an opportunity to return to who we are and not what some folks who never knew Chukwu Okike Abiama wanted to make us believe of ourselves. That ought not be the way of the world. We're children of the most high God, Chukwu Okike Abiama. If he liveth, he had not abandoned us to ourselves."

"Believe me, it ain't gonna work," repeated Turnkey.

"We shall see! We just have to give it a shot in the arm. But that aside. Business and officialdom aside, we'll find time to sit down and relive good old days, Golan," said Atinga as the men turned to meet their respective parties.

As Chance also bade bye to his compatriot, he turned to his friend and said, "I now know why you introduced yourself to him as Golan. You've known him forever."

"Oh, he's a good old sport, even before you," said Turnkey.

As Atinga turned the corner, he thought to himself, *What a small world!*

CHAPTER 38

It was a few months later when Turnkey moved into his estate. Construction was still going on in some part of the palatial estate. The police post was open. The supermarket center, nothing of its size seen in any part of the continent Africa, was thrown open to the public. The furl over the signpost to the estate was completely unfurled, which in bold letters read, "Welcome to Ghoostte Town." It was conspicuous for all to see. Then it became the talk of the whole town. Market women and children took turns to take a swipe at it. Bordered on one side by Umuagbara, on another side by Umulihilihi, and on the other side by the people of Umunkenke, and on the other side by the tributaries to the sea, it was different in a lot of ways. The inhabitants of these places had never seen anything like that before.

At the entrance of the estate, the American flag was hoisted at one end, and at the other end, the Biafran flag flustered in the evening sky, as a group of women came to pass.

"What a name?" scoffed Nwanyinna, whose mother came from the town of Umuagbara, meaning children of the spirit.

"It was not different from the name of the town of your mother," Ezenwanyi reminded her.

"That sounds true. But you know that I never gave it a thought," Nwanyinna recollected.

"That's the way of the world. For most things, we never gave them a thought because…"

"That's true anyway. What a name! But who cares about what's in a name?" said Nwanyinna resignedly as they skirted their way around the estate with their kids in tow.

The children Nwanyinna had with herself were her youngest kids. The older kids had wandered off to other places and far-off lands. She was not sure that they would ever come back to the place of their birth to live and call home and to die, so she had gone on and on to beget more children. She was not alone. Every family in the land had this kind of story to tell. As the young men wandered off the land, foreigners whose sole aim was to despoil it moved in to fill the void. A people so endowed had abandoned their land to foreigners to pillage, foreigners they were better off. They had got themselves to blame. A people set apart had become a people given to self-destruct. Dispirited, suddenly lily-livered, baited with their own lucre and in its pursuit, they had abandoned the essential things that made them a special heritage, a people set apart. Continually baited and falling for it, a lot among them had become perverted people, ingratiating themselves, with some sort of mind boggling glee, to foxes and jackals as if yielding their places to those who wanted to devour them was a badge of honor. Now, fawners! Now, bondservants! Now, men without cojones. Now, women of easy virtue. A laughing stock, made mockery of by those who inwardly envied them and wished they were like them. How this could have come to be was the crux of the matter. Like the children of the most high in the olden days, they had been dispersed in the wind to the fringes of the earth, faint and suffering. Seemed accustomed to the vicissitudes of their predicaments as fait accompli they bore their yoke as a way of life. Teased themselves with their own suffering, almost detached, as if those were all that were to living and dying. The story of Judah was for forty years in the wilderness. However, in this age, the children of Chukwu Okike had gone more than forty years for thousands of dusks and dawns and noons and evenings in the wilderness of sin. If Chukwu Okike were to cry like men his eyes would shed blood for the indigenous inhabitants of this land, the people of Biafra. Their untold hardship they brought it out on themselves. Now they had sold their minds for paltriness, and they had made themselves worse than senseless things. These ubiquitous people, roaming the face of the earth, scavenging. Now, they had a mountain to climb, in part for the expiation of their sins. They had wandered away effortlessly, but now they had to come back to their old places, faint but fighting. At a point in time, the glorious lineage of new fools become wise and face up to the challenges of their lives. Arduous the task but the rising sun beckoned on them to hie and hie to their land like the gathering of the children of ancient Judah. If they must reclaim that which was theirs, they must master the truth in a tooth for a tooth, the doctrine of our forbearers. A people given to offering the other cheek were bound to lose their sight completely and perhaps their neck, and since there would always be one neck, they would be bound to be no more. But when their detractor understood that there was vengeance to come, they were bound to be left alone, to live their lives to their fullest potentials. That was what the people the American investor was quoted as calling a people set apart needed to understand to have a lineage to be left for their next generation. The indigenous people of this land must master the essence of threatening vengeance and willingness to mete it out, or they will be consigned to mere myth and told by those whose fathers eviscerated them, by those who washed their hands in their blood. Never had a people so endowed allowed that sort of fate to befall them. Never! Now, they had a chance to say, never again!

Ghoostte Town was a breath of fresh air in this parch of the land. There used to be a shortcut for these women, but since Ghoostte Town began to spring up these women had had to take the longest route which was now, in any case, the shortest and the only route out there for them to get home, as they waited for the homecoming of their other children.

The End

About the Author

Chimezie Anosike was born in Biafra in 1965, a year before the events that precipitated the genocidal Biafran war. Just like every other child born in Biafra right about that time, the day-to-day living for parents was a rigor and life was uncertain. Death seemed more certain than survival due largely to starvation as a weapon of war. Having survived the war and starvation, and their attendant kwashiorkor he proceeded to elementary school in Abakuru where his parents pitched their tent even before the war. Life was a drudgery, and he was later taken to the big city of Onitsha by one of his elder brothers, Joe, where he completed both elementary and high school education.

He holds a bachelor's degree in linguistics, and a master's degree in international law and diplomacy from the University of Jos, Nigeria. He emigrated to the United States of America in 1998 where he enrolled and obtained another postgraduate degree in pharmacy at Texas Southern University in Houston.

His first effort at storytelling is not published and remains a stillborn. He is married to beautiful and lovely, innate and eternal soulmate, Dr. Augusta Anosike, née Ukaigwe, the bone of his bones, and they have four children. He hails from Umudurunna, Abba in Okigwe Province of Biafra. He holds an American citizenship, and they reside in Richmond, Texas.

www.ingramcontent.com/pod-product-compliance
Lightning Source LLC
Chambersburg PA
CBHW051129120626
46547CB00012B/722